INTRODUC
MODERN ENGLIS
FOR STUDENTS

Modern Novels

Alex Martin and Robert Hill

ENGLISH LANGUAGE TEACHING

Prentice Hall

New York London Toronto Sydney Tokyo Singapore

Published 1996 by
Prentice Hall International
Campus 400, Spring Way
Maylands Avenue, Hemel Hempstead
Hertfordshire, HP2 7EZ

Typeset in 10/12pt Syntax, 10/12pt Plantin and 12/13pt Bembo
by Derek Lee

Printed and bound in Great Britain by
Redwood Books, Trowbridge, Wiltshire

Library of Congress Cataloging-in-Publication Data

Martin, Alex. 1953–
Modern novels: introductions to modern English literature for students of English/Alex Martin and Robert Hill.
p. cm. — (English language teaching)
ISBN 0-13-017831-4
1. English language–Textbooks for foreign speakers. 2. Readers–Fiction. I. Hill, Robert, 1953 Mar. 31– II. Title. III. Series: English language teaching (Englewood Cliffs, N.J.)
PE1128.M3512 1996
428.6 ′4—dc20
95-46412
CIP

British Library Cataloguing in Publication Data

A catalogue record for this book is available from the British Library

ISBN 0-13-017831-4

6 5 4 3 2 1
2000 1999 98 97 96

Cover illustration: *The Yellow Window* by Stephen McKenna, reproduced by kind permission of the artist and Kerlin Gallery, Dublin

For
Jennie Gascoigne

Acknowledgements

The Editors and Publishers would like to thank the following for their kind permission to reproduce the following extracts:

Hamish Hamilton Ltd for *Farewell, My Lovely* by Raymond Chandler (Hamish Hamilton, 1940), copyright © Raymond Chandler, 1940 and for 'The Simple Art of Murder' from *Pearls Are A Nuisance* by Raymond Chandler (Hamish Hamilton, 1950) copyright © Raymond Chandler, 1950; William Heinemann Ltd for *The Third Man* by Graham Greene and for *Things Fall Apart*, by Chinua Achebe; Jonathan Cape for *A Farewell to Arms* by Ernest Hemingway, for *Catch-22* by Joseph Heller and for *The Handmaid's Tale* by Margaret Atwood; Merriam-Webster Inc for the entry on 'game' from *Merriam-Webster's Collegiate ® Dictionary*, Tenth Edition © 1994 by Merriam-Webster Inc; George Weidenfeld & Nicolson Ltd for *The Danger Tree* by Olivia Manning; Abner Stein for *The Joy Luck Club* by Amy Tan, published by William Heinemann Ltd; John Murray for *The Householder* by Ruth Prawer Jhabvala; The Bodley Head and the Estate of the author for *Ulysses* by James Joyce; Oxford University Press for *James Joyce And The Making Of Ulysses* by Frank Budgen; The Samuel Beckett Estate and The Calder Educational Trust, London for *Molloy* by Samuel Beckett, published by John Calder (Publishers) Ltd, London; The Estate of the late Sonia Browenll Orwell and Martin Secker & Warburg for *Nineteen Eighty-Four* by George Orwell.

The Editors and Publishers are grateful to the following for permission to reproduce photographs:
Warner Bros: *Bullets or Ballots* (top, p 31); Turner Entertainment Co: *Murder My Sweet* (bottom left, p 31); Polygram Television: *Farewell, My Lovely* (bottom right, p 31); Tropix Photographic Library (p 115); Mary Evans Picture Library (top, p 141); Camera Press / Stefan Richter (bottom, p 141); National Library of Ireland (Lawrence Collection) (p 171); The Kobal Collection: *The Handmaid's Tale* (p 203).

While every endeavour has been made to trace copyright owners, the Publishers would be pleased to hear from any other parties who may feel they hold rights in any of the material that has been included.

Contents

Introduction

1 To The Student

This book is for those who either want to read some novels in English or need to for school, university or exams. You don't need to have studied literature before. The aim of the book is help you understand and enjoy reading novels, and to give you tools and methods for appreciating them in the future.

You can use the book with or without a teacher. If you are studying alone, you will need to check your answers in the Key at the end of the book. The study of literature sometimes requires a purely personal response, however, so not all the exercises have a single correct answer. In these cases it will be useful to discuss your ideas with a teacher or another student.

Like the other books in this series (*Modern Poetry*, *Modern Short Stories* and *Modern Plays*) , this one adopts a double approach: literary and linguistic. Each chapter contains a *Language practice* section divided into *Structures* (ie grammar) and *Vocabulary*, in addition to the literary section on *Close reading*. The Language section is always based on the literature in the chapter and leads back into it. The two approaches feed each other, the language study helping you to appreciate the literature, and the literature helping you to appreciate (and use) the possibilities of the language.

After the *Language practice* section in each chapter there is a section called *Extension*, which gives you the chance to discuss or write about themes raised by the novels. A final section, *Beyond the text*, offers you an extract from a similar or contrasting novel.

You can work on the chapters in any order you like, but we suggest that you begin with Chapter 1, *Anatomy of a Novel*, which introduces some of the basic language of criticism of the novel.

At the back of the book you will find a *Glossary*. In this section are listed the most essential vocabulary items for each novel, together with words and phrases which are not usually included in a standard dictionary, such as slang and dialect. These words are listed in the order that they appear in the text, rather than alphabetically.

In order to make the best of this book, you need to have a good monolingual English dictionary, a good bilingual dictionary, and a handbook of English grammar and usage. You may also want to know more about the historical and cultural background to the novels. Here are some suggestions:

Monolingual English dictionaries
Oxford Advanced Learner's Dictionary
Longman Dictionary of Contemporary English

Bilingual dictionaries
This will depend on what is available in your language, but buy a large, modern dictionary if possible. Ask the advice of someone who knows both

languages well. A good dictionary is an indispensable intellectual tool which will serve you for many years. It should (a) translate a large number of words, (b) give all possible meanings for these words, and (c) reflect past as well as present usage. Avoid mini-dictionaries, therefore, which have their place in the tourist's suitcase but are useless for the study of literature.

Grammar and usage

Jake Allsop, *Students' English Grammar* (Prentice Hall)
Collins Cobuild English Grammar
Collins Cobuild English Usage
Raymond Murphy, *English Grammar In Use* (Cambridge)
Michael Swan, *Practical English Usage* (Oxford)
A J Thomson & A V Martinet, *A Practical English Grammar* (Oxford)

Historical and cultural background

(a) General
Harry Blamires, *Twentieth Century English Literature* (Macmillan)
Boris Ford (editor), *The New Pelican Guide to English Literature*, Volumes 7, 8 and 9 (Penguin)

(b) History of the novel
Ian Watt, *The Rise of the Novel* (Penguin)
Walter Allen, *The English Novel* (Penguin)
Malcolm Bradbury, *The Modern American Novel* (Penguin)
Malcolm Bradbury, *The Modern British Novel* (Penguin)

(c) Theory and practice
Wayne C Booth, *The Rhetoric of Fiction* (University of Chicago Press)
Geoffrey N Leech and Michael H Short, *Style in Fiction* (Longman)
Jeremy Hawthorn, *Studying the Novel* (Edward Arnold)
David Lodge, *Language of Fiction* (Routledge & Kegan Paul)
Roger Fowler, *Linguistics and the Novel* (Methuen)

2 To The Teacher

Little needs to be added, except to note that although this book is written with the possibility of private study in mind, practically every exercise will work in the classroom with little or no adaptation. Many of the individual exercises can be transformed by the addition of simple instructions: 'discuss this with a partner', 'report your conclusions', etc.

The use of literature in the language class is now very widely accepted as one of the most effective tools for cultural and linguistic enrichment. Yet in many schools and universities all over the world, literary study is still too often regarded as a form of magic, into which the students are initiated through the ritual repetition of weird and impenetrable spells – otherwise known as critical terminology. This can be the case even at a humble level. How many of us remember being told, at school, to 'analyze the character of Mrs ———

without the faintest idea of (a) what a 'character' is, (b) how to analyze one, or (c) why anyone should want to do this in the first place? And how many of us, who still smart at such memories, continue to set our students such mystifying tasks? There must be a better way of doing things.

One alternative is suggested in this book. The essence of our approach is to apply communicative teaching techniques to the study of literature. To us this means (a) reducing critical jargon to a minimum, (b) defining and thoroughly practising any critical terms that are used, (c) setting practical exercises that are challenging, achievable, and personally engaging, (d) encouraging students to develop and share their ideas with each other. Broadly, it means that the students should talk more and the teacher less. One might add that an ideal class would be like a conversation, or a group of friends out on a walk, rather than the traditional lecture + interrogation format.

Making this approach actually work in the classroom is, of course, up to the teacher – it is ultimately beyond the powers of even the most fanatically thorough textbook writer. Still, we have done what we can. This book is full of classroom activities. You can of course add your own. Time spent on thinking up suitable ways to introduce games, drama improvizations, surveys, quizzes, puzzles, debates, role-plays and projects will almost always pay handsome returns. [For a wealth of further practical ideas on this, see J Collie & S Slater, *Literature Teaching in the Language Classroom*; Françoise Grellet, *Developing Reading Skills*; and Penny Ur, *Discussions that Work* (all Cambridge University Press).] In setting up any group activity, however (especially a discussion), it is essential to give the student a specific goal – a decision to be reached, in a specific time. The approach of 'discuss Question Four', followed inevitably by 'discuss Question Five' is unlikely to be much of a success in any context.

Unlike the first two books in the series, *Modern Novels* – like *Modern Plays* – is based on extracts rather than full-length works. This is inevitable in a book of this size, but it also offers certain advantages, allowing students to examine a variety of novels, to go into some depth within that variety, and to sample each novelist's work as a prelude to further reading. Ideally, they will go on to do that further reading on their own initiative (perhaps with a little encouragement from you).

The *While reading* questions that occur during the main extracts can be done individually, in pairs, groups or as class brainstorming. They are there to:

a) give the students achievable portions of text to be read

b) encourage students to engage in the mechanics of the plot

c) aid, rather than test, comprehension by highlighting the questions that a practised reader would be asking her/himself.

These questions should therefore be dealt with fairly rapidly, and the students should carry on reading the novel at the first sign of the class discussion or pair/group work flagging. A more leisurely and deeper analysis of the novel is always provided in the *Close reading* section.

The *First reaction* exercise should also be dealt with quickly. The aim of this exercise is to harness that moment when any reader (even the least practised) tends to want to make a subjective response. We hope that this will encourage the less confident students to express their reactions. Detailed discussion of these reactions, however, should be left till after the *Close reading*, when students will have looked at key moments in the extract and should be able to take a more informed critical stance.

Finally, if you find yourself disagreeing violently with the answers in the Key, you can of course treat them as further discussion points. It is probably unwise to suggest that all literary questions are debatable, but a good many certainly are, at least to the extent that there is always more to be said.

Alex Martin
Robert Hill

1 Anatomy of a Novel

The aim of this chapter is to introduce some of the basic language of criticism of the novel. It should enable you to talk and write more confidently about the major elements of a novel: plot and setting, narrator and point of view, characters and characterization, style, structure and theme. (A deeper exploration of these terms, and more advanced critical terminology, can be found in the books recommended in the Introduction.)

There are seven sections in this chapter. You can certainly read them, and do the exercises, on your own, but it would be better to compare your ideas with other people. If you are studying on your own, stop and reflect after each section, and only check with the Key after you have really thought about the exercises. It is also a good idea to relate the ideas in this chapter to novels you have read in your own language. The novel is a universal art-form.

Background

What is a novel?

1 Write a definition for the noun 'novel' in no more than fifteen words. Compare your definition with a partner, then look up 'novel' in a dictionary.

Now read on.

When you looked up 'novel' in a dictionary in Exercise 1 you probably found a brief definition such as

'a long, written story, about imaginary people and events'

We would probably all agree with a basic definition like this, although we might want to add some ideas ...

- 'long': what does it mean, exactly? We know that a novel can be extremely long (for example, *War and Peace* by Leo Tolstoy is over a thousand pages long) but we might want to define more exactly the lower limit: a story up to about eighty pages long we normally call an extended **short story**, rather than a novel. A novel can allow the writer to include more people and events, and is generally more complex than a short story.
- 'written': this distinguishes novels from stories that are told orally but we should add that novels are written in **prose** (the continuous way of writing that you are reading now) rather than **verse** (the way of writing used for **poetry**, broken into rhythmic lines that may or may not rhyme).
- 'imaginary people and events': This does not strictly apply to **historical novels** (for example, Napoleon and the war between France and Russia appear in *War and Peace*), but real people and events are described in an imaginative way so that the reader feels a sense of participation. So the historical novel conveys more than just 'facts'.

But whatever definition we finally agree on, it is clear that the word 'novel' covers an enormous range. A novel can make us cry, laugh, or think, or all of them – it can be tragic, comic, satirical, romantic, a combination of these, or something difficult to define with just these words. A novel can fall into one of the easily defined categories that bookshops often use to display novels – **historical**, **science fiction**, **crime**, **horror**, **spy**, **best-sellers**, **classics**, and so on – or it can be defined according to the categories of academic literary criticism, such as **social realism** (an accurate and unromantic picture of life as it really is), or **Bildungsroman** (a German term meaning novels about the process of growing up – many novels deal with this), or **anti-novel** (novels that remind us they they are simply fictions, not representations of reality; writers playing with our expectations derived from traditional novels), and so on. In short, the range is endless.

Where does the novel come from? The earliest long stories are in verse.

Probably the choice of verse was first made to help the memory of oral storytellers, and then verse became a standard form of writing stories for several centuries. Examples are Homer's *Iliad* and *Odyssey*, Virgil's *Aeneid*, the Anglo-Saxon *Beowulf*, Chaucer's *The Canterbury Tales*, Milton's *Paradise Lost*, and so on. But from the early Middle Ages onwards, longer stories started to be written in prose as well. Outside Europe, the first examples are from Japan (for example the story of Genji from about 1000 AD, a woman's story about the love-affairs at the imperial court) and from Egypt (the collection of Arabian stories known as *The Thousand and One Nights*), while in Europe the Spanish **picaresque narrative** was an immediate ancestor of the modern novel. (*'Pícaro'* is the Spanish word for an immoral person who makes his living by deceiving people.) These stories were often a series of **episodes** relating the adventures of the main character. A parody of this kind of story, containing a main character who is noble but ingenuous rather than a deceiver, was *Don Quixote de la Mancha* (1605) by the Spanish writer Miguel de Cervantes. This book is not just a series of episodes: the main character develops during the course of the book. For this reason it is often considered the first example of the novel in Europe.

In England the first examples of the novel were written in the first half of the eighteenth century: *Robinson Crusoe* (1719) and *Moll Flanders* (1722) by Daniel Defoe, *Gulliver's Travels* (1726) by Jonathan Swift, *Pamela* (1740–41) and *Clarissa* (1747–8) by Samuel Richardson, and *Joseph Andrews* (1742) and *Tom Jones* (1749) by Henry Fielding. Already in *Tristram Shandy* (1759–67), the novelist Laurence Sterne was beginning to experiment with the novel, and pushing it to the limits as a form of telling a story. From then on the novel became *the* form of telling a story, and the nineteenth century produced such well-known novelists in Britain as Jane Austen, Sir Walter Scott, William Thackeray, the Brontë sisters, George Eliot and Charles Dickens. The development of the novel written in English in the twentieth century is the subject of this book.

(The books mentioned in the Introduction, or any good history of literature, will give details about the historical background of the novel.)

Nowadays there is a rival to the novel as the most popular way of telling a story – the **film**. However, films are not always based on original **screenplays** (stories invented without any reference to another source such as a novel) – many films are in fact adaptations of novels. And it seems that a successful film will inspire many people to go and read the novel it is based on (publishers often bring out a new printing of a novel that has been successfully filmed, with a scene from the film on the cover). Of the fourteen extracts from novels you will read in this book, eleven have been adapted for the screen. If you can, do try and see the film version. Remember that you are seeing something that may be different from the novelist's original intentions, but this will allow you to see more clearly, from what has been added or taken away, what the qualities of the novel are. (There is a list of film versions based on the novels included in this book on page 288.)

And finally, why do we use the word 'novel' in English? The word derives from the Italian word 'novella' (literally meaning 'a new little thing'), which was the medieval term in Europe for a short story told in prose: a well-known collection is the *Decameron* (1349–51) by the Italian Giovanni Boccaccio. Other languages derive their word for 'novel' from other sources. Several European languages use a word like *'roman'*: this term derives from the medieval French word *'romance'*, which was used in Europe to refer to stories told in verse or prose about the battles and love-affairs of courageous knights (for example, the various versions of the adventures of King Arthur and his knights).

'Romance' in modern English is not used for serious works of art: it refers to sentimental 'love-stories'. The word 'novella' is still used in modern English to refer to a piece of writing longer than an extended short story but shorter than an average novel. (An example of a novella is Joseph Conrad's *Heart of Darkness*, which you will look at in Chapter 5.)

Plot and setting

As in a short story, play or film, the **plot** of a novel is what happens in it. When describing what happens, it is important to specify certain things. These can be summed up in four simple questions: Who? Where? What? When?

- Who are the characters?
- Where are they?
- What do they do?
- When does the action take place?

Summarizing a novel, or an extract from a novel, usually means describing these four things. It is very useful to be able to do this quickly and without too many irrelevant details. Like describing character, this is something we all do in ordinary conversation – when telling a joke or a story, or describing an incident we have seen.
A summary of a plot is called a **synopsis.**

Sometimes the time and place, the 'when and where' of the plot, are called the **setting**. This is generally established at the beginning of a novel, but in certain novels the reader is constantly made aware of the setting all the way through. The *atmosphere* created by the setting is often very important. The novels of Graham Greene, for example, are well known for their atmospheric settings – often unhealthy, shabby, post-colonial backwaters – which provide the ideal ground for the development of Greene's favourite theme of the ambiguity of morality.

Sometimes the setting is so essential it almost becomes a character in itself. This is the case in Lawrence Durrell's series of four novels set in the Egyptian city of Alexandria, *The Alexandria Quartet* (1957–60).

2 Read this description of Alexandria.

> Six o'clock. The shuffling of white-robed figures from the station yards. The shops filling and emptying like lungs in the Rue des Soeurs. The pale lengthening rays of the afternoon sun smear the long curves of the Esplanade, and the dazzled pigeons, like rings of scattered paper, climb above the minarets to take the last rays of the waning light on their wings. ...
>
> The city unwrinkles like an old tortoise and peers about it. For a moment it relinquishes the torn rags of the flesh, while from some hidden alley by the slaughter-house, above the moans and screams of the cattle, comes the nasal chipping of a Damascus love-song.
>
> Lawrence Durrell, *Justine* (1957)

a Can you suggest one or two adjectives of your own to describe the city of Alexandria as it is presented by Durrell?

b Compare your ideas with a partner.

Narrators and points of view

Do you always believe everything that people tell you? Or everything you read in newspapapers and magazines, or see on television, or hear on the radio? Probably not. Consciously or unconsciously, you might ask yourself these questions:

- Who is telling me this?
- Do I trust this person's judgment?
- Am I being told facts, or opinions?
- Is this the complete version of events, or is there another side to the story?

The same sort of questions are relevant when you are reading a novel. Ever since novels were first written, novelists have explored different ways of telling their stories. They have used different characters to tell the stories – **narrators** – and presented the events from different 'angles' – from different **points of view**.

Here are the main ways that novelists use to tell their stories.

First-person narrator

The story is told by an 'I', who may be the main character in the novel, as you can see clearly in this opening sentence.

> If you really want to hear about it, the first thing you'll really want to know is where I was born, and what my lousy childhood was like, and how my parents and all were occupied before they had

> me, and all that David Copperfield kind of crap.
>
> J D Salinger, *The Catcher in the Rye* (1951)

Alternatively the 'I' may be a minor character in the novel, an observer of events that happen to others. Examples of this are Nick in F Scott Fitzgerald's *The Great Gatsby* (1925), and Marlow in many of the novels of Joseph Conrad. (See Chapter 5.)

The choice of the first person can bring the reader very close to the personality of the narrator, and can also make events seem more vivid, since they are described by an 'eye-witness'. Of course the first-person narrator is supposed to be just an ordinary person: he/she cannot know what is going on inside the heads of other characters, or know all the facts of a situation. But this 'limited' knowledge has its advantages: it is often used in novels about growing up, where the psychological development of the narrator is the central element. It is also a common choice for detective novels, where the detective-narrator is trying to find something out, and suspense and surprise depend on the gradual revelation of the facts.

Third-person narrator

The story is told by a narrator outside the story, who refers to the characters by their names, or by 'he', 'she' or 'they'. An advantage over the first-person narrator is that there is greater liberty to move around in time and space, and to include more characters.

In novels written in the third person, two main points of view are normally used: the **omniscient point of view** and the **limited point of view**.

The **omniscient point** of view means that the narrator knows everything about the events and the characters, and knows all their thoughts and motives. But how much of all this does the narrator choose to reveal? There is a lot of room for variety here! These are the two extremes (with the terms critics use to describe them), but there are many possible variations in between:

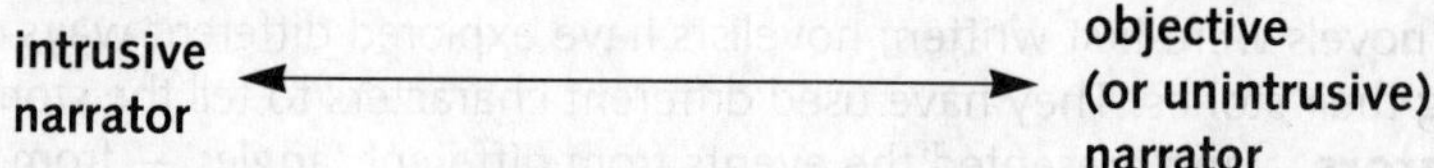

An **intrusive narrator** explicitly *tells* the reader things, commenting on the characters and explaining events. An **objective** (or **unintrusive**) **narrator** simply *shows* things, without commenting or explaining: he is more like a camera. Here are two examples.

In the following extract notice how the **intrusive narrator** tells us about the village, the author Henry Babbacombe's reputation and psychology, all about the harvesting machines, and where Henry works.

> In the tiny and depressing hill-village where Henry Babbacombe, an author virtually unknown, even to himself, lived and breathed and had his being, they were cutting the corn.
>
> Great gantry-like machines, high-powered combine harvesters with great front teeth, stereo in the cab, central locking and racing stripes were thundering through the nearby fields, shaking the soil, shuddering the trees, and rocking the foundations, if there were some, of the small and gloomy garden shed amid the weeds at the bottom of Henry's cottage garden, beside the graveyard, where he sat and wrote his books.
>
> Malcolm Bradbury, *Cuts* (1987)

Contrast the extract above with the following extract, where the **objective narrator** *tells* us nothing except what is immediately observable: he simply shows us the scene.

> The door of Henry's lunch-room opened and two men came in. They sat down at the counter.
>
> 'What's yours?' George asked them.
>
> 'I don't know,' one of the men said. 'What do you want to eat, Al?'
>
> 'I don't know,' said Al. 'I don't know what I want to eat.'
>
> Outside it was getting dark. The street-light came on outside the window. The two men at the counter read the menu.
>
> Ernest Hemingway, *The Killers* (1928)

Generally speaking, modern novelists tend to be more objective.

The **limited point of view** means that, although the narrator tells the story in the third person, he confines himself to the impressions and feelings of *one* character in the novel: he presents only one point of view of events. The effect of this can be similar to that created by a first-person narrator (although the narrator still has greater liberty to move around in time and space). In the following extract, the events of the Second World War in China are limited to the point of view of a young boy, Jim, who cannot possibly know what is going on.

> For two days Jim had wandered along the Shanghai waterfront. ... His only hope of seeing his parents again was to find one of their Swiss or Swedish friends. Although the European neutrals drove through the streets of Shanghai, Jim had not seen a single British or American face. Had they all been sent to prison camps in Japan?
>
> J G Ballard, *Empire of the Sun* (1984)

You will find all these kinds of third-person points of view in this book: an omniscient point of view, intrusive narrator in *Catch-22* (Chapter 4); an omniscient point of view, objective narrator in *Things Fall Apart* (Chapter 5); and a limited point of view in *The Householder* (Chapter 6) and *Nineteen Eighty-Four* (Chapter 8).

Multiple narrators and multiple points of view

Experimenting with the various effects produced by different narrators and points of view is probably the most significant development in the modern novel. (Perhaps this reflects typically twentieth century concerns: the complex nature of reality; the decline of belief in absolute truth; a fascination with psychological analysis; a belief in the importance of individual experience and opinion.) Some modern novelists emphasize the complexity – and richness – of experience by using **multiple narrators** and **multiple points of view**. In *The Sound and the Fury* (1929) and *As I Lay Dying* (1930), William Faulkner described events through the eyes of different narrators, including children and a mentally retarded character. Lawrence Durrell's *The Alexandria Quartet* (see Exercise 2) is composed of four novels, each with a different narrator describing the same characters and sequence of events. In John Fowles's *The Collector* (1963), a kidnapping is described in the first half of the novel by the kidnapper, in the second half by the victim.

3 Read the following ways of describing an event (***a–e***). Then match them with the five points of view listed underneath (***1–5***).

a Mary Evans was driving home along Seymour Road. There had been problems at the office again that day. And at home, the behaviour of her husband, Nick, had changed recently. Suddenly a man stepped out in front of the car. Mary braked, but the car hit the man and he fell to the ground. The blood drained from Mary's face, and she sat motionless behind the steering-wheel. A woman ran over and shouted to her through the window, but she didn't reply.

b I was walking home along Seymour Road. The evening was fine, and I was looking forward to dinner at my local Greek restaurant. Suddenly I heard a screech of brakes and looked around. I recognized Mary Evans's car, and saw a man in front of it, and then heard the horrible thud of body against car. I ran over. Mary had gone completely white. I shouted 'Mary, Mary!' through the window, but she was obviously in a state of shock, and didn't seem to recognize me at all.

c Mary Evans was driving home after yet another difficult day. Doubts and fears about her job and her marriage tormented her. Her worries were well founded: her boss was increasingly dissatisfied with her work, and more importantly, her husband, Nick, was thinking of leaving her. Suddenly, a man on the pavement, lost in worries of his own, stepped into the road without looking. Mary braked hard, but too late. The man was knocked to the ground. Mary's friend Anna, who was passing, ran over to her, but Mary was too shocked to speak or even think.

d Mary Evans was driving home, wondering what to do about the problems that had come up at the office that day, and her boss's obvious displeasure. And Nick, her husband, how would he behave when she got home? If only she knew why he was behaving so strangely! Suddenly there was a man in front of the car. Instinctively, her foot pushed hard on the brake. The man's terrified face appeared in front of her for an instant, then disappeared again. Everything seemed to go blank. From what seemed a million miles away, someone was calling her name.

e It had been another awful day at the office, one problem after another, and my boss criticizing me all the time. And I wasn't looking forward to my evening very much either. My husband, Nick, had been acting strangely all week – I really worry about losing him. I just wasn't thinking about my driving, and the next thing I knew there was a man right in front of me. I remember braking, but it was too late – there was nothing I could do. I can't remember any more.

1 first-person narrator: a minor character in the story
2 first-person narrator: a main character in the story
3 third-person narrator: omniscient, intrusive
4 third-person narrator: omniscient, objective
5 third-person narrator: limited

4 Choose one of the following moments. Imagine who is there and what happens. Choose a point of view and narrate the scene in 5–10 lines. If you a working with a partner, choose different points of view, write your own version, and then compare your results.
a an hour later, Mary at the hospital
b Mary at home, later that evening
c any other moment from how you think the plot might develop

Characters and characterization

5 Before you read this section think about some people you know. You may have a good opinion of them, or a bad opinion, or any of the wide variety of opinions in between. You may also find them interesting or boring, or something in between, and so on.
a Make a brief list of the main ways you arrive at your opinions.
b What do you think are the similarities and differences between the ways we evaluate people in real life, and the way we evaluate the 'people' in a novel?
c Compare your list in ***a***, and your ideas in ***b***, with a partner.
Now read on.

The 'people' in a novel are referred to as **characters**, and the way the novelist presents them to us is called **characterization**.

The novelist E M Forster, in his critical work *Aspects of the Novel* (1927), made a useful distinction between **flat characters** and **round characters**. **Flat characters** are two-dimensional and do not change during the course of a novel. They are often described briefly, with one or two vivid details. **Round characters** have complex personalities, are characterized in more subtle ways, and develop during the course of a novel. Like people in real life, they reveal themselves gradually, they can surprise us, but just like people we do not expect them to behave totally erratically, without any motivation.

The characters in a novel are usually a mixture of main characters, who tend to be 'round', and minor characters, who tend to be 'flat'. Great novelists like Charles Dickens are able to create a host of memorable 'flat' characters. You will find an enormous number of minor, 'flat' characters in the extracts from *Catch-22* (Chapter 4). Notice that in some kinds of novel, such as adventure novels or popular thrillers, even the main characters are 'flat'. We do not expect much psychological complexity from Ian Fleming's James Bond!

Before you look at the following methods of characterization, remember what was said about **intrusive** and **objective narrators** in the preceding section. The narrator can simply *show* us a character in action, and leave the interpretation up to us, or can also *tell* us about a character – give us background information and make judgments for us. Often a novel can contain both moments of *showing* and moments of *telling*.

When we read a novel we take our ideas about a character from the following indications.

Appearance and possessions: Physical appearance – eyes, face, hair, body, movements, etc – as well as clothes, where the character lives, and any personal objects he/she has. Flat characters are often described briefly in this way.

Here is a description of the wife of a British Consul in a provincial African capital. She seems rather intimidating; no longer young; determined to 'keep up appearances' in a foreign land.

> She was tall and palely fleshy, a moderately 'handsome' woman gone to fat, with short, dyed black hair swept back in a dramatic wave from her face and held immovably in position by a fear-somely strong lacquer; even in the most intemperate breezes Morgan had never seen a single hair stir from the solid lapidary mass of her coiffed head.
>
> William Boyd, *A Good Man in Africa* (1981)

Action: Certain 'big' actions such as falling in love, marrying, resigning from a job – even murder, suicide and so on – have dramatic impact, but often it is what builds up to and follows such moments that tells us more about a character. Particularly in the modern novel, it is the observation of small particulars and everyday actions that are used for characterization.

Look at Tom Ripley, the psychopathic hero of a series of novels by Patricia Highsmith, in action. In the following extract he has a suitcase full of money intended to pay for the release of a boy who has been kidnapped. But, at the arranged meeting, instead of paying, Tom chooses a more drastic solution ...

> Tom picked up the suitcase and gripped its handle, and as the man rounded the corner, Tom swung the suitcase and caught him

> on the left side of his head with it. The impact made not a loud thud but a solid one, and there was a second bump as the man's head hit the back of the shed. Tom brought the suitcase down once more, aiming at the left side of the man's head as he was falling.
>
> Patricia Highsmith, *The Boy Who Followed Ripley* (1980)

This is certainly dramatic and exciting, and we also infer that Tom is used to violence, and can be quite rational – indeed, clinically violent – in such extreme circumstances. But to complete the picture of Tom, look at him a few pages later in the novel, where he has come back to the apartment of a friend called Eric ...

> 'Back again!' Tom whispered cheerfully, and set the suitcase down in Eric's hall, near where it became the living room. ...
>
> 'A drink first, I think. Could you manage a gin and tonic?'
>
> Eric could, and while he was making it, Tom went to the bathroom and washed his hands with warm water and soap.

Here we see a curious mixture: casualness – the cheerfulness, the polite request for a drink (a 'sophisticated' gin and tonic, which he can wait for, not an immediate, desperate gulp of whisky) – but in the need to wash his hands there is a suggestion of guilt, remorse or distaste. It is the everyday actions which imply the complexity of his character.

Conversation: What a character says reveals a great deal. But, just as in life, a character might *say* one thing, *mean* something else, or indeed be *thinking* something completely different. In the following example the omniscient narrator makes this explicit for the reader.

Holman, a young university professor, is talking with his wife, Emmy, one evening.

> 'Did you have a good day today?' she finally said.
>
> 'All right,' lied Holman. All through graduate school he had talked freely to Emmy about his work which she was not at all interested in, though she did what she could to show interest because she was interested in Holman. ...
>
> 'That's good,' Emmy finally said. She knew, or suspected, that he was lying. She knew it without thinking, as she knew most things.
>
> Alison Lurie, *Love and Friendship* (1962)

But on many occasions the difference between what is said and what is intended or thought is not explicit, and readers must often be ready to make their own interpretations.

6 In presenting conversation, the writer has a wide choice between *showing* and *telling*. What differences do you notice between the way the following two examples of conversation are presented to the reader? Compare your ideas with a partner, and then check your ideas with the Key.

> 'Simon sometimes seems to me rather a heartless person.'
> 'He is only honest,' said Fanny.
> 'It can be heartless to be that, as you seem to have found.'
> 'He shows what he is, and not many of us do.'
> 'Surely you and I do. We have not so much to hide.'
> 'About the usual amount. And we are wise to hide it.'
>
> Ivy Compton-Burnett, *A Heritage and its History* (1959)

> ... a quiet knocking came at the door. 'Come in,' Dixon said with reflex promptness.
>
> Michie entered. 'Good afternoon, Mr Dixon,' he said, then added politely 'Good afternoon' to the still-prostrate Bertrand, who at this stimulus struggled to his feet. 'I seem to have come at an inconvenient time.'
>
> 'Not at all,' Dixon said smoothly. 'Mr Welch is just going.'
>
> Kingsley Amis, *Lucky Jim* (1954)

Thought: What a character thinks may reveal more than what is said, and 'getting inside the head' of a character has been a main concern of the modern novel.

An important development in narrative was the **stream of consciousness technique**. The phrase was first used by the American psychologist William James in his *Principles of Psychology* (1890) to define the flow of thoughts in a person's mind. The term is used by literary critics to describe a technique used especially in the early 20th century by experimental writers such as James Joyce, Virginia Woolf and William Faulkner, who presented narrative as the mixture of thoughts and sense perceptions of one or more characters' minds. Events are conveyed to the reader through the memories, associations, feelings and expectations of characters. Some critics use the term **interior monologue** interchangeably with **stream of consciousness**, while other critics use *stream of consciousness* as the general term for any technique that uses a character's thoughts as the backbone of a narrative, and reserve interior monologue to describe the 'ungrammatical' kind of prose which is intended to represent the way people really think.

Here is an example of stream of consciousness writing from Virginia Woolf's *Mrs Dalloway*. Clarissa Dalloway is seen here with her old friend Peter Walsh, who, unknown to her, is in love with her. He is nervously playing with his penknife.

> For Heaven's sake, leave your knife alone! she cried to herself in irrepressible irritation; it was his silly unconventionality, his weakness; his lack of the ghost of a notion what anyone else was feeling that annoyed her, had always annoyed her; and now at his age, how silly!
>
> I know all that, Peter thought; I know what I'm up against, he thought, running his finger along the blade of his knife, Clarissa and Dalloway and all the rest of them; but I'll show Clarissa – and then to his utter surprise, suddenly thrown by

> those uncontrollable forces, thrown through the air, he burst into tears; wept; wept without the least shame, sitting on the sofa, the tears running down his cheeks.
>
> Virginia Woolf, *Mrs Dalloway* (1925)

The reader is shown 'inside the heads' of both characters, but the grammar is not deviant. On the other hand, interior monologue deviates from conventional grammar, as you can see in this example from James Joyce's *Ulysses*, where Leopold Bloom is thinking about his absent daughter's birthday.

> Fifteen yesterday. Curious, fifteenth of the month too. Her first birthday away from home. Separation. Remember the summer morning she was born, running to knock up Mrs Thornton in Denzille street. Jolly old woman.
>
> James Joyce, *Ulysses* (1922)

The experiments with ways of presenting thought that you have just seen often produced novels which are thought of as 'difficult'. Such experiments that extend over entire novels are now rare, but contemporary novelists have been influenced by these experiments, and often move freely among a variety of techniques for presenting thought.

Style

Style is a word that we use every day. We talk about different styles of clothes, cooking, furniture, playing football, ... and different styles of writing. Instinctively, we probably all agree on identifying styles of writing such as 'romantic', simple, journalistic, bureaucratic, scientific, and so on. But to talk about the style, or styles, used in a novel, we need to be more explicit. It is a useful first step to look at the **syntax** and the **vocabulary**.

Syntax means the way that words are organized into sentences. An enormous range of possibilities is open to the writer: sentences can be short or long, simple (using just co-ordination with words such as *and* or *but*) or complex (using subordination with relative clauses, or a clauses of time, contrast, reason or result, etc), or combinations of these possibilities. The writer can also alternate the various possible forms of sentences within a paragraph.

7 ***a*** Experiment with different ways of extending the following sentence. How long can you make it? At what point does your sentence start to seem too long?
David ate the sandwich.
(You may want think about details such as: who is David? where was he? what was in the sandwich? how did he eat it? did he enjoy it? what was he thinking about? etc.)

b Compare your results with a partner.

Vocabulary (often called **lexis**) means, quite simply, *words*. Words such as articles, demonstratives, pronouns, auxiliary verbs and co-ordinators are called **grammatical words**, but what we notice more when we read are the **semantic words** – nouns, adjectives, verbs and adverbs. When you look in a dictionary the first meaning you find for these words is the **denotation** (the most basic, literal meaning). Literature, however, communicates more than plain facts: it uses the **connotations** of words (the associations, ideas and emotions that they suggest) to influence our thoughts and feelings in more subtle ways. In the following two examples, the essential factual information is the same:

a He cried all night. His girlfriend had left him.
b He wept until dawn. His love had abandoned him.

But different ideas are suggested. Is the character in ***b*** more 'romantic' and 'tragic'? Or more self-dramatizing? Or simply a character from a novel of a previous century, when this style was more prevalent? Or a character in a novel by a novelist making fun of a romantic style – and therefore comic? The connotations rather than the denotations of the words make us ask these questions. These questions are answered in the context of the novel as a whole.

As you can see, style is not just decoration added to a basic idea; it is an integral part of the meaning. The choice of style is generally the result of other choices. Read the following two extracts.

> I met Bobby Callahan on Monday of that week. By Thursday, he was dead. He was convinced someone was trying to kill him and it turned out to be true, but none of us figured it out in time to save him. I've never worked for a dead man before and I hope I won't have to do it again. This report is for him, for whatever it's worth.
>
> Sue Grafton, *C is for Corpse* (1986)

> The Consul sat on the broken green rocker facing Yvonne. Perhaps it was just the soul, he thought, slowly emerging out of the strychnine into a form of detachment, to dispute with Lucretius, that grew older, while the body could renew itself many times unless it had acquired an unalterable habit of age.
>
> Malcolm Lowry, *Under the Volcano* (1947)

The **plain** style of the first extract, with its simple syntax and vocabulary, indicates the character of the tough, private-detective narrator. The style of the second extract, with its complex syntax and vocabulary, reflects the melancholic, philosophical – and often alcoholic – point of view of the Consul.

Similes and **metaphors** can be seen as ways of using the **denotations** and **connotations** of words to produce a special, powerful effect. Words whose denotations are quite different are put together to create vivid or startling comparisons. Similes are explicit comparisons, where the two things compared are linked by *like*, *as*, or *as if/as though*. Metaphors are implicit comparisons, where the linking words are missing. When used well, a variety of connotations is created. Look at how the writer Laurie Lee (born 1914) describes the sombre Spanish city, Valladolid:

> Valladolid: a dark square city hard as its syllables – a shut box, full of the pious dust and preserved breath of its dead whose expended passions once ruled a world which now seemed of no importance.
>
> Laurie Lee, *As I Walked Out One Midsummer's Morning* (1969)

With the simile, Lee implies that the city is as harsh as the sound of its name, suggesting a correspondence between name and place. The 'shut box' metaphor suggests many things: secrecy, darkness, a coffin, a musty smell, a city not 'open' to modernity but 'closed' in its past, and so on.

8 Read the following extract, the beginning of Laurie Lee's account of his childhood in a small English village just after the First World War.

> I was set down from the carrier's cart at the age of three; and there with a sense of bewilderment and terror my life in the village began. The June grass, amongst which I stood, was taller than I was, and I wept. I had never been so close to grass before. It towered above me and all around me, each blade tattooed with tiger-skins of sunlight. It was knife-edged, dark, and a wicked green, thick as a forest and alive with grasshopppers that chirped and chattered and leapt through the air like monkeys.
>
> Laurie Lee, *Cider With Rosie* (1959)

a Underline all the similes and metaphors.
b What general efffect do you think is Lee trying to create?
c Here we have a **first-person narrator**. But do you think the **point of view** is that of a child, or an adult looking back on childhood experiences? Why do you think so?
d Do you think any of his metaphors or similes are particularly effective? Do you think any of them are not successful?
e Compare your ideas with a partner, then check with the Key.

Generally speaking, **symbols** are signs – words or pictures – which represent something else. The use of symbols is called **symbolism**. Some traditional symbols are the dove (symbolizing peace), the heart (symbolizing love), the lion (symbolizing strength), and so on. In literature we often find traditional symbols (for example, spring and winter often symbolize birth and death), as well as symbols from more literary traditions (for example, a rose symbolizing love). More originally, writers can create their own symbols, which we interpret from the context. In novels, symbolic force can be given to characters, buildings, objects of all kinds. They might symbolize one idea, or a variety of ideas, and help us to appreciate the **theme(s)** of the novel. (For **theme**, see the last section of this chapter.)

9 The English novelist E M Forster (1879–1970) used symbolism to great effect. In *A Passage to India* the character Aziz, a young Indian doctor and a Muslim, feels a part of a minority in his own town, where British colonialists hold the power and Hindus outnumber Muslims. In the following extract he is enjoying a moment of peace while sitting outside a mosque. Read the extract and answer the questions.

> There were owls, the Punjab mail … and flowers smelt deliciously in the station-master's garden. But the mosque – that alone signified, and he returned to it from the complex appeal of the night, and decked it with meanings the builder had never intended. Some day he too would build a mosque, smaller than this but in perfect taste, so that all who passed by should experience the happiness he felt now. And near it, under a low dome, should be his tomb, with a Persian inscription:
>
> Alas, without me for thousands of years
> The Rose will blossom and the Spring will bloom,
> But those who have secretly understood my heart –
> They will approach and visit the grave where I lie.
>
> E M Forster, *A Passage to India* (1924)

a What symbolism can you see in the Persian inscription that Aziz thinks of for his tomb?
b What do you think the mosque might symbolize?
c Compare your ideas with a partner, then check with the Key.

In everyday English, an **image** is a picture, a visual representation of something. In literary criticism, **imagery** is a commonly used term, but critics tend to use it in two different ways:

a) as a general term to refer to metaphors, similes and symbols
b) to refer to any of a series of sense impressions created through words, not just visual, but also to do with taste, touch, hearing and smell

The second definition of **imagery** is used in this book.

Imagery is often used to create *setting*. It can also be a means of *characterization*, and can lead us to appreciate the **theme(s)** of the novel. (For **theme**, see the last section of this chapter.)

10 Read the following extract from a story by D H Lawrence about the relationship between a captain and the soldier who is his personal servant, his 'orderly'.

> The Captain sat on horseback, watching. He needed to see his orderly. His helmet threw a dark shadow over his light fierce eyes,

> but his moustache and mouth and chin were distinct in the sunshine. The orderly must move under the presence of the figure of the horseman. It was not that he was afraid or cowed. It was as if he was disembowelled, made empty, like an empty shell. He felt himself as nothing, a shadow creeping under the sunshine. And, thirsty as he was, he could scarcely drink, feeling the Captain near him. He would not take off his helmet to wipe his wet hair. He wanted to stay in shadow, not to be forced into consciousness. Starting, he saw the light heel of the officer prick the belly of the horse; the Captain cantered away, and he himself could relapse into vacancy.
>
> D H Lawrence, *The Prussian Officer* (1914)

a Underline all the imageries of light/dark, emptiness and wetness/dryness.
b The images help us to understand the relationship between the Captain and the orderly. How would you describe their relationship?
c Compare your ideas with a partner.

11 The American novelist William Faulkner (1897–1962) set most of his work in a fictional **setting**, Yoknapatawpha County in the Deep South of the USA (it is a fictionalized version of Faulkner's own state, Mississippi). The capital of Faulkner's invented county is called Jefferson. Read the following opening of one of his stories, and answer the questions.

> Monday is no different from any other weekday in Jefferson now. The streets are paved now, and the telephone and electric companies are cutting down more and more of the shade trees – the water oaks, the maples and locusts and elms – to make room for iron poles bearing clusters of bloated and ghostly and bloodless grapes, and we have a city laundry which makes the rounds on Monday morning, gathering the bundles of clothes into bright-coloured, specially-made motor cars: the soiled wearing of a whole week now flees apparitionlike behind alert and irritable electric horns, with a long diminishing noise of rubber and asphalt like tearing silk, and even the Negro women who still take in white people's washing after the old custom, fetch and deliver it in automobiles.
>
> William Faulkner, *That Evening Sun* (1933)

a The narrator does not explicitly say whether he prefers Jefferson now or as it used to be. Which do you think he prefers?
b In answering ***a***, did you base your ideas on any examples of simile, metaphor, imagery or symbolism? If so, which ones did you notice, and how did you interpret them?
c Compare your ideas with a partner, and check with the Key.

Structure

So far, you have looked at various 'elements' of a novel – but in reality the elements are interdependent and many are working together at the same time.

Structure refers to the way a novel is organized, the way the various elements combine together to make the complete novel. One obvious example of structure is something you can see when you pick up any novel: the organization into chapters. Some novels have many chapters, and some none at all. Sometimes the chapters are long, sometimes short. These choices are not arbitrary: a change in the organization would result in a different novel.

You will see three complete chapters from *The Handmaid's Tale* in Chapter 8 of this book and two complete chapters from *Catch-22* in Chapter 4.

Here are some other elements on which structure depends. They are not so immediately visible as chapter divisions, but they are fundamental.

The balance of characters: The characters interact in the overall structure, often complementing or contrasting with each other.

You will see interesting balances of complement and contrast in the extracts from *Farewell, My Lovely* and *The Third Man* (Chapter 2), *Women in Love* and *A Farewell to Arms* (Chapter 3), *Heart of Darkness* (Chapter 5), *The Householder* (Chapter 6) and *Ulysses* (Chapter 7).

Imagery and symbolism: As with characters, there may be contrasting or complementary sets of images or symbols, or there may be one major symbol which unites the ideas. In Virginia Woolf's *To the Lighthouse* (1927), very little actually happens in the plot, and the structure is based on the imagery and central symbol of the lighthouse which represents the different aspirations – spiritual, artistic and emotional – of the characters.

Plot – suspense and surprise: Novelists often play on the predictions readers constantly make. A novel's structure will often include moments of **suspense** (a tense feeling in the reader, caused by wondering what may happen), and **surprise** (the feeling in the reader caused by something unexpected happening).

Plot – narrative structure: Novels from previous centuries tended to follow the chronological order of events (from beginning to end, in the order they would occur in real time):

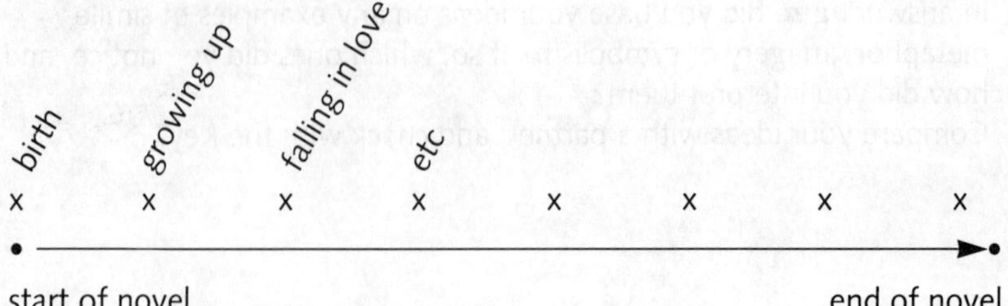

This is still a common way of telling a story, but modern writers often structure their novels in a non-chronological way, with the result that the **narrative order** and the **chronological order** are not the same. Previous events outside the time-scale of the novel are included as **flashbacks** (either through the characters' thoughts, conversation, or the narrator's comments). Developments later in the story can be suggested through **anticipation**.

flashbacks

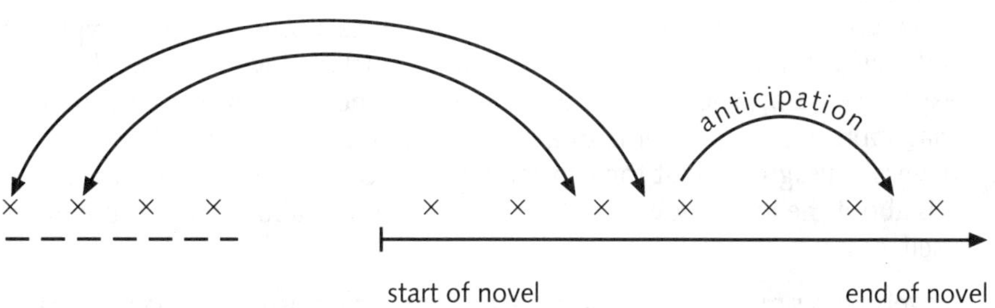

A classic example of a novel where the chronological order is full of flashbacks is *Ulysses*, which you will look at in Chapter 7.

Narrators and points of view: Changing the narrator or point of view will change the structure radically. You have already seen that modern novelists sometimes employ multiple narrators and points of view. This means there are almost infinite ways of structuring the same story.

An example in this book is *The Joy Luck Club*, a novel composed of experiences recounted by eight different narrators, an extract from which you will read in Chapter 6.

So, in addition to the chronological and narrative structures, the story can be represented both through different patterns of time-scale and by different narrators.

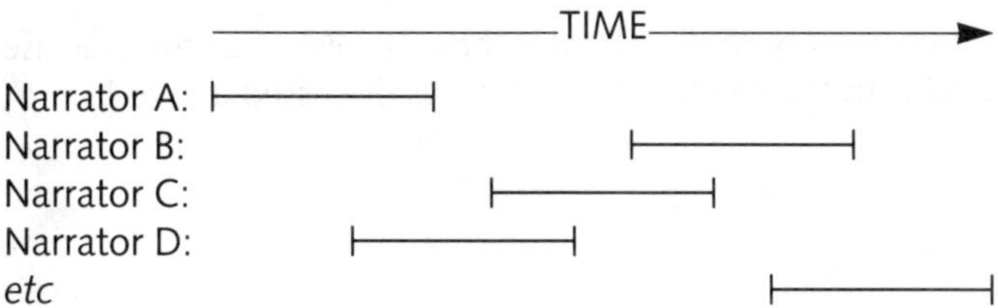

Theme

The **theme** of a novel is often defined as the central philosophical or moral idea of a novel, what the novel is really 'about'. The reader responds to the theme by interpreting the plot, the characters, the symbolism, the imagery, … in short, all the elements of the novel working together (what we have called the *structure*). Identifying the **theme** – or **themes** – is often a subjective, personal process. Readers hardly ever disagree about the plot of a novel, what happens in it, but they sometimes disagree about the theme, what seems to be the point of it. This is part of the personal response of the reader to the novel.

A great novel may have many themes. Joyce's *Ulysses*, for example, does not have a complicated plot, yet the themes include love, loss, death, art, exile, a sense of belonging, and many more. And as an example of the fact that appreciating the theme of a novel is a personal matter, two great novelists disagree about the central theme of *Ulysses*. For Vladimir Nabokov, it is about the loss of love. For Samuel Beckett, it is about the art of writing itself.

Novels with similar subject matter are often distinguished by their themes. Take, for example, the spy novels of Ian Fleming and those of John Le Carré, both very popular. There are, of course enormous differences in the settings, plots and characters (Fleming appeals to fantasy, Le Carré emphasizes realism), but while the James Bond novels are exciting, they are not really 'about' anything: in contrast, Le Carré's novels are about loyalty, the tension between public and individual morality, betrayal and loneliness, and this explains their reputation as more serious and significant works of art. As a further example, the novels in Chapter 2 are seen by most readers as something more than 'entertainments' because of their theme of individual morality and integrity in a corrupt world.

12 ***a*** Choose a novel both you and your partner have read. How do you personally interpret the theme(s) of the novel ?

b Compare your ideas with your partner. Are they similar or different?

[Note: at the end of the Key to this chapter there is a list of all the exercises in this book that deal with the elements of the novel discussed above.]

2 Mean Streets

Before you read

1 Look at the film stills on the previous page. Which do you think are the 'heroes'? Which do you think are the 'villains'? What makes you think so?

2 One afternoon the private investigator Philip Marlowe receives a phone call in his Los Angeles office ...

See the Glossary section at the back of the book for vocabulary.

... I heard a cool, supercilious voice that sounded as if it thought it was pretty good. It said drawlingly, after I had answered:

'You are Philip Marlowe, a private detective?'

'Check.'

'Oh – you mean, yes. You have been recommended to me as a man who can be trusted to keep his mouth shut. I should like you to come to my house at seven o'clock this evening. We can discuss a matter. My name is Lindsay Marriott and I live at 4212 Cabrillo Street, Montemar Vista. Do you know where that is?'

'I know where Montemar Vista is, Mr Marriott.'

'Yes. Well, Cabrillo Street is rather hard to find. The streets down here are all laid out in a pattern of interesting but intricate curves. I should suggest that you walk up the steps from the sidewalk café. If you do that, Cabrillo is the third street you come to and my house is the only one on the block. At seven then?'

'What is the nature of the employment, Mr Marriott?'

'I should prefer not to discuss that over the phone.'

'Can't you give some idea? Montemar Vista is quite a distance.'

'I shall be glad to pay your expenses, if we don't agree. Are you particular about the nature of the employment?'

'Not as long as it's legitimate.'

The voice grew icicles. 'I should not have called you, if it were not.'

A Harvard boy. Nice use of the subjunctive mood. The end of my foot itched, but my bank account was still trying to crawl under a duck. I put honey into my voice and said:

'Many thanks for calling me, Mr Marriott. I'll be there.'

(From *Farewell, My Lovely* by Raymond Chandler)

a Imagine you are Marlowe.

1 Why have you agreed to go and see Marriott?
2 What is your opinion of him?
3 Think of three things that you want to ask him during the meeting.

b Imagine you are Marriott.

1 Why have you contacted Marlowe?

2 What is your opinion of him?

3 Think of three things that you want to ask him during the meeting.

Later the same evening Marlowe drives out to Montemar Vista ...

Farewell, My Lovely (1940) Raymond Chandler

See the Glossary section at the back of the book for vocabulary.

CHAPTER 8

I got down to Montemar Vista as the light began to fade, but there was still a fine sparkle on the water and the surf was breaking far out in long smooth curves. A group of pelicans was flying bomber formation just under the creaming lip of the waves. A lonely yacht was taking in toward the yacht harbour at Bay City. Beyond it the huge emptiness of the Pacific was purple-grey.

Montemar Vista was a few dozen houses of various sizes and shapes hanging by their teeth and eyebrows to a spur of mountain and looking as if a good sneeze would drop them down among the box lunches on the beach.

Above the beach the highway ran under a wide concrete arch which was in fact a pedestrian bridge. From the inner end of this a flight of concrete steps with a thick galvanized handrail on one side ran straight as a ruler up the side of the mountain. Beyond the arch the sidewalk café my client had spoken of was bright and cheerful inside, but the iron-legged tile-topped tables outside under the striped awning were empty save for a single dark woman in slacks who smoked and stared moodily out to sea, with a bottle of beer in front of her. A fox terrier was using one of the iron chairs for a lamp-post. She chided the dog absently as I drove past and gave the sidewalk café my business to the extent of using its parking space.

I walked back through the arch and started up the steps. It was a nice walk if you liked grunting. There were two hundred and eighty steps up to Cabrillo Street. They were drifted over with windblown sand and the handrail was as cold and wet as a toad's belly.

When I reached the top the sparkle had gone from the water and a seagull with a broken trailing leg was twisting against the offsea breeze. I sat down on the damp cold top step and shook the sand out of my shoes and waited for my pulse to come down into the low hundreds. When I was breathing more or less normally again I shook my shirt loose from my back and went along to the lighted house which was the only one within yelling distance of the steps.

It was a nice little house with a salt-tarnished spiral of staircase going up to the front door and an imitation coach-lamp for a porch light. The garage was underneath and to one side. Its door was lifted up and rolled back and the light of the porch-lamp shone obliquely on a huge black battleship of a car with chromium trimmings, a coyote tail tied to the Winged Victory on the radiator cap and engraved initials where the emblem should be. The car had a right-hand drive and looked as if it had cost more than the house.

I went up the spiral steps, looked for a bell, and used a knocker in the shape of a tiger's head. Its clatter was swallowed in the early evening fog. I heard no steps in the house. My damp shirt felt like an icepack on my back. The door opened silently, and I was looking at a tall blond man in a white flannel suit with a violet satin scarf around his neck.

There was a cornflower in the lapel of his white coat and his pale blue eyes looked faded out by comparison. The violet scarf was loose enough to show that he wore no tie and that he had a thick, soft brown neck, like the neck of a strong woman. His features were a little on the heavy side, but handsome; he had an inch more of height than I had, which made him six feet one. His blond hair was arranged, by art or nature, in three precise blond ledges which reminded me of steps, so that I didn't like them. I wouldn't have liked them anyway. Apart from all this he had the general appearance of a lad who would wear a white flannel suit with a violet scarf round his neck and a cornflower in his lapel.

He cleared his throat lightly and looked past my shoulder at the darkening sea. His cool supercilious voice said. 'Yes?'

'Seven o'clock,' I said. 'On the dot.'

'Oh yes. Let me see, your name is ——' he paused and frowned in the effort of memory. The effect was as phony as the pedigree of a used car. I let him work at it for a minute, then I said:

'Philip Marlowe. The same as it was this afternoon.'

He gave me a quick darting frown, as if perhaps something ought to be done about that. Then he stepped back and said coldly:

'Ah yes. Quite so. Come in, Marlowe. My house boy is away this evening.'

He opened the door wide with a fingertip, as though opening the door himself dirtied him a little.

What do you think Marriott's house will be like? What kind of furniture and possessions is he likely to have?

I went in past him and smelled perfume. He closed the door. The entrance put us on a low balcony with a metal railing that ran around three sides of a big studio living-room. The fourth side contained a big fireplace and two doors. A fire was crackling in the fireplace. The balcony was lined with bookshelves and there were pieces of glazed metallic-looking bits of sculpture on pedestals.

We went down three steps to the main part of the living room. The carpet almost tickled my ankles. There was a concert grand piano, closed down. On one corner of it stood a tall silver vase on a strip of peach-coloured velvet, and a single yellow rose in the vase. There was plenty of nice soft furniture, a great many floor cushions, some with golden tassels and some just naked. It was a nice room, if you didn't get rough. There was a wide damask covered divan in a shadowy corner, like a casting couch. It was the kind of room where people sit with their feet in their laps and sip absinthe through lumps of sugar and talk with high affected voices and sometimes just squeak. It was a room where anything could happen except work.

Mr Lindsay Marriott arranged himself in the curve of the grand piano, leaned over to sniff at the yellow rose, then opened a French enamel cigarette case and lit a long brown cigarette with a gold tip. I sat down on a pink chair and hoped I wouldn't leave a mark on it. I lit a Camel, blew smoke through my nose and looked at a piece of black shiny metal on a stand. It showed a full, smooth curve with a shallow fold in it and two protuberances on the curve. I stared at it. Marriott saw me staring at it.

'An interesting bit,' he said negligently, 'I picked it up just the other day. Asta Dial's *Spirit of Dawn*.'

'I thought it was Klopstein's *Two Warts on a Fanny*,' I said.

Mr Lindsay Marriott's face looked as if he had swallowed a bee. He smoothed it out with an effort.

'You have a somewhat peculiar sense of humour,' he said.

'Not peculiar,' I said. 'Just uninhibited.'

'Yes,' he said very coldly. 'Yes – of course. I've no doubt. … Well, what I wished to see you about is, as a matter of fact, a very slight matter indeed. Hardly worth bringing you down here for. I am meeting a couple of men tonight and paying them some money. I thought I might as well have someone with me. You carry a gun?'

'At times. Yes,' I said. I looked at the dimple in his broad, fleshy chin. You could have lost a marble in it.

'I shan't want you to carry that. Nothing of that sort at all. This is a purely business transaction.'

'I hardly ever shoot anybody,' I said. 'A matter of blackmail?'

He frowned. 'Certainly not. I'm not in the habit of giving people grounds for blackmail.'

'It happens to the nicest people. I might say particularly to the nicest people.'

He waved his cigarette. His aquamarine eyes had a faintly thoughtful expression, but his lips smiled. The kind of smile that goes with a silk noose.

He blew some more smoke and tilted his head back. This accentuated the soft firm lines of his throat. His eyes came down slowly and studied me.

'I'm meeting these men – most probably – in a rather lonely place. I don't know where yet. I expect a call giving me the particulars. I have to be ready to leave at once. It won't be very far away from here. That's the understanding.'

'You've been making this deal some time?'

'Three or four days, as a matter of fact.'

'You left your bodyguard problem until pretty late.'

He thought that over. He snicked some dark ash from his cigarette. 'That's true. I had some difficulty making my mind up. It would be better for me to go alone, although nothing has been said definitely about my having someone with me. On the other hand I'm not much of a hero.'

'They know you by sight, of course?'

'I – I'm not sure. I shall be carrying a large amount of money and it is not my money. I'm acting for a friend. I shouldn't feel justified in letting it out of my possession, of course.'

I snubbed out my cigarette and leaned back in the pink chair and twiddled my thumbs. 'How much money – and what for?'

'Well, really – ' it was a fairly nice smile now, but I still didn't like it. 'I can't go into that.'

'You just want me to go along and hold your hat?'

His hand jerked again and some ash fell off on his white cuff. He shook it off and stared down at the place where it had been.

I'm afraid I don't like your manner,' he said, using the edge of his voice.

'I've had complaints about it,' I said. 'But nothing seems to do any good. Let's look at this job a little. You want a bodyguard, but he can't wear a gun. You want a helper, but he isn't supposed to know what he's supposed to do. You want me to risk my neck without knowing why or what for or what the risk is. What are you offering for all this?'

'I hadn't really got around to thinking about it.' His cheekbones were dusky red.

'Do you suppose you could get around to thinking about it?'

He leaned forward gracefully and smiled between his teeth. 'How would you like a swift punch on the nose?'

Do you think Marriott will hit Marlowe? Why, or why not?

I grinned and stood up and put my hat on. I started across the carpet towards the front door, but not very fast.

His voice snapped at my back. 'I'm offering you a hundred dollars for a few hours of your time. If that isn't enough, say so. There's no risk. Some jewels were taken from a friend of mine in a hold-up – and I'm buying them back. Sit down and don't be so touchy.'

I went back to the pink chair and sat down again.

'All right,' I said. 'Let's hear about it.'

We stared at each other for all of ten seconds. 'Have you ever heard of Fei Tsui jade?' he asked slowly, and lit another of his dark cigarettes.

'No.'

'It's the only really valuable kind. Other kinds are valuable to some extent for the material, but chiefly for the workmanship on them. Fei Tsui is valuable in itself. All known deposits were exhausted hundreds of years ago. A friend of mine owns a necklace of sixty beads of about six carats each, intricately carved. Worth eighty or ninety thousand dollars. The Chinese Government has a very slightly larger one valued at a hundred and twenty-five thousand. My friend's necklace was taken in a hold-up a few nights ago. I was present, but quite helpless. I had driven my friend to an evening party and later to the Trocadero and we were on our way back to her home from there. A car brushed the left front fender and stopped, as I thought, to apologize. Instead of that it was a very quick and very neat hold-up. Either three or four men, I really saw only two, but I'm sure another stayed in the car behind the wheel, and I thought I saw a glimpse of still a fourth at the rear window. My friend was wearing the jade necklace. They took that and two rings and a bracelet. The one who seemed to be the leader looked the things over without any apparent hurry under a small flashlight. Then he handed one of the rings back and said that would give us an idea what kind of people we were dealing with and to wait for a phone call before reporting to the police or the insurance company. So we obeyed their instructions. There's plenty of that sort of thing going on, of course. You keep the affair to yourself and pay ransom, or you never see your jewels again. If they're fully insured, perhaps you don't mind, but if they happen to be rare pieces, you would rather pay ransom.'

I nodded. 'And this jade necklace is something that can't be picked up every day.'

He slid a finger along the polished surface of the piano with a dreamy expression, as if touching smooth things pleased him.

'Very much so. It's irreplaceable. She shouldn't have worn it out – ever. But she's a reckless sort of woman. The other things were good but ordinary.'

'Uh-huh. How much are you paying?'

'Eight thousand dollars. It's dirt cheap. But if my friend couldn't get another like it, these thugs couldn't very easily dispose of it either. It's probably known to everyone in the trade, all over the country.'

This friend of yours – does she have a name?'

'I'd prefer not to mention it at the moment.'

'What are the arrangements?'

He looked at me along his pale eyes. I thought he seemed a bit scared, but I didn't know him very well. Maybe it was a hangover. The hand that held the dark cigarette couldn't keep still.

'We have been negotiating by telephone for several days through me. Everything is settled except the time and place of meeting. It is to be some time tonight. I shall presently be getting a call to tell me of that. It will not be very far away, they say, and I must be prepared to leave at once. I suppose that is so that no plant could be arranged. With the police, I mean.'

'Uh-huh. Is the money marked? I suppose it is money?'

'Currency, of course. Twenty dollar bills. No, why should it be marked?'

'It can be done so that it takes black light to detect it. No reason – except that the cops like to break up these gangs – if they can get any co-operation. Some of the money might turn up on some lad with a record.'

He wrinkled his brow thoughtfully. 'I'm afraid I don't know what black light is.'

'Ultra-violet. It makes certain metallic inks glisten in the dark. I could get it done for you.'

'I'm afraid there isn't time for that now,' he said shortly.

'That's one of the things that worries me.'

'Why?'

'Why you only called me this afternoon. Why you picked on me. Who told you about me?'

He laughed. His laugh was rather boyish, but not a very young boy. 'Well, as a matter of fact I'll have to confess I merely picked your name at random out of the phone book. You see I hadn't intended to have anyone go with me. Then this afternoon I got to thinking why not.'

I lit another of my squashed cigarettes and watched his throat muscles. 'What's the plan?'

He spread his hands. 'Simply to go where I am told, hand over the package of money, and receive back the jade necklace.'

'Uh-huh.'

'You seem fond of that expression.'

'What expression?'

'Uh-huh.'

'Where will I be – in the back of the car?'

'I suppose so. It's a big car. You could easily hide in the back of it.'

What do you think Marlowe's opinion of this plan will be?

'Listen,' I said slowly. 'You plan to go out with me hidden in your car to a destination you are to get over the phone some time tonight. You will have eight grand in currency on you and with that you are supposed to buy back a jade necklace worth ten or twelve times that much. What you will probably get will be a package you won't be allowed to open – providing you get anything at all. It's just as likely they will simply take your money, count it over in some other place, and mail you the necklace, if they feel big-hearted. There's nothing to prevent them double-crossing you. Certainly nothing I could do would stop them. These are heist guys. They're tough. They might even knock you on the head – not hard – just enough to delay you while they go on their way.'

'Well, as a matter of fact, I'm a little afraid of something like that,' he said quietly, and his eyes twitched. 'I suppose that's really why I wanted somebody with me.'

'Did they put a flash on you when they pulled the stick-up?'

He shook his head, no.

'No matter. They've had a dozen chances to look you over since. They probably knew all about you before that anyway. These jobs are cased. They're cased the way a dentist cases your tooth for a gold inlay. You go out with this dame much?'

'Well – not infrequently,' he said stiffly.

'Married?'

'Look here,' he snapped. 'Suppose we leave the lady out of this entirely.'

'Okey,' I said. 'But the more I know the fewer cups I break. I ought to walk away from this job, Marriott. I really ought. If the boys want to play ball, you don't need me. If they don't want to play ball, I can't do anything about it.'

'All I want is your company,' he said quickly.

I shrugged and spread my hands. 'Okey – but I drive the car and carry the money – and you do the hiding in the back. We're about the same height. If there's any question, we'll just tell them the truth. Nothing to lose by it.'

'No.' He bit his lip.

'I'm getting a hundred dollars for doing nothing. If anybody gets conked, it ought to be me.'

He frowned and shook his head, but after quite a long time his face cleared slowly and he smiled.

'Very well,' he said slowly. 'I don't suppose it matters much. We'll be together. Would you care for a spot of brandy?'

'Uh-huh. And you might bring me my hundred bucks. I like to feel money.'

He moved away like a dancer, his body almost motionless from the waist up.

The phone rang as he was on his way out. It was in a little alcove off the living-room proper, cut into the balcony. It wasn't the call we were thinking about though. He sounded too affectionate.

He danced back after a while with a bottle of Five-Star Martell and five nice crisp twenty-dollar bills. That made it a nice evening – so far.

How do you think Marlowe is feeling?

CHAPTER 9

The house was very still. Far off there was a sound which might have been beating surf or cars zooming along a highway, or wind in pine trees. It was the sea, of course, breaking far down below. I sat there and listened to it and thought long, careful thoughts.

The phone rang four times within the next hour and a half. The big one came at eight minutes past ten. Marriott talked briefly, in a very low voice, cradled the instrument without a sound and stood up with a sort of hushed movement. His face looked drawn. He had changed to dark clothes now. He walked silently back into the room and poured himself a stiff drink in a brandy glass. He held it against the light a moment with a queer unhappy smile, swirled it once quickly and tilted his head back to pour it down his throat.

'Well – we're all set, Marlowe. Ready?'

'That's all I've been all evening. Where do we go?'

'A place called Purissima Canyon.'

'I never heard of it.'

'I'll get a map.' He got one and spread it out quickly and the light blinked in his brassy hair as he bent over it. Then he pointed with his finger. The place was one of the many canyons off the foothill boulevard that turns into town from the coast highway north of Bay City. I had a vague idea where it was, but no more. It seemed to be at the end of a street called Camino de la Costa.

'It will be not more than twelve minutes from here,' Marriott said quickly. 'We'd better get moving. We only have twenty minutes to play with.'

He handed me a light-coloured overcoat which made me a fine target. It fitted pretty well. I wore my own hat. I had a gun under my arm, but I hadn't told him about that.

While I put the coat on, he went on talking in a light nervous voice and dancing on his hands the thick manila envelope with the eight grand in it.

'Purissima Canyon has a sort of level shelf at the inner end of it, they say. This is walled off from the road by a white fence of four-by-fours, but you can just squeeze by. A dirt road winds down into a little hollow and we are to wait there without lights. There are no houses around.'

'We?'

'Well, I mean "I" – theoretically.'

'Oh.'

He handed me the manila envelope and I opened it up looked at what was inside. It was money all right, a huge wad of currency. I didn't count it. I snapped the rubber around again and stuffed the packet down inside my overcoat. It almost caved in a rib.

We went to the door and Marriott switched off all the lights. He opened the front door cautiously and peered out at the foggy air. We went out and down the salt-tarnished spiral stairway to the street level and the garage.

It was a little foggy, the way it always is down there at night. I had to start up the windshield wiper for a while.

The big foreign car drove itself, but I held the wheel for the sake of appearances. …

Marlowe drives Marriott towards Purissima Canyon.

What do you think will happen at the appointment?

... There was a house to a block, then a house to two blocks, then no houses at all. A vague window or two was still lighted, but the people around there seemed to go to bed with the chickens. Then the paved avenue ended abruptly in a dirt road packed as hard as concrete in dry weather. The dirt road narrowed and dropped slowly downhill between walls of brush. The lights of the Belvedere Beach Club hung in the air to the right and far ahead there was a gleam of moving water. The acrid smell of the sage filled the night. Then a white-painted barrier loomed across the dirt road and Marriott spoke at my shoulder again.

'I don't think you can get past it,' he said. 'The space doesn't look wide enough.'

I cut the noiseless motor, dimmed the lights and sat there, listening. Nothing. I switched the lights off altogether and got out of the car. The crickets stopped chirping. For a little while the silence was so complete that I could hear the sound of tyres on the highway at the bottom of the cliffs, a mile away. Then one by one the crickets started up again until the night was full of them.

'Sit tight. I'm going down there and have a look see,' I whispered into the back of the car.

I touched the gun butt inside my coat and walked forward. There was more room between the brush and the end of the white barrier than there had seemed to be from the car. Some one had hacked the brush away and there were car marks in the dirt. Probably kids going down there to neck on warm nights. I went on past the barrier. The road dropped and curved. Below was darkness and a vague far off sea-sound. And the lights of cars on the highway. I went on. The road ended in a shallow bowl entirely surrounded by brush. It was empty. There seemed to be no way into it but the way I had come. I stood there in the silence and listened.

Minute passed slowly after minute, but I kept on waiting for some new sound. None came. I seemed to have that hollow entirely to myself.

I looked across to the lighted beach club. From its upper windows a man with a good night glass could probably cover this spot fairly well. He could see a car come and go, see who got out of it, whether there was a group of men or just one. Sitting in a dark room with a good night glass you can see a lot more detail than you would think possible.

I turned to go back up the hill. From the base of a bush a cricket chirped loud enough to make me jump. I went on up around the curve and past the white barricade. Still nothing. The black car stood dimly shining against a greyness which was neither darkness nor light. I went over to it and put a foot on the running board beside the driver's seat.

'Looks like a tryout,' I said under my breath, but loud enough for Marriott to hear me from the back of the car. 'Just to see if you obey orders.'

There was a vague movement behind but he didn't answer. I went on trying to see something besides bushes.

Whoever it was had a nice easy shot at the back of my head. Afterwards I thought I might have heard the swish of a sap. Maybe you always think that – afterwards.

First reaction

3 Which of these statements do you think is most likely?

a Marriott was telling the truth all the time. Marlowe was hit on the head because he wasn't expected to be there.

b Marriott had been told to trick Marlowe into going to Purissima Canyon, but Marriott was the real target. He was shot, and Marlowe was hit on the head.

c Marlowe was the real target, and Marriott had been tricking him. However, by mistake Marlowe was hit on the head and Marriott shot instead of the other way round.

d It was Marriott who hit Marlowe on the head.

Check your answer with the Key.

Close reading

Dialogue

4 ***a*** The scene at Marriott's house is typical of all the scenes where Marlowe meets suspects or clients. Put a mark on the line to show your impression of what is going on.

The dialogue between Marlowe and Marriott is:

b Compare your impression with a partner.

5 Imagine you are a police officer interrogating Marriott about the theft of the jade necklace (lines 162–219). What questions would you ask? Make a list, and compare your questions with a partner or in groups.
Examples: *What time did you leave home that evening?*
What time did you get back?
Where did you go?

6 Which of the questions you thought of in Exercise 5 are answered in the extract?

7 Now imagine you are Marlowe. What answers have you got from your client to these questions?
a What do you want me to do?
b How much will I get paid?
c Is the job dangerous, suspicious, illegal – or straightforward?

8 But their conversation is not only an exchange of information. Marlowe and Marriott also express hostility, suspicion and other emotions. Look at these moments and choose from the interpretations 1–3.

*WHAT THEY **SAY***	*WHAT THEY **MEAN***
lines 60–68	
a Marlowe: Seven o'clock. On the dot.	***1*** I'm Philip Marlowe. ***2*** I'm punctual and efficient. ***3*** Can you have forgotten the time we arranged to meet?
b Marriott: Oh yes. Let me see, your name is ———?	***1*** This business is of very little importance to me. ***2*** You must excuse me, my memory is not very good. ***3*** I don't normally associate with people like you.
c Marlowe: Philip Marlowe. The same as it was this afternoon.	***1*** What a terrible memory you have! ***2*** Let me remind you of my name; you seem to have forgotten. ***3*** You remember my name, but you're pretending not to.
d Marriott: Ah yes. Quite so. Come in, Marlowe. My house boy is away this evening.	***1*** I'm alone this evening. ***2*** I don't normally come to the door for people like you. ***3*** I'm nervous about opening the door to strangers.

lines 96–101

e Marriott: An interesting bit. I picked it up just the other day. Asta Dial's *Spirit of Dawn*.

1. Are you a connoisseur of modern art?
2. I imagine you know nothing about art.
3. I'm an artistic type of person.

f Marlowe: I thought it was Klopstein's *Two Warts on a Fanny*.

1. Modern art doesn't interest me.
2. What pretentious nonsense!
3. It doesn't look like a piece by Asta Dial.

g Marriott: You have a somewhat peculiar sense of humour.

1. How vulgar you are!
2. You have no sense of humour.
3. I've never come across such an original sense of humour as yours before!

9 Write your own interpretations for the following extracts from the dialogue between Marlowe and Marriott. You can write more than one sentence.

WHAT THEY ***SAY***	*WHAT THEY* ***MEAN***
lines 113–16 ***a*** Marriott: Certainly not. I'm not in the habit of giving people grounds for blackmail. ***b*** Marlowe: It happens to the nicest people. I might say particularly to the nicest people.	______________________
line 129 ***c*** Marlowe: You left your bodyguard problem until pretty late.	______________________
lines 143–9 ***d*** Marlowe: You want me to go along and hold your hat? ***e*** Marlowe: I've had complaints about it. But nothing seems to do any good.	______________________
line 155 ***f*** Marlowe: Do you suppose you could get around to thinking about it?	______________________

Characterization

10 Marriott is not only characterized through what he says; other details are significant too. Make notes under these headings, and compare your ideas with a partner. Some examples are given.

his appearance (lines 44–57)

Example: … he had a thick, soft brown neck, like the neck of a strong woman. (lines 49–50)
This suggests that although he is muscular he is rather effeminate.

a His blond hair was arranged, by art or nature, in three precise blond ledges … I wouldn't have liked them anyway. (lines 52–5)

___

b … he had the general appearance of a lad who would wear a white flannel suit … and a cornflower in his lapel. (lines 55–7)

___

his home and possessions (lines 71–87)

Example: I went in past him and smelled perfume. (line 71)
This suggests either that he has recently entertained a woman, or reinforces the suggestion that he is effeminate.

c The balcony was lined with bookshelves and there were pieces of glazed metallic-looking bits of sculpture on pedestals. (lines 75–6)

___

d The carpet almost tickled my ankles. (line 78)

___

e It was a nice room, if you didn't get rough. … It was a room where anything could happen except work. (lines 82–7)

___

his behaviour

Example: Mr Lindsay Marriott arranged himself in the curve, leaned over to sniff at the yellow rose … and lit a long brown cigarette with a gold tip. (lines 88–90)
This suggests that he is graceful, 'artistic' and used to luxury (and perhaps effeminate): perhaps he also wants to to give Marlowe the impression that he is not worried about anything – which might indicate that he is worried.

(Notice how Marlowe's character is so completely contrasted in the description of similar behaviour in lines 91–3.)

f He slid a finger along the polished surface of the piano with a dreamy expression, as if touching smooth things pleased him. (lines 199–200)

____

g The hand that held the dark cigarette couldn't keep still. (line 213)

____

h His laugh was rather boyish, but not a very young boy. (lines 236–7)

____

Language practice – structures

Structures for comparing and describing

11 Look at these two comparisons from the passage:

(Marriott) frowned in the effort of memory. The effect was *as phony as* the pedigree of a used car. (lines 61–3)

He moved away *like a dancer*, his body almost motionless from the waist up. (lines 294–5)

A What is the grammar rule about the use of *like* and *as*? Check your ideas in the Key.

B Now look at the following comparisons that Marlowe uses in other parts of *Farewell, My Lovely*. Join the beginnings ***a–k*** with the endings ***1–11***, using *like* or *as*. The first one is done for you.

Notice that Marlowe is always colourful, but in addition to explicit comparisons (such as 'he was as strong as a lion' meaning 'he was very strong') he sometimes makes ironic comparisons (such as 'he was as strong as a mouse' meaning 'he was not very strong').

a 'Don't say that, pal,' the big man purred softly,
b A Colt Army .45 looked
c She swished before me in a tight dress that fitted her
d 'Uh-huh,' the voice dragged itself out of her throat
e His smile was as cunning
f Then suspicion climbed all over her face,
g She's a charming middle-aged lady with a face

1 a plumber's handkerchief.
2 a hen having hiccups.
3 a bucket of mud …
4 a frozen fish.
5 fleas.
6 a toy pistol in his hand.
7 a sick man getting out of bed
8 a mermaid's skin …
9 a broken mousetrap.
10 four tigers after dinner.
11 a kitten, but not so playfully.

h His smile was as stiff
i My stomach burned from the last drink. I wasn't hungry. I lit a cigarette. It tasted
j I left her laughing. The sound was
k He had small, hungry, heavy-lidded eyes, as restless

a ***10 (+like)*** ***b*** ________ ***c*** ________ ***d*** ________
e ________ ***f*** ________ ***g*** ________ ***h*** ________
i ________ ***j*** ________ ***k*** ________

12 Now look at these two comparisons.
Montemar Vista was a few dozen houses … looking *as if* a good sneeze would drop them down among the box lunches on the beach. (lines 7–10)
He opened the door wide with a fingertip, *as though* opening the door dirtied him a little. (lines 69–70)

A What is the grammar rule about the use of *as if* and *as though*? Check your ideas in the Key.
B Imagine you are Marlowe, and describe some of the following moments using a sentence with the *as if/as though* structure.
Examples: Marlowe's exhaustion (lines 29–30)
I felt as though my lungs would never forgive me.
I felt as if my body was asking for a divorce on grounds of cruelty.
a Marriott's appearance (lines 45–57)
b Marriott's living-room (lines 77–87)
c Marriott's reaction to mention of money (lines 153–4)
d Marriott's reaction to Marlowe's question (lines 236–7)
e Marriott's way of talking on the phone (lines 296–8)
f Marriott's description (suspiciously precise?) of the meeting-place (lines 333–7)
g the blow to Marlowe's head (lines 403–5)

13 Now look at another two comparisons.
It was *the kind of room where* people sit with their feet in their laps … and sometimes just squeak. (lines 84–7)
(Marriott's) lips smiled. *The kind of smile that* goes with a silk noose. (lines 118–19)

A What grammatical construction is used here? Check your ideas with the Key.
B Imagine you are Marlowe, and describe some of the following using the structure above.
Example: Marriott's car
It was the kind of car that would cost me a year's salary – if I bought it second-hand.

a Marriott's woman friend
b the jade necklace
c the men who stole the necklace
d Purissima Canyon
e the beach club (lines 386–91)

Language practice – vocabulary

Describing 'good' and 'bad' characters

14 ***a*** Sort the following characters into 'heroes' and 'villains'. Then add other examples to your lists.

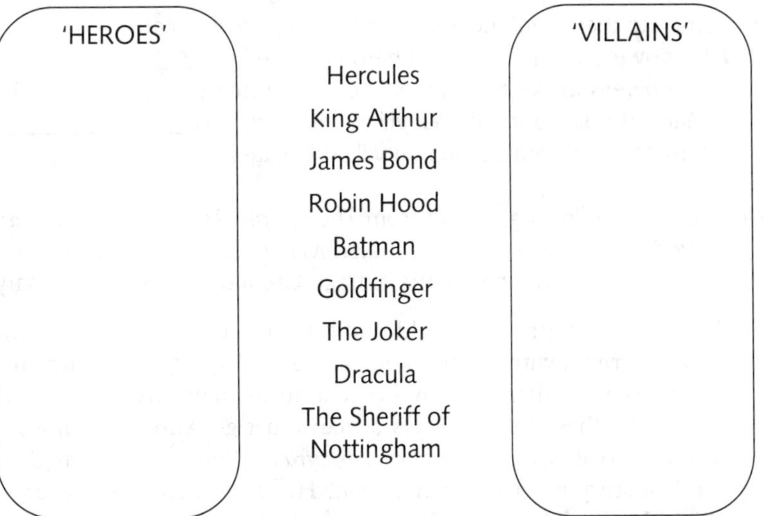

b Write the words in the box below in the columns on page 50 that you think most suitable. You can put a word in more than one column if you want. You can also add words of your own.

short of money *kind* *corrupt* *pure* *hypocritical* *selfish* *witty* *observant* *ugly* *honest* *scheming* *cynical* *smooth-talking* *ostentatious* *handsome* *cowardly* *rich* *strong* *dishonest* *brave* *naïve* *modest* *cruel*

'TRADITIONAL HERO'	MARLOWE	MARRIOTT	'TRADITIONAL VILLAIN'
brave			*cruel*

c Complete these sentences in as many ways as you can.
1 Marlowe is like a traditional hero because he is ____________________
2 Marlowe is unlike a traditional hero because he is ____________________
3 Marriott is like a traditional villain because he is ____________________
4 Marriott is unlike a traditional villain because he is ____________________

15 Now read the following extract from *The Simple Art of Murder*, an essay on detective fiction by Raymond Chandler. Match the words and phrases in *italics* with those given below the extract. Use a dictionary if necessary.

It is not a very fragrant world, but it is the world you live in, and certain writers with tough minds and a cool spirit of detachment can make very interesting and even amusing patterns out of it. ... But down these mean streets a man must go who is *not himself mean*, who is *neither tarnished nor afraid*. The detective in this kind of story must be such a man. He is the hero, he is everything. He must be a complete man and a *common* man and yet an *unusual* man. He must be, to use a rather weathered phrase, *a man of honour*, by instinct, by inevitability, without thought of it, and certainly without saying it. He must be *the best man in his world* and *a good enough man for any world*. I do not care much about his private life; he is *neither a eunuch nor a satyr*; I think he might seduce a duchess and I am quite sure he would not spoil a virgin; if he is a man of honour in one thing, he is that in all things.

He is a *relatively poor* man, or he would not be a detective at all. He is a common man or he could not go among common people. He *has a sense of character*, or he would not know his job. He *will take no man's money dishonestly and no man's insolence* without a due and dispassionate revenge. He is a *lonely* man and his *pride* is that you will treat him as a proud man or be very sorry that you ever saw him. He talks as a man of his age talks, that is, with *rude wit*, *a lively sense of the grotesque*, *a disgust for sham*, and *a contempt for pettiness*.

The story is this man's adventure in search of a hidden truth and it would be no adventure if it did not happen to a man *fit for adventure*. He has *a range of awareness that startles you*, but it belongs to him by right, because it belongs to the world he lives in. If there were enough like him, I think the world would be a very safe place to live in, and yet not too dull to be worth living in.

Example:
solitary ***lonely***

a deserves respect in any society ________
b uncorrupt and courageous ________
c surprising perception ________
d out of the ordinary ________
e a disdain for small-mindedness ________
f ready to take risks ________
g average ________
h certainly not well-off ________
i a hatred of pretence ________
j superior to those around him ________
k is a good judge of people ________
l not sordid or ignoble ________
m self-respect ________
n has an interest in sex, but is not excessive ________
o is honest, and does not tolerate lack of respect ________
p someone with a moral code ________
q a vivid sense of humour some people would consider vulgar ________

16 Does Philip Marlowe conform to the ideal described in *The Simple Art of Murder*? Try to find some examples of these qualities in the extracts from *Farewell, My Lovely*.

Extension

17 **Essay/class discussion**: Chandler wrote the following comment about another great writer of detective stories, Dashiell Hammett (1894–1961, author of *The Maltese Falcon*):

'And there are still quite a few people around who say that Hammett did not write detective stories at all, merely hard-boiled chronicles of mean streets with a perfunctory mystery element dropped in like the olive in a martini.'

a If you like the detective genre, make a list of detective novels and films you have enjoyed, or:

b If you don't like the detective genre, make a list of detective novels and films that have been successful with the public.

c What are the main ingredients that make them enjoyable? Choose from the following, or add other ideas of your own. Discuss your ideas in class, or write a short essay.

the style of writing/filming the plot suspense and surprise
the figure of the 'hero' the figure of the 'villain' the setting
the dialogue the action the moral 'message'

18 Imagine that you have gone to see Marlowe at his home. What sort of place do you imagine he lives in? What do you think he looks like? Why have you gone there? Write a paragraph about your visit. You can use Marlowe's description of his visit to Marriott at lines 41–95 as a model if you like.

19 Imagine one of the phone calls that Marriott receives (lines 296–8, 306–9). Write it in dialogue form. Give a name to the other person.

Marriott:	*Hello? Lindsay Marriott speaking.*
Other person:	________________
Marriott:	________________
Other person:	________________
(and so on)	

Beyond the text

In Graham Greene's novel, *The Third Man*, Rollo Martins, an American writer of cheap Western novels, has gone to post-war Vienna on the invitation of his old friend Harry Lime, who has promised him business opportunities there. When he arrives he is informed that Lime was killed in a road accident the previous day. Lime's death, however, is a bluff, and has been stage-managed by Lime himself as a way of escaping from the police. They have discovered that he is a black market profiteer, selling fake penicillin that disfigures or kills patients. At first, Martins cannot believe his childhood friend is a criminal, but the police show him the proof. Eventually he manages to persuade Lime's black market accomplices to arrange a meeting with Lime, who has abandoned his girlfriend, Anna, and gone into hiding in the Russian sector of the city.

In the following extract, the narrator, the police officer investigating Lime, tells us how Martins waits in the pleasure park (the 'Prater') for Lime.

20 As you read, notice especially what Lime says. Give line references and make notes under these headings.

a comments that make him seem human and generous

b comments that make him seem ruthless

c comments that you find ambiguous

The Third Man (1950)
Graham Greene

Joseph Cotten and Orson Welles in the scene on the Big Wheel from Carol Reed's 1949 film version of *The Third Man*.

See the Glossary section at the back of the book for vocabulary.

Somewhere behind the cakestall a man was whistling, and Martins knew the tune. He turned and waited. Was it fear or excitement that made his heart beat – or just the memories that tune ushered in, for life had always quickened when Harry came, came just as he came now, as though nothing much had happened, nobody had been lowered into a grave or found with cut throat in a basement, came with his amused, deprecating, take-it-or-leave-it manner – and of course one always took it.

'Harry.'

'Hullo, Rollo.'

Don't picture Harry Lime as a smooth scoundrel. He wasn't that. The picture I have of him on my files is an excellent one: he is caught by a street photographer with his stocky legs apart, big shoulders a little hunched, a belly that has known too much good food for too long, on his face a look of cheerful rascality, a geniality, a recognition that *his* happiness will make the world's day. Now he didn't make the mistake of putting out a hand that might have been rejected, but instead just patted Martins on the elbow and said, 'How are things?'

'We've got to talk, Harry.'

'Of course.'

'Alone.'

'We couldn't be more alone than here.'

He had always known the ropes, and even in the smashed pleasure park he knew them, tipping the woman in charge of the Wheel, so that they might have a car to themselves. He said, 'Lovers used to do this in the old days, but they haven't the money to spare, poor devils, now,' and he looked out of the window of the swaying, rising car at the figures diminishing below with what looked like genuine commiseration.

Very slowly on one side of them the city sank; very slowly on the other the great cross-girders of the Wheel rose into sight. As the horizon slid away the Danube became visible, and the piers of the Reichsbrücke lifted above the houses. 'Well,' Harry said, 'it's good to see you, Rollo.'

'I was at your funeral.'

'That was pretty smart of me, wasn't it?'

'Not so smart for your girl. She was there too – in tears.'

'She's a good little thing,' Harry said. 'I'm very fond of her.'

'I didn't believe the police when they told me about you.'

Harry said, 'I wouldn't have asked you to come if I'd known what was going to happen, but I didn't think the police were on to me.'

'Were you going to cut me in on the spoils?'

'I've never kept you out of anything, old man, yet.' He stood with his back to the door as the car swung upwards, and smiled back at Rollo Martins, who could remember him in just such an attitude in a secluded corner of the school-quad, saying, 'I've learned a way to get out at night. It's absolutely safe. You are the only one I'm letting in on it.' For the first time Rollo Martins looked back through the years without admiration, as he thought: He's never grown up. Marlowe's devils wore squibs attached to their tails: evil was like Peter Pan – it carried with it the horrifying and horrible gift of eternal youth.

Martins said, 'Have you ever visited the children's hospital? Have you seen any of your victims?'

Harry took a look at the toy landscape below and came away from the door. 'I never feel quite safe in these things,' he said. He felt the back of the door with his hand, as though he were afraid that it might fly open and launch him into that iron-ribbed space. 'Victims?' he asked. 'Don't be melodramatic, Rollo. Look down there,' he went on, pointing through the window at the people moving like black flies at the base of the Wheel. 'Would you really feel any pity if one of those dots stopped moving – for ever? If I said you can have twenty thousand pounds for every dot that stops, would you really, old man, tell me to keep my money – without hesitation? Or would you calculate how many dots you could afford to spare? Free of income tax, old man. Free of income tax.' He gave his boyish conspiratorial smile. 'It's the only way to save nowadays.'

'Couldn't you have stuck to tyres?'

'Like Cooler? No, I've always been ambitious.'

'You are finished now. The police know everything.'

'But they can't catch me, Rollo, you'll see. I'll pop up again. You can't keep a good man down.'

The car swung to a standstill at the highest point of the curve and Harry turned his back and gazed out of the window. Martins thought: One good shove and I could break the glass, and he pictured the body falling, falling, through the iron struts, a piece of carrion dropping among the flies. He said, 'You know the police are planning to dig up your body. What will they find?'

'Harbin,' Harry replied with simplicity. He turned away from the window and said, 'Look at the sky.'

The car had reached the top of the Wheel and hung there motionless, while the stain of the sunset ran in streaks over the wrinkled papery sky beyond the black girders.

'Why did the Russians try to take Anna Schmidt?'

'She had false papers, old man.'

'Who told them?'

'The price of living in this zone, Rollo, is service. I have to give them a little information now and then.'

'I thought perhaps you were just trying to get her here – because she was your girl? Because you wanted her?'

Harry smiled. 'I haven't all that influence.'

'What would have happened to her?'

'Nothing very serious. She'd have been sent back to Hungary. There's nothing against her really. A year in a labour camp perhaps. She'd be infinitely better off in her own country than being pushed around by the British police.'

'She hasn't told them anything about you.'

'She's a good little thing,' Harry repeated with satisfaction and pride.

'She loves you.'

'Well, I gave her a good time while it lasted.'

'And I love her.'

'That's fine, old man. Be kind to her. She's worth it. I'm glad.' He gave the impression of having arranged everything to everybody's satisfaction. 'And you can help to keep her mouth shut. Not that she knows anything that matters.'

'I'd like to knock you through the window.'

'But you won't, old man. Our quarrels never last long. You remember that fearful one in the Monaco, when we swore we were through. I'd trust you anywhere, Rollo. Kurtz tried to persuade me not to come, but I know you. Then he tried to persuade me to, well, arrange an accident. He told me it would be quite easy in this car.'

'Except that I'm the stronger man.'

'But I've got the gun. You don't think a bullet wound would show when you hit *that* ground?' Again the car began to move, sailing slowly down, until the flies were midgets, were recognizable human beings. 'What fools we are, Rollo, talking like this, as if I'd do that to you – or you to me.' He turned his back and leaned his face against the glass. One thrust. … 'How much do you earn a year with your Westerns, old man?'

'A thousand.'

'Taxed. I earn thirty thousand free. It's the fashion. In these days, old man, nobody thinks in terms of human beings. Governments don't, so why should we? They talk of the people and the proletariat, and I talk of the mugs. It's the same thing. They have their five-year plans and so have I.'

'You used to be a Catholic.'

'Oh, I still *believe*, old man. In God and mercy and all that. I'm not hurting anybody's soul by what I do. The dead are happier dead. They don't miss much here, poor devils,' he added with that odd touch of genuine pity, as the car reached the platform and the faces of the doomed-to-be-victims, the tired pleasure-hoping Sunday faces, peered in at them. 'I could cut you in, you know. It would be useful. I have no one left in the Inner City.'

'Except Cooler? And Winkler?'

'You really mustn't turn policeman, old man.' They passed out of the car and he put his hand again on Martins' elbow. 'That was a joke: I know you won't. Have you heard anything of old Bracer recently?'

'I had a card at Christmas.'

'Those were the days, old man. Those were the days. I've got to leave you here. We'll see each other sometime. If you are in a jam, you can always get me at Kurtz's.' He moved away and, turning, waved the hand he had had the tact not to offer: it was like the whole past moving off under a cloud. Martins suddenly called after him, 'Don't trust me, Harry,' but there was too great a distance now between them for the words to carry.

21 Look at the comments of the narrator at lines 11–16 and of Martins at lines 49–53. What do they suggest about Lime?

22 Philip Marlowe is perhaps not a 'typical' hero, and in the same way Harry Lime is not a 'typical' villain. Use Chandler's description in Exercise 16 as a model and write about 50–100 words describing the kind of villain Lime represents.

23 Martins doesn't answer Lime's questions at lines 62–8, or comment on his statement at lines 130–2. What would *you* say at these moments?

24 Which extract in this chapter did you prefer, and why?

Authors

Raymond Chandler (1888–1959) was born in Chicago, but his parents emigrated to England when he was still young. He attended Dulwich College, London, and completed his education in France and Germany. After a brief period in London spent as a reporter, book reviewer and essayist he returned to the USA in 1912 and settled in California. In the First World War he served in the Canadian army, and afterwards became an executive for an oil company before turning again to writing in the 1930s. He published sixteen crime stories for the 'pulp fiction' magazine *Black Mask* before his first novel, *The Big Sleep* (1939), came out. It was an immediate hit, and introduced the character of the private detective Philip Marlowe. This was followed by other novels describing Marlowe's investigations down the 'mean streets' of superficially glittering California: *Farewell, My Lovely* (1940), *The High Window* (1942), *The Lady in* *the Lake* (1943), *The Little Sister* (1949), *The Long Good-Bye* (1954). All of these were soon filmed, and some of them later re-filmed (*The Long Good-Bye* again in 1973, directed by Robert Altman with Elliot Gould as Marlowe; *Farewell, My Lovely* again in 1975 with Robert Mitchum), yet everybody's screen image of Marlowe is surely Humphrey Bogart, even though he played the part once only, in Howard Hawks' 1946 version of *The Big Sleep*. Chandler himself wrote screenplays for Hollywood, including those for the cult 'films noirs' *Double Indemnity* (1944) and *The Blue Dahlia* (1946). There is no doubt about Philip Marlowe's place in the detective genre – Anthony Burgess rightly described him as 'as immortal as Sherlock Holmes' – and the place of Chandler's novels in the canon of 'serious' literature is equally unquestionable. The English poet W H Auden classified them as 'serious studies of a criminal milieu, the Great Wrong Place, and his powerful but extremely depressing books should be read and judged, not as escape literature, but as works of art'.

Graham Greene (1904–1991) was born in Hertfordshire and educated at Oxford. In 1926 he converted to Roman Catholicism, and after four years working at *The Times* he left to become a full-time writer. These early years are described in the first volume of his autobiography *A Sort of Life* (1971), which gives a picture of a young man with a manic-depressive temperament who even indulged in private games of Russian roulette to relieve the sense of boredom he suffered from. In later life he combined his writing with extensive foreign travel, especially in Africa and Central America, often as an antidote to attacks of boredom: his second volume of autobiography, *Ways of Escape* (1980), describes this period. He spent his last years in Antibes, France.

Greene himself divided his work into two categories: 'serious' novels, and 'entertainments' or 'literary thrillers'. In the former Greene created characters facing the dilemma of choosing between right and wrong, but where the choices are not clear-cut and morality is an ambiguous value. Notable examples are *Brighton Rock* (1938), *The Power and the Glory* (1940), *The Heart of the Matter* (1948), *The End of the Affair* (1951), *A Burnt-Out Case* (1961), and *The Honorary Consul* (1973). Greene said, quoting the English poet Robert Browning, that all his novels explored the characters of 'The honest thief, the tender murderer,/The superstitious atheist ...', and even in his 'entertainments', such as *Stamboul Train* (1932), *The Confidential Agent* (1939), *The Third Man* (marvellously filmed from Greene's screenplay by Carol Reed in 1949), and *Our Man in Havana* (1958), the dominant theme is of the ambivalence of good and evil, the grey area between right and wrong.

3 'It Was Never Love'

Oliver Reed and Glenda Jackson in a scene from Ken Russell's 1969 film version of *Women in Love*

Before you read

1 Look at the film still on the previous page. What different kinds of emotions do you see in it?

2 Read the following quotations. What different attitudes to love do you see in them? Group or classify them in any way you like: for example, romantic/non-romantic; idealistic/pragmatic/bitter; love brings happiness/love brings misery, etc. Do you think any of the quotations seem to go with the film still on the previous page?

a I hate and love. And if you ask me how,
I do not know: I only feel it, and I'm torn in two.
Catullus (c. 84–54BC)

b Love means not ever having to say you're sorry.
Erich Segal, *Love Story* (1970)

c A pity beyond all telling
Is hid in the heart of love.
W B Yeats, *The Pity of Love* (1892)

d Those who have some means think that the most important thing in the world is love. The poor know that it is money.
Gerald Brenan, *Thoughts in a Dry Season* (1978)

e We must love one another or die.
W H Auden, *September 1, 1939* (1940)

f Love is heaven, and heaven is love.
Sir Walter Scott, *The Lay of the Last Minstrel* (1805)

g By heaven, I do love, and it hath taught me to rhyme, and to be melancholy.
William Shakespeare, *Love's Labour's Lost* (1593–1596)

h You know very well that love is, above all, the gift of oneself!
Jean Anouilh, *Ardèle* (1949)

i Experience shows us that love does not consist in gazing at each other but in looking together in the same direction.
Antoine de Saint Exupéry, *Wind, Sand and Stars* (1939)

j 'Tis better to have loved and lost than never to have loved at all.
Alfred, Lord Tennyson, *In Memoriam* (1850)

k Love is like linen often changed, the sweeter.
Phineas Fletcher (1582–1650), *Sicelides*

l Love is the wisdom of the fool, and the folly of the wise.
Dr Samuel Johnson (1709–84)

m Lovers may be, and, indeed, generally *are* enemies, but they can never be friends; because there must always be a spice of jealousy and a something of self in all their speculations.
Lord Byron, *Letters* (November 10, 1822)

3 ***a*** Which of the quotations in Exercise 2 most appeals to you? Why?

b What is *your* definition of love? Write one in not more than twenty words.

c Compare your definitions with others in the class, then choose the five best definitions.

Women in Love (1921)
D H Lawrence

The sisters Ursula and Gudrun Brangwen live in a coal-mining town in the English Midlands, and teach at the local school. In the following passage they encounter Gerald Crich, the son of the owner of the local coal-mine.

See the Glossary section at the back of the book for vocabulary.

CHAPTER 9
COAL DUST

Going home from school in the afternoon, the Brangwen girls descended the hill between the picturesque cottages of Willey Green till they came to the railway crossing. There they found the gate shut, because the colliery train was rumbling nearer. They could hear the small locomotive panting hoarsely as it advanced with caution between the embankments. The one-legged man in the little signal-hut by the road stared out from his security, like a crab from a snail-shell.

Whilst the two girls waited, Gerald Crich trotted up on a red Arab mare. He rode well and softly, pleased with the delicate quivering of the creature between his knees. And he was very picturesque, at least in Gudrun's eyes, sitting soft and close on the slender red mare, whose long tail flowed on the air. He saluted the two girls, and drew up at the crossing to wait for the gate, looking down the railway for the approaching train. In spite of her ironic smile at his picturesqueness, Gudrun liked to look at him. He was well set and easy, his face with its warm tan showed up his whitish, coarse moustache, and his blue eyes were full of sharp light as he watched the distance.

The locomotive chuffed slowly between the banks, hidden. The mare did not like it. She began to wince away, as if hurt by the unknown noise. But Gerald pulled her back and held her head to the gate. The sharp blasts of the chuffing engine broke with more and more force on her. The repeated sharp blows of unknown, terrifying noise struck through her till she was rocking with terror. She recoiled like a spring let go. But a glistening, half-smiling look came into Gerald's face. He brought her back again, inevitably.

The noise was released, the little locomotive with her clanking steel connecting-rod emerged on the highroad, clanking sharply. The mare rebounded like a drop of water from hot iron. Ursula and Gudrun pressed back into the hedge, in fear. But Gerald was heavy on the mare, and forced her back. It seemed as if he sank into her magnetically, and could thrust her back against herself.

'The fool!' cried Ursula loudly. 'Why doesn't he ride away till it's gone by?'

Gudrun was looking at him with black-dilated, spellbound eyes. But he sat glistening and obstinate, forcing the wheeling mare, which spun and swerved like a wind, and yet could not get out of the grasp of his will, nor escape from the mad clamour of terror that resounded through her, as the trucks thumped slowly, heavily, horrifying, one after the other, one pursuing the other, over the rails of the crossing.

The locomotive, as if wanting to see what could be done, put on the brakes, and back came the trucks rebounding on the iron buffers, striking like horrible cymbals, clashing nearer and nearer in frightful strident concussions. The mare opened her mouth and rose slowly, as if lifted up on a wind of terror. Then suddenly her forefeet struck out, as she convulsed herself utterly away from the horror. Back she went, and the two girls clung to each other, feeling she must fall backwards on top of him. But he leaned forward, his face shining with fixed amusement, and at last he brought her down, sank her down, and was bearing her back to the mark. But as strong as the pressure of his compulsion was the repulsion of her utter terror, throwing her back away from the railway, so that she spun round and round on two legs, as if she were in the centre of some whirlwind. It made Gudrun faint with poignant dizziness, which seemed to penetrate to her heart.

'No – ! No – ! Let her go! Let her go, you fool, you *fool* –!' cried Ursula at the top of her voice, completely outside herself. And Gudrun hated her bitterly for being outside herself. It was unendurable that Ursula's voice was so powerful and naked.

A sharpened look came on Gerald's face. He bit himself down on the mare like a keen edge biting home, and *forced* her round. She roared as she breathed, her nostrils were two wide, hot holes, her mouth was apart, her eyes frenzied. It was a repulsive sight. But he held on her unrelaxed, with an almost mechanical relentlessness, keen as a sword pressing into her. Both man and horse were sweating with violence. Yet he seemed calm as a ray of cold sunshine.

Meanwhile the eternal trucks were rumbling on, very slowly, treading one after the other, one after the other, like a disgusting dream that has no end. The connecting chains were grinding and squeaking as the tension varied, the mare pawed and struck away mechanically now, her terror fulfilled in her, for now the man encompassed her; her paws were blind and pathetic as she beat the air, the man closed round her, and brought her down, almost as if she were part of his own physique.

'And she's bleeding! She's bleeding!' cried Ursula, frantic with opposition and hatred of Gerald. She alone understood him perfectly, in pure opposition.

Gudrun looked and saw the trickles of blood on the sides of the mare, and she turned white. And then on the very wound the bright spurs came down, pressing relentlessly. The world reeled and passed into nothingness for Gudrun, she could not know any more.

How do you think this scene will end?

When she recovered, her soul was calm and cold, without feeling. The trucks were still rumbling by, and the man and the mare were still fighting. But she herself was cold and separate, she had no more feeling for them. She was quite hard and cold and indifferent. They could see the top of the hooded guard's-van approaching, the sound of the trucks was diminishing, there was hope of relief from the intolerable noise. The heavy panting of the half-stunned mare sounded automatically, the man seemed to be relaxing confidently, his will bright and unstained. The guard's-van came up, and passed slowly, the guard staring out in his transition on the spectacle in the road. And, through the man in the closed wagon Gudrun could see the whole scene spectacularly, isolated and momentary, like a vision isolated in eternity.

Lovely, grateful silence seemed to trail behind the receding train. How sweet the silence is! Ursula looked with hatred on the buffers of the diminishing wagon. The gate-keeper stood ready at the door of his hut, to proceed to open the gate. But Gudrun sprang suddenly forward, in front of the struggling horse, threw off the latch and flung the gates asunder, throwing one-half to the keeper, and running with the other half forwards. Gerald suddenly let go the horse and leaped forwards, almost on to Gudrun. She was not afraid. As he jerked aside the mare's head, Gudrun cried, in a strange, high voice, like a gull, or like a witch screaming out from the side of the road:

'I should think you're proud.'

The words were distinct and formed. The man, twisting aside on his dancing horse, looked at her in some surprise, some wondering interest. Then the mare's hoofs had danced three times on the drum-like sleepers of the crossing, and man and horse were bounding springily, unequally up the road.

The two girls watched them go. The gate-keeper hobbled thudding over the logs of the crossing, with his wooden leg. He had fastened the gate. Then he also turned, and called to the girls:

'A masterful young jockey, that'll have his own road, if ever anybody would.'

'Yes,' cried Ursula, in her hot, overbearing voice. 'Why couldn't he take the horse away, till the trucks had gone by? He's a fool, and a bully. Does he think it's manly, to torture a horse? It's a living thing, why should he bully it and torture it?'

There was a pause, then the gate-keeper shook his head, and replied:

'Yes, it's as nice a little mare as you could set eyes on – beautiful little thing, beautiful. Now you couldn't see his father treat any animal like that – not you. They're as different as they welly can be, Gerald Crich and his father – two different men, different made.'

Then there was a pause.

'But why does he do it?' cried Ursula, 'why does he? Does he think he's grand, when he's bullied a sensitive creature, ten times as sensitive as himself?'

Again there was a cautious pause. Then again the man shook his head, as if he would say nothing, but would think the more.

'I expect he's got to train the mare to stand to anything,' he replied. 'A pure-bred Harab – not the sort of breed as is used to round here – different sort from our sort altogether. They say as he got her from Constantinople.'

'He would!' said Ursula. 'He'd better have left her to the Turks, I'm sure they would have had more decency towards her.'

The man went in to drink his can of tea, the girls went on down the lane, that was deep in soft black dust. Gudrun was as if numbed in her mind by the sense of indomitable soft weight of the man, bearing down into the living body of the horse: the strong, indomitable thighs of the blond man clenching the palpitating body of the mare into pure control; a sort of soft white magnetic domination from the loins and thighs and calves, enclosing and encompassing the mare heavily into unutterable subordination, soft-blood-subordination, terrible.

On the left, as the girls walked silently, the coal-mine lifted its great mounds and its patterned head-stocks, the black railway with the trucks at rest looked like a harbour just below, a large bay of railroad with anchored wagons.

First reaction

4 Who do you sympathize with? Put ticks (✓) in the table below.

		GERALD	GUDRUN	URSULA	THE GATE-KEEPER	THE HORSE
I sympathize most with	*a*					
	b					
	c					
	d					
I sympathize least with	*e*					

Close reading

Points of view

5 **The Brangwen sisters' point of view**

a Look at the following moments from lines 9–113. Put a tick (✓) in the last two columns on the right to describe the sisters' reactions. The first three are done for you.

			LINE(S)	INDIGNATION OR ANGER	ANOTHER REACTION
	Gudrun	And he was very picturesque, at least in Gudrun's eyes, …	11–12		✓
	Gudrun	In spite of her ironic smile at his picturesqueness, Gudrun liked to look at him.	15–16		✓
	Ursula	'The fool!' cried Ursula loudly. 'Why doesn't he ride away till it's gone by?'	34–5	✓	
1	Gudrun	Gudrun was looking at him with black-dilated, spellbound eyes.	36		
2	Gudrun	It made Gudrun faint with poignant dizziness, which seemed to penetrate to her heart.	56–7		
3	Ursula	'No – ! No – ! Let her go! …' cried Ursula at the top of her voice, completely outside herself.	58–9		

			LINE(S)	INDIGNATION OR ANGER	ANOTHER REACTION
4	Gudrun	And Gudrun hated her bitterly … It was unendurable that Ursula's voice was so powerful and naked.	59–61		
5	Ursula	'And she's bleeding! ...' She alone understood him perfectly, in pure opposition.	78–80		
6	Gudrun	Gudrun looked and saw the trickles of blood … nothingness for Gudrun, she could not know any more.	81–4		
7	Gudrun	When she recovered, her soul was calm and cold … She was quite hard and cold and indifferent.	85–9		
8	Gudrun	And, through the man in the closed wagon ... momentary, like a vision isolated in eternity.	95–7		
9	Ursula	Ursula looked with hatred on the buffers of the diminishing wagon.	99–100		
10	Gudrun	She was not afraid. ... a witch screaming out from the side of the road: 'I should think you're proud.'	105–8		

b Which sister's reactions seem more complex?

c Here are some interpretations of the reactions you put in the second column in Exercise 5a.

- a feeling of superiority
- sadistic identification with Gerald
- sexual attraction to Gerald
- an immense effort of self-control
- envy of Gerald
- masochistic identification with the horse
- sensual abandon
- deliberate detachment from the scene
- disgust, but not condemnation
- an almost hypnotic sensation

Which do you think are likely? Are there any that might be likely, but you are not sure about? Sort them into the two boxes on the next page, then discuss your choices with a partner.

LIKELY INTERPRETATIONS	I'M NOT SURE

6 **The gate-keeper's point of view**
Look at lines 114–40.

a How does the gate-keeper react to Gerald's behaviour? Is his opinion critical, neutral, admiring or something else? Find some examples.

b Which sister does the talking in this scene? Does she express any different opinions from before, or not?

7 **Gudrun's point of view**
Look at lines 141–9. Which of the interpretations in Exercise 5c seem most relevant to this paragraph?

8 **The narrator's point of view**
Can you find anything in the extract that suggests what the narrator's opinion might be? Note down any words or phrases.

9 **Your own point of view**
In your opinion is Gerald 'manly', or 'a fool and a bully', or something else? Discuss your opinion with a partner.

Before you read

10 Later in the novel, Ursula falls in love with and marries Rupert Birkin, a school inspector, while Gudrun and Gerald start a love affair. What do you guess the relationship between Gudrun and Gerald is like? Tick (✓) any of the following that you think are likely, add any predictions of your own, then compare ideas with a partner.

- they are happy
- they are unhappy
- their relationship is passionate
- their relationship is dull
- they agree on most things

- they disagree on most things
- they respect each other
- one partner tries to dominate the other
- your own prediction(s): ______________________________

All four characters go on holiday together to the Swiss Alps. Ursula and Rupert decide to go on to Italy, leaving Gudrun and Gerald to stay on at the hotel. As you read the following extract, check whether your predictions in Exercise 10 were right.

See the Glossary section at the back of the book for vocabulary.

CHAPTER 30
SNOWED UP

When Ursula and Birkin were gone, Gudrun felt herself free in her contest with Gerald. As they grew more used to each other, he seemed to press upon her more and more. At first she could manage him, so that her own will was always left free. But very soon, he began to ignore her female tactics, he dropped his respect for her whims and her privacies, he began to exert his own will blindly, without submitting to hers.

Already a vital conflict had set in, which frightened them both. But he was alone, whilst already she had begun to cast round for external resource.

When Ursula had gone, Gudrun felt her own existence had become stark and elemental. She went and crouched alone in her bedroom, looking out of the window at the big, flashing stars. In front was the faint shadow of the mountain-knot. That was the pivot. She felt strange and inevitable, as if she were centred upon the pivot of all existence, there was no further reality.

Presently Gerald opened the door. She knew he would not be long before he came. She was rarely alone, he pressed upon her like a frost, deadening her.

'Are you alone in the dark?' he said. And she could tell by his tone he resented it, he resented this isolation she had drawn round herself. Yet, feeling static and inevitable, she was kind towards him.

'Would you like to light the candle?' she asked.

He did not answer, but came and stood behind her, in the darkness.

'Look,' she said, 'at that lovely star up there. Do you know its name?'

He crouched beside her, to look through the low window.

'No,' he said. 'It is very fine.'

Isn't it beautiful! Do you notice how it darts different coloured fires – it flashes really superbly –'

They remained in silence. With a mute, heavy gesture she put her hand on his knee, and took his hand.

'Are you regretting Ursula?' he asked.

'No, not at all,' she said. Then, in a slow mood, she asked:

'How much do you love me?'

He stiffened himself further against her.

'How much do you think I do?' he asked.

'I don't know,' she replied.

'But what is your opinion?' he asked.

There was a pause. At length, in the darkness, came her voice, hard and indifferent:

'Very little indeed,' she said coldly, almost flippant. His heart went icy at the sound of her voice.

'Why don't I love you ?' he asked, as if admitting the truth of her accusation, yet hating her for it.

'I don't know why you don't – I've been good to you. You were in a *fearful* state when you came to me.'

Her heart was beating to suffocate her, yet she was strong and unrelenting.

'When was I in a fearful state?' he asked.

'When you first came to me. I *had* to take pity on you. But it was never love.'

It was that statement 'It was never love', which sounded in his ears with madness.

'Why must you repeat it so often, that there is no love?' he said in a voice strangled with rage.

'Well you don't *think* you love, do you?' she asked.

He was silent with cold passion of anger.

'You don't think you *can* love me, do you?' she repeated almost with a sneer.

'No,' he said.

'You know you never *have* loved me, don't you?'

'I don't know what you mean by the word "love",' he replied.

'Yes, you do. You know all right that you have never loved me. Have you, do you think?'

'No,' he said, prompted by some barren spirit of truthfulness and obstinacy.

'And you never *will* love me,' she said finally, 'will you?' There was a diabolic coldness in her, too much to bear.

'No,' he said.

'Then,' she replied, 'what have you against me?'

He was silent in cold, frightened rage and despair. 'If only I could kill her,' his heart was whispering repeatedly. 'If only I could kill her – I should be free.'

It seemed to him that death was the only severing of this Gordian knot.

'Why do you torture me?' he said.

She flung her arms round his neck.

'Ah, I don't want to torture you,' she said pityingly, as if she were comforting a child. The impertinence made his veins go cold, he was insensible. She held her arms round his neck, in a triumph of pity. And her pity for him was as cold as stone, its deepest motive was hate of him, and fear of his power over her, which she must always counterfoil.

'Say you love me,' she pleaded. 'Say you will love me for ever – won't you – won't you?'

But it was her voice only that coaxed him. Her senses were entirely apart from him, cold and destructive of him. It was her overbearing *will* that insisted.

'Won't you say you'll love me always?' she coaxed. 'Say it, even if it isn't true – say it, Gerald, do.'

'I will love you always,' he repeated, in real agony, forcing the words out.

She gave him a quick kiss.

'Fancy your actually having said it,' she said with a touch of raillery.

He stood as if he had been beaten.

'Try to love me a little more, and to want me a little less,' she said, in a half contemptuous, half coaxing tone.

The darkness seemed to be swaying in waves across his mind, great waves of darkness plunging across his mind. It seemed to him he was degraded at the very quick, made of no account.

'You mean you don't want me?' he said.

'You are so insistent, and there is so little grace in you, so little fineness. You are so crude. You break me – you only waste me – it is horrible to me.'

'Horrible to you?' he repeated.

'Yes. Don't you think I might have a room to myself, now Ursula has gone? You can say you want a dressing-room.'

'You do as you like – you can leave altogether if you like,' he managed to articulate.

'Yes, I know that,' she replied. 'So can you. You can leave me whenever you like – without notice even.'

The great tides of darkness were swinging across his mind, he could hardly stand upright. A terrible weariness overcame him, he felt he must lie on the floor. Dropping off his clothes, he got into bed, and lay like a man suddenly overcome by drunkenness, the darkness lifting and plunging as if he were lying upon a black, giddy sea. He lay still in this strange horrific reeling for some time, purely unconscious.

At length she slipped from her own bed and came over to him. He remained rigid, his back to her. He was all but unconscious.

She put her arms round his terrifying, insentient body, and laid her cheek against his hard shoulder.

'Gerald,' she whispered. 'Gerald.'

There was no change in him. She caught him against her. She pressed her breasts against his shoulders, she kissed his shoulder, through the sleeping jacket. Her mind wondered over his rigid, unliving body. She was bewildered, and insistent, only her will was set for him to speak to her.

'Gerald, my dear' she whispered, bending over him, kissing his ear.

Her warm breath playing, flying rhythmically over his ear seemed to relax the tension. She could feel his body gradually relaxing a little, losing its terrifying, unnatural rigidity. Her hands clutched his limbs, his muscles, going over him spasmodically.

The hot blood began to flow again through his veins, his limbs relaxed.

'Turn round to me,' she whispered, forlorn with insistence and triumph.

So at last he was given again, warm and flexible. He turned and gathered her in his arms. And feeling her soft against him, so perfectly and wondrously soft and recipient, his arms tightened on her. She was as if crushed, powerless in him. His brain seemed hard and invincible now like a jewel, there was no resisting him.

His passion was awful to her, tense and ghastly, and impersonal like a destruction, ultimate. She felt it would kill her. She was being killed.

'My God, my God,' she cried, in anguish, in his embrace, feeling her life being killed within her. And when he was kissing her, soothing her, her breath came slowly, as if she were really spent, dying.

'Shall I die, shall I die?' she repeated to herself.

And in the night, and in him, there was no answer to the question.

How do you think she will feel the next day?

And yet, next day, the fragment of her which was not destroyed remained intact and hostile, she did not go away, she remained to finish the holiday, admitting nothing. He scarcely ever left her alone, but followed her like a shadow, he was like a doom upon her, a continual 'thou shalt', 'thou shalt not'. Sometimes it was he who seemed strongest, whilst she was almost gone, creeping near the earth like a spent wind; sometimes it was the reverse. But always it was this eternal see-saw, one destroyed that the other might exist, one ratified because the other was nulled.

'In the end,' she said to herself, 'I shall go away from him.'

'I can be free of her,' he said to himself in his paroxysms of suffering.

And he set himself to be free. He even prepared to go away, to leave her in the lurch. But for the first time there was a flaw in his will.

'Where shall I go?' he asked himself.

'Can't you be self-sufficient?' he replied to himself, putting himself upon his pride.

'Self-sufficient!' he repeated.

It seemed to him that Gudrun was sufficient unto herself, closed round and completed, like a thing in a case. In the calm, static reason of his soul, he recognized this, and admitted it was her right, to be closed round upon herself, self-complete, without desire. He realized it, he admitted it, it only needed one last effort on his own part, to win for himself the same completeness. He knew that it only needed one convulsion of his will for him to be able to turn upon himself also, to close upon himself as a stone fixes upon itself, and is impervious, self-completed, a thing isolated.

This knowledge threw him into a terrible chaos. Because, however much he might mentally *will* to be immune and self-complete, the desire for this state was lacking, and he could not create it. He could see that, to exist at all, he must be perfectly free of Gudrun, leave her if she wanted to be left, demand nothing of her, have no claim upon her.

But then, to have no claim upon her, he must stand by himself, in sheer nothingness. And his brain turned to nought at the idea. It was a state of nothingness. On the other hand, he might give in, and fawn to her. Or, finally, he might kill her. Or he might become just indifferent, purposeless, dissipated, momentaneous. But his nature was too serious, not gay enough or subtle enough for mocking licentiousness.

A strange rent had been torn in him; like a victim that is torn open and given to the heavens, so he had been torn apart and given to Gudrun. How should he close again? This wound, this strange, infinitely-sensitive opening of his soul, where he was exposed, like an open flower, to all the universe, and in which he was given to his complement, the other, the unknown, this wound, this disclosure, this unfolding of his own covering, leaving him incomplete, limited, unfinished, like an open flower under the sky, this was his cruellest joy. Why then should he forgo it? Why should he close up and become impervious, immune, like a partial thing in a sheath, when he had broken forth, like a seed that has germinated, to issue forth in being, embracing the unrealized heavens.

He would keep the unfinished bliss of his own yearning even through the torture she inflicted upon him. A strange obstinacy possessed him. He would not go away from her whatever she said or did. A strange, deathly yearning carried him along with her. She was the determinating influence of his very being, though she treated him with contempt, repeated rebuffs and denials, still he would never be gone, since in being near her, even, he felt the quickening, the going forth in him, the release, the knowledge of his own limitation and the magic of the promise, as well as the mystery of his own destruction and annihilation.

She tortured the open heart of him even as he turned to her. And she was tortured herself. It may have been her will was stronger. She felt, with horror, as if he tore at the bud of her heart, tore it open, like an irreverent persistent being. Like a boy who pulls off a fly's wings, or tears open a bud to see what is in the flower, he tore at her privacy, at her very life, he would destroy her as an immature bud, torn open, is destroyed.

She might open towards him, a long while hence, in her dreams, when she was a pure spirit. But now she was not to be violated and ruined. She closed against him fiercely.

They climbed together, at evening, up the high slope, to see the sun set. In the finely breathing, keen wind they stood and watched the yellow sun sink in crimson and disappear. Then in the east the peaks and ridges glowed with living rose, incandescent like immortal flowers against a brown-purple sky, a miracle, whilst down below the world was a bluish shadow, and above, like an annunciation, hovered a rosy transport in mid-air.

Do you think that there will be a moment of reconciliation, or another confrontation?

To her it was so beautiful, it was a delirium, she wanted to gather the glowing, eternal peaks to her breast, and die. He saw them, saw they were beautiful. But there arose no clamour in his breast, only a bitterness that was visionary in itself. He wished the peaks were grey and unbeautiful, so that she should not get her support from them. Why did she betray the two of them so terribly, in embracing the glow of the evening? Why did she leave him standing there, with the ice wind blowing through his heart, like death, to gratify herself among the rosy snow-tips?

'What does the twilight matter?' he said. 'Why do you grovel before it? Is it so important to you?'

She winced in violation and in fury.

'Go away,' she cried, 'and leave me to it. It is beautiful, beautiful,' she sang in strange, rhapsodic tones. 'It is the most beautiful thing I have ever seen in my life. Don't try to come between it and me. Take yourself away, you are out of place –'

He stood back a little, and left her standing there, statue-like, transported into the mystic glowing east. Already the rose was fading, large white stars were flashing out. He waited. He would forgo everything but the yearning.

'That was the most perfect thing I have ever seen,' she said in cold, brutal tones, when at last she turned round to him. 'It amazes me that you should want to destroy it. If you can't see it yourself, why try to debar me?' But in reality, he had destroyed it for her, she was straining after a dead effect.

'One day,' he said, softly, looking up at her, 'I shall destroy *you* as you stand looking at the sunset; because you are such a liar.'

There was a soft, voluptuous promise to himself in the words. She was chilled but arrogant.

'Ha!' she said. 'I am not afraid of your threats!'

She denied herself to him, she kept her room rigidly private to herself. But he waited on, in a curious patience, belonging to his yearning for her.

'In the end,' he said to himself with real voluptuous promise, 'when it reaches that point, I shall do away with her.' And he trembled delicately in every limb, in anticipation, as he trembled in his most violent accesses of passionate approach to her, trembling with too much desire.

First reaction

11 Who do you sympathize with more, Gudrun or Gerald? Can you say why?

12 Lawrence talks of a 'contest' (line 155) and a 'conflict' (line 161). Who do you think has 'won'?
- ***a*** Gudrun
- ***b*** Gerald
- ***c*** Neither of them

Close reading

Theme: contest and conflict

13 a In this exercise the 'contest' or 'conflict' between Gerald and Gudrun is shown in the form of a graph. The vertical axis represents who is stronger at any particular moment:

2 = much stronger; 1 = a little stronger; 0 (stalemate) = neither is stronger.

The horizontal axis represents line references to different moments in their 'contest'. You choose three more moments to complete the axis.

Put crosses (✗) on the graph to show who you think is 'winning' at each moment.

b When you have finished show your completed graph to a partner.

Gudrun is stronger	***2***												
	1												
stalemate	***0***												
	1												
Gerald is stronger	***2***												
		155 to 160	170 to 175	188 to 196	208 to 224	231 to 237	243 to 251	260 to 265	283 to 292	301 to 306	— to —	— to —	— to —

14 a Do you remember who is 'pressing' whom at these moments? Check with the text.

'... keen as a sword pressing into her.' (line 67)
'... pressing relentlessly.' (line 83)
'... he seemed to press upon her more and more.' (lines 156–7)

b Find one or two other parallels between Gerald's treatment of the horse in the first extract and the way Gudrun and Gerald treat each other in the second extract.

c What do these parallels suggest to you about their attitudes to love?

15 Write down your personal responses to the following, then discuss your ideas with a partner.

a What is the most hurtful thing that Gudrun says to Gerald?

b What is the most hurtful thing that Gerald says to Gudrun?

c Do they ever say anything tender to each other?

16 'I don't know what you mean by the word "love".' (line 216)
Look back to the quotations in Exercise 2. Which of them

a give an idea of what Gudrun and Gerald might mean by 'love'?

b certainly do not apply to Gudrun and Gerald's attitudes to love?

Alternatively, find other quotations or write definitions of your own to describe their attitude to love.

Language practice – structures

Reported speech

17 *a* Make sure you know what these verbs mean. Use a dictionary if necessary.

accuse deny agree confess refuse complain ask
admit doubt beg insist plead tell

b Which verbs might be used by someone being aggressive? Which by someone who is a victim? Can you think of any other ways of grouping them?

18 The following sentences summarize the scene between Gerald and Gudrun at lines 186–265. Use the verbs from Exercise 17 to fill in the gaps. Discuss your choices with a partner.

a Gerald __________ that Gudrun tells him what she thinks of his love for her.

b Gudrun __________ that he loves her very much at all.

c Gerald half __________ that this is true.

d She __________ him that it was pity rather than love she felt for him.

e She __________ him of not being able to love her, of never having loved her.

f He __________ that he can't love her.

g He __________ her not to torture him.

h She __________ torturing him.

i She __________ with him to say he loves her.
j At first he __________ to say it, but when he gives in, she makes fun of him for having said it.
k She __________ that he wants her physically instead of loving her, and that his desire is oppressive.
l She __________ him to let her have a room to herself.
m They __________ that they can leave each other whenever they want.

Check your answers with the Key. Do you agree with this summary of the scene? Is there anything you want to add, take away, or change?

19 What grammatical patterns follow the verbs as they are used in Exercise 18? Fill in the following table.

	GRAMMATICAL PATTERNS	VERBS
1	reporting verb + person (+ **that**) + finite clause	***tell***
2	reporting verb (no person) (+ **that**) + finite clause	***admit,***
3	reporting verb + person + infinitive	
4	reporting verb (no person) + infinitive	
5	reporting verb + **with** + person + infinitive	
6	reporting verb + person + **of** + gerund	
7	reporting verb (no person) + gerund	

20 Here are some more reporting verbs. Make sure you know what they mean, using a dictionary if necessary. Fill in the brackets with a number ***1–7*** from Exercise 19 to indicate the grammatical pattern that follows the verb (use your knowledge or instinct, or make hypotheses – then check with the Key).

claim [ ] *explain [ ]* *order [ ]* *promise [ ]* or *[ ]* *realise [ ]* *state [ ]* *threaten [ ]* *warn [ ]* *fear [ ]*

21 a Use the words and expressions given below and write sentences that report the conversation between Gerald and Gudrun at lines 394–422.
Example:

Gerald	accuses refuses complains	(Gudrun)	recognize/beauty/sunset. prefer/sunset/to him. exclude/him.

Gerald accuses Gudrun of preferring the sunset to him.
Gerald accuses Gudrun of excluding him.
Gerald refuses to recognize … etc.

1	Gudrun	explains accuses orders	(Gerald)	leave/her alone. be/insensitive. sunset/most beautiful thing/she/ever seen.
2	Gudrun	states admits claims	(Gerald)	spoil/pleasure/sunset for her. sunset/more important to her/than Gerald. only she/appreciate beautiful things.
3	Gerald	threatens promises warns	(Gudrun)	kill/her. he/win. take/his revenge on her.
4	Gudrun	claims denies	(Gerald)	frighten/her. be/intimidated. be/not afraid of him.
5	Gerald	realizes promises fears		have/last word. their affair/finish badly their affair/only end in one way.

b Write some sentences of your own to report the conversation at lines 117–40.

22 What do you think Lawrence gains by using direct speech rather than reported speech in these scenes?

23 Write a brief report of an emotional scene that you have been involved in or have observed. Try to use verbs from Exercises 17 and 20.

Language practice – vocabulary

Imagery and symbolism; style

24 Look at the diagram on page 79. This represents some aspects of Lawrence's use of imagery and symbols in the scene between Gerald and Gudrun at lines 154–306. (For the terms **style**, **imagery** and **symbols** see Chapter 1, *Anatomy of a Novel*, pages 23–27.)

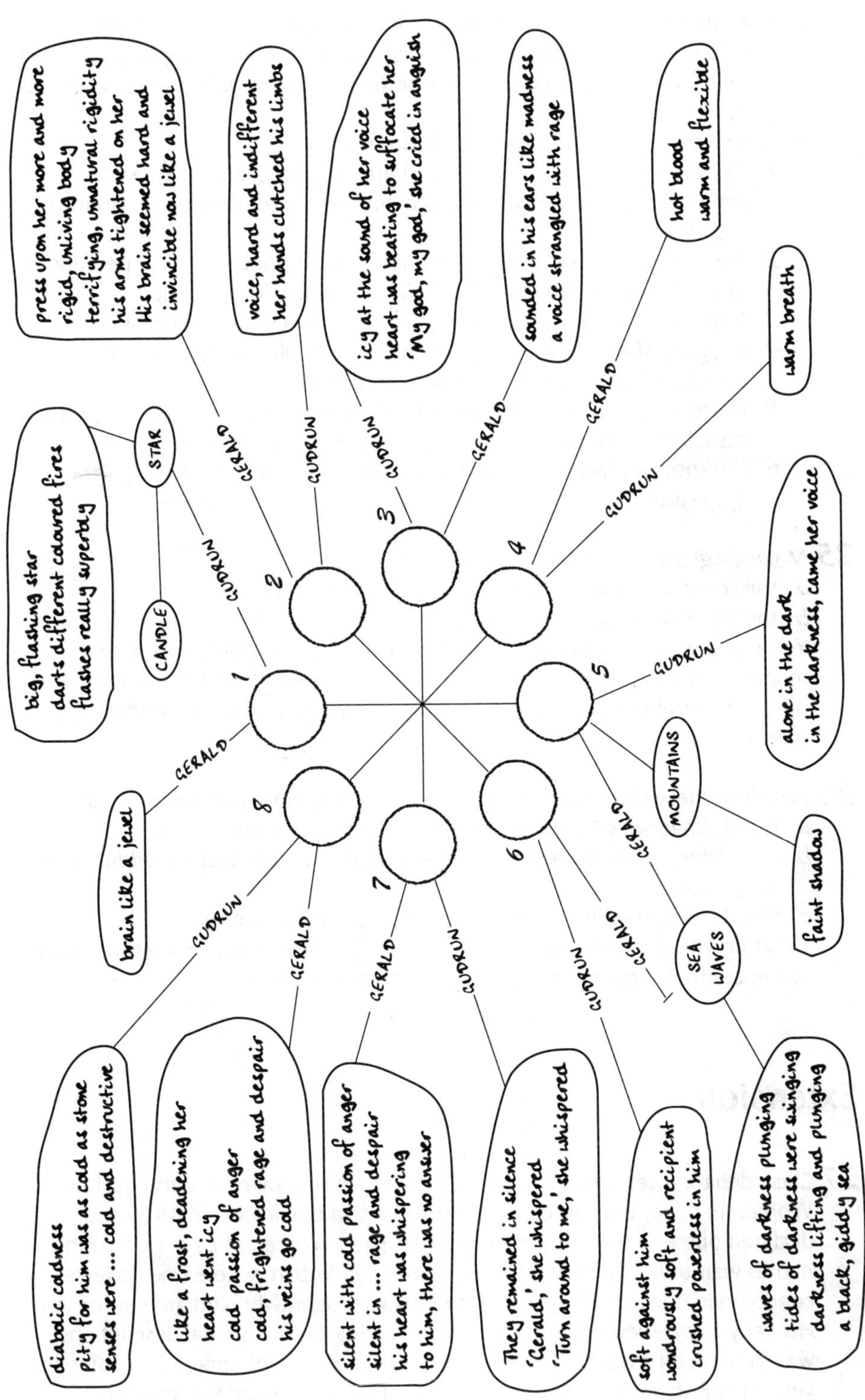

1
2
3
4
5
6
7
8
GERALD
GUDRUN
STAR
CANDLE
MOUNTAINS
SEA WAVES
big, flashing star
darts different coloured fires
flashes really superbly
press upon her more and more
rigid, unliving body
terrifying, unnatural rigidity
his arms tightened on her
His brain seemed hard and
invincible now like a jewel
voice, hard and indifferent
her hands clutched his limbs
icy at the sound of her voice
heart was beating to suffocate her
'My god, my god,' she cried in anguish
sounded in his ears like madness
a voice strangled with rage
hot blood
warm and flexible
warm breath
alone in the dark
in the darkness, came her voice
faint shadow
waves of darkness plunging
tides of darkness were swinging
darkness lifting and plunging
a black, giddy sea
soft against him
wondrously soft and recipient
crushed powerless in him
They remained in silence
'Gerald,' she whispered
'Turn around to me,' she whispered
silent with cold passion of anger
silent in ... rage and despair
his heart was whispering
to him, there was no answer
like a frost, deadening her
heart went icy
cold passion of anger
cold, frightened rage and despair
his veins go cold
diabolic coldness
pity for him was as cold as stone
senses were ... cold and destructive
brain like a jewel

a Each pair of circles, connected by a line, represents a pair of opposed qualities, for example *hard – soft*. Can you fill in the missing words in each circle? Compare your ideas with a partner, then check the Key before you go on.

b Which of the following statements are true?

1 The two characters have different imagery associated with each of them: Gerald is always associated with one kind of imagery, Gudrun with the opposite.

2 The star symbolizes something beautiful but unobtainable – perhaps an ideal of love. In any case, it sets Gudrun apart from Gerald.

3 Hardness is associated with aggression, softness with submission.

4 Imagery of heat is associated with anger, while imagery of cold is associated with calmer, more tender moments.

5 Noise is associated with moments of passion and anger, but quiet is also associated with Gerald's impotent anger and frustration.

6 Darkness represents moments of relief for Gerald from Gudrun's aggression.

25 Make diagrams for one of the following passages.

a the scene with the horse (lines 1–113 and 141–9)

b the scene at sunset (lines 378–422)

You can use the diagram on page 79 as a guide, but you can make any modifications you want to. When you have finished, note down some observations about Lawrence's use of imagery and symbolism in these scenes.

26 Which of these statements do you think best describes Lawrence's style?

a It is distinguished by simple repetition of the same key words.

b It is distinguished by repetition of key words, varied with the addition of other words.

c It is distinguished by constant variety in the use of words.

What do you think of Lawrence's style? Do you find it dull, interesting, suited to the content, oppressive, exciting, or something else?

Extension

27 **Class debate – censorship:** *The Rainbow*, which Lawrence wrote just before *Women in Love*, was seized by the police upon publication in 1915 and declared obscene. Although Lawrence finished *Women in Love* in 1916 he had to wait until 1921 for it to be published in Britain, where one reviewer condemned it as an 'analytical study of sexual depravity' and an 'epic of vice'. His *Lady Chatterley's Lover*, a novel containing explicit sexual descriptions, was published privately in Florence in 1928, but did not appear in a complete version in Britain until 1960, after the publishers (Penguin Books) had successfully defended a prosecution under the Obscene Publications Act of 1959.

Copies of the first English language edition of James Joyce's *Ulysses* (see Chapter 7) were burned by the New York post office authorities, and the British Customs authorities confiscated the second edition in 1923: it was not published in England until 1936.

a All the books mentioned above were banned for obscenity, but what other reasons for censorship can you think of?

b Divide into two teams, each team taking one of the following positions.

- Censorship is never justifiable in any context, for any reason.
- Censorship can be justified in certain contexts, for certain reasons.

Either ask your teacher to decide which team has debated more persuasively, or appoint a third, small team of students as judges. This team should prepare themselves by thinking about both sides of the argument while the two major teams prepare their debate.

28 **Discussion/essay**:

'Where love rules, there is no will to power, and where power predominates, love is lacking. The one is the shadow of the other.'
Carl Gustav Jung, *On the Psychology of the Unconscious* (1917)

How far are 'will', 'power' and 'love' connected in real-life love affairs?

29 **Writing:** Choose one of the following tasks.

a How will Gudrun and Gerald's love affair end? Write a prediction in about 100 words. (If you are curious, the Key gives Lawrence's ending.)

b Assume that during their stay in the Alps Gerald decides to leave Gudrun, or that Gudrun decides to leave Gerald. Imagine you are either Gerald or Gudrun. Write a letter giving reasons for leaving, and saying goodbye.

Beyond the text

30 Before reading, look at the dictionary entry for the word 'game' on page 82. Which of the definitions could have anything to do with a love-affair? Discuss your ideas with a partner, then read the extract.

[1]**game** \'gām\ [ME, fr. OE *gamen*; akin to OHG *gaman* amusement] (bef. 12*c*) **1 a** (1) : activity engaged in for diversion or amusement : PLAY (2) : the equipment for a game **b** : often derisive or mocking; jesting : FUN, SPORT < make ~ of a nervous player> **2 a** : a procedure or strategy for gaining an end : TACTIC **b** : an illegal or shady scheme or maneuver : RACKET **3 a** (1) : a physical or mental competition conducted according to rules with the participants in direct opposition to each other (2) : a division of a larger contest (3) : the number of points necessary to win (4) : points scored in certain card games (as in all fours) by a player whose cards count up the highest (5) : the manner of playing in a contest (6) : the set of rules governing a game (7) : a particular aspect or phase of play in a game or sport < a football team's kicking ~ > **b** *pl* : organized athletics **c** (1) : a field of gainful activity : LINE < the newspaper ~ > (2) : any activity undertaken and regarded as a contest involving rivalry, strategy, or struggle < the dating ~ > < the ~ of politics >; *also* : the course or period of such an activity < got into aviation early in the ~ > (3) : area of expertise : SPECIALTY < comedy is not my ~ > **4 a** (1) : animals under pursuit or taken in hunting; esp : wild animals hunted for sport or food (2) : the flesh of game animals **b** *archaic* : PLUCK **c** : a target or object esp. of ridicule or attack ~ often used in the phrase *fair game* ***syn*** see FUN – **gamelike** \ -līk\ *adj*

A Farewell to Arms (1929)
Ernest Hemingway

An American lieutenant, Frederic Henry, is serving with the Italian army in northern Italy during the First World War. He has spent a couple of evenings with a British nurse, Catherine Barkley, and after a few days at the front comes back to see her again.

See the Glossary section at the back of the book for vocabulary.

I saw Catherine Barkley coming town the hall, and stood up. She did not seem tall walking toward me but she looked very lovely.

'Good evening, Mr Henry,' she said.

'How do you do?' I said. The orderly was listening behind the desk.

'Shall we sit here or go out in the garden?'

'Let's go out. It's much cooler.'

I walked behind her out into the garden, the orderly looking after us. When we were out on the gravel drive she said, 'Where have you been?'

'I've been out on post.'

'You couldn't have sent me a note?'

'No,' I said. 'Not very well. I thought I was coming back.'

'You ought to have let me know, darling.'

We were off the driveway, walking under the trees. I took her hands, then stopped and kissed her.

'Isn't there anywhere we can go?'

'No,' she said. 'We have to just walk here. You've been away a long time.'

'This is the third day. But I'm back now.'

She looked at me. 'And you do love me?'

'Yes.'

'You did say you loved me, didn't you?'

'Yes,' I lied. 'I love you.' I had not said it before.

'And you call me Catherine?'

'Catherine.' We walked on a way and were stopped under a tree.

'Say, "I've come back to Catherine in the night."'

'I've come back to Catherine in the night.'

'Oh, darling, you have come back, haven't you?'

'Yes.'

'I love you so and it's been awful. You won't go away?'

'No. I'll always come back.'

'Oh, I love you so. Please put your hand there again.'

'It's not been away.' I turned her so I could see her face when I kissed her and I saw that her eyes were shut. I kissed both her shut eyes. I thought she was probably a little crazy. It was all right if she was. I did not care what I was getting into. This was better than going every evening to the house for officers where the girls climbed all over you and put your cap on backward as a sign of affection between their trips upstairs with brother officers. I knew I did not love Catherine Barkley nor had any idea of loving her. This was a game, like bridge, in which you said things instead of playing cards. Like bridge, you had to pretend you were playing for money or playing for some stakes. Nobody had mentioned what the stakes were. It was all right with me.

'I wish there was some place we could go,' I said. I was experiencing the masculine difficulty of making love very long standing up.

'There isn't any place,' she said. She came back from wherever she had been.

'We might sit there just for a little while.'

We sat on the flat stone bench and I held Catherine Barkley's hand She would not let me put my arm around her.

'Are you very tired?' she asked.

'No.'

She looked down at the grass.

'This is a rotten game we play, isn't it?'

'What game?'

'Don't be dull.'

'I'm not, on purpose.'

'You're a nice boy,' she said. 'And you play it as well as you know how. But it's a rotten game.'

'Do you always know what people think?'

'Not always. But I do with you. You don't have to pretend you love me. That's over for the evening. Is there anything you'd like to talk about?'

'But I do love you.'

'Please let's not lie when we don't have to. I had a very fine little show and I'm all right now. You see I'm not mad and I'm not gone off. It's only a little sometimes.'

I pressed her hand, 'Dear Catherine.'

'It sounds very funny now – Catherine. You don't pronounce it very much alike. But you're very nice. You're a very good boy.'

'That's what the priest said.'

'Yes, you're very good. And you will come and see me?'

'Of course.'

'And you don't have to say you love me. That's all over for a while.' She stood up and put out her hand. 'Good night.'

I wanted to kiss her.

'No,' she said. 'I'm awfully tired.'

'Kiss me, though,' I said.

'I'm awfully tired, darling.'

'Kiss me.'

'Do you want to very much?'

'Yes.'

We kissed and she broke away suddenly. 'No. Good night, please, darling.' We walked to the door and I saw her go in and down the hall. I liked to watch her move. She went on down the hall. I went on home. It was a hot night and there was a good deal going on up in the mountains. I watched the flashes on San Gabriele.

31 *a* Write a short definition of what the man means by 'game'. (lines 42–6)
b Write a short definition of what the woman means by 'game'. (lines 57–62)
c Is the man happy with the game that is being played?
d Is the woman happy with the game that is being played?
e Do you see any similarities or differences between Lawrence's use of 'contest' and 'conflict' and the use of the word 'game' in this extract?

32 Compare the way Catherine and Gudrun ask their men to say 'I love you'. Why do you think they do this? (You may want to look again at *A Farewell to Arms*, lines 22–34 and 64–78, and *Women in Love*, lines 187–95 and 238–48.)

33 Do you think the couple in *A Farewell to Arms* will be happier or less happy than Gerald and Gudrun?

34 Do you think that male writers can understand and write successfully about the feelings of women? Compare your ideas with a partner or friend.

Authors

D(avid) H(erbert) Lawrence (1885–1930) was born in Eastwood, Nottinghamshire. His father was a coal-miner, and his mother was an ex-schoolteacher who came from a middle-class family; the tension between the often drunk father and the gentle but possessive mother are described in his autobiographical novel *Sons and Lovers* (1913), along with the complex and troubled relationships between mother and son and between the son and other women. After working as a clerk Lawrence studied for a teacher's certificate, but gave up teaching when his novel *The White Peacock* was published in 1911. A year later he met Frieda von Richthofen, the German wife of a professor at Nottingham University College. They eloped to Europe, married in 1914, and spent the next year in Italy. Back in England, Lawrence was extremely critical of World War I, and he and Frieda were even prosecuted as alleged German agents. After the war they left England, and travelled to Italy, Australia, Ceylon, the USA, Mexico and France, Lawrence being continually attracted and disappointed in his quest for a home and 'congenial associates', and also in search of warm climates for his growing illness. He died of tuberculosis in a sanatorium in the south of France.

Despite ill-health, money troubles and constant travelling, Lawrence's output was remarkably high. His other novels include *The Lost Girl* (1920), *Aaron's Rod* (1922), *Kangaroo* (1923), *The Plumed Serpent* (1926); in addition to these he also wrote short stories, poetry, criticism and travel books (*Mornings in Mexico, Sea and Sardinia, Etruscan Places*). Lawrence's 'world-view' derives from an instinctive rejection of the mechanical and artificial aspects of industrial civilization and a passionate belief in the value of physical experience, and his explicit descriptions of physical love often led to censorship trouble (see

Exercise 27). He wrote in 1913: 'My great religion is a belief in the blood, the flesh, as being wiser than intellect. We can go wrong in our minds. But what our blood feels and believes and says is always true.'

Ernest Hemingway (1898–1961) was born in Illinois in the USA, and after working as a journalist in Kansas City he joined a volunteer ambulance unit on the Italian front during the First World War, where he was severely wounded: his experiences there provide the background to *A Farewell to Arms*. After the war he was sent to Paris as a newspaper correspondent for *The Toronto Star*, where he mixed with leading figures in contemporary culture such as Ezra Pound, Gertrude Stein, James Joyce, Pablo Picasso and Henri Matisse, a period described in his memoirs *A Moveable Feast* (1964). Along with Scott Fitzgerald he soon came to be recognized as representative of the so-called 'Lost Generation' of writers of the 1920s. In Paris he wrote *The Sun Also Rises* (1926), describing the rootless and promiscuous life of English and American expatriates, and *A Farewell to Arms* (1929). During the Spanish Civil War he fought on the Republican side against the Fascists: *For Whom the Bell Tolls* (1940) is his novel based on this experience. During the Second World War Hemingway was a war correspondent in Europe, and afterwards lived mostly in Cuba, where he wrote *The Old Man and the Sea* (1952), in which a Cuban fisherman's struggle to catch a giant marlin becomes an allegory of man's struggle against nature. After a long illness he shot himself in 1961.

Hemingway's style in his novels and highly-regarded short stories *(Men without Women* and *Winner Take Nothing*) is unmistakable: short, very simple sentences; dialogue that is terse, colloquial and colourful; very objective, with little narratorial comment. Few writers have been so closely identified as Hemingway with the 'macho' values of 'the man of action': he pursued a lifestyle – four marriages, African safaris, hunting, boxing, love of bullfighting, heavy drinking – that brought him the status of a modern-day romantic hero in the same mould as a classic 19th century equivalent, Byron. Yet his work is full of death and disillusion: what is important is how the Hemingway 'hero' behaves – his directness, his courage, his endurance in the face of pain and loss. Hemingway was awarded the Nobel Prize for Literature in 1954.

4 War Games

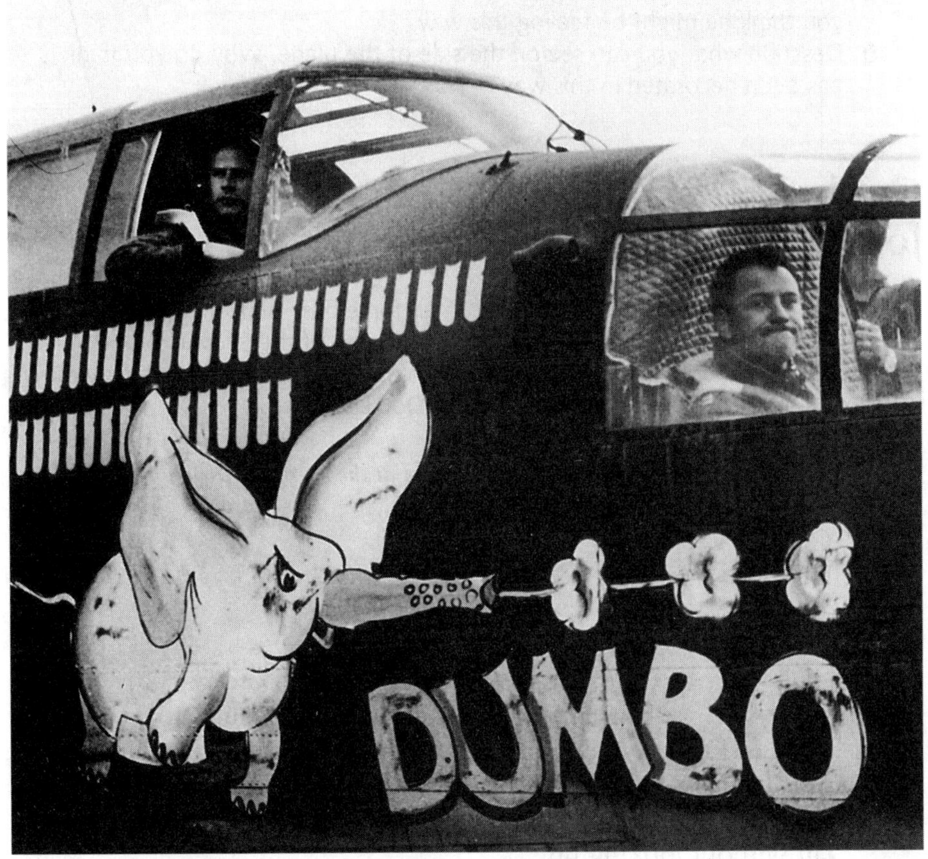

A scene from Mike Nichols' 1970 film version of *Catch-22*

Before you read

1 Look at the film still on the previous page.

a How would you describe the expression of the man on the right? Why do you think he might be feeling this way?

b Describe what you can see on the side of the plane. Why do you think it has been decorated in this way?

Catch-22 (1961)
Joseph Heller

Catch-22 describes life on an American air force base on a small Mediterranean island during the Italian campaign of the Second World War. The main character is an airman, Captain Yossarian, but there are many other characters, including the medical officer, Doc Daneeka …

See the glossary section at the back of the book for vocabulary.

CHAPTER 4
DOC DANEEKA

Hungry Joe was crazy, and no one knew it better than Yossarian, who did everything he could to help him. Hungry Joe just wouldn't listen to Yossarian. Hungry Joe just wouldn't listen because he thought Yossarian was crazy.

'Why should he listen to you ?' Doc Daneeka inquired of Yossarian without looking up.

'Because he's got troubles.'

Doc Daneeka snorted scornfully. 'He thinks he's got troubles? What about me?' Doc Daneeka continued slowly with a gloomy sneer. 'Oh, I'm not complaining. I know there's a war on. I know a lot of people are going to have to suffer for us to win it. But why must I be one of them? Why don't they draft some of these old doctors who keep shooting their kissers off in public about what big sacrifices the medical game stands ready to make? I don't want to make sacrifices. I want to make dough.'

Doc Daneeka was a very neat, clean man whose idea of a good time was to sulk. He had a dark complexion and a small, wise, saturnine face with mournful pouches under both eyes. He brooded over his health continually and went almost daily to the medical tent to have his temperature taken by one of the two enlisted men there who ran things for him practically on their own, and ran it so efficiently that he was left with little else to do but sit in the sunlight with his stuffed nose and wonder what other people were so worried about. Their names were Gus and Wes and they had succeeded in elevating medicine to an exact science. All men reporting on sick call with temperatures above 102 were rushed to the hospital. All those except Yossarian reporting on sick call with temperatures below 102 had their gums and toes painted with gentian violet solution and were given a laxative to throw away into the bushes. All those reporting on a sick call with temperatures of exactly I02 were asked to return in an hour to have their temperatures taken again. Yossarian, with his temperature of 101, could go to the hospital whenever he wanted to because he was not afraid of them.

The system worked just fine for everybody, especially for Doc Daneeka, who found himself with all the time he needed to watch old Major —— de Coverley pitching horseshoes in his private horseshoe-pitching pit, still wearing the transparent eye patch Doc Daneeka had fashioned for him from the strip of celluloid stolen from Major Major's orderly room window months before when Major —— de Coverley had returned from Rome with an injured cornea after renting two apartments there for the officers and enlisted men to use on their rest leaves. The only time Doc Daneeka ever went to the medical tent was the time he began to feel he was a very sick man each day and stopped in just to have Gus and Wes look him over. They could never find anything wrong with him. His temperature was always 96.8, which was perfectly all right with them, as long as he didn't mind. Doc Daneeka did mind. He was beginning to lose confidence in Gus and Wes and was thinking of having them both transferred back to the motor pool and replaced by someone who *could* find something wrong.

Doc Daneeka was personally familiar with a number of things that were drastically wrong. In addition to his health, he worried about the Pacific Ocean and flight time. Health was something no one ever could be sure of for a long enough time. The Pacific Ocean was a body of water surrounded on all sides by elephantiasis and other dread diseases to which, if he ever displeased Colonel Cathcart by grounding Yossarian, he might suddenly find himself transferred. And flight time was the time he had to spend in airplane flight each month in order to get his flight pay. Doc Daneeka hated to fly. He felt imprisoned in an airplane. In an airplane there was absolutely no place in the world to go except to another part of the airplane. Doc Daneeka had been told that people who enjoyed climbing into an airplane were really giving vent to a subconscious desire to climb back into the womb. He had been told this by Yossarian, who made it possible for Dan Daneeka to collect his flight pay each month without ever climbing back into the womb. Yossarian would persuade McWatt to enter Doc Daneeka's name on his flight log for training missions or trips to Rome.

'You know how it is,' Doc Daneeka had wheedled, with a sly, conspiratorial wink. 'Why take chances when I don't have to?'

'Sure,' Yossarian agreed.

'What difference does it make to anyone if I'm in the plane or not?'

'No difference.'

What do you think of this idea? Does it make any difference if Doc Daneeka is in the plane?

'Sure, that's what I mean,' Doc Daneeka said. 'A little grease is what makes this world go round. One hand washes the other. Know what I mean? You scratch my back, I'll scratch yours.'

Yossarian knew what he meant.

'That's not what I meant,' Doc Daneeka said, as Yossarian began scratching his back. 'I'm talking about co-operation. Favors. You do a favor for me, I'll do one for you. Get it?'

'Do one for me,' Yossarian requested.

'Not a chance,' Doc Daneeka answered.

There was something fearful and minute about Doc Daneeka as he sat despondently outside his tent in the sunlight as often as he could, dressed in khaki summer trousers and a short-sleeved summer shirt that was bleached almost to an antiseptic gray by the daily laundering to which he had it subjected. He was like a man who had grown frozen with horror once and had never come completely unthawed. He sat all tucked up into himself, his slender shoulders huddled halfway around his head, his suntanned hands with their luminous silver fingernails massaging the backs of his bare, folded arms gently as though he were cold. Actually he was a very warm, compassionate man who never stopped feeling sorry for himself.

'Why me ?' was his constant lament, and the question was a good one.

Yossarian knew it was a good one because Yossarian was a collector of good questions and had used them to disrupt the educational sessions Clevinger had once conducted two nights a week in Captain Black's intelligence tent with the corporal in eyeglasses who everybody knew was probably a subversive. Captain Black knew he was a subversive because he wore eyeglasses and used words like *panacea* and *utopia*, and because he disapproved of Adolf Hitler, who had done such a great job of combating un-American activities in Germany. Yossarian attended the educational sessions because he wanted to find out why so many people were working so hard to kill him. A handful of other men were also interested, and the questions were many and good when Clevinger and the subversive corporal finished and made the mistake of asking if there were any.

'Who is Spain?'

'Why is Hitler?'

'When is right?'

'Where was that stooped and mealy-colored old man I used to call Poppa when the merry-go-round broke down?'

'How was trump at Munich?'

'Ho-ho beriberi.'

and

'Balls!'

all rang out in rapid succession, and then there was Yossarian with the question that had no answer:

'Where are the Snowdens of yesteryear?'

The question upset them, because Snowden had been killed over Avignon when Dobbs went crazy in mid-air and seized the controls away from Huple.

The corporal played it dumb. 'What?' he asked.

'Where are the Snowdens of yesteryear?'

'I'm afraid I don't understand.'

'*Où sont les Neigedens d'antan?*' Yossarian said to make it easier for him.

'*Parlez en anglais*, for Christ's sake,' said the corporal. '*Je ne parle pas français*.'

'Neither do I,' answered Yossarian, who was ready to pursue him through all the words in the world to wring the knowledge from him if he could, but Clevinger intervened, pale, thin, and laboring for breath, a humid coating of tears already glistening in his undernourished eyes.

Group Headquarters was alarmed, for there was no telling what people might find out once they felt free to ask whatever questions they wanted to. Colonel Cathcart sent Colonel Korn to stop it, and Colonel Korn succeeded with a rule governing the asking of questions. Colonel Korn's rule was a stroke of genius, Colonel Korn explained in his report to Colonel Cathcart. Under Colonel Korn's rule, the only people permitted to ask questions were those who never did. Soon the only people attending were those who never asked questions, and the sessions were discontinued altogether, since Clevinger, the corporal and Colonel Korn agreed that it was neither possible nor necessary to educate people who never questioned anything.

Colonel Cathcart and Lieutenant Colonel Korn lived and worked in the Group Headquarters building, as did all the members of the headquarters staff, with the exception of the chaplain. The Group Headquarters building was an enormous, windy, antiquated structure built of powdery red stone and banging plumbing. Behind the building was the modern skeet-shooting range that had been constructed by Colonel Cathcart for the exclusive recreation of the officers at Group and at which every officer and enlisted man on combat status now, thanks to General Dreedle, had to spend a minimum of eight hours a month.

Yossarian shot skeet, but never hit any. Appleby shot skeet and never missed. Yossarian was as bad at shooting skeet as he was at gambling. He could never win money gambling either. Even when he cheated he couldn't win, because the people he cheated against were always better at cheating too. These were two disappointments to which he had resigned himself: he would never be a skeet shooter, and he would never make money.

'It takes brains *not* to make money,' Colonel Cargill wrote in one of the homiletic memoranda he regularly prepared for circulation over General Peckem's signature. 'Any fool can make money these days and most of them do. But what about people with talent and brains? Name, for example, one poet who makes money.'

'T. S. Eliot,' ex-P.F.C. Wintergreen said in his mail-sorting cubicle at Twenty-seventh Air Force Headquarters, and slammed down the telephone without identifying himself.

Colonel Cargill, in Rome was perplexed.

'Who was it?' asked General Peckem.

'I don't know,' Colonel Cargill replied.

'What did he want?'

'I don't know.'

'Well, what did he say?'

'"T. S. Eliot,"' Colonel Cargill informed him.

'What's that?'

'"T. S. Eliot,"' Colonel Cargill repeated.

'Just "T. S.—"'

'Yes, sir. That's all he said. Just "T. S. Eliot."'

'I wonder what it means,' General Peckem reflected.

Colonel Cargill wondered, too.

'T. S. Eliot,' General Peckem mused.

'T. S. Eliot,' Colonel Cargill echoed with the same funereal puzzlement.

What do you think General Peckem will do now?

General Peckem roused himself after a moment with an unctuous and benignant smile. His expression was shrewd and sophisticated. His eyes gleamed maliciously. 'Have someone get me General Dreedle,' he requested Colonel Cargill. 'Don't let him know who's calling.'

Colonel Cargill handed him the phone.

'T. S. Eliot,' General Peckem said, and hung up.

'Who was it?' asked Colonel Moodus.

General Dreedle, in Corsica, did not reply. Colonel Moodus was General Dreedle's son-in-law, and General Dreedle, at the insistence of his wife and against his own better judgment, had taken him into the military business. General Dreedle gazed at Colonel Moodus with level hatred. He detested the very sight of his son-in-law, who was his aide and therefore in constant attendance upon him. He had opposed his daughter's marriage to Colonel Moodus because he disliked attending weddings. Wearing a menacing and pre-occupied scowl, General Dreedle moved to the full-length mirror in his office and stared at his stocky reflection. He had a grizzled, broad-browed head with iron-gray tufts over his eyes and a blunt and belligerent jaw. He brooded in ponderous speculation over the cryptic message he had just received. Slowly his face softened with an idea, and he curled his lips with wicked pleasure.

'Get Peckem,' he told Colonel Moodus. 'Don't let the bastard know who's calling.'

'Who was it?' asked Colonel Cargill, back in Rome.

'That same person,' General Peckem replied with a definite trace of alarm. 'Now he's after me.'

'What did he want?'

'I don't know.'

'What did he say?'

'The same thing.'

'" T.S. Eliot"?'

'Yes, "T. S. Eliot." That's all he said.' General Peckem had a hopeful thought. 'Perhaps it's a new code or something, like the colors of the day. Why don't you have someone check with Communications and see if it's a new code or something or the colors of the day?'

Communications answered that T. S. Eliot was not a new code or the colors of the day.

Colonel Cargill had the next idea. 'Maybe I ought to phone Twenty-seventh Air Force Headquarters and see if they know anything about it. They have a clerk up there named Wintergreen I'm pretty close to. He's the one who tipped me off that our prose was too prolix.'

Ex-P.F.C. Wintergreen told Cargill that there was no record at Twenty-seventh Air Force Headquarters of a T. S. Eliot.

'How's our prose these days?' Colonel Cargill decided to inquire while he had ex-P.F.C. Wintergreen on the phone.

'It's much better now, isn't it?'

'It's still too prolix,' ex-P.F.C. Wintergreen replied.

'It wouldn't surprise me if General Dreedle were behind the whole thing,' General Peckem confessed at last. 'Remember what he did to that skeet-shooting range?'

General Dreedle had thrown open Colonel Cathcart's private skeet-shooting range to every officer and enlisted man in the group on combat duty. General Dreedle wanted his men to spend as much time out on the skeet-shooting range as the facilities and their flight schedule would allow. Shooting skeet eight hours a month was excellent training for them. It trained them to shoot skeet.

Dunbar loved shooting skeet because he hated every minute of it and the time passed so slowly. He had figured out that a single hour on the skeet-shooting range with people like Havermeyer and Appleby could be worth as much as eleven-times-seventeen years.

How do you think this will be explained?

'I think you're crazy,' was the way Clevinger had responded to Dunbar's discovery.

'Who wants to know?' Dunbar answered.

'I mean it,' Clevinger insisted.

'Who cares?' Dunbar answered.

'I really do. I'll even go so far as to concede that life seems longer i—'

'—*is* longer i—'

'— *is* longer — *Is* longer? All right, *is* longer if it's filled with periods of boredom and discomfort, b—'

'Guess how fast?' Dunbar said suddenly.

'Huh?'

'They go,' Dunbar explained.

'Who?'

'Years.'

'Years.'

'Years,' said Dunbar. 'Years, years, years.'

'Clevinger, why don't you let Dunbar alone?' Yossarian broke in. 'Don't you realize the toll this is taking?'

'It's all right,' said Dunbar magnanimously. 'I have some decades to spare. Do you know how long a year takes when it's going away?'

'And you shut up also,' Yossarian told Orr, who had begun to snigger.

'I was just thinking about that girl,' Orr said. 'That girl in Sicily. That girl in Sicily with the bald head.'

'You'd *better* shut up also,' Yossarian warned him.

'It's your fault,' Dunbar said to Yossarian. 'Why don't you let him snigger if he wants to? It's better than having him talking.'

'All right. Go ahead and snigger if you want to.'

'Do you know how long a year takes when it's going away?' Dunbar repeated to Clevinger. 'This long.' He snapped his fingers. 'A second ago you were stepping into college with your lungs full of fresh air. Today you're an old man.'

'Old?' asked Clevinger with surprise. 'What are you talking about?'

'Old.'

'I'm not old.'

'You're inches away from death every time you go on a mission. How much older can you be at your age? A half minute before that you were stepping into high school, and an unhooked brassiere was as close as you ever hoped to get to Paradise. Only a fifth of a second before that you were a small kid with a ten-week summer vacation that lasted a hundred thousand years and still ended too soon. Zip! They go rocketing by so fast. How the hell else are you ever going to slow time down ?' Dunbar was almost angry when he finished.

'Well, maybe it is true,' Clevinger conceded unwillingly in a subdued tone. 'Maybe a long life does have to be filled with many unpleasant conditions if it's to seem long. But in that event, who wants one?'

'I do,' Dunbar told him.

'Why?' Clevinger asked.

'What else is there?'

First reaction

2 Which character(s) do you find most interesting? Can you say why?

Close reading

Narrative structure 1

3 ***a*** Match the line references on the left with the descriptions of what happens on the right. The first one is done for you.

1) 1–9	a) disruption of the educational sessions
2) 10–15	b) Doc Daneeka's hypochondria, and the temperature tests in the medical tent
3) 16–50	c) compulsory skeet shooting and Yossarian's attitude to it
4) 51–64	d) Hungry Joe's refusal to listen to Yossarian
5) 64–83	e) Group Headquarters' reaction to the questions at the educational sessions
6) 84–97	f) Doc Daneeka's deal with Yossarian about flight time
7) 98–137	g) compulsory skeet shooting mentioned again
8) 138–54	h) Doc Daneeka's complaint about being drafted into the armed services
9) 155–71	i) Dunbar's theory of the brevity of life, and how to make it longer
10) 172–242	j) Doc Daneeka's fears about being transferred and flying
11) 243–8	k) confusion caused by 'T. S. Eliot'
12) 249–304	l) description of Doc Daneeka's self-pity

1) *d)* 2) ____ 3) ____ 4) ____ 5) ____ 6) ____ 7) ____
8) ____ 9) ____ 10) ____ 11) ____ 12) ____

b How would you describe the narrative structure?

1 chronological: one event follows another in time, and this carries the plot forward.

2 non-chronological: associations of ideas and flashbacks carry the plot forward.

Characters 1

4 ***a*** Without looking back at the extract, have a guess at how many characters are mentioned. Compare your guess with the rest of the class, and then check with the Key.

b Do you find this number usual or unusual in comparison with other novels you know?

c Describe your reaction to this number of characters: were you confused, irritated, amused, or what?

5 ***a*** Scan the extract again and pick out some phrases and sentences which indicate the the kind of person Doc Daneeka is.
b Compare your choices with a partner.

Before you read

Do you remember how Doc Daneeka picks up his flight pay? If necessary, re-read lines 58–77.

The plane flown by a pilot called McWatt has just crashed …

See the Glossary section at the back of the book for vocabulary.

CHAPTER 31
MRS DANEEKA

When Colonel Cathcart learned that Doc Daneeka too had been killed in McWatt's plane, he increased the number of missions to seventy.

The first person in the squadron to find out that Doc Daneeka was dead was Sergeant Towser, who had been informed earlier by the man in the control tower that Doc Daneeka's name was down as a passenger on the pilot's manifest McWatt had filed before taking off. Sergeant Towser brushed away a tear and struck Doc Daneeka's name from the roster of squadron personnel. With lips still quivering, he rose and trudged outside reluctantly to break the bad news to Gus and Wes, discreetly avoiding any conversation with Doc Daneeka himself as he moved by the flight surgeon's slight sepulchral figure roosting despondently on his stool in the late-afternoon sunlight between the orderly room and the medical tent. Sergeant Towser's heart was heavy; now he had *two* dead men on his hands – Mudd, the dead man in Yossarian's tent who wasn't even there, and Doc Daneeka, the new dead man in the squadron, who most certainly was there and gave every indication of proving a still thornier administrative problem for him.

Gus and Wes listened to Sergeant Towser with looks of stoic surprise and said not a word about their bereavement to anyone else until Doc Daneeka himself came in about an hour afterward to have his temperature taken for the third time that day and his blood pressure checked. The thermometer registered a half degree lower than his usual subnormal temperature of 96.8. Doc Daneeka was alarmed. The fixed, vacant, wooden stares of his two enlisted men were even more irritating than always.

'Goddammit,' he expostulated politely in an uncommon excess of exasperation, 'what's the matter with you two men anyway? It just isn't right for a person to have a low temperature all the time and walk around with a stuffed nose.' Doc Daneeka emitted a glum, self-pitying sniff and strolled disconsolately across the tent to help himself to some aspirin and sulphur pills and paint his own throat with Argyrol. His downcast face was fragile and forlorn as a swallow's, and he rubbed the back of his arms rhythmically. 'Just look how cold I am right now. You're sure you're not holding anything back?'

'You're dead, sir,' one of his two enlisted men explained.

Doc Daneeka jerked his head up quickly with resentful distrust. 'What's that?'

'You're dead, sir,' repeated the other. 'That's probably the reason you always feel so cold.'

'That's right, sir. You've probably been dead all this time and we just didn't detect it.'

'What the *hell* are you both talking about?' Doc Daneeka cried shrilly with a surging, petrifying sensation of some onrushing unavoidable disaster.

'It's true, sir,' said one of the enlisted men. 'The records show that you went up in McWatt's plane to collect some flight time. You didn't come down in a parachute, so you must have been killed in the crash.'

'That's right, sir,' said the other. 'You ought to be glad you've got any temperature at all.'

Doc Daneeka's mind was reeling in confusion. 'Have you both gone crazy?' he demanded. 'I'm going to report this whole insubordinate incident to Sergeant Towser.'

'Sergeant Towser's the one who told us about it,' said either Gus or Wes. 'The War Department's even going to notify your wife.'

Doc Daneeka yelped and ran out of the medical tent to remonstrate with Sergeant Towser, who edged away from him with repugnance and advised Doc Daneeka to remain out of sight as much as possible until some decision could be reached relating to the disposition of his remains.

'Gee, I guess he really is dead,' grieved one of his enlisted men in a low, respectful voice. 'I'm going to miss him. He was a pretty wonderful guy, wasn't he?'

'Yeah, he sure was,' mourned the other. 'But I'm glad the little fuck is gone. I was getting sick and tired of taking his blood pressure all the time.'

Mrs Daneeka, Doc Daneeka's wife, was not glad that Doc Daneeka was gone and split the peaceful Staten Island night with woeful shrieks of lamentation when she learned by War Department telegram that her husband had been killed in action. Women came to comfort her, and their husbands paid condolence calls and hoped inwardly that she would soon move to another neighborhood and spare them the obligation of continuous sympathy. The poor woman was totally distraught for almost a full week. Slowly, heroically, she found the strength to contemplate a future filled with dire problems for herself and her children. Just as she was growing resigned to her loss, the postman rang with a bolt from the blue – a letter from overseas that was signed with her husband's signature and urged her frantically to disregard any bad news concerning him. Mrs Daneeka was dumfounded. The date on the letter was illegible. The handwriting throughout was shaky and hurried, but the style resembled her husband's and the melancholy, self-pitying tone was familiar, although more dreary than usual. Mrs Daneeka was overjoyed and wept irrepressibly with relief and kissed the crinkled, grubby tissue of V-mail stationery a thousand times. She dashed a grateful note off to her husband pressing him for details and sent a wire informing the War Department of its error. The War Department replied touchily that there had been no error and that she was undoubtedly the victim of some sadistic and psychotic forger in her husband's squadron. The letter to her husband was returned unopened, stamped KILLED IN ACTION.

How do you think Mrs Daneeka will react?

Mrs Daneeka had been widowed cruelly again, but this time her grief was mitigated somewhat by a notification from Washington that she was sole beneficiary of her husband's $10,000 GI insurance policy, which amount was obtainable by her on demand. The realization that she and the children were not faced immediately with starvation brought a brave smile to her face and marked the turning point in her distress. The Veterans Administration informed her by mail the very next day that she would be entitled to pension benefits for the rest of her natural life because of her husband's demise, and to a burial allowance for him of $250. A government check for $250 was enclosed. Gradually, inexorably, her prospects brightened. A letter arrived that same week from the Social Security Administration stating that, under the provisions of the Old Age and Survivors Insurance Act of 1935, she would receive monthly support for herself and her dependent children until they reached the age of eighteen, and a burial allowance of $250. With these government letters as proof of death, she applied for payment on three life insurance policies Doc Daneeka had carried, with a value of $50,000 each; her claim was honored and processed swiftly. Each day brought new unexpected treasures. A key to a safe-deposit box led to a fourth life insurance policy with a face value of $50,000, and to $18,000 in cash on which income tax had never been paid and need never be paid. A fraternal lodge to which he had belonged gave her a cemetery plot. A second fraternal organization of which he had been a member sent her a burial allowance of $250. His county medical association gave her a burial allowance of $250.

The husbands of her closest friends began to flirt with her. Mrs Daneeka was simply delighted with the way things were turning out and had her hair dyed. Her fantastic wealth just kept piling up, and she had to remind herself daily that all the hundreds of thousands of dollars she was acquiring were not worth a single penny without her husband to share this good fortune with her. It astonished her that so many separate organizations were willing to do so much to bury Doc Daneeka, who, back in Pianosa, was having a terrible time trying to keep his head above the ground and wondered with dismal apprehension why his wife did not answer the letter he had written.

He found himself ostracized in the squadron by men who cursed his memory foully for having supplied Colonel Cathcart with provocation to raise the number of combat missions. Records attesting to his death were pullulating like insect eggs and verifying each other beyond all contention. He drew no pay or PX rations and depended for life on the charity of Sergeant Towser and Milo, who both knew he was dead. Colonel Cathcart refused to see him, and Colonel Korn sent word through Major Danby that he would have Doc Daneeka cremated on the spot if he ever showed up at Group Headquarters. Major Danby confided that Group was incensed with all flight surgeons because of Dr Stubbs, the bushy-haired, baggy-chinned, slovenly flight surgeon in Dunbar's squadron who was deliberately and defiantly brewing insidious dissension there by grounding all men with sixty missions on proper forms that were rejected by Group indignantly with orders restoring the confused pilots, navigators, bombardiers and gunners to combat duty. Morale there was ebbing rapidly, and Dunbar was under surveillance. Group was glad Doc Daneeka had been killed and did not intend to ask for a replacement.

Not even the chaplain could bring Doc Daneeka back to life under the circumstances. Alarm changed to resignation, and more and more Doc Daneeka acquired the look of an ailing rodent. The sacks under his eyes turned hollow and black, and he padded through the shadows fruitlessly like a ubiquitous spook. Even Captain Flume recoiled when Doc Daneeka sought him out in the woods for help. Heartlessly, Gus and Wes turned him away from their medical tent without even a thermometer for comfort, and then, only then, did he realize that, to all intents and purposes, he really was dead, and that he had better do something damned fast if he ever hoped to save himself.

There was nowhere else to turn but to his wife, and he scribbled an impassioned letter begging her to bring his plight to the attention of the War Department and urging her to communicate at once with his group commander, Colonel Cathcart, for assurances that—no matter what else she might have heard—it was indeed he, her husband, Doc Daneeka, who was pleading with her, and not a corpse or some impostor. Mrs Daneeka was stunned by the depth of emotion in the almost illegible appeal. She was torn with compunction and tempted to comply, but the very next letter she opened that day was from that same Colonel Cathcart, her husband's group commander, and began:

Dear Mrs, Mr, Miss, or Mr and Mrs Daneeka: Words cannot express the deep personal grief I experienced when your husband, son, father or brother was killed, wounded or reported missing in action.

Mrs. Daneeka moved with her children to Lansing, Michigan, and left no forwarding address.

First reaction

6 Which of these reactions do you agree with?

- ***a*** This is poetic justice: Doc Daneeka gets exactly what he deserves.
- ***b*** Even Doc Daneeka is a victim, and deserves some of our sympathy.
- ***c*** We are not expected to have any moral reaction to this episode: we are either amused or not, that is all.

Close reading

Narrative structure 2

7 ***a*** Match the line references on the left with the descriptions of what happens on the right. The first one is done for you.

1) 305 – 8	a) Doc Daneeka's second letter to Mrs Daneeka
2) 309 – 23	b) Sergeant Towser's reaction to Doc Daneeka's 'death'
3) 324 – 72	c) Doc Daneeka's first letter to Mrs Daneeka
4) 373 – 82	d) Mrs Daneeka's move to Michigan
5) 382 – 93	e) insurance, pension benefits and other payments for Mrs Daneeka
6) 393 – 7	f) Colonel Cathcart's reaction to Doc Daneeka's 'death'
7) 398 – 431	g) Doc Daneeka's complete rejection by everyone
8) 431 – 63	h) Mrs Daneeka's reaction to the War Department telegram informing her of Doc Daneeka's 'death'
9) 464 – 71	i) the War Department's confirmation of Doc Daneeka's 'death', and return of his letter
10) 471 – 7	j) Colonel Cathcart's letter to Mrs Daneeka
11) 478 – 9	k) Gus and Wes' reaction to Doc Daneeka's 'death'

1) *f)* 2) ____ 3) ____ 4) ____ 5) ____ 6) ____ 7) ____
8) ____ 9) ____ 10) ____ 11) ____

b How would you describe the narrative structure used in the second extract? Choose one of the options in Exercise 3b.

Characters 2

8 Does Doc Daneeka have the kind of wife he deserves? Does Mrs Daneeka have the kind of husband she deserves? (You may find it useful to look back to your answers to Exercise 5.)

The world of *Catch-22*

9 Put a tick (✓) next to the expressions below which you think best describe the world of *Catch-22*. Find one or two examples from the extracts to justify each of your choices. You can use your examples more than once if you want.

- reason and logic
- the enemy = your own side
- bureaucracy replaces common sense
- successful communication
- instinctive dislike and mistrust of other people
- self-interest
- common sense modifies bureaucracy
- the enemy = the Nazis
- perverse logic
- spontaneous like and trust of other people

- mutual incomprehension
- altruism and generosity

Do you want to add any ideas of your own?

10 On the basis of what you have read, which statement do you agree with most – ***a***, ***b*** or ***c***? Write your own interpretation if you like.

a *Catch-22* describes the absurd, brutal and surreal world of war; fundamentally it is an anti-war novel.

b The world of *Catch-22* is an exaggerated but recognizable version of the real world, an allegory of human behaviour in peacetime too.

c The world of *Catch-22* is a comic, lunatic creation which has nothing to do with the real world we live in.

d your own interpretation: ______________________________

____

Language practice – structures

Analyzing and writing complex sentences

11 a Every now and again Heller uses long, complex sentences. Look at the following sentence.

> The system worked just fine for everybody, especially for Doc Daneeka, [who found himself with all the time he needed to watch old Major —— de Coverley pitching horseshoes in his private horseshoe-pitching pit,] [still wearing the transparent eye patch] [Doc Daneeka had fashioned for him from the strip of celluloid] [stolen from Major Major's orderly room window months before] [when Major ______ de Coverley had returned from Rome with an injured cornea after renting two apartments there for the officers and enlisted men to use on their rest leaves.] (lines 34–42)

Now look at this grammatical analysis.

1 The system links this sentence with what goes before it: it refers back to the temperature-taking of the preceeding passage.

2 The brackets [ ] enclose relative clauses. There are five of them. Note how the relative clauses are introduced: by the pronouns *who* and *when* (= 'at the time which'); by absence of pronoun (eg *eye patch Doc Daneeka had fashioned*); by present and past participles (*wearing* and *stolen*).

3 Past perfect tenses are circled.

4 Two clauses of purpose are underlined. These are expressed by the infinitive form of the verb.

b Now make a similar analysis of the following passage.

1 Box words which link the passage with what goes before it in the extract. What do they refer to?

2 Put brackets [ ] around the relative clauses.

3 Circle the past perfect tenses.

4 Underline the clauses of reason (introduced with 'because').

Yossarian knew it was a good one because Yossarian was a collector of good questions and had used them to disrupt the educational sessions Clevinger had once conducted two nights a week in Captain Black's intelligence tent with the corporal in eyeglasses who everybody knew was probably a subversive. Captain Black knew he was a subversive because he wore eyeglasses and used words like *panacea* and *utopia*, and because he disapproved of Adolf Hitler, who had done such a great job of combating un-American activities in Germany. (lines 98–106)

c How does the grammar of the sentences in ***a*** and ***b*** above contribute to the narrative structure and overall effects of *Catch-22*? Exchange ideas in pairs or groups, then check with the Key. (You may find it useful to look back to your answers to Exercises 3b, 4, 9 and 10.)

d If you want to examine some other complex sentences, here are some examples.
There was something fearful ... he had it subjected. (lines 84–8)
Behind the building ... eight hours a month. (lines 154–9)
Major Danby confided ... to combat duty. (lines 443–9)

What is 'Catch-22'?

12 A 'catch' is a difficulty or complication in a situation that is not immediately obvious. For example, if offered an arrangement or a bargain that seems too good to be true, you might say 'Where is the catch?' Now read the following sentences, which explain how Yossarian discovered what 'Catch-22' was, and his reaction to it.

a Yossarian went to Doc Daneeka and asked to be grounded.

b Yossarian's reason for asking to be grounded was that he was crazy and therefore not fit to fly.

c Doc Daneeka said he couldn't ground him.

d Doc Daneeka couldn't ground Yossarian because of a rule.

e This rule was called 'Catch-22'.

f 'Catch-22' obliged pilots to *ask* personally to be grounded.
g 'Catch-22' recognized that you had to be crazy to keep on flying missions.
h As soon as you *asked* to be grounded you proved you weren't crazy.
i Asking to be grounded meant you had to keep on flying combat missions.

j Yossarian could not help being impressed by what he called the 'elliptical precision' of this rule.
k Yossarian had always appreciated intellectual elegance.
l Yossarian compared 'Catch-22' to good modern art.
m The reason for his comparison was that it was both 'graceful' and 'shocking' at the same time.

Now combine them into one paragraph made up of three sentences: ***a–e***; ***f–i***; ***j–m***. Make any changes necessary, such as omitting and substituting words.

13 Try to remember an incident or situation that really frustrated you. Write a paragraph describing it in the style of the sentences in Exercises 11 and 12. Try to get Heller's feeling of controlled confusion.

Language practice – vocabulary

Impressions of novels

14 On the cover of a novel you will find the **blurb** – a description of the novel and often some favourable extracts from reviews. Read the following examples from the blurb of a paperback edition of *Catch-22*. Use a dictionary if necessary.

a 'Remarkable, mind-spinning, rave of a novel. Uniquely funny.' Kenneth Allsop, *Daily Mail*
b 'Comic, macabre, knockabout, nightmarish, ironic, bawdy, illogical, formless, Shavian.' *Books and Bookmen*
c 'A wild, moving, shocking, hilarious, raging, exhilarating, giant roller-coaster of a book.' *New York Herald Tribune*
d 'Wildly original, brutally gruesome, a dazzling performance that will outrage as many readers as it delights. Vulgarly, bitterly, savagely funny, it will not be forgotten by those who can take it.' *New York Times*
e 'Brilliantly written anti-war novel … a masterpiece.' *Bristol Evening News*
f 'A book of enormous richness and art, of deep thought and brilliant writing.' *Spectator*
g 'Devastatingly original novel, with a felicity of comic invention … deeply impressive.' *Irish Times*
h 'Extremely funny, sad, frightening – and above all, funny.' *Sunday Telegraph*
i 'Stands comparison with the most memorable works in satire.' *Belfast Telegraph*

j 'A crazy, wonderful, yet cruelly sane story, written with wit and wonder.' *Newsday*

k 'Absolutely original ... a disturbing insight into the larger struggle of today: the survival of mankind.' *Richmond Times Despatch*

15 Now classify the words and expressions from the blurb comments under the following headings. Some are done for you.

a It makes you laugh
Uniquely funny; comic; knockabout; ____________________

b It can disturb you
macabre; nightmarish; ____________________

c It makes you think
mind-spinning; ____________________

d It's different from other novels
Remarkable; ____________________

e It's well-written
a dazzling performance; ____________________

f Other words and expressions
rave of a novel; ____________________

16 When choosing comments for the 'blurb', publishers look for phrases which will publicize the novel and arouse interest, rather than phrases which represent sober, critical opinions. They are particularly interested in two features:

a favourable expressions listed one after the other with little or nothing in between. All the comments in Exercise 15 exemplify this, but comments ***a***, ***b*** and ***c*** are particularly extreme examples.

b *exaggeratedly* favourable expressions (expressions that would not be found in, for example, a serious critical essay). What expressions of this kind can you find in Exercise 15?

17 Do one of the following tasks.

a Choose one of the comments ***a–k*** from Exercise 15 that best represents your opinion of *Catch-22*.

b Write a sentence of your own that might be used for the blurb of a new edition of *Catch-22*.

c If you didn't like the chapters you have read, write a *critical* 'blurb-style' comment of your own.

18 Collect the names of some novels that most of the class know. Write some 'blurb-style' comments for them. Ask other students in the class to guess what novel you are referring to. If they can't guess immediately, give them some clues before you tell them the title.

Extension

19 Because of the influence of Heller's novel the phrase 'Catch-22' (or sometimes, 'a Catch-22 situation') has become part of the language. Other 'Catch-22s' have been formulated to apply to particular situations: for example, young actors struggling to find work often come up against 'the show-business Catch-22' – 'no work unless you have an agent, no agent unless you've worked'.
Choose one of the following tasks.

a Write a dictionary definition of 'a Catch-22'. (Some authentic dictionary definitions are given in the Key.)

b Formulate 'a Catch-22' that applies to a particularly frustrating situation you know well (for example, in your school or job, in dealings with bureaucracy, etc).

20 **Class project**: Divide into three groups. Using your own experience, reference books and anthologies, and by asking friends and relations, do some research on how war has been represented in different art-forms.
Group 1: visual forms – paintings, photographs and sculpture
Group 2: 'popular' forms – films and songs
Group 3: literature – novels, short stories, plays and poems

When you have finished your research, present it to the class in the form of a poster or wall display. (If you are studying on your own, choose one of the three group works above to research.)

21 **Writing**: Choose one of the following tasks.

a Write one of Doc Daneeka's letters to his wife (see lines 382–91 and 464–71).

b Write an entry from Yossarian's diary describing the episode of Doc Daneeka's 'death'.

22 Design a cover for a new paperback printing of *Catch-22*.

Beyond the text

23 Briefly look back to Exercise 9 and the expressions you chose from to describe *Catch-22*. As you read the following extract, ask yourself which you would choose to apply to the people and situation described here.

The Danger Tree (1977)
Olivia Manning

The Danger Tree is set in Egypt during the Second World War. Simon Boulderstone, a young British officer, has gone to look for his brother, Hugo, who is serving in another regiment.

See the Glossary section at the back of the book for vocabulary.

At the Operations truck, a New Zealand major, a tall, thin, grave-faced man, listened with lowered head as Simon explained that he was looking for a Captain Boulderstone. The major, jerking his head up, smiled on him. 'You think he's your brother, do you? Well, son, I think maybe he is. You're as like as two peas. But I don't know where he's got to – someone will have to look around for him. If you have a snack in the mess, we'll let you know as soon as we find him. OK?'

'OK, and thank you, sir.'

The mess was a fifteen hundred-weight truck from which an awning stretched to cover a few fold-up tables and chairs. Simon seated himself in shade that had the colour and smell of stewed tea. The truck itself served as a cook-house and Simon said to the man inside, 'Lot of flies about here.'

'Yes, they been a right plague this month. Our CO said something got to be done about them, but he didn't say what. I sprays flit around and the damn things laugh at it.'

The flies were lethargic with the heat. Simon, having eaten his bully-beef sandwich and drunk his tea, had nothing better to do than watch them sinking down on to the plastic table tops. He remembered what Harriet Pringle had said about the plagues coming to Egypt and staying there. The flies had been the third plague, 'a grievous swarm', and here they still were, crawling before him so slowly they seemed to be pulling themselves through treacle. The first excitement of arrival had left him and he could not understand why Hugo was so long in coming. Boredom and irritation came over him and seeing a fly swat on the truck counter, he borrowed it in order to attack the flies.

A dozen or so crawled on his table and no matter how many he killed, the numbers never grew less. When the swat hit the table, the surviving flies would lift themselves slowly and drift a little before sinking down again. He pushed the dead flies off the table and they dropped to the tarpaulin which covered the ground. When he looked down to count his bag of flies, he found they had all disappeared. He killed one more and watched to see what became of it. It had scarcely touched the floor when a procession of ants veered purposefully to it, surrounded it and, manoeuvring the large body between them, bore it away.

Simon laughed out loud. The ants did not pause to ask where the manna came from, they simply took it. The sky rained food and Simon, godlike, could send down an endless supply of it. He looked forward to telling Hugo about the flies and ants. He killed till teatime and the flies were as numerous as ever, then, all in a moment, the killing disgusted him. He had tea and, still waiting, he thought of the German youth he had killed on the hill. Away from the heat of battle, that killing too, disgusted him, and he would have sworn, had the situation permitted, never to kill again.

The mess filled with officers but none of them was Hugo. About five o'clock a corporal came to tell him that Captain Boulderstone had gone out with a patrol to bring in wounded.

'Has there been a scrap, then?'

The corporal did not look directly at Simon as he said, 'There was a bit of a scrap at the Mierir Depression two days ago. Last night we heard shelling. Could be, sir, the patrol's holed up there.'

'You mean, he's been gone some time?'

The man gave Simon a quick, uneasy glance before letting him know that the patrol had left camp the previous morning. Hugo had, in fact, been away so long, his batman had gone out in the evening to look for him.

A sense of disaster came down on Simon and he got to his feet. 'They should be coming back soon. I'll go and meet them.'

'With respect, sir, you'd do better to stay. The wind's rising and there could be a storm brewing.'

Simon refused to wait. He wanted to move, as though by moving he could hasten Hugo's return to the camp. He had sent Hugman to the canteen and decided to let him stay there. The corporal told him that there was a gap in the mine fields where the track ran through the forward positions into no-man's-land and continued on to the enemy positions at El Mierir and Mitediriya. As Simon went to the car, the corporal followed him.

'You're not going alone, sir?'

'Yes.'

The car, its steering wheel almost too hot to handle, stood beside the Operations truck. The corporal said, 'Like me to come with you, sir? Only take a tick to get permission.'

'Thank you, no. I'll be all right.'

Even a tick was too long to wait while he had hope of meeting Hugo. The sand was lifting along the banks between the gun pits. Small sand devils were whirling across the track, breaking up, dropping and regathering with every change in the wind. The sky was growing dark and before he could reach the forward position, his view was blotted out. He had driven into the storm and there was nothing to do but pull to the side, stop and stare into the sand fog, watching for the batman's truck to come through it. Nothing came. He got out of the car and tried to walk down the track but the wind was furious, driving the searing particles of sand into his eyes and skin, forcing him back to shut himself in the car. He was trapped and would remain trapped until the storm blew itself out.

At sunset the sand-clogged air turned crimson. When the colour died, there was an immediate darkness and in darkness he would have to remain. He could see nothing. He could hear nothing but the roar of the wind. He opened the car door an inch expecting a light to switch on but the sand blew in and there was no light. He switched on the headlamps that showed him a wall of sand. Realizing that no one was likely to see them, he switched them off to save the battery. Then, aware there was nothing more to be done, he subsided into blackness that was like nonexistence. The luminous hands of his watch showed that it was nearly nine o'clock. He climbed over to the back seat and put his head down and slept.

He awoke to silence and the pellucid silver of first light. He was nearer the perimeter than he realized. Before him was a flat expanse of desert where the light was rolling out like a wave across the sand. Two tanks stood in the middle distance and imagining they had stopped for a morning brew-up, he decided to cross to them and ask if they had seen anything of the patrol or the batman's truck. It was too far to walk so he went by car, following the track till he was level with the tanks, then walking across the mardam. A man was standing in one of the turrets, motionless, as though unaware of Simon's approach. Simon stopped at a few yards' distance to observe the figure, then saw it was not a man. It was a man-shaped cinder that faced him with white and perfect teeth set in a charred black skull. He could make out the eye-sockets and the triangle that had once supported a nose then, returning at a run, he swung the car round and drove back between the batteries, so stunned that for a little while his own private anxiety was forgotten.

The major was waiting for him at the Operations truck, his long grave face more grave as though to warn Simon that Hugo had been found. He had been alive, but not for long. All the major could do was try and soften the news by speaking highly of Hugo, telling Simon that Hugo had been a favourite with everyone, officers and men. His batman, Peters, was so attached to him, he was willing to risk his own life to find him. And he was alive when Peters came on him, but both legs had been shot away. The sand around him was soaked with blood. He didn't stand a chance.

'And the rest of the patrol? Couldn't they have done something?'

'All dead. Young Boulderstone just had to lie there with his life-blood running out till someone found him.'

The major sent for Peters so Simon could be told all that remained to be told. Peters was a thin youth who choked on his words. 'When I found him, he said, quite cheerfully, "Hello, Peters old chap, I knew you'd come."' Tears filled Peters's eyes and Simon felt surprise that this stranger could weep while he himself felt nothing.

Peters, regaining himself, explained that the patrol had been returning to the camp at sunset when it was attacked by German mortars. The ambulance moving against the red of the sky must have been an irresistible target. 'They knew what it was, the bastards. And they went on firing till they'd got the lot.'

Peters, having found Hugo, could not move him because movement would increase the haemorrhage. He intended to return to the camp for help but the storm blew up, so he had to spend the night with the wounded man.

'He told you what happened?'

'He did, sir. His speech was quite clear, right to the end. About two a.m., he said, "I think I'm going, Peters. Just as well. A chap's not much use with two wooden pins," I said, "You hold on, sir. They can do wonders these days with pins," and he laughed. He didn't speak again.'

'Thank you, Peters.

Peters had brought in the body. The burial party bad already set out. There was nothing for Simon to see and he felt Thank God for that. Knowing that his presence was an embarrassment in the camp, he held out his hand to the major and said he would be on his way. Hugman, who had been waiting for him, eyed him with furtive sympathy and muttered, 'Sorry to hear what happened, sir.'

Simon nodded, 'Rotten luck', then there was silence between them until they reached the coast road and he said, 'Don't wait, Hugman. The car's due back. You might tell Ridley what happened. He'll understand.'

A truck appeared on the road before Hugman was out of sight. The squaddie beside the driver offered Simon his seat but Simon refused and said he would ride in the rear. The back flap was let down for him. He threw his kit aboard, jumped after it, and the truck went on again.

Simon, sitting with his back to the cabin, looked out over the desert that had become as familiar to him as his childhood streets. He was reconciled to its neutral colour, its gritty wind, the endless stretches of arid stone and sand, but now a darkness hung over it all. He felt death as though he and Hugo had been one flesh and he was possessed by the certainty that if he returned here, he, too, would be killed.

'Both of us. They would lose both of us.'

He thought of his mother going into the greenhouse to read the wire, imagining perhaps that one of her sons was coming home on leave. He found a pad in his rucksack and began to write.

'Dear Mum and Dad, By the time you get this you will have heard about Hugo. I was there in the NZ camp when he didn't come in. His batman found him, legs blown off …' Simon stopped, not knowing if he should tell them that, and started on another page.

'Dear Mum and Dad, By the time you get this, you'll know that Hugo is …' but he could not write the word 'dead', and what else could he say?

Hugo was dead. The reality of Hugo's death came down on him and his unfeeling calm collapsed. He gulped and put his hands over his face. Tears ran through his fingers. There was no one to see him and the men in front would not hear his sobs above the engine noise. He gave himself up to grief. He wept for Hugo – but Hugo was safely out of it. He wept for his parents who must live with their sorrow, perhaps for years.

In the end, having stupefied himself with weeping, he lay on the floor of the truck and slept. He was wakened by passing traffic and, sitting up, he read what he had written and knew that neither letter would do.

There was nothing to be said. He tore the pages into fragments and threw them to the desert wind.

24 Make notes under the following headings. If you see a clear contrast or similarity with *Catch-22*, include that in your notes as well.

a Who are the enemy? What is the attitude towards them?
The Danger Tree ______________________________

____

Catch-22 ______________________________

____

b How do people behave towards each other?
The Danger Tree ______________________________

____

Catch-22 ______________________________

____

c How do people react to death?
The Danger Tree ______________________________

____

Catch-22 ______________________________

____

d Do people behave rationally or irrationally?
The Danger Tree ______________________________

____

Catch-22 ______________________________

____

25 Why does Simon tear up the letters he has written to his parents? Can you make any connection with *Catch-22* here?

26 Which of the two novels in this chapter would you like to read more of? Why?

Authors

Joseph Heller (1923 –) was born into a family of Jewish immigrants in New York in 1923. After the war he attended university, and then worked as an executive in advertising, all the time writing short stories. *Catch-22* was his first novel; it took him eight years to write and on its publication in 1961 became an instant commercial and critical success. At the age of 19 Heller had joined the Air Force as a bombardier, and when writing *Catch-22* in the 1950s he drew upon his war experiences for the setting of his novel. *Catch-22* is not, however, in the tradition of realist war novels, such as Norman Mailer's *The Naked and the Dead* (1948); Heller himself sees his work more as an allegory of America in the 1950s, which happens to be set in the Second World War. Yet *Catch-22* has appealed in many ways: it became a key text of the 1960s, both for those who saw in it a satirical vision of corporate America, where authority has no moral basis and the majority of people simply look after their own interests, and for opponents of the Vietnam War who saw in it a fierce condemnation of war.

Other novels have been *Something Happened* (1974), the domestic tragicomedy of a middle-aged New York executive; *Good as Gold* (1979), a surreal satire about Jewish New York and Washington politics; and *Picture This* (1988). In 1994 Heller published a kind of sequel to *Catch-22 – Closing Time*. Set in the world of big business and politics, it once again features Yossarian, the captain who at the end of *Catch-22* finally deserted and ran away to Sweden. He is now a consultant for another character from *Catch-22*, the entrepreneurial Milo Minderbinder (who once accepted payment from the Germans to bomb his own airfield), now the owner of a business conglomerate. Critical opinion, perhaps inevitably, found *Closing Time* less powerful than the 1961 novel, one review pointing out that it is no longer necessary to reveal that those in power are dishonest and inefficient. At one point in the novel the President of the USA resigns, and a particularly unintelligent Vice President takes charge. He wants to be sworn in by the Chief Justice, but this cannot be done because the Chief Justice has also resigned, and a new one cannot be sworn in until there is a sworn-in President to do so. After this has been explained many times to the Vice President, he finally gets the idea and, pleased by his own inspiration, summarizes the situation with the phrase 'Then it's just like *Catch-22*, isn't it?'

Olivia Manning (1908–1980) was born and brought up in Portsmouth, England. In 1939 she married R D Smith, a lecturer for the British Council, and accompanied him on his various postings during the Second World War to Bucharest, Athens, Alexandria and Jerusalem. Her experiences provided ideas for the characters and setting of the series of novels on which her reputation is based: The Balkan Trilogy (*The Great Fortune*, 1960; *The Spoilt City*, 1962; *Friends and Heroes*, 1965), followed by the sequel The Levant Trilogy (*The Danger Tree*, 1977; *The Battle Lost and Won*, 1978; *The Sum of Things*, 1980). The sequence charts the fortunes of Harriet Pringle, through whose eyes the events are mostly narrated, and her impulsive, generous, and rather unreliable husband Guy Pringle, who works for the British Council. The narrative begins with the recently-married Pringles in Romania, follows their flight to Athens as the German army advances, describes their accidental separation in North Africa and concludes with them re-united in the Near East. The novels include a large cast of comic minor characters whose displacements and discomforts are seen against the larger scenario of a world at war and its horrors. A sense of time and place are vividly present: the battle of El Alamein is described through the eyes of Simon Boulderstone in *The Battle Lost and Won*. Olivia Manning wrote five other novels and two volumes of short stories (*Growing Up*, 1948; *A Romantic Hero*, 1966).

5 'The White Man's Burden'

Before you read

1 Look at the photographs on the previous page.

- ***a*** When and where do you think they were taken?
- ***b*** Why do you think the people on the boat in the first photograph have come to this place?
- ***c*** In the second photograph, what do you think is the relationship between the two men in hats and the people around them? What do you think they are doing there?

2 Read the following three verses from Rudyard Kipling's *The White Man's Burden*. This poem, written in 1899, was addressed to the United States, which had just colonized the Philippines.

Take up the White Man's Burden –
 Send forth the best ye breed –
Go bind your sons to exile
 To serve your captives' need;
To wait in heavy harness
 On fluttered folk and wild –
Your new-caught, sullen peoples,
 Half devil and half child.

Take up the White Man's Burden –
 In patience to abide,
To veil the threat of terror
 And check the show of pride;
By open speech and simple,
 An hundred times made plain,
To seek another's profit,
 And work another's gain.

Take up the White Man's Burden –
 The savage wars of peace –
Fill full the mouth of Famine
 And bid the sickness cease;
And when your goal is nearest
 The end for others sought,
Watch Sloth and heathen Folly
 Bring all your hope to nought.

1 *burden*: literally, a heavy load; metaphorically, a duty or responsibility
2 *forth*: out (ie to the Philippines)
2 *ye*: you
3 *bind*: tie
5 *harness*: literally, the leather bands which tie a horse to a cart
6 *fluttered*: volatile, excited
7 *sullen*: resentful and unhappy
10 *abide*: live
11 *veil*: cover, hide
12 *check*: restrain
20 *bid*: order
22 *sought*: (past participle of 'to seek') tried to obtain
23 *Sloth*: laziness
23 *heathen*: pagan, not Christian
24 *nought*: nothing

3

- ***a*** What do you think Kipling means by the phrase 'The White Man's Burden'?
- ***b*** Note down some of the ways that Kipling describes the people of the Philippines.
- ***c*** Compare your ideas with a partner, and check with the Key before going on.

4 Which of the following opinions do you agree with? You can write your own opinion if you like.

- ***a*** Kipling's philosophy is completely unacceptable. The future of humanity depends on forgetting racist ideas like these.
- ***b*** Kipling was expressing a common view of his time: he sincerely believed that the white races were superior. We should see these ideas in their historical context, and study and try to understand them.
- ***c*** Kipling was right. The white man did have a duty to civilize the rest of the world.
- ***d*** Your opinion: ____

____

5 Imagine you have the job of finding illustrations for an anthology of poetry – would you choose the first or second photograph on page 115 to illustrate Kipling's poem?
If you think neither of these photographs is suitable, find (or describe) an alternative picture which you think would go well with the poem.

Heart of Darkness (1902)
Joseph Conrad

On a boat anchored in the Thames the narrator, Marlow, tells a group of colleagues the story of a journey he made when he was a young man. He had been employed by a Belgian trading company as captain of a steamboat, and his job was to sail up the River Congo and collect ivory to bring back to the coast. In the following extract he describes his arrival in Africa.

See the Glossary section at the back of the book for vocabulary.

'I left in a French steamer, and she called in every blamed port they have out there, for, as far as I could see, the sole purpose of landing soldiers and custom-house officers. I watched the coast. Watching a coast as it slips by the ship is like thinking about an enigma. There it is before you – smiling, frowning, inviting, grand, mean, insipid, or savage, and always mute with an air of whispering, Come and find out. This one was almost featureless, as if still in the making, with an aspect of monotonous grimness. The edge of a colossal jungle, so dark-green as to be almost black, fringed with white surf, ran straight, like a ruled line, far, far away along a blue sea whose glitter was blurred by a creeping mist. The sun was fierce, the land seemed to glisten and drip with steam. Here and there greyish-whitish specks showed up clustered inside the white surf, with a flag flying above them perhaps. Settlements some centuries old, and still no bigger than pin-heads on the untouched expanse of their background. We pounded along, stopped, landed soldiers; went on, landed custom-house clerks to levy toll in what looked like a God-forsaken wilderness, with a tin shed and a flag-pole lost in it; landed more soldiers – to take care of the custom-house clerks, presumably. Some, I heard, got drowned in the surf; but whether they did or not, nobody seemed particularly to care. They were just flung out there, and on we went. Every day the coast looked the same, as though we had not moved; but we passed various places – trading places – with names like Gran' Bassam, Little Popo; names that seemed to belong to some sordid farce acted in front of a sinister back-cloth. The idleness of a passenger, my isolation amongst all these men with whom I had no point of contact, the oily and languid sea, the uniform sombreness of the coast, seemed to keep me away from the truth of things, within the toil of a mournful and senseless delusion. The voice of the surf now and then was a positive pleasure, like the speech of a brother. It was something natural, that had its reason, that had a meaning. Now and then a boat from the shore gave one a momentary contact with reality. It was paddled by black fellows. You could see from afar the white of their eyeballs glistening. They shouted, sang; their bodies streamed with perspiration; they had faces like grotesque masks – these chaps; but they had bone, muscle, a wild vitality, an intense energy of movement, that was as natural and true as the surf along their coast. They wanted no excuse for being there. They were a great comfort to look at. For a time I would feel I belonged still to a world of straight-forward facts; but the feeling would not last long. Something would turn up to scare it away. Once, I remember, we came upon a man-of-war anchored off the coast. There wasn't even a shed there, and she was shelling the bush. It appears the French had one of their wars going on thereabouts. Her ensign dropped limp like a rag; the muzzles of the long six-inch guns stuck out all over the low hull; the greasy, slimy swell swung her up lazily and let her down, swaying her thin masts. In the empty immensity of earth, sky, and water, there she was, incomprehensible, firing into a continent. Pop, would go one of-the six-inch guns; a small flame would dart and vanish, a little white smoke would disappear, a tiny projectile would give a feeble screech – and nothing happened. Nothing could happen. There was a touch of insanity in the proceeding, a sense of lugubrious drollery in the sight; and it was not dissipated by somebody on board assuring me earnestly there was a camp of natives – he called them enemies! – hidden out of sight somewhere.

'We gave her her letters (I heard the men in that lonely ship were dying of fever at the rate of three a-day) and went on. We called at some more places with farcical names, where the merry dance of death and trade goes on in a still and earthy atmosphere as of an overheated catacomb; all along the formless coast bordered by dangerous surf, as if Nature herself had tried to ward off intruders; in and out of rivers, streams of death in life, whose banks were rotting into mud, whose waters, thickened into slime invaded the contorted mangroves, that seemed to writhe at us in the extremity of an impotent despair. Nowhere did we stop long enough to get a particularized impression, but the general sense of vague and oppressive wonder grew upon me. It was like a weary pilgrimage amongst hints for nightmares.

'It was upward of thirty days before I saw the mouth of the big river. We anchored off the seat of the government. But my work would not begin till some two hundred miles farther on. So as soon as I could I made a start for a place thirty miles higher up.

What do you think this place will be like?

'I had my passage on a little sea-going steamer. Her captain was a Swede, and knowing me for a seaman, invited me on the bridge. He was a young man, lean, fair, and morose, with lanky hair and a shuffling gait. As we left the miserable little wharf, he tossed his head contemptuously at the shore. "Been living there?" he asked. I said, "Yes." "Fine lot these government chaps are they not?" he went on, speaking English with great precision and considerable bitterness. "It is funny what some people will do for a few francs a-month. I wonder what becomes of that kind when it goes up country?" I said to him I expected to see that soon. "So-o-o!" he exclaimed. He shuffled athwart, keeping one eye ahead vigilantly. "Don't be too sure," he continued. "The other day I took up a man who hanged himself on the road. He was a Swede, too." "Hanged himself! Why, in God's name?" I cried. He kept on looking out watchfully. "Who knows? The sun too much for him, or the country perhaps."

'At last we opened a reach. A rocky cliff appeared, mounds of turned-up earth by the shore, houses on a hill, others with iron roofs, amongst a waste of excavations, or hanging to the declivity. A continuous noise of the rapids above hovered over this scene of inhabited devastation. A lot of people, mostly black and naked, moved about like ants. A jetty projected into the river. A blinding sunlight drowned all this at times in a sudden recrudescence of glare. "There's your Company's station," said the Swede, pointing to three wooden barrack-like structures on the rocky slope. "I will send your things up. Four boxes did you say? So. Farewell."

'I came upon a boiler wallowing in the grass, then found a path leading up the hill. It turned aside for the boulders, and also for an undersized railway-truck lying there on its back with its wheels in the air. One was off. The thing looked as dead as the carcass of some animal. I came upon more pieces of decaying machinery, a stack of rusty rails. To the left a clump of trees made a shady spot, where dark things seemed to stir feebly. I blinked, the path was steep. A horn tooted to the right, and I saw the black people run. A heavy and dull detonation shook the ground, a puff of smoke came out of the cliff, and that was all. No change appeared on the face of the rock. They were building a railway. The cliff was not in the way or anything; but this objectless blasting was all the work going on.

'A slight clinking behind me made me turn my head. Six black men advanced in a file, toiling up the path. They walked erect and slow, balancing small baskets full of earth on their heads, and the clink kept time with their footsteps. Black rags were wound round their loins, and the short ends behind waggled to and fro like tails. I could see every rib, the joints of their limbs were like knots in a rope; each had an iron collar on his neck, and all were connected together with a chain whose bights swung between them, rhythmically clinking. Another report from the cliff make me think suddenly of that ship of war I had seen firing into a continent. It was the same kind of ominous voice; but these men could by no stretch of imagination be called enemies. They were called criminals, and the outraged law, like the bursting shells, had come to them, an insoluble mystery from the sea. All their meagre breasts panted together, the violently dilated nostrils quivered, the eyes stared stonily up-hill. They passed me within six inches, without a glance, with that complete, deathlike indifference of unhappy savages. Behind this raw matter one of the reclaimed, the product of the new forces at work, strolled despondently, carrying a rifle by its middle. He had a uniform jacket with one button off, and seeing a white man on the path, hoisted his weapon to his shoulder with alacrity. This was simple prudence, white men being so much alike at a distance that he could not tell who I might be. He was speedily reassured, and with a large, white, rascally grin, and a glance at his charge, seemed to take me into partnership in his exalted trust. After all, I also was a part of the great cause of these high and just proceedings.

'Instead of going up, I turned and descended to the left. My idea was to let that chain-gang get out of sight before I climbed the hill. You know I am not particularly tender; I've had to strike and to fend off. I've had to resist and to attack sometimes – that's only one way of resisting – without counting the exact cost, according to the demands of such sort of life as I had blundered into. I've seen the devil of violence, and the devil of greed, and the devil of hot desire; but, by all the stars! these were strong, lusty, red-eyed devils, that swayed and drove men – men, I tell you. But as I stood on this hill-side, I foresaw that in the blinding sunshine of that land I would become acquainted with a flabby, pretending, weak-eyed devil of a rapacious and pitiless folly. How insidious he could be, too, I was only to find out several months later and a thousand miles farther. For a moment I stood appalled, as though by a warning. Finally I descended the hill, obliquely, towards the trees I had seen.

Marlow is going to see something else that will shock him. What kind of thing do you think it might be?

'I avoided a vast artificial hole somebody had been digging on the slope, the purpose of which I found it impossible to divine. It wasn't a quarry or a sandpit, anyhow. It was just a hole. It might have been connected with the philanthropic desire of giving the criminals something to do. I don't know. Then I nearly fell into a very narrow ravine, almost no more than a scar in the hillside. I discovered that a lot of imported drainage-pipes for the settlement had been tumbled in there. There wasn't one that was not broken. It was a wanton smash-up. At last I got under the trees. My purpose was to stroll into the shade for a moment; but no sooner within than it seemed to me I had stepped into the gloomy circle of some Inferno. The rapids were near, and an uninterrupted, uniform, headlong, rushing noise filled the mournful stillness of the grove, where not a breath stirred, not a leaf moved, with a mysterious sound – as though the tearing pace of the launched earth had suddenly become audible.

'Black shapes crouched, lay, sat between the trees leaning against the trunks, clinging to the earth, half coming out, half effaced within the dim light, in all the attitudes of pain, abandonment, and despair. Another mine on the cliff went off, followed by a slight shudder of the soil under my feet. The work was going on. The work! And this was the place where some of the helpers had with-drawn to die.

'They were dying slowly – it was very clear. They were not enemies, they were not criminals, they were nothing earthly now, –

nothing but black shadows of disease and starvation, lying confusedly in the greenish gloom. Brought from all the recesses of the coast in all the legality of time contracts, lost in uncongenial surroundings, fed on unfamiliar food, they sickened, became inefficient, and were then allowed to crawl away and rest. These moribund shapes were free as air – and nearly as thin. I began to distinguish the gleam of the eyes under the trees. Then, glancing down, I saw a face near my hand. The black bones reclined at full length with one shoulder against the tree, and slowly the eyelids rose and the sunken eyes looked up at me, enormous and vacant, a kind of blind, white flicker in the depths of the orbs, which died out slowly. The man seemed young – almost a boy – but you know with them it's hard to tell. I found nothing else to do but to offer him one of my good Swede's ship's biscuits I had in my pocket. The fingers closed slowly on it and held – there was no other movement and no other glance. He had tied a bit of white worsted round his neck – Why? Where did he get it? Was it a badge – an ornament – a charm – a propitiatory act? Was there any idea at all connected with it? It looked startling round his black neck, this bit of white thread from beyond the seas.

'Near the same tree two more bundles of acute angles sat with their legs drawn up. One, with his chin propped on his knees, stared at nothing, in an intolerable and appalling manner: his brother phantom rested its forehead, as if overcome with a great weariness; and all about others were scattered in every pose of contorted collapse, as in some picture of a massacre or a pestilence. While I stood horror-struck, one of these creatures rose to his hands and knees, and went off on all-fours towards the river to drink. He lapped out of his hand, then sat up in the sunlight, crossing his shins in front of him, and after a time let his woolly head fall on his breastbone.

'I didn't want any more loitering in the shade, and I made haste towards the station. When near the buildings I met a white man, in such an unexpected elegance of get-up that in the first moment I took him for a sort of vision. I saw a high starched collar, white cuffs, a light alpaca jacket, snowy trousers, a clear necktie, and varnished boots. No hat. Hair parted, brushed, oiled, under a green-lined parasol held in a big white hand. He was amazing, and had a penholder behind his ear.

What kind of opinion do you think Marlow will have of this man?

'I shook hands with this miracle, and I learned he was the Company's chief accountant, and that all the book-keeping was done at this station. He had come out for a moment, he said, "to get a breath of fresh air." The expression sounded wonderfully odd, with its suggestion of sedentary desk-life. I wouldn't have mentioned the fellow to you at all, only it was from his lips that I first heard the name of the man who is so indissolubly connected with the memories of that time. Moreover, I respected the fellow. Yes; I respected his collars, his vast cuffs, his brushed hair. His appearance was certainly that of a hairdresser's dummy; but in the great demoralization of the land he kept up his appearance. That's backbone. His starched collars and got-up shirt-fronts were achievements of character. He had been out nearly three years; and later, I could not help asking him how he managed to sport such linen. He had just the faintest blush, and said modestly, "I've been teaching one of the native women about the station. It was difficult. She had a distaste for the work." Thus this man had verily accomplished something. And he was devoted to his books, which were in apple-pie order.

'Everything else in the station was in a muddle – heads, things, buildings. Strings of dusty niggers with splay feet arrived and departed; a stream of manufactured goods, rubbishy cottons, beads, and brass-wire sent into the depths of darkness, and in return came a precious trickle of ivory.

'I had to wait in the station for ten days – an eternity. I lived in a hut in the yard, but to be out of the chaos I would sometimes get into the accountant's office. It was built of horizontal planks, and so badly put together that, as he bent over his high desk, he was barred from neck to heels with narrow strips of sunlight. There was no need to open the big shutters to see. It was hot there, too; big flies buzzed fiendishly, and did not sting, but stabbed. I sat generally on the floor, while, of faultless appearance (and even slightly scented), perching on a high stool, he wrote. Sometimes he stood up for exercise. When a truckle-bed with a sick man (some invalid agent from up-country) was put in there, he exhibited a gentle annoyance. "The groans of this sick person," he said, "distract my attention. And without that it is extremely difficult to guard against clerical errors in this climate."

'One day he remarked, without lifting his head, "In the interior you will no doubt meet Mr Kurtz." On my asking who Mr Kurtz was, he said he was a first-class agent; and seeing my disappointment at this information, he added slowly, laying down his pen, "He is a very remarkable person." Further questions elicited from him that Mr Kurtz was at present in charge of a trading post, a very important one, in the true ivory-country, at "the very bottom of there. Sends in as much ivory as all the others put together …" He began to write again. The sick man was too ill to groan. The flies buzzed in a great peace.

'Suddenly there was a growing murmur of voices and a great tramping of feet. A caravan had come in. A violent babble of uncouth sounds burst out on the other side of the planks. All the carriers were speaking together, and in the midst of the uproar the lamentable voice of the chief agent was heard "giving it up" tearfully for the twentieth time that day … He rose slowly. "What a frightful row," he said. He crossed the room gently to look at the sick man, and returning, said to me, "He does not hear." "What! Dead?" I asked, startled. "No, not yet," he answered, with great composure. Then, alluding with a toss of the head to the tumult in the station-yard, "When one has got to make correct entries, one comes to hate those savages – hate them to the death." He remained thoughtful for a moment. "When you see Mr Kurtz," he went on, "tell him from me that everything here" – he glanced at the desk – "is very satisfactory. I don't like to write to him – with those messengers of ours you never know who may get hold of your letter – at that Central Station." He stared at me for a moment with his mild, bulging eyes. "Oh, he will go far, very far," he began again. "He will be a somebody in the Administration before long. They, above – the Council in Europe, you know – mean him to be."

'He turned to his work. The noise outside had ceased, and presently in going out I stopped at the door. In the steady buzz of flies the homeward-bound agent was lying flushed and insensible; the other, bent over his books, was making correct entries of perfectly correct transactions; and fifty feet below the doorstep I could see the still tree-tops of the grove of death.

'Next day I left that station at last, with a caravan of sixty men, for a two-hundred-mile tramp.'

First reaction

6 Imagine that you are Marlow. What would you be thinking as you left the station? Write your thoughts down (maximum 25 words), and compare them with others in the class.

Close reading

Setting

7 Look at lines 1–41. Pick out words and phrases which show Marlow's attitude to what he sees. Are his impressions mostly positive or negative?

a words and phrases showing a positive impression	***b*** words and phrases showing a negative impression
______________________	______________________
______________________	______________________
______________________	______________________
______________________	______________________
______________________	______________________
______________________	______________________
______________________	______________________

Theme: colonialism

8 Make short notes about the process of colonization as presented in the following four moments ***a–d***.
Example: the man-of-war shelling the bush (lines 42–59):
'Once, I remember, we came upon a man-of war ... and went on.'
The shelling is presented as ***useless***, ***arbitrary*** *('There wasn't even a shed there, and she was shelling the bush'),* ***wasteful*** *and* ***ineffectual*** *('Pop, would go one of the six-inch guns ... – and nothing happened'). Marlow explicitly calls it 'insanity' –* ***senseless***. *The European values are* ***inappropriate*** *to the circumstances (' – he called them enemies!') – perhaps this is a hypocritical justification for colonization. There is even* ***indifference*** *to the well-being of the white sailors ('the men in that lonely ship were dying of fever at the rate of three a-day').*

a arrival at the Company station (lines 100–11):
'I came upon a boiler ... but this objectless blasting was all the work going on.'

b the chain gang (lines 112–37):
'A slight clinking behind me made me turn my head. ... these high and just proceedings.'

c outside the Company station – the sick natives (lines 168–81):
'Black shapes crouched, ... and were then allowed to crawl away and rest.'

d life at the Company station (lines 224–52):
'His appearance was certainly ... to guard against clerical errors in this climate.'

9 ***a*** Look through your answers to Exercise 8. Choose just three or four words to sum up the process of colonization as described by Marlow. Compare your choices with a partner.

b Look back at Kipling's poem in Exercise 2. Which lines contrast most with the picture presented by Marlow?

The narrator

10 (For a discussion of the role of **narrators**, see Chapter 1, *Anatomy of a Novel*, page 15.)
Look at lines 138–52. At this point, the reader assesses both the character of Marlow, and the importance of what he witnesses. Write some ideas in the following table. The first one is done for you.

	1	*2*	*3*
	MARLOW'S WORDS	IMPLICATIONS ABOUT THE KIND OF MAN MARLOW IS	IMPLICATIONS ABOUT THE EVENTS OF THE STORY
a	I'm not particularly tender … (line 140)	I'm tough, not easily moved	This was a really horrifying moment, even for a man of experience
b	I've had to strike and fend off … without counting the exact cost (lines 140–2)		
c	such sort of life as I had blundered into … (line 143)		
d	For a moment I stood appalled … (line 151)		

11 Re-read the following parts of the extract where the Africans are described: lines 32–41, 125–37, 175–207 and 234–8.

a How would you describe Marlow's attitude to these people? Do you think he regards them as his equals, inferiors or superiors? Note down some words from the passage to illustrate your opinions.

b Compare your impressions with a partner.

12 This is how Joseph Conrad once described his own feelings about Marlow:

'Of all my people (ie characters created by Conrad in his novels) he's the one that has never been a vexation to my spirit. A most discreet, understanding man. …'

a What is your opinion of Marlow? What do you like or admire about him? Is there anything you dislike about him?

b Compare your opinions with a partner.

Anticipation

13 (For the term **anticipation** see Chapter 1, *Anatomy of a Novel*, page 29.)

Marlow often anticipates what is going to happen later in his story. The anticipation is, however, implicit and incomplete, and it increases suspense about later developments. Here are some examples.

'But my work would not begin till some two hundred miles farther on.' (lines 72–3)

' "I wonder what becomes of that kind when it goes up country?" I said to him I expected to see that soon.' (lines 82–4)

'But as I stood on this hillside, I foresaw that in the blinding sunshine of that land I would become acquainted with a flabby, pretending, weak-eyed devil of a rapacious and pitiless folly.' (lines 146–9)

a Find some other examples of anticipation in lines 216–88.
b A character who seems as if he will be important in the novel is introduced by this technique. Who is he? What kind of expectations are built up about him?

Language practice – structures

Clauses of contrast, reason and result

14 Look at the following ways of expressing contrast, reason and result.

contrast
'Settlements some centuries old, and still no bigger than pin-heads on the untouched expanse of their background.' (lines 14–16)

→ *In spite of/Despite* the age of the settlements, they had not grown, and the interior had still not been penetrated.
→ *Although/Even though* the settlements were very old, they had not grown, and the interior had still not been penetrated.

a What are the grammatical differences between the use of *in spite of/despite* and *although/even though*?

reason
'(the black fellows) … had bone, muscle, a wild vitality, … that was as natural and true as the surf along their coast. They wanted no excuse for being there. They were a great comfort to look at.' (lines 37–40)

→ Marlow felt an affinity with the Africans *because of* their vitality and naturalness.
→ Marlow felt an affinity with the Africans *because* they were vital and natural.

b What are the grammatical differences between the use of *because of* and *because*?

result
'I met a white man, in such an unexpected elegance of get-up that in the first moment I took him for a sort of vision.' (lines 209–11)

→ The accountant looked *so elegant that* Marlow thought he was dreaming.
→ The accountant had *such an elegant appearance that* Marlow thought he was dreaming.

c What are the grammatical differences between the use of *so … that* and *such … that*?

15 Combine the following sentences using expressions of contrast, reason and result. (The sentences are not the same as the text, but if you want to check the actual context, the line references are given.)
Example: Some soldiers were drowned when disembarking. *<contrast>* Nobody seemed to care. (lines 20–1)
<u>Even though/Although</u> *some soldiers were drowned when disembarking, nobody seemed to care.*

a A man-of-war was shelling the bush. *<contrast>* There wasn't even a shed there. (lines 42–4)
b Men on board were dying at the rate of three-a-day. *<contrast>* The ship stayed there. (lines 58–9)
c The Swedish captain suggested the Swede might have hanged himself. *<reason>* The heat. (lines 86–9)
d The blasting was going on. *<contrast>* The cliff was not in the way. (lines 109–11)
e Marlow felt disgust at the sight of the chain gang *<result>* He couldn't bear to see them again. (lines 138–9)
f The treatment, surroundings and food were unfamiliar to the natives. *<result>* They had lost the will to live. (lines 178–81)
g Marlow mentions the accountant. *<reason>* He first heard about Kurtz from him. (lines 220–23)
h Marlow respected the accountant. *<reason>* His 'backbone'. (lines 223–6)
i The accountant kept up his appearance. *<contrast>* The demoralization among the other Europeans. (lines 226–7)
j The accountant's office was very badly built. *<result>* The light came in. (lines 241–4)
k The sick agent made a lot of noise. *<result>* The accountant claimed he couldn't concentrate. (lines 250–2)

l The invalid agent from up-country was unconscious. <*contrast*> The accountant did not seem concerned. (lines 269–72)

m The accountant had come to hate the Africans. <*reason*> They interfered with his concentration. (lines 272–4)

n The accountant didn't write to Kurtz. <*reason*> His distrust of the messengers. (lines 277–9)

16 Fill in the blanks in the passage below with the words and expressions in the box. The first one is done for you.

so even though such that because because of in spite of
that although because even though ~~despite~~

In the fifteenth and sixteenth centuries Europeans were already settling in America and were doing business – often as pirates – in Africa and Asia.***Despite*** (a) their small numbers, they were able to dominate __________ (b) their superior fire-power. This advantage was __________ (c) clear to Europeans __________ (d), as early as 1481, the Pope ruled that arms should not be sold to Africans. Government support for expansion was prevalent only in Europe; in contrast, the Arabs and Chinese, __________ (e) they were skilful navigators, were not competitors in this phase of world history.

The search for land and precious metal motivated Spanish imperialism in Central and South America. __________ (f) he only had a few hundred men, Cortès managed to conquer the Aztec empire in Mexico __________ (g) the Aztecs had no guns, horses or steel and were susceptible to imported diseases. The resources found in Mexico and Peru were of __________ (h) great value __________ (i), by 1650, 16,000 tonnes of silver and 180 tonnes of gold objects had been brought to Spain. The Church played an important role in the colonization of South America, __________ (j) the fact that its intentions were religious rather than political. For example, __________ (k) they didn't want the Indians to be corrupted by their conquerors, missionaries didn't teach them Spanish, __________ (l) this effectively prevented them from becoming integrated into the administrative system.

17 Combine the following sentences to bring out the relationship of contrast, reason or result.

Example: Settlers in North America initially collaborated with the original inhabitants. They quite soon started taking over their territories.
Although settlers in North America initially collaborated with the original inhabitants, they quite soon started taking over their territories.

a The Church defended the status of South American Indians. No such feelings were extended towards black slaves from Africa.

b Europeans took over nine million black slaves to the Americas. They needed them as labourers on their plantations.

c The sugar plantations in the Caribbean became very prosperous. Piracy of ships returning to Europe became common.

d Until the end of the nineteenth century the interior of Africa, with all its wealth of ivory and gold, remained unexplored. Disease and climate kept Europeans out.

e Both the use of steam – for railways and ships – and treatment for tropical diseases made great progress in the nineteenth century. The colonization of the interior of Africa, particularly the Congo, started in the 1880s.

f Europeans had great confidence in the superiority of their own religion and customs. They thought these should be imposed on their colonies.

g Europeans imposed a wage-earning economy on the peoples they colonized. The peoples they colonized were used to a different economy, based on hunting, farming and trading.

h Paradoxically, missionary activity had the effect of encouraging rebellion among natives. Missionary activity showed the difference between the morality of the colonizers and their practice.

Language practice – vocabulary

Denotation and connotation

18 The **denotation** of a word is its most basic meaning – it is the first definition of a word given in a dictionary. (In everyday English we sometimes use the expression 'literal meaning'.) The **connotation** of a word is the range of associations it provokes, the ideas and emotions it suggests. This can depend on the context the word is used in, and on people's attitudes to, and experiences of, the word or what it refers to. (For more on **denotation** and **connotation**, see Chapter 1, *Anatomy of a Novel*, pages 24–5.)

19 Look at the following words and their denotations.

devil: the most powerful evil spirit in Christianity and Judaism
child: a young human being, not yet fully-grown
man: a fully-grown male human being

Now look again at how the words are used by Marlow and Kipling in these examples.

the *devil* of violence, and the *devil* of greed, and the *devil* of hot desire; but … these were strong, lusty, red-eyed *devils*, that swayed and drove *men* – *men*, I tell you. (*Heart of Darkness*, lines 143–6)

Your new-caught, sullen peoples
Half *devil* and half *child.* (*The White Man's Burden*, lines 7–8)

a What do you think Marlow means by the words 'devil' and 'men'?
b What do you think Kipling means by the words 'devil' and 'child'?

20 **Changing connotations**: Denotations of words generally remain fixed for a very long time – if not, different generations would find it impossible to communicate with each other! The connotations of certain words, however, may change as attitudes in society change. If necessary, use a dictionary for the following questions.

a Which of the following uses of the word 'savage' are normal today, and which not? Why?

1 a coast ... insipid, or *savage*, ... (*Heart of Darkness*, lines 4–6)
2 ... unhappy *savages*. (*Heart of Darkness*, line 128)
3 ... *savage* wars ... (*The White Man's Burden*, line 18)

b Are the connotations that Kipling puts on 'heathen' (*The White Man's Burden*, line 23) shared by readers today?

c Are the connotations that Marlow puts on 'men' (see Exercise 19a) shared by readers today?

21 Think of the denotation and connotations of the words underlined in the following sentences, then note down a few ideas about what you think Marlow means when he uses these words. Compare your ideas with a partner before checking with the Key.

a 'The voice of the surf now and then was a positive pleasure, like the speech of a brother.' (lines 30–1)

b 'Black shapes crouched, lay, sat between the trees ...' (line 168)

c 'Behind this raw matter one of the reclaimed, the product of the new forces at work, strolled despondently, ... ' (lines 128–30)

d 'It was like a weary pilgrimage amongst hints for nightmares.' (lines 69–70)

e 'It might have been connected with the philanthropic desire of giving the criminals something to do.' (lines 155–7)

22 a Work on your own. What personal response do you have to the words in the box below? Put one of the following symbols next to each word.

The connotations I put on this word are:

+ +	almost always positive
+	generally positive
Ø	neither positive nor negative: it depends on the context
–	generally negative
– –	almost always negative

profit [ ] primitive [ ] efficiency [ ] foreign [ ] traditional [ ]
discrimination [ ] appearance [ ] civilized [ ] trade [ ] clan [ ]
passionate [ ] development [ ] pride [ ]

b Compare and explain your responses with a partner or in groups.

c On your own, think of one other word that has both negative and positive connotations. Write two sentences that clearly show both connotations.
d Now blank out the word you thought of in *c* from your two sentences. Show the sentences to other students, who should try to guess the word that you have blanked out.

Extension

23 **Class discussion**: Some people consider the following as contemporary manifestations of colonialism.

- '**cultural imperialism**' This means the spread of the culture of a world-power. A particular example is the worldwide proliferation of the more banal aspects of American culture, sometimes referred to as 'Coca-Colonization'.
- '**linguistic imperialism**' Artificial languages, such as Esperanto, which are not connected to a particular country or culture, have never had much success. On the other hand, conservative estimates indicate that while more than three hundred million people speak English as their mother tongue, another four hundred million speak it as a second or foreign language. (English is the official language of air traffic control; two-thirds of the world's scientists write in English; three-quarters of the world's mail is written in English; it has become the dominant language of the international electronic highway, the Internet. English words find their way into most of the world's languages.)
- '**economic imperialism**' This means that major industrialized countries such as the USA, Japan or Germany, influence trade or commodity prices. (Such countries, or giant multinational companies based in them, often have significant economic interests in developing countries.)

a Do you agree that these are forms of 'imperialism'?
b Do you think that they should be resisted or accepted?

24 **Role-play**: Imagine that before Marlow leaves the station an important manager from the Company arrives. He wants to speak to Marlow. What do they say to each other?

25 **Writing**: Write one of the following letters (150–200 words).
a a letter from the Company's accountant to a friend or member of his family about Marlow
b a letter from Marlow to his employers

Beyond the text

The following extract from *Things Fall Apart* is set in Nigeria, among the Ibo people, in roughly the same period as *Heart of Darkness*. The main character, Okonkwo, lives in the village society of Umuofia and has risen to a high position in his clan. But one day, at the funeral of a village elder, his gun goes off accidentally and kills the elder's son. Even though this was a complete accident, killing a clansman is considered a crime against the earth goddess, and Okonkwo must go into exile for seven years. Consequently, he and his family go to the village of Mbanta, where his mother came from. During their time there, white missionaries arrive all over Nigeria – one of their converts is Okonkwo's eldest son, Nwoye. The missionaries are followed by British colonial administrators.

In the following extract Okonkwo reflects on recent events, and is visited by Obierika, a close friend from Umuofia.

26 As you read the extract, make notes about Okonkwo's feelings in the two columns below. Compare your notes with a partner when you have finished reading.

a Okonkwo's worries about what he personally might have lost, and about his community	***b*** Okonkwo's consolations, and his hopes for when he returns
______________________	______________________
______________________	______________________
______________________	______________________
______________________	______________________
______________________	______________________
______________________	______________________
______________________	______________________
______________________	______________________
______________________	______________________
______________________	______________________
______________________	______________________

Things Fall Apart (1958)
Chinua Achebe

See the Glossary section at the back of the book for vocabulary.

CHAPTER 20

Seven years was a long time to be away from one's clan. A man's place was not always there, waiting for him. As soon as he left, someone else rose and filled it. The clan was like a lizard; if it lost its tail it soon grew another.

Okonkwo knew these things. He knew that he had lost his place among the nine masked spirits who administered justice in the clan. He had lost the chance to lead his warlike clan against the new religion, which, he was told, had gained ground. He had lost the years in which he might have taken the highest titles in the clan. But some of these losses were not irreparable. He was determined that his return should be marked by his people. He would return with a flourish, and regain the seven wasted years.

Even in his first year in exile he had begun to plan for his return. The first thing he would do would be to rebuild his compound on a more magnificent scale. He would build a bigger barn than he had before and he would build huts for two new wives. Then he would show his wealth by initiating his sons in the *ozo* society. Only the really great men in the clan were able to do this. Okonkwo saw clearly the high esteem in which he would be held, and he saw himself taking the highest title in the land.

As the years of exile passed one by one it seemed to him that his *chi* might now be making amends for the past disaster. His yams grew abundantly, not only in his motherland but also in Umuofia, where his friend gave them out year by year to sharecroppers.

Then the tragedy of his first son had occurred. At first it appeared as if it might prove too great for his spirit. But it was a resilient spirit, and in the end Okonkwo overcame his sorrow. He had five other sons and he would bring them up in the way of the clan.

He sent for the five sons and they came and sat in his *obi*. The youngest of them was four years old.

'You have all seen the great abomination of your brother. Now he is no longer my son or your brother. I will only have a son who is a man, who will hold his head up among my people. If any one of you prefers to be a woman, let him follow Nwoye now while I am alive so that I can curse him. If you turn against me when I am dead I will visit you and break your neck.'

Okonkwo was very lucky in his daughters. He never stopped regretting that Ezinma was a girl. Of all his children she alone understood his every mood. A bond of sympathy had grown between them as the years had passed.

Ezinma grew up in her father's exile and became one of the most beautiful girls in Mbanta. She was called Crystal of Beauty, as her mother had been called in her youth. The young ailing girl who had caused her mother so much heartache had been transformed, almost overnight, to a healthy, buoyant maiden. She had, it was true, her moments of depression when she would snap at everybody like an angry dog. These moods descended on her suddenly and for no apparent reason. But they were very rare and short-lived. As long as they lasted, she could bear no other person but her father.

Many young men and prosperous middle-aged men of Mbanta came to marry her. But she refused them all, because her father had called her one evening and said to her: 'There are many good and prosperous people here, but I shall be happy if you marry in Umuofia when we return home.'

That was all he had said. But Ezinma had seen clearly all the thought and hidden meaning behind the few words. And she had agreed.

'Your half-sister, Obiageli, will not understand me,' Okonkwo said. 'But you can explain to her.'

Although they were almost the same age, Ezinma wielded a strong influence over her half-sister. She explained to her why they should not marry yet, and she agreed also. And so the two of them refused every offer of marriage in Mbanta.

'I wish she were a boy,' Okonkwo thought within himself. She understood things so perfectly. Who else among his children could have read his thought so well? With two beautiful grown-up daughters his return to Umuofia would attract considerable attention. His future sons-in-law would be men of authority in the clan. The poor and unknown would not dare to come forth.

Umuofia had indeed changed during the seven years Okonkwo had been in exile. The church had come and led many astray. Not only the low-born and the outcast but sometimes a worthy man had joined it. Such a man was Ogbuefi Ugonna, who had taken two titles, and who like a madman had cut the anklet of his titles and cast it away to join the Christians. The white missionary was very proud of him and he was one of the first men in Umuofia to receive the sacrament of Holy Communion, or Holy Feast as it was called in Ibo. Ogbuefi Ugorma had thought of the Feast in terms of eating and drinking, only more holy than the village variety. He had therefore put his drinking-horn into his goatskin bag for the occasion.

But apart from the church, the white men had also brought a government. They had built a court where the District Commissioner judged cases in ignorance. He had court messengers who brought men to him for trial. Many of these messengers came from Umuru on the bank of the Great River, where the white men first came many years before and where they had built the centre of their religion and trade and government. These court messengers were greatly hated in Umuofia because they were foreigners and also arrogant and high-handed. They were called *kotma*, and because of their ash-coloured shorts they earned the additional name of Ashy-Buttocks. They guarded the prison, which was full of men who had offended against the white man's law. Some of these prisoners had thrown away their twins and some had molested the Christians. They were beaten in the prison by the *kotma* and made to work every morning clearing the government compound and fetching wood for the white Commissioner and the court messengers. Some of these prisoners were men of title who should be above such mean occupation. They were grieved by the indignity and mourned for their neglected farms. As they cut grass in the morning the younger men sang in time with the strokes of their matchets:

Kotma of the ash buttocks,
He is fit to be a slave
The white man has no sense,
He is fit to be a slave

The court messengers did not like to be called Ashy-Buttocks, and they beat the men. But the song spread in Umuofia.

Okonkwo's head was bowed in sadness as Obierika told him these things.

'Perhaps I have been away too long,' Okonkwo said, almost to himself. 'But I cannot understand these things you tell me. What is it that has happened to our people? Why have they lost the power to fight?'

'Have you not heard how the white man wiped out Abame?' asked Obierika.

'I have heard,' said Okonkwo. 'But I have also heard that Abame people were weak and foolish. Why did they not fight back? Had they no guns and matchets? We would be cowards to compare ourselves with the men of Abame. Their fathers had never dared to stand before our ancestors. We must fight these men and drive them from the land.' .

'It is already too late,' said Obierika sadly. 'Our own men and our sons have joined the ranks of the stranger. They have joined his religion and they help to uphold his government. If we should try to drive out the white men in Umuofia we should find it easy. There are only two of them. But what of our own people who are following their way and have been given power? They would go to Umuru and bring the soldiers, and we would be like Abame.' He paused for a long time and then said: 'I told you on my last visit to Mbanta how they hanged Aneto.'

'What has happened to that piece of land in dispute?' asked Okonkwo.

'The white man's court has decided that it should belong to Nnama's family, who had given much money to the white man's messengers and interpreter.'

'Does the white man understand our customs about land?'

'How can he when he does not even speak our tongue? But he says that our customs are bad; and our own brothers who have taken up his religion also say that our customs are bad. How do you think we can fight when our own brothers have turned against us? The white man is very clever. He came quietly and peaceably with his religion. We were amused at his foolishness and allowed him to stay. Now he has won our brothers, and our clan can no longer act like one. He has put a knife on the things that held us together and we have fallen apart.'

'How did they get hold of Aneto to hang him?' asked Okonkwo.

'When he killed Oduche in the fight over the land, he fled to Aninta to escape the wrath of the earth. This was about eight days after the fight, because Oduche had not died immediately from his wounds. It was on the seventh day that he died. But everybody knew that he was going to die and Aneto got his belongings together in readiness to flee. But the Christians had told the white man about the accident, and he sent his *kotma* to catch Aneto. He was imprisoned with all the leaders of his family. In the end Oduche died and Aneto was taken to Umuru and hanged. The other people were released, but even now they have not found the mouth with which to tell of their suffering.'

The two men sat in silence for a long while afterwards.

27 Make brief notes about how the following are presented in the extract.

a the white man's law
b the white man's religion

c the reaction of the Africans to colonization
What comparisons can you make with the extract from *Heart of Darkness*?

28 Achebe once said that he hoped his novels would teach his African readers that 'their past – with all its imperfections – was not one of a long night of savagery from which the first Europeans acting on God's behalf delivered them. ...'
Look at the following quotations from the extract, and say what they imply about Okonkwo's society.
Example: Then he would show his wealth by initiating his sons in the *ozo* society. Only the really great men in the clan were able to do this. (lines 16–18)
Wealth is important in this society, and it should be displayed because status is measured by it. The family is fundamental, and sons are particularly important. Society is organized according to class or rank.

a 'I will only have a son who is a man, ... If any one of you prefers to be a woman, let him follow Nwoye now while I am alive so that I can curse him.' (lines 32–5)
b His future sons-in-law would be men of authority in the clan. The poor and unknown would not dare to come forth. (lines 67–9)
c These court messengers were greatly hated in Umuofia because they were foreigners and also arrogant and high-handed. (lines 87–9)
d Some of these prisoners were men of title who should be above such mean occupation. They were grieved by the indignity and mourned for their neglected farms. (lines 96–9)
e 'When he killed Oduche in the fight over the land, he fled to Aninta to escape the wrath of the earth.' (lines 146–7)

29 In a lecture given at the University of Massachusetts in 1975, Chinua Achebe called *Heart of Darkness* an 'offensive and deplorable book', and its author 'a thoroughgoing racist'. He quoted several passages from the book, including two from the extract in this chapter: lines 32–40 are criticized because the blacks are seen as admirable only as long as they remain in a primitive context, and lines 175–81 are dismissed as 'bleeding-heart sentiments' – ie the conventional compassion of a superior for inferiors.

Achebe went on to say that Africans are 'dehumanized', 'depersonalized' and regarded as 'rudimentary souls'. Africa itself, he said, is presented as 'the antithesis of Europe and therefore of civilization', a place of 'triumphant bestiality'. Achebe pointed out that in the part of Africa described there were 'strikingly successful' native societies, but that Conrad preferred not to notice or report this fact to his European readers. The result is 'a book which parades in the most vulgar fashion prejudices and insults from which a section of mankind has suffered untold agonies and atrocities in the past and continues to do so in many ways and many places today ... a story in which the humanity of black people is called in question'.

What is your reaction to Achebe's accusations? (You may want to look again at the extract and your answers to Exercise 11.)

30 Now compare the two extracts from any point of view you like. If you preferred one to the other, try to explain why.

Authors

Joseph Conrad (1857–1924) was born to Polish parents in the Ukraine – his real name was Teodor Jozef Konrad Korzeniowski. His father's nationalist politics provoked brutal and repressive treatment from the Russian authorities, and Conrad's mother died when he was seven, his father when he was twelve. In 1874, at the age of seventeen, he fulfilled an early ambition to go to sea by going to Marseilles to become a sailor on a French ship. In 1878 he joined an English merchant ship, and subsequently served in the British merchant service in the East and the Mediterranean, and became a British subject in 1886. An interlude from British service came in 1890, when he was in command of a river steamer on the river Congo for a Belgian company, the experience which was to produce *Heart of Darkness*. In 1894 Conrad left the sea, settled in England, and devoted himself to writing at the age of thirty-seven. However, he had to wait until the publication of the novel *Chance* in 1913 for popular recognition, but by his death he was well established as a major novelist.

His best-known novels are *The Nigger of the 'Narcissus'* (1898), *Lord Jim* (1900), *Nostromo* (1904), *The Secret Agent* (1907), *Under Western Eyes* (1911) and *The Shadow Line* (1917). Short novels are *Youth* (1902), *Heart of Darkness* (1902) and *Typhoon* (1903).

The sea provides the setting for most of his writing, but Conrad's main concern is not the evocation of exotic settings: he uses life at sea or in remote settlements to explore profound moral problems and ambiguities in human experience. Conrad's constant concern is with testing people in extreme situations: 'I insist not on the events,' he said, 'but on their effect on the persons of the tale'. Conrad also explored new narrative techniques. He frequently made use of narrators – Marlow is one of his favourites – and this use of limited points of view is a way of suggesting the complexity of experience and the difficulty of judging human actions: there is always something unfathomable and uncommunicable in life.

Conrad did not learn English until he was twenty, and is one of those rare authors who have written successfully in a foreign language. (Other novelists who chose English are the Russian novelist Vladimir Nabokov, and the Polish novelist Ruth Prawer Jhabvala (see Chapter 6), while Samuel Beckett (see Chapter 7) wrote some of his major works first in French.)

Chinua Achebe was born in 1930 and brought up in Nigeria, where his father, a member of the Ibo people of Eastern Nigeria, taught in a school run by the Church Missionary Society. He studied medicine and English Literature at the

University of Ibadan, and spent a few years in broadcasting. His so-called 'African Trilogy' established a new voice in world literature: *Things Fall Apart* (1958, since translated into forty languages), *No Longer at Ease* (1960) and *Arrow of God* (1964) describe the gradual decay of traditional society as a result of the confrontation with colonial European society. Achebe does not, however, paint a simplistic, sentimental picture of noble Africans and corrupt white people: the whites are seen more as a catalyst than the active destroyers of African society. In *A Man of the People* (1966) Achebe satirizes the contemporary Lagos scene, where the euphoria following independence from Britain in 1960 is replaced by bitterness and disillusionment at Nigerian politics.

After the Nigerian civil war of 1970, ending with the surrender of the Eastern area which had declared independence as the Republic of Biafra in 1967, he turned to poetry – the collection *Beware Soul-Brother* won the Commonwealth Poetry Prize in 1972. A return to the novel was *Anthills of the Savanna* (1987), short-listed for the Booker Prize. Achebe has also written children's books and short stories (*The Sacrificial Egg*, 1962, and *Girls at War*, 1972). His lectures at the Universities of Nigeria, Connecticut and Massachusetts have been published in various collections: the lecture on Conrad, 'An Image of Africa: Racism in Conrad's *Heart of Darkness*', is in the collection *Hopes and Impediments, Selected Essays 1965–1987* (1988).

6 'Bad Wife!'

A Chinese wedding procession in the 1850s

An Indian wedding feast in the 1950s

Before you read

1 *a* Describe a wedding that you have seen. You can use the following headings to guide your description, but add any other ideas of your own. Then compare your description with a partner. (Note: the woman who gets married is called the *bride*, the man is called the *bridegroom* or *groom*.)

presents: did anybody give presents to the bride and/or groom?
the bride leaves from ... : did the bride leave from any special place to join the ceremony?
transport: did the bride and/or groom arrive or leave in any special kind of transport?
clothes: what did the bride and groom wear?
place: where did the wedding take place?
wedding guests: who was invited to the wedding?
good luck and bad luck: was anything that happened at the wedding supposed traditionally to bring good or bad luck (eg the weather)?
marriage symbols: was there anything that symbolized the solemnity of the wedding (eg a ring)?
speech-makers: who made a speech? A priest, the father of the bride, ... ?
food, drink and entertainment: was there a kind of 'party' before or after the ceremony?
afterwards: when it was time for the bride and groom to be alone, did guests or friends do anything that was supposed to be humorous or lucky?
anything else?: ______________________________

b Now imagine what would be an ideal wedding for you. In what ways would it be similar to, or different from, what you have just described? Compare your ideas with a partner.

The Joy Luck Club (1989)
Amy Tan

In China in the 1920s it was still the custom in some parts of the country for marriage to be a contract between two families rather than an expression of romantic love; as a result, marriages were often fixed years in advance by a professional matchmaker.

In *The Joy Luck Club*, Lindo, the daughter of a farmer, is promised at the age of two as the future wife of Tyan-yu, the one-year-old son of the wealthy Huang family. When Lindo is twelve years old a flood destroys her parents' house, forcing them to leave the village and go to live with relations in another part of China. They decide that Lindo is old enough to be left behind with the Huang family and to be taken care of by her future mother-in-law, Huang Taitai. (Any future contact between Lindo and her family will in any case be made difficult by the Japanese invasion of China in 1937.)

Lindo's mother says goodbye to her with the words 'Obey your family. Do not disgrace us. Act happy when you arrive. Really, you're very lucky.' In the following extract Lindo has just arrived at the Huangs' house.

See the Glossary section at the back of the book for vocabulary.

No big celebration was held when I arrived. Huang Taitai didn't have red banners greeting me in the fancy room on the first floor. Tyan-yu was not there to greet me. Instead, Huang Taitai hurried me upstairs to the second floor and into the kitchen, which was a place where family children didn't usually go. This was a place for cooks and servants. So I knew my standing.

That first day, I stood in my best padded dress at the low wooden table and began to chop vegetables. I could not keep my hands steady. I missed my family and my stomach felt bad, knowing I had finally arrived where my life said I belonged. But I was also determined to honor my parents' words, so Huang Taitai could never accuse my mother of losing face. She would not win that from our family.

As I was thinking this I saw an old servant woman stooping over the same low table gutting a fish, looking at me from the corner of her eye. I was crying and I was afraid she would tell Huang Taitai. So I gave a big smile and shouted, 'What a lucky girl I am. I'm going to have the best life.' And in this quick-thinking way I must have waved my knife too close to her nose because she cried angrily, '*Shemma bende ren!*' – What kind of fool are you? And I knew right away this was a warning, because when I shouted that declaration of happiness, I almost tricked myself into thinking it might come true.

I saw Tyan-yu at the evening meal. I was still a few inches taller than he, but he acted like a big warlord. I knew what kind of husband he would be, because he made special efforts to make me cry. He complained the soup was not hot enough and then spilled the bowl as if it were an accident. He waited until I had sat down to eat and then would demand another bowl of rice. He asked why I had such an unpleasant face when looking at him.

Over the next few years, Huang Taitai instructed the other servants to teach me how to sew sharp corners on pillowcases and to embroider my future family's name. How can a wife keep her husband's household in order if she has never dirtied her own hands, Huang Taitai used to say as she introduced me to a new task. I don't think Huang Taitai ever soiled her hands, but she was very good at calling out orders and criticism.

'Teach her to wash rice properly so that the water runs clear. Her husband cannot eat muddy rice,' she'd say to a cook servant.

Another time, she told a servant to show me how to clean a chamber pot: 'Make her put her own nose to the barrel to make sure it's clean.' That was how I learned to be an obedient wife. I learned to cook so well that I could smell if the meat stuffing was too salty before I even tasted it. I could sew such small stitches it looked as if the embroidery had been painted on. And even Huang Taitai complained in a pretend manner that she could scarcely throw a dirty blouse on the floor before it was cleaned and on her back once again, causing her to wear the same clothes every day.

After a while I didn't think it was a terrible life, no, not really. After a while, I hurt so much I didn't feel any difference. What was happier than seeing everybody gobble down the shiny mushrooms and bamboo shoots I had helped to prepare that day? What was more satisfying than having Huang Taitai nod and pat my head when I had finished combing her hair one hundred strokes? How much happier could I be after seeing Tyan-yu eat a whole bowl of noodles without once complaining about its taste or my looks? It's like those ladies you see on American TV these days, the ones who are so happy they have washed out a stain so the clothes look better than new.

Can you see how the Huangs almost washed their thinking into my skin? I came to think of Tyan-yu as a god, someone whose opinions were worth much more than my own life. I came to think of Huang Taitai as my real mother, someone I wanted to please, someone I should follow and obey without question.

When I turned sixteen on the lunar new year, Huang Taitai told me she was ready to welcome a grandson by next spring. Even if I had not wanted to marry, where would I go live instead? Even though I was strong as a horse, how could I run away? The Japanese were in every corner of China.

What do you think Lindo would prefer to do: run away or stay and marry Tyan-yu? What do you think she will do?

'The Japanese showed up as uninvited guests,' said Tyan-yu's grandmother, 'and that's why nobody else came.' Huang Taitai had made elaborate plans, but our wedding was very small.

She had asked the entire village and friends and family from other cities as well. In those days, you didn't do RSVP. It was not polite not to come. Huang Taitai didn't think the war would change people's good manners. So the cook and her helpers prepared hundreds of dishes. My family's old furniture had been shined up into an impressive dowry and placed in the front parlor. Huang Taitai had taken care to remove all the water and mud marks. She had even commissioned someone to write felicitous messages on red banners, as if my parents themselves had draped these decorations to congratulate me on my good luck. And she had arranged to rent a red palanquin to carry me from her neighbor's house to the wedding ceremony.

A lot of bad luck fell on our wedding day, even though the matchmaker had chosen a lucky day, the fifteenth day of the eighth moon, when the moon is perfectly round and bigger than any other time of the year. But the week before the moon arrived, the Japanese came. They invaded Shansi province, as well as the provinces bordering us. People were nervous. And the morning of the fifteenth, on the day of the wedding celebration, it began to rain, a very bad sign. When the thunder and lightning began, people confused it with Japanese bombs and would not leave their houses.

I heard later that poor Huang Taitai waited many hours for more people to come, and finally, when she could not wring any more guests out of her hands, she decided to start the ceremony. What could she do? She could not change the war.

I was at the neighbor's house. When they called me to come down and ride the red palanquin, I was sitting at a small dressing table by an open window. I began to cry and thought bitterly about my parents' promise. I wondered why my destiny had been decided, why I should have an unhappy life so someone else could have a happy one. From my seat by the window I could see the Fen River with its muddy brown waters. I thought about throwing my body into this river that had destroyed my family's happiness. A person has very strange thoughts when it seems that life is about to end.

It started to rain again, just a light rain. The people from downstairs called up to me once again to hurry. And my thoughts became more urgent, more strange.

I asked myself, What is true about a person? Would I change in the same way the river changes color but still be the same person? And then I saw the curtains blowing wildly, and outside rain was falling harder, causing everyone to scurry and shout. I smiled. And then I realized it was the first time I could see the power of the wind. I couldn't see the wind itself, but I could see it carried the water that filled the rivers and shaped the countryside. It caused men to yelp and dance.

I wiped my eyes and looked in the mirror. I was surprised at what I saw. I had on a beautiful red dress, but what I saw was even more valuable. I was strong. I was pure. I had genuine thoughts inside that no one could see, that no one could ever take away from me. I was like the wind.

I threw my head back and smiled proudly to myself. And then I draped the large embroidered red scarf over my face and covered these thoughts up. But underneath the scarf I still knew who I was. I made a promise to myself: I would always remember my parents' wishes, but I would never forget myself.

When I arrived at the wedding, I had the red scarf over my face and couldn't see anything in front of me. But when I bent my head forward, I could see out the sides. Very few people had come. I saw the Huangs, the same old complaining relatives now embarrassed by this poor showing, the entertainers with their violins and flutes. And there were a few village people who had been brave enough to come out for a free meal. I even saw servants and their children, who must have been added to make the party look bigger.

Someone took my hands and guided me down a path. I was like a blind person walking to my fate. But I was no longer scared. I could see what was inside me.

A high official conducted the ceremony and he talked too long about philosophers and models of virtue. Then I heard the matchmaker speak about our birthdates and harmony and fertility. I tipped my veiled head forward and I could see her hands unfolding a red silk scarf and holding up a red candle for everyone to see.

The candle had two ends for lighting. One length had carved gold characters with Tyan-yu's name, the other with mine. The matchmaker lighted both ends and announced, 'The marriage has begun.' Tyan yanked the scarf off my face and smiled at his friends and family, never even looking at me. He reminded me of a young peacock I once saw that acted as if he had just claimed the entire courtyard by fanning his still-short tail.

I saw the matchmaker place the lighted red candle in a gold holder and then hand it to a nervous-looking servant. This servant was supposed to watch the candle during the banquet and all night to make sure neither end went out. In the morning the matchmaker was supposed to show the result, a little piece of black ash, and then declare, 'This candle burned continuously at both ends without going out. This is a marriage that can never be broken.'

I still can remember. That candle was a marriage bond that was worth more than a Catholic promise not to divorce. It meant I couldn't divorce and I couldn't ever remarry, even if Tyan-yu died. That red candle was supposed to seal me forever with my husband and his family, no excuses afterward.

And sure enough, the matchmaker made her declaration the next morning and showed she had done her job. But I know what really happened, because I stayed up all night crying about my marriage.

What do you think might have 'really happened' on their wedding night?

After the banquet, our small wedding party pushed us and half carried us up to the third floor to our small bedroom. People were shouting jokes and pulling boys from underneath the bed.

The matchmaker helped small children pull red eggs that had been hidden between the blankets. The boys who were about Tyan-yu's age made us sit on the bed side by side and everybody made us kiss so our faces would turn red with passion. Firecrackers exploded on the walkway outside our open window and someone said this was a good excuse for me to jump into my husband's arms.

After everyone left, we sat there side by side without words for many minutes, still listening to the laughing outside. When it grew quiet, Tyan-yu said, 'This is my bed. You sleep on the sofa.' He threw a pillow and a thin blanket to me. I was so glad! I waited until he fell asleep and then I got up quietly and went outside, down the stairs and into the dark courtyard.

Outside it smelled as if it would soon rain again. I was crying, walking in my bare feet and feeling the wet heat still inside the bricks. Across the courtyard I could see the matchmaker's servant through a yellow-lit open window. She was sitting at a table, looking very sleepy as the red candle burned in its special gold holder. I sat down by a tree to watch my fate being decided for me.

I must have fallen asleep because I remember being startled awake by the sound of loud cracking thunder. That's when I saw the matchmaker's servant running from the room, scared as a chicken about to lose its head. Oh, she was asleep too, I thought, and now she thinks it's the Japanese. I laughed. The whole sky became light and then more thunder came, and she ran out of the courtyard and down the road, going so fast and hard I could see pebbles kicking up behind her. Where does she think she's running to, I wondered, still laughing. And then I saw the red candle flickering just a little with the breeze.

I was not thinking when my legs lifted me up and my feet ran me across the courtyard to the yellow-lit room. But I was hoping – I was praying to Buddha, the goddess of mercy, and the full moon – to make that candle go out. It fluttered a little and the flame bent down low, but still both ends burned strong. My throat filled with so much hope that it finally burst and blew out my husband's end of the candle.

I immediately shivered with fear. I thought a knife would appear and cut me down dead. Or the sky would open up and blow me away. But nothing happened, and when my senses came back, I walked back to my room with fast guilty steps.

The next morning the matchmaker made her proud declaration in front of Tyan-yu, his parents, and myself. 'My job is done,' she announced, pouring the remaining black ash onto the red cloth. I saw her servant's shame-faced mournful look.

> *How do you think Tyuan-yu will behave from now on? How do you think Lindo will behave?*

I learned to love Tyan-yu, but it is not how you think. From the beginning, I would always become sick thinking he would someday climb on top of me and do his business. Every time I went into our bedroom, my hair would already be standing up. But during the first months, he never touched me. He slept in his bed, I slept on my sofa.

In front of his parents, I was an obedient wife, just as they taught me. I instructed the cook to kill a fresh young chicken every morning and cook it until pure juice came out. I would strain this juice myself into a bowl, never adding any water. I gave this to him for breakfast, murmuring good wishes about his health. And every night I would cook a special tonic soup called *tounau,* which was not only very delicious but has eight ingredients that guarantee long life for mothers. This pleased my mother-in-law very much.

But it was not enough to keep her happy. One morning, Huang Taitai and I were sitting in the same room, working on our embroidery. I was dreaming about my childhood, about a pet frog I once kept named Big Wind. Huang Taitai seemed restless, as if she had an itch in the bottom of her shoe. I heard her huffing and then all of a sudden she stood up from her chair, walked over to me, and slapped my face.

'Bad wife!' she cried. 'If you refuse to sleep with my son, I refuse to feed you or clothe you.' So that's how I knew what my husband had said to avoid his mother's anger. I was also boiling with anger, but I said nothing, remembering my promise to my parents to be an obedient wife.

That night I sat on Tyan-yu's bed and waited for him to touch me. But he didn't. I was relieved. The next night, I lay straight down on the bed next to him. And still he didn't touch me. So the next night, I took off my gown.

That's when I could see what was underneath Tyan-yu. He was

scared and turned his face. He had no desire for me, but it was his fear that made me think he had no desire for any woman. He was like a little boy who had never grown up. After a while I was no longer afraid. I even began to think differently toward Tyan-yu. It was not like the way a wife loves a husband, but more like the way a sister protects a younger brother. I put my gown back on and lay down next to him and rubbed his back. I knew I no longer had to be afraid. I was sleeping with Tyan yu. He would never touch me and I had a comfortable bed to sleep on.

After more months had passed and my stomach and breasts remained small and flat, Huang Taitai flew into another kind of rage. 'My son says he's planted enough seeds for thousands of grandchildren. Where are they? It must be you are doing something wrong.' And after that she confined me to the bed so that her grandchildren's seeds would not spill out so easily.

Oh, you think it is so much fun to lie in bed all day, never getting up. But I tell you it was worse than a prison. I think Huang Taitai became a little crazy.

She told the servants to take all sharp things out of the room, thinking scissors and knives were cutting off her next generation. She forbade me from sewing. She said I must concentrate and think of nothing but having babies. And four times a day, a very nice servant girl would come into my room, apologizing the whole time while making me drink a terrible-tasting medicine.

I envied this girl, the way she could walk out the door. Sometimes as I watched her from my window, I would imagine I was that girl, standing in the courtyard, bargaining with the traveling shoe mender, gossiping with other servant girls, scolding a handsome delivery man in her high teasing voice.

One day, after two months had gone by without any results, Huang Taitai called the old matchmaker to the house. The matchmaker examined me closely, looked up my birthdate and the hour of my birth, and then asked Huang Taitai about my nature. Finally, the matchmaker gave her conclusions: 'It's clear what has happened. A woman can have sons only if she is deficient in one of the elements. Your daughter-in-law was born with enough wood, fire, water, and earth, and she was deficient in metal, which was a good sign. But when she was married, you loaded her down with gold bracelets and decorations and now she has all the elements, including metal. She's too balanced to have babies.'

This turned out to be joyous news for Huang Taitai, for she liked nothing better than to reclaim all her gold and jewelry to help me become fertile. And it was good news for me too. Because after the gold was removed from my body, I felt lighter, more free. They say this is what happens if you lack metal. You begin to think as an independent person. That day I started to think about how I would escape this marriage without breaking my promise to my family.

It was really quite simple. I made the Huangs think it was their idea to get rid of me, that they would be the ones to say the marriage contract was not valid.

I thought about my plan for many days. I observed everyone around me, the thoughts they showed in their faces, and then I was ready. I chose an auspicious day, the third day of the third month. That's the day of the Festival of Pure Brightness. On this day, your thoughts must be clear as you prepare to think about your ancestors. That's the day when everyone goes to the family graves. They bring hoes to clear the weeds and brooms to sweep the stones and they offer dumplings and oranges as spiritual food. Oh, it's not a somber day, more like a picnic, but it has special meaning to someone looking for grandsons.

On the morning of that day, I woke up Tyan-yu and the entire house with my wailing. It took Huang Taitai a long time to come into my room. 'What's wrong with her now,' she cried from her room. 'Go make her be quiet.' But finally, after my wailing didn't stop, she rushed into my room, scolding me at the top of her voice.

> *Why do you think Lindo is wailing? How do you think this fits into her plan?*

I was clutching my mouth with one hand and my eyes with another. My body was writhing as if I were seized by a terrible pain. I was quite convincing, because Huang Taitai drew back and grew small like a scared animal.

'What's wrong, little daughter? Tell me quickly,' she cried.

'Oh, it's too terrible to think, too terrible to say,' I said between gasps and more wailing.

After enough wailing, I said what was so unthinkable. 'I had a dream,' I reported. 'Our ancestors came to me and said they wanted to see our wedding. So Tyan-yu and I held the same ceremony for our ancestors. We saw the matchmaker light the candle and give it to the servant to watch. Our ancestors were so pleased, so pleased. …'

Huang Taitai looked impatient as I began to cry softly again. 'But then the servant left the room with our candle and a big wind came and blew the candle out. And our ancestors became very angry. They shouted that the marriage was doomed! They said that Tyan-yu's end of the candle had blown out! Our ancestors said Tyan-yu would die if he stayed in this marriage!'

Tyan-yu's face turned white. But Huang Taitai only frowned. 'What a stupid girl to have such bad dreams!' And then she scolded everybody to go back to bed.

'Mother,' I called to her in a hoarse whisper. 'Please don't leave me! I am afraid! Our ancestors said if the matter is not settled, they would begin the cycle of destruction.'

'What is this nonsense!' cried Huang Taitai, turning back toward me. Tyan-yu followed her, wearing his mother's same frowning face. And I knew they were almost caught, two ducks leaning into the pot.

'They knew you would not believe me,' I said in a remorseful tone, 'because they know I do not want to leave the comforts of my marriage. So our ancestors said they would plant the signs, to show our marriage is now rotting.'

'What nonsense from your stupid head,' said Huang Taitai, sighing. But she could not resist. 'What signs?'

'In my dream, I saw a man with a long beard and a mole on his cheek.'

'Tyan-yu's grandfather?' asked Huang Taitai. I nodded, remembering the painting I had observed on the wall.

'He said there are three signs. First, he has drawn a black spot on Tyan-yu's back, and this spot will grow and eat away Tyan-yu's flesh just as it ate away our ancestor's face before he died.'

Huang Taitai quickly turned to Tyan-yu and pulled his shirt up. 'Ai-ya!' she cried, because there it was, the same black mole, the size of a fingertip, just as I had always seen it these past five months of sleeping as sister and brother.

'And then our ancestor touched my mouth,' and I patted my cheek as if it already hurt. 'He said my teeth would start to fall out one by one, until I could no longer protest leaving this marriage.'

Huang Taitai pried open my mouth and gasped upon seeing the open spot in the back of my mouth where a rotted tooth fell out four years ago.

'And finally, I saw him plant a seed in a servant girl's womb. He said this girl only pretends to come from a bad family. But she is really from imperial blood, and …'

I lay my head down on the pillow as if too tired to go on. Huang Taitai pushed my shoulder, 'What does he say?'

'He said the servant girl is Tyan-yu's true spiritual wife. And the seed he has planted will grow into Tyan-yu's child.'

By mid-morning they had dragged the matchmaker's servant over to our house and extracted her terrible confession.

And after much searching they found the servant girl I liked so much, the one I had watched from my window every day. I had seen her eyes grow bigger and her teasing voice become smaller whenever the handsome delivery man arrived. And later, I had watched her stomach grow rounder and her face become longer with fear and worry.

So you can imagine how happy she was when they forced her to tell the truth about her imperial ancestry. I heard later she was so struck with this miracle of marrying Tyan-yu she became a very religious person who ordered servants to sweep the ancestors' graves not just once a year, but once a day.

There's no more to the story. They didn't blame me so much. Huang Taitai got her grandson. I got my clothes, a rail ticket to Peking, and enough money to go to America. The Huangs asked only that I never tell anybody of any importance about the story of my doomed marriage.

It's a true story, how I kept my promise, how I sacrificed my life. See the gold metal I can now wear. I gave birth to your brothers and then your father gave me these two bracelets. Then I had you. And every few years, when I have a little extra money, I buy another bracelet. I know what I'm worth. They're always twenty-four carats, all genuine.

But I'll never forget. On the day of the Festival of Pure Brightness, I take off all my bracelets. I remember the day when I finally knew a genuine thought and could follow where it went. That was the day I was a young girl with my face under a red marriage scarf. I promised not to forget myself.

How nice it is to be that girl again, to take off my scarf, to see what is underneath and feel the lightness come back my body!

First reaction

2 'Then I had you' (line 383). Lindo is telling this story to her daughter from her second marriage, a young woman in her early thirties, who has grown up in the USA.
What advice about life do you think Lindo wants to give her daughter by telling this story? Summarize this advice in 20–30 words, and compare your ideas with a partner.

Close reading: themes – cultural differences and family relationships

Lindo's 'training'

3 Look at lines 1–67. Find some sentences that show
a the social status that Lindo has in the Huang household.
b the way Lindo feels when she arrives.
c the way Lindo feels after a few years.
Discuss them with a partner, then check with the Key before going on to the next exercise.

4 *a* What do you think of the way Huang Taitai and Tyuan-yu treat Lindo?
b Would you have felt the same way as Lindo?
c Compare your ideas with a partner.

The wedding

5 Look at lines 68–98 and 116–72. Make notes under the following headings (the same ones as in Exercise 1) to describe the wedding.

a **presents**: ______________________________
____
b **the bride leaves from** ... : ______________________________
____
c **transport**: ______________________________
____
d **clothes**: ______________________________
____
e **place**: ______________________________
____
f **wedding guests**: ______________________________
____
g **good luck and bad luck**: ______________________________
____
h **marriage symbols**: ______________________________
____
i **speech-makers**: ______________________________
____
j **food, drink and entertainment**: ______________________________
____
k **afterwards**: ______________________________
____

6 Compare your notes in Exercise 5 with the notes you made in Exercise 1. Note down a few ideas in the following boxes, and compare them with a partner.

DIFFERENCES FROM MY CULTURE	SIMILARITIES WITH MY CULTURE

The wedding night

7 Look at lines 173–204. Lindo's language is simple, but is her character simple? Which of the following interpretations do you agree with? You can choose more than one, or add your own.

a I was crying. (line 179)

1 She was crying because Tyan-yu had rejected her.
2 She was crying because she realised that she was trapped.
3 She was crying because she missed her parents.

b I laughed. (line 189) and … still laughing. (line 192)

1 She laughed with amusement at another person's stupidity.
2 She laughed bitterly, because she saw another person afraid and feeling trapped.
3 She laughed hysterically.

8 Now write your own interpretations of the following. Compare them with a partner.

a … with so much hope … (lines 198–9)
She was hoping ________________________________

b I immediately shivered with fear. (line 201)
She was afraid because ________________________________

Married life

9 Look at lines 173–8 and 209–86. Look at this diagram and the arrows connecting the three characters.

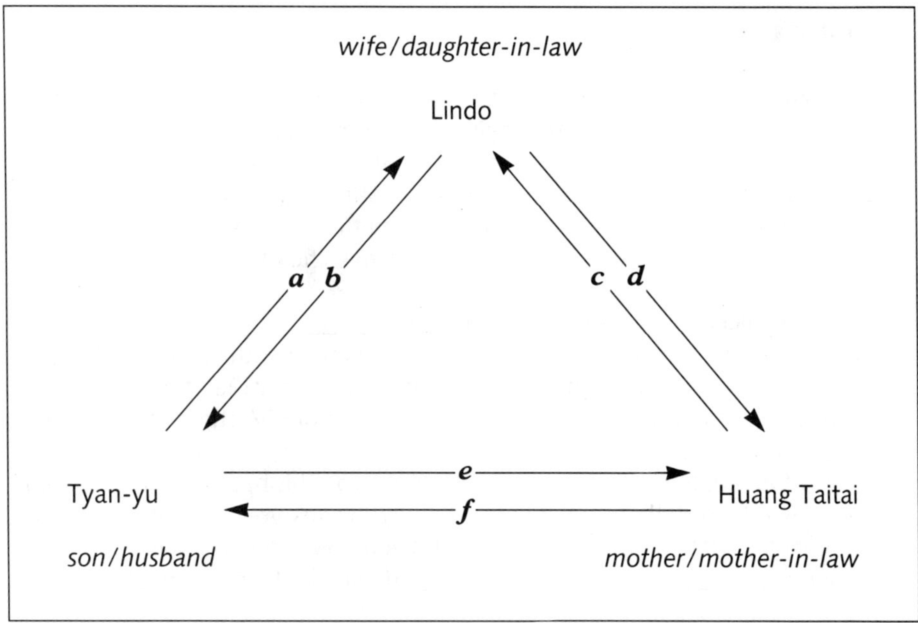

Make brief notes to show the attitude and behaviour of the three characters towards each other.

a Tyan-yu towards Lindo
b Lindo towards Tyan-yu
c Huang Taitai towards Lindo
d Lindo towards Huang Taitai
e Tyan-yu towards Huang Taitai
f Huang Taitai towards Tyan-yu

10 a Which character do you feel most sympathy with?
b Which character do you judge most critically? Do you really blame him/her, or is he/she just a product of their culture?
c Compare your ideas with a partner.

Escape

11 Look at lines 287–393. In this last episode Lindo seems to have changed: she seems much more 'clever' than she did before. Look at this example:
'I observed everyone around me, the thoughts they showed in their faces, and then I was ready.' (lines 290–2)
This shows Lindo's powers of observation, her insight into human nature, and her sense of timing.

Find two other sentences from lines 293–370 that show this 'new' Lindo. Discuss them with a partner. (A character who develops is often called a 'round' character. For a description of this term see Chapter 1, *Anatomy of a Novel*, pages 19–22.)

The 'message'

12 The extract you have read comes from a chapter in *The Joy Luck Club* called 'The Red Candle'. This chapter begins with the passage below, where Lindo addressess her daughter (see Exercise 2). The spaces (a)–(h) represent just *two* missing words. One word is a verb, the other is used as a verb and a noun (both singular and plural). What do you think the two missing words are? Fill in the spaces, using one word five times, the other three times.

I once sacrificed my life to keep my parents' __________ (a). This means nothing to you, because to you __________ (b) mean nothing. A daughter can __________ (c) to come to dinner, but if she has a headache, if she has a traffic jam, if she wants to watch a favorite movie on TV, she no longer has a __________ (d). …

It's too late to change you, but I'm telling you this because I worry about your baby. I worry that someday she will say, 'Thank you, Grandmother, for the gold bracelet. I'll never __________ (e) you.' But later, she will __________ (f) her __________ (g). She will __________ (h) she had a grandmother.

Check your answer with the Key before going on to the next exercise.

13 Which of the following do you think describe Lindo's purpose in telling the story you have read? You can choose more than one, and add your own idea if you like. (You may want to look back to your answers to Exercises 2 and 12.)

a encouragement to her daughter to be independent
b criticism of her daughter
c a warning about how families can grow apart
d a demonstration of cultural differences between countries
e a nostalgic celebration of times past
f your own idea: ______________________________

Language practice – structures

Presenting how characters think

14 Look at the following five ways of presenting the same thought.

A 'Can I be happy with him?'

B 'Can I be happy with him?' I wondered.
C Could I be happy with him?
D I wondered if I could be happy with him.
E I wondered about my future happiness with him.

a What differences in grammar and vocabulary can you see between the five ways **A–E**?

b What different effects can a writer create by using the different ways of presenting thought? Choose ideas from the box below and match them with the sentences **A–E** above. Add any ideas of your own about the effects created.

immediate a general idea dramatic *the presence of the writer is more apparent vague* *a report rather than the actual thought precise* *a character in dialogue with himself/herself vivid*

15 Writers often present characters' thoughts in different ways in order to create variety, drama, and to emphasize sudden moments of realization. Amy Tan does this in Lindo's moment of revelation in lines 96–125. For each of the following thoughts, put a letter **B–E** (as in Exercise 14) in the brackets to indicate which way Amy Tan is using (note she does not use **A**).

Example: I began to cry and thought bitterly about my parents' promise. (lines 98–99) **[E]**

a I wondered why my destiny had been decided, why I should have an unhappy life so someone else could have a happy one. (lines 99–101) [ ]

b I thought about throwing my body into this river that had destroyed my family's happiness. (lines 102–3) [ ]

c I asked myself, What is true about a person? (line 108) [ ]

d Would I change in the same way the river changes color but still be the same person? (lines 108–9) [ ]

e And then I realized it was the first time I could see the power of the wind. (lines 111–13) [ ]

f I was strong. I was pure. I had genuine thoughts inside that no one could see, that no one could ever take away from me. I was like the wind. (lines 118–20) [ ]

g I made a promise to myself: I would always remember my parents' wishes, but I would never forget myself. (lines 124–5) [ ]

16 The following are all thoughts that Lindo might have had, expressed directly. Change them into indirect thoughts (**D** in Exercise 14).

Example: 'I'll never be happy here.' [*realize*]
I realised (that) I would never be happy there.

a 'Why is it only my cooking that they appreciate?' [*wonder*]

b 'I can't run away – the Japanese are everywhere.' [*realize*]

c 'He looks as ridiculous as a young peacock.' [*think*]

d 'Something terrible will happen to me because I've blown out the candle.' [*believe*]
e 'Is he going to try and touch me?' [*be afraid*]
f 'I must respect my promise to my parents.' [*remember*]
g 'I don't have to be afraid of him any more.' [*know*]
h 'What would it be like to be that servant girl?' [*wonder*]
i 'If I talk about our ancestors, they'll believe me.' [*think*]

17 One effect of using a first-person narrator is that the reader identifies more with the narrator – we know his/her thoughts – and less with other characters – we don't know what they are thinking. (See Chapter 1, *Anatomy of a Novel*, pages 15–16 for a discussion of first-person narrators.)
For each of the following moments suggest what might be going through the mind of Huang Taitai or Tyan-yu. Experiment with using some of the different ways of presenting their thoughts.
Example: **Huang Taitai**: … poor Huang Taitai waited many hours for more people to come, and finally, when she could not wring any more guests out of her hands, she decided to start the ceremony. (lines 92–4)
'How can I possibly start the wedding with so few guests?' she wondered.
What could she do in this situation?
She wondered whether anybody else would come.

a **Tyan-yu**: Tyan yanked the scarf off my face and smiled at his friends and family, never even looking at me. (lines 145–6)

b **Huang Taitai**: Huang Taitai seemed restless, as if she had an itch in the bottom of her shoe. (lines 226–7)

c **Tyan-yu**: He was scared and turned his face. … I put my gown back on and lay down next to him and rubbed his back. (lines 239–46)

d **Huang Taitai**: I think Huang Taitai became a little crazy. (lines 256–7) *e* **Huang Taitai**: This turned out to be joyous news for Huang Taitai, for she liked nothing better than to reclaim all her gold and jewelry to help me become fertile. (lines 280–2)

____

____

f **Huang Taitai and Tyan-yu**: Tyan-yu's face turned white. But Huang Taitai only frowned. (line 324)

____

____

g **Huang Taitai and Tyan-yu**: By mid-morning they had dragged the matchmaker's servant over to our house and extracted her terrible confession. (lines 363–4)

____

____

h **Huang Taitai and Tyan-yu**: … they forced her (ie *the pregnant servant girl*) to tell the truth about her imperial ancestry. (lines 371–2)

____

____

Language practice – vocabulary

Adjectives of character

18 a Look at the adjectives in the box on page 160. Use a dictionary to check any meanings you don't know, and then experiment with grouping them in any way you like. Some of the ways you could try are:

- words similar in meaning
- words contrasting in meaning

- words which are always positive
- words which are always negative
- words which can be positive or negative

- words you would like to hear used about yourself
- words you wouldn't like to hear used about yourself

vulnerable patronizing kind insecure demanding shrewd rebellious nervous sensitive aggressive tough assertive pompous patient confident polite gullible vain selfish easygoing class-conscious industrious sadistic materialistic careless loyal bossy short-tempered generous cheerful indulgent strict domineering critical

b Compare your groupings with a partner.

19 Lindo, the narrator of this chapter of *The Joy Luck Club*, mostly communicates her own character and that of the others by showing us how they behave (and sometimes by telling us her thoughts). She does not use many adjectives: it is up to the reader to make interpretations.

a From the adjectives given in Exercise 18 (you do not have to use all of them) decide which *definitely apply* to each of the three main characters, and which you think *definitely do not apply*. There may also be some adjectives that you are not sure about.

b Compare your ideas with a partner when you have finished.

	adjectives that definitely apply	*adjectives that definitely don't apply*	*adjectives that I'm not sure about*
Lindo	__________	__________	__________
	__________	__________	__________
	__________	__________	__________
	__________	__________	__________
Tyan-yu	__________	__________	__________
	__________	__________	__________
	__________	__________	__________
	__________	__________	__________
Huang Taitai	__________	__________	__________
	__________	__________	__________
	__________	__________	__________
	__________	__________	__________

20 a What qualities do you like people close to you to have? Choose two or three of the following, and think about their ideal qualities.

mother father brother sister grandfather grandmother wife husband daughter son cousin aunt uncle best friend colleague at work girlfriend boyfriend

Refer to the adjectives in Exercise 18, and, adding any adjectives of your own, note down some ideas like this:
I think an ideal mother should be ____________________
I think an ideal mother should *not* be ____________________

b Compare your ideas with the rest of the class.

21 a Make a brief character analysis of yourself. Here are some phrases you might want to use. Write your self-analysis on a piece of paper without your name on it.

I try to be __________, but sometimes …
I think I'm too __________.
I don't think I'm __________ enough.
I'd like to be more __________.
I'd like to be less __________.
My good points are that I'm __________.
Some people think I'm __________, but …
My bad points are that I'm __________.

b Now the class should collect the anonymous self-analyses, mix them up, and re-distribute them, one for each student. Each student should then try to identify the student who wrote his/her self-analysis.

Extension

22 **Class discussion**: How much of Lindo's story would be possible in the culture that you live in? Exchange ideas with a partner.

23 **Class discussion/project**: *The Joy Luck Club* contains the views of four elderly Chinese women coming to terms with what it means to be an immigrant in the USA, and their four daughters finding out what it means to be first-generation Chinese Americans.

Racial tension in the USA is often seen as a conflict between 'whites' and 'blacks', with recent years seeing the gradual erosion of prejudice. But the true picture is more complex. Hispanic and Asian ethnic minorities can be both victims and perpetrators of racial prejudice, not always involving the white community. For example, in the savage race riots that shook Los Angeles in 1993, black rioters, outraged at a white jury's decision to acquit white policemen of a charge of using excessive violence against an Afro-American, Rodney King, also targeted the Vietnamese community.

What do you think divides people in contemporary society? Look at the following:

sex class colour political convictions language religion place of birth money education age

a Which do you think are the most divisive in the society you live in? Which are the least divisive?

b Which do you think are the most divisive and the least divisive in the world?
c Which would you most like to eliminate?
d Can you think of anything else which divides people?

24 **Role-play/writing**: Choose one of the following.
a In pairs or groups of three imagine that you are Lindo and Lindo's mother and/or father. You meet again thirty years after the events described in the passage you have read. What do you say to each other?
b In groups of three imagine that you are the pregnant servant girl and Huang Taitai and Tyan-yu (see lines 371–5). What do you say to each other?

25 **Writing – epiphanies**: With reference to the modern novel, the word **epiphany** has been used to describe a moment where a character has a sudden revelation while observing an everyday object. James Joyce (see Chapter 7) was the first to use this term – he defined it as 'a sudden spiritual manifestation' – and his novels and short stories often describe characters experiencing an epiphany. In *The Joy Luck Club* Lindo experiences an epiphany while observing the effects of wind (lines 96–125).

Describe a moment in your life where you had a sudden revelation which changed your outlook on life (100–200 words).

Beyond the text

The main character in Ruth Prawer Jhabvala's novel *The Householder* is Prem, a young teacher in New Delhi in India in the late 1950s. He is married to Indu, who is expecting a baby, and although the marriage was arranged by their parents, they are genuinely fond of each other. But life is not so easy for Prem in his ambition to become a 'householder' – a responsible family man with a steady job. He has little authority with his students, he gets little respect from his colleagues, his salary is low, and the rent for his small flat is too high. Added to this, he has just quarrelled with Indu, who has been insisting on going back to stay with her mother for the period of her pregnancy. Prem has refused to let her go, because *his* mother has promised to come and visit them soon.

26 Before you read, look at the following sentences taken from the extract. Which interpretation do you think is more likely, ***1*** or ***2***? Explain your choices to a partner.
a She is not even very good at household duties.
1 a daughter-in-law talking about her mother-in-law
2 a mother-in-law talking about her daughter-in-law
b 'Eat eat,' he said indulgently. He took out another sweetmeat and offered it to her between finger and thumb.

1 a son giving his mother something to eat
2 a husband giving his wife something to eat

c … turned away her face and drew up her sari to hide her bashful look.
1 a daughter-in-law reacting to her mother-in-law's gaze
2 a mother-in-law reacting to her daughter-in-law's gaze

d 'Be careful with that jar,' … 'It is your favourite pickle.'
1 a mother talking to her son
2 a wife talking to her husband

e He wondered what he could do to placate her. Perhaps, he thought, he should bring her some present.
1 a husband thinking about his wife
2 a son thinking about his mother

f She gave one short look, then turned away again. She said, 'I don't want.'
1 a wife refusing something from her husband
2 a mother refusing something from her son

g … she sighed, 'I know how much you like these things.' Her sigh at once made clear the infinite labour she had undergone in the preparation of them.
1 a wife giving something to her husband
2 a mother giving something to her son

h When she served his breakfast, she did so with a defiant little slam.
1 a mother giving breakfast to her son
2 a wife giving breakfast to her husband

i He was wondering when she would allow him to go to bed.
1 a son thinking about his mother
2 a husband thinking about his wife

j To almost every question he asked, she pursed her mouth and said, 'What do I know of these things?'
1 a mother replying to her son
2 a wife replying to her husband

Now read the extract and check your responses with the sentences in context.

The Householder (1960)
Ruth Prawer Jhabvala

Next morning it appeared they were not on speaking terms. He had forgotten all about her quarrel with him but she, he now found out, had not. When she served his breakfast, she did so with a defiant little slam. He looked up in surprise, but saw only her retreating back with the pigtail swinging aggressively. After a while he made an excuse to talk to her. He followed her into the kitchen where she squatted stirring something in the fire. 'The puris were very good this morning,' he said sheepishly. It was the first time he had ever praised her cooking, but she gave no indication of having heard. Only her lips tightened, and she leant forward to peer into the pot in which she was stirring. Prem waited a bit longer, but finally saw nothing for it but to leave for college. He was about to go down the stairs, when a voice hissed behind him. 'Bibiji's puris are always very good.' He turned round and there was the servant-boy glaring at him with angry eyes.

So all morning he thought more about Indu than he did about the swami. He wondered what he could do to placate her. Perhaps, he thought, he should bring her some present. Only he did not know what she would like. He might have consulted Sohan Lal if, after yesterday's visit, he had not felt a little ashamed to show his concern over these trivial worldly matters. But he could not help being concerned: he wanted Indu to think kindly of him again. He had had no experience of giving presents to women, and the only thing he could think of that might please her was a sari. But that took rather more money than he at present had. He had still not decided on anything when he went home at midday. On the way, as he went through the bazaar, he passed a sweetmeat stall where people stood outside drinking frothy buttermilk out of tall, brass tumblers or eating sweetmeats, swimming in syrup, out of earthenware pots. Prem made his selection of sweetmeats and spent rather more than he could afford.

But when he got home, he did not know how to present his gift to her. His lunch was served to him with the same slam as his breakfast had been, and she walked away with the same swing of her hips and of her pigtail. Afterwards, though, he followed her into the bedroom and, holding out the earthenware pot of sweetmeats to her, he said in a shy appealing voice, 'I brought this for you.'

She gave one short look, then turned away again. She said, 'I don't want.'

'Take it,' Prem urged, going one step nearer and still holding it out to her.

After a while she said, 'What is it?'

'Sweetmeats,' he replied eagerly. 'Rasgullas and gulab jamuns and jelabis …'

'All right. Give it.'

She sat down on the edge of the bed and at once began to eat. He watched her, first with gratification then with surprise at the amount and speed with which she was eating. She finished each sweetmeat in two neat bites, then at once fished for another one. In between she licked her lips and her fingertips with a pink and greedy little tongue.

He said, 'You are very hungry?'

'No,' she said. 'But I long for sweetmeats. I long and long and long for them,' she said passionately, fishing out another one.

He sat down beside her on the bed. 'Why didn't you tell me before? I would have brought for you'; and when she merely shrugged in reply added, 'You must tell me everything.'

'You want?' she said and held out a piece of rasgulla, wet and wounded where she had just bitten into it. He opened his mouth and allowed her to lay it on his tongue, managing to lick her fingers before she withdrew them.

'If you don't tell me, how am I to know what you want?' he urged her. After a while a new thought struck him, 'You don't feel ill any time?' he anxiously asked; and when she shook her head, 'Or do you have a pain – here?' he whispered, shyly pointing at that part of her where she was carrying her baby.

'No no,' she laughed. 'Only I want to eat sweetmeats all the time.'

'Every day I will bring for you.' Midday heat lay hot and close in the room. Indu smelt of perspiration and a very sweet scent, rather like vanilla essence, which she used.

'Please take them away from me,' she begged, giving him the earthenware pot in which there were now only a few sweetmeats left.

'Eat eat,' he said indulgently. He took out another sweetmeat a offered it to her between finger and thumb. 'No,' she said. 'Yes,' said, and gently forced it between her lips. She ate with relish, moaning. 'I have had too many already.' He kissed her cheek and then her neck. She did not push him away, nor did he feel at all ashamed, though it was daytime.

Then there was a loud knock on the outer door and a voice call 'Telegram!' Prem started up and took it and tore it open. He went back into the bedroom and told her: 'My mother is coming this evening on the Punjab Mail.'

'Oh,' she said. And he, too, to his surprise, found he was not as pleased as he thought he would have been.

'Be careful with that jar,' Prem's mother said. 'It is your favourite pickle.' Prem smiled rather sheepishly, and helped her to climb in the tonga. 'Are all my things here?' she asked. 'They won't fall out?' She had a lot of baggage: there was a steel trunk with a big padlock it, a roll of bedding, a great number of cloth bundles tied with thick string, a basket and an earthenware water-container. Prem did his best to accommodate all these things safely in the tonga, while the tonga-driver sat perched up on his seat, with his whip in his hand,

and watched him. The horse stood with its head patiently lowered and the porter stood waiting for his money.

At last they started off and Prem's mother asked, 'How much did you pay him?' When Prem told her, she said, 'That is too much. I never give more than two annas to a porter. They don't expect more.' Prem said nothing, only lowered his eyes as if he felt the justice of her rebuke. 'You must learn not to be extravagant,' she said. 'Now that you will soon have a family of your own.'

When they got home, she looked Indu up and down. 'You don't show,' she said, almost accusingly.

Indu turned away her face and drew up her sari to hide her bashful look. Prem hovered around them; he felt nervous, without quite knowing why.

Prem's mother sighed and said, 'May it be a healthy boy.'

A string-cot had been put up for her in the living-room, and she had soon accommodated herself, her steel trunk, her earthenware water-container and her basket. She sat on the bed and began to untie her many cloth bundles. There were Prem's favourite biscuits, pickles, chutneys, guava cheese, sherbet – all of which she had made at home for him before she came. As she unpacked and displayed them, she sighed, 'I know how much you like these things.' Her sigh at once made clear the infinite labour she had undergone in the preparation of them.

Indu went to bed early. Prem was tired and would have liked to follow her soon after, but his mother had a lot to tell him. She gave him all the news about his four sisters and complained about her four sons-in-law. One did not earn enough, another spent too much time at the Club, the third expected his wife to massage his legs every evening, the fourth made too many children. All of them were lacking in respect towards their mother-in-law. 'If your father had been alive,' she kept saying, 'things would have been different'; and she wiped her eyes with a corner of her sari.

Prem's sisters were all considerably older than he was, and though he was fond of them, he was not as interested in their affairs as his mother's lengthy recital assumed. On the other hand, he very much wanted to know about some other aspects of his Ankhpur life, but when he asked about these, she was not able to give him any information. 'And Rajinder – he is still in his uncle's business?' 'Have they made Ganpat's marriage yet?' 'Has the new cinema been opened?' 'Who has replaced Mr Williams as station-master?' To almost every question he asked, she pursed her mouth and said, 'What do I know of these things?'

Besides his sisters and their families, the only other topic on which she cared to dwell was that of Ankhpur College and its Principal. 'Things are becoming worse and worse,' she reported. 'He is ruining that college. All your father's lifework he is undoing.' Prem shook his head and tried to look troubled. Though really he had never had affection for Ankhpur College. It was housed in a grim nineteenth-century Gothic building which had once been the municipal offices and its main purpose was to turn out graduates to fill the lower-rank posts in the U.P. Civil Service. 'Just think,' his mother said, 'in this year's B.A. results there was no one in the first division and only four students in the second division!' Prem clicked his tongue, as seemed expected of him. 'What sort of man is he to replace your father?' his mother demanded. 'And his wife …' Here she had a lot more to say. Prem did not listen very carefully. He was wondering when she would allow him to go to bed. Indu was probably asleep by now. At last his mother said, 'Come, son, I have had a tiring journey.' Prem left her and lay down next to Indu in their bedroom. He fell asleep in a somewhat gloomy state of mind.

The following night Indu again went to bed much earlier than she usually did. As soon as she had gone, Prem's mother said in a flat and melancholy way, 'She seems a good girl.' Prem made no comment; as a matter of fact, he felt very much embarrassed and pretended that there was something wrong with the leg of the little cane table which urgently needed his attention.

'I did my best for you, son,' his mother said with a sigh. 'If your father had been alive, perhaps …' and she gave another deeper sigh. Prem turned the table right round and hit at its leg with the flat of his hand.

'Her family could have given you some more things,' she said 'Look at this room – how bare it is …'

Prem mumbled, 'They have given us a bed.'

'*One* bed,' his mother said. She added, 'It is not as if the girl is very pretty.' Prem bent his head lower to hide his flushed face. What could he say?

'And she is not very much educated,' his mother said. She scratched under her bun of hair with her fingernail, then looked at the fingernail as if she expected to find something in it. 'She is not even very good at household duties.'

Prem said in a strangled voice, 'I think I will go to bed. I have to get up early in the morning.'

'My poor son. You work so hard.' She heaved another sigh. 'God's will,' she said, and laid herself sadly to sleep.

Prem very much wanted to say something to Indu. She seemed to be asleep, but he hoped that she was only pretending. 'Listen,' he urgently whispered, and when there was no response: 'Listen, it is very important.' 'What?' she whispered back, rather suspiciously. He tried to think what he could tell her that was of any importance. 'You have not forgotten Sunday the fourth,' he finally said.

'What?' she said sleepily.

'Sunday the fourth – the Principal's tea-party.'

'You have woken me up because of that?'

'You don't understand – it is very important. You see, we must make a good impression so that Mr Khanna will give us –'

'Please let me sleep.'

'Listen to me.'

'Son?' inquired Prem's mother from thc living-room. Prem sank back on to the pillow. Indu flung herself to the extreme edge of the bed, where she again pretended to be asleep.

'Son? Is something wrong?' Prem shut his eyes and kept silent. 'Shall I come, son?'

'We are sleeping, Mother!'

There was a slight mutter from the living-room, then silence. Prem did not dare talk again to Indu. He could only lie there, feeling guilty towards her; he knew he should have said something to his mother to let her know that Indu was not such an inferior girl as she seemed to suppose.

27 Choose some sentences from the extract which you think are typical of the attitude and behaviour of the three characters towards each other.

a Prem towards Indu
b Indu towards Prem
c Prem towards his mother
d Prem's mother towards Prem
e Indu towards Prem's mother
f Prem's mother towards Indu

28 How would you describe their attitudes and behaviour in the sentences you chose in Exercise 27? Choose some expressions from the box below, or add ideas of your own.

sulky embarrassed apologetic reluctant in praise awkward concerned petulant generous indulgent a martyr critical complaining interfering bossy guilty always comparing the past to the present*

*a martyr = a person who suffers to gain admiration or sympathy

29 What do you think the characters might be thinking at these moments? (Follow the same procedure as in Exercise 17.)

a **Indu**: Only her lips tightened, and she leant forward to peer into the pot in which she was stirring. (lines 10–11)

b **Prem's mother**: When they got home, she looked Indu up and down. ... Prem's mother sighed and said, 'May it be a healthy boy.' (lines 101–6)

c **Prem**: Prem said in a strangled voice, 'I think I will go to bed. I have to get up early in the morning.' (lines 173–4)

d Choose one or two other moments for each of the characters and suggest what they might be thinking. Compare your ideas with a partner.

30 **Pair/group work**: Discuss these questions. (You may want to use ideas you had in Exercises 27–9.)

a Which of the three characters do feel most sympathy with? Why?

b Would you criticize any of the three characters? If so, why?

c Do you think the characters and situation are realistic and true-to-life, or stereotypical?

d Do you find the extract amusing, amusing with moments of sadness, ... or do you have another reaction?

31 Do you think that Prem's and Indu's relationship will survive the visit of Prem's mother, and the other problems they have? Check your answers with the Key.

32 *a* Compare the two extracts from *The Joy Luck Club* and *The Householder* in any way you like. Follow up any of these ideas, or choose your own points of comparison.

themes	family life, marriage, differences between generations, family loyalties, ...
narrative structure	narrator and point of view, suspense and surprise
characterization	use of physical details, conversation, actions, thoughts, ...
feelings	humour, pathos, passion, ...
setting	representation of culture, life-style, ...
style	use of language, syntax, ...

b Which passage do you prefer? Give your reasons.

Authors

Amy Tan was born in 1952 in Oakland, California, two and and half years after her Chinese parents, John and Daisy Tan, had emigrated to the United States. Like the parents represented in *The Joy Luck Club*, Tan's parents had great ambitions for their daughter – they wanted her to become a neurosurgeon, and a concert pianist in her spare time! Rebelling against her parents' expectations, Tan studied English and linguistics at San José University, started a doctorate at the Univeristy of Berkeley, California, but dropped out in 1976. She worked as a consultant on programmes for disabled children until 1981, and then became a highly succesful freelance business writer for six years. Fearing she was becoming a workaholic – she was working 90 hours a week – and dissatisfied with the professional therapy she received, she took up jazz piano lessons and writing short stories. She visited China for the first time with her mother in 1987, where she felt 'a sense of completeness, like having a mother and a father ... it was instant bonding, ... there was something about this country that I belonged to'. Her short story writing and the visit to China resulted in *The Joy Luck Club* (1989), which was an immediate success with both public and critics (it has been translated into 17 languages, including Chinese). She followed this up with a well-received second novel, *The Kitchen God's Wife* (1991). Her latest book is *The Hundred Secret Senses* (1996).

Two themes run through Tan's writing: tensions between generations and differences between cultures. As regards culture, Tan has said that although she once tried to distance herself from her ethnic background, writing *The Joy Luck Club* helped her discover 'How very Chinese I was. And how much had stayed with me that I had tried to deny'. As regards generations, one critic has said about *The Joy Luck Club*: 'These moving and powerful stories share the irony, pain, and sorrow of the imperfect ways in which mothers and daughters love each other.' *The Joy Luck Club* is set in San Francisco in the late 1980s: four Chinese mothers, immigrants in the USA, had set up a kind of social club for themselves, 'The Joy Luck Club', and now try to involve their Americanized daughters in it. The sixteen interrelated stories that make up the novel, told by the four mothers and their daughters, describe the expectations and disappointments of the mothers, and the initial impatience and rejection of the daughters, who gradually come to realize the suffering their mothers have experienced and the strength they have shown.

Ruth Prawer Jhabvala was born in Germany in 1927 to Polish parents. Her family came to England in 1939 as refugees, and she was educated in London. After graduating from London University, she married an Indian architect and went to live in Delhi in 1951, where she stayed for twenty-four years. Since 1975 she has divided her time between New York, London and Delhi.

Apart from the novel *In Search of Love and Beauty* (1983), which is set in New York, most of her fiction relates to India, whose inhabitants – both Indian and European – she views with a mixture of affection and impatience from the viewpoint of an informed outsider. Significant novels include *To Whom She Will* (1955), *Esmond in India* (1958), *The Householder* (1960), *A New Dominion* (1973), and *Heat and Dust* (1975), which won the Booker Prize. Her most recent novels are *Three Continents*, *Poet and Dancer* and *Shards of Memory*. She has also written four volumes of short stories, from which she has made her own selection of favourites, published as *Out of India*.

She is equally well known as a film scriptwriter, collaborating with the producer-director team Ishmael Merchant and James Ivory. An original screenplay was *Shakespeare Wallah* (1965), about a group of travelling actors in India, while her adaptations have included *The Europeans* (1979), *Quartet* (1981), *Heat and Dust* (1982), *The Bostonians* (1984), *A Room with a View* (1985), *Howards End* (1992), and *The Remains of the Day* (1993).

7 Thinking Aloud

Street traders near Nelson's Pillar, Dublin, c 1900

Before you read

1 ***a*** What do you think of when you hear or see the word 'morning'? Make a list of five ideas that come into your head.

b Which of your senses is most sensitive in the morning:
taste touch smell sight hearing
Write down an example or two to show this.

c Write one or two true sentences about your early morning routine that you think other people would find interesting or surprising.

d Now compare your answers with a partner.

2 James Joyce's *Ulysses* describes a day in the lives of two people: Leopold Bloom, a thirty-eight-year old salesman of advertising space, and Stephen Dedalus, a young writer.
In the following extract, the beginning of Chapter 4, we meet Bloom for the first time. The setting is his home in Dublin. It is 8 o'clock in the morning, 16 June 1904. Read the following summary of the first part of the extract. Is there anything in it which is similar to your early morning routine? Are there any great differences?

lines	*summary*
1–5	A description of what Bloom likes to eat.
6–14	Bloom, thinking of breakfast, cuts bread and butter for his wife, Molly, and puts the kettle on to boil.
15–45	Bloom 'talks' with his cat. He speculates about the nature of cats while he gives her some milk.
46–52	While the cat is having the milk, Bloom decides on a pork kidney for breakfast.
53–61	Bloom goes upstairs and asks Molly if she wants anything special for breakfast. She doesn't.
62–70	Molly turning over makes the bed jingle. The noise reminds Bloom of where the old-fashioned bed came from – Gibraltar. He thinks of Molly's childhood there, and of her father, an army officer (and an astute investor in stamps) who bought the bed.
71–6	Bloom gets his hat, and checks if he has the receipt that he needs to collect a letter from the Post Office later that day. (He has been secretly corresponding with a woman he contacted through the 'lonely hearts' column of the *Irish Times*.)
77–82	Bloom realizes his key is in another pair of trousers in the bedroom, but he does have his 'lucky' potato on him. Not wanting to disturb Molly by opening the wardrobe to get the key, he leaves the front door unlocked but looking closed.

Now read the extract.

Ulysses (1922)
James Joyce

See the Glossary section at the back of the book for vocabulary.

CHAPTER 4

Mr Leopold Bloom ate with relish the inner organs of beasts and fowls. He liked thick giblet soup, nutty gizzards, a stuffed roast heart, liverslices fried with crustcrumbs, fried hencods' roes. Most of all he liked grilled mutton kidneys which gave to his palate a fine tang of faintly scented urine.

Kidneys were in his mind as he moved about the kitchen softly righting her breakfast things on the humpy tray. Gelid light and air were in the kitchen but out of doors gentle summer morning everywhere. Made him feel a bit peckish.

The coals were reddening.

Another slice of bread and butter: three, four: right. She didn't like her plate full. Right. He turned from the tray, lifted the kettle off the hob and set it sideways on the fire. It sat there, dull and squat, its spout stuck out. Cup of tea soon. Good. Mouth dry.

The cat walked stiffly round a leg of the table with tail on high.

—Mkgnao!

—O, there you are, Mr Bloom said, turning from the fire.

The cat mewed in answer and stalked again stiffly round a leg of the table, mewing. Just how she stalks over my writingtable. Prr. Scratch my head. Prr.

Mr Bloom watched curiously, kindly the lithe black form. Clean to see: the gloss of her sleek hide, the white button under the butt of her tail, the green flashing eyes. He bent down to her, his hands on his knees.

— Milk for the pussens, he said.

—Mrkgnao! the cat cried.

They call them stupid. They understand what we say better than we understand them. She understands all she wants to. Vindictive too. Cruel. Her nature. Curious mice never squeal. Seem to like it. Wonder what I look like to her. Height of a tower? No, she can jump me.

— Afraid of the chickens she is, he said mockingly. Afraid of the chookchooks. I never saw such a stupid pussens as the pussens.

– Mrkrgnao! the cat said loudly.

She blinked up out of her avid shameclosing eyes, mewing plaintively and long, showing him her milkwhite teeth. He watched the dark eyeslits narrowing with greed till her eyes were green stones. Then he went to the dresser, took the jug Hanlon's milkman had just filled for him, poured warmbubbled milk on a saucer and set it slowly on the floor.

—Gurrhr! she cried, running to lap.

He watched the bristles shining wirily in the weak light as she tipped three times and licked lightly. Wonder is it true if you clip them they can't mouse after. Why? They shine in the dark, perhaps, the tips. Or kind of feelers in the dark, perhaps.

He listened to her licking lap. Ham and eggs, no. No good eggs with this drouth. Want pure fresh water. Thursday: not a good day either for a mutton kidney at Buckley's. Fried with butter, a shake of pepper. Better a pork kidney at Dlugacz's. While the kettle is boiling. She lapped slower, then licking the saucer clean. Why are their tongues so rough? To lap better, all porous holes. Nothing she can eat? He glanced round him. No.

On quietly creaky boots he went up the staircase to the hall, paused by the bedroom door. She might like something tasty. Thin bread and butter she likes in the morning. Still perhaps: once in a way.

He said softly in the bare hall:

—I'm going round the corner. Be back in a minute.

And when he had heard his voice say it he added:

—You don't want anything for breakfast?

A sleepy soft grunt answered:

—Mn.

No. She didn't want anything. He heard then a warm heavy sigh, softer, as she turned over and the loose brass quoits of the bedstead jingled. Must get those settled really. Pity. All the way from Gibraltar. Forgotten any little Spanish she knew. Wonder what her father gave for it. Old style. Ah yes! of course. Bought it at the governor's auction. Got a short knock. Hard as nails at a bargain, old Tweedy. Yes, sir. At Plevna that was. I rose from the ranks, sir, and I'm proud of it. Still he had brains enough to make that corner in stamps. Now that was farseeing.

His hand took his hat from the peg over his initialled heavy overcoat and his lost property office secondhand waterproof. Stamps: stickyback pictures. Daresay lots of officers are in the swim too. Course they do. The sweated legend in the crown of his hat told him mutely: Plasto's high grade ha. He peeped quickly inside the leather headband. White slip of paper. Quite safe.

On the doorstep he felt in his hip pocket for the latchkey. Not there. In the trousers I left off. Must get it. Potato I have. Creaky wardrobe. No use disturbing her. She turned over sleepily that time. He pulled the halldoor to after him very quietly, more, till the footleaf dropped gently over the threshold, a limp lid. Looked shut. All right till I come back anyhow.

Bloom's relish for 'inner organs', his behaviour with the cat, his behaviour towards his wife, his secret correspondence, his 'lucky' potato: which aspect of Bloom have you found most striking so far?

He crossed to the bright side, avoiding the loose cellarflap of number seventyfive. The sun was nearing the steeple of George's church. Be a warm day I fancy. Specially in these black clothes feel it more. Black conducts, reflects, (refracts is it?), the heat. But I couldn't go in that light suit. Make a picnic of it. His eyelids sank quietly often as he walked in happy warmth. Boland's breadvan delivering with trays our daily but she prefers yesterday's loaves turnovers crisp crowns hot. Makes you feel young. Somewhere in the east: early morning: set off at dawn. Travel round in front of the sun, steal a day's march on him. Keep it up for ever never grow a day older technically. Walk along a strand, strange land, come to a city gate, sentry there, old ranker too, old Tweedy's big moustaches, leaning on a long kind of a spear. Wander through awned streets. Turbaned faces going by. Dark caves of carpet shops, big man, Turko the terrible, seated crosslegged, smoking a coiled pipe. Cries of sellers in the streets. Drink water scented with fennel, sherbet. Dander along all day. Might meet a robber or two. Well, meet him. Getting on to sundown. The shadows of the mosques among the pillars: priest with a scroll rolled up. A shiver of the trees, signal, the evening wind. I pass on. Fading gold sky. A mother watches me from her doorway. She calls her children home in their dark language. High wall: beyond strings twanged. Night sky, moon, violet colour of Molly's new garters. Strings. Listen. A girl playing one of those instruments what do you call them: dulcimers. I pass.

Probably not a bit like it really. Kind of stuff you read: in the track of the sun. Sunburst on the titlepage. He smiled, pleasing himself. What Arthur Griffith said about the headpiece over the *Freeman* leader: a homerule sun rising up in the northwest from the laneway behind the bank of Ireland. He prolonged his pleased smile. Ikey touch that: homerule sun rising up in the northwest.

He approached Larry O'Rourke's. From the cellar grating floated up the flabby gush of porter. Through the open doorway the bar squirted out whiffs of ginger, teadust, biscuitmush. Good house, however: just the end of the city traffic. For instance M'Auley's down there: n. g. as position. Of course if they ran a tramline along the North Circular from the cattlemarket to the quays value would go up like a shot.

Baldhead over the blind. Cute old codger. No use canvassing him for an ad. Still he knows his own business best. There he is, sure enough, my bold Larry, leaning against the sugarbin in his shirtsleeves watching the aproned curate swab up with mop and bucket. Simon Dedalus takes him off to a tee with his eyes screwed up. Do you know what I'm going to tell you? What's that, Mr O'Rourke? Do you know what? The Russians they'd only be an eight o'clock breakfast for the Japanese.

Stop and say a word: about the funeral perhaps. Sad thing about poor Dignam, Mr O'Rourke.

Turning into Dorset street he said freshly in greeting through the doorway:

— Good day, Mr O'Rourke.

— Good day to you.

— Lovely weather, sir.

— 'Tis all that.

Where do they get the money? Coming up redheaded curates from the county Leitrim, rinsing empties and old man in the cellar. Then, lo and behold, they blossom out as Adam Findlaters or Dan Tallons. Then think of the competition. General thirst. Good puzzle would be cross Dublin without passing a pub. Save it they can't. Off the drunks perhaps. Put down three and carry five. What is that, a bob here and there, dribs and drabs. On the wholesale orders perhaps. Doing a double shuffle with the town travellers. Square it you with the boss and we'll split the job, see?

How much would that tot to off the porter in the month? Say ten barrels of stuff. Say he got ten per cent off. O more. Fifteen. He passed Saint Joseph's National school. Brats' clamour. Windows open. Fresh air helps memory. Or a lilt. Ahbeesee defeegee kelomen opeecue rustyouvee doubleyou. Boys are they? Yes. Inishturk. Inishark. Inishboffin. At their joggerfry. Mine. Slieve Bloom.

He halted before Dlugacz's window, staring at the hanks of sausages, polonies, black and white. Fifteen multiplied by. The figures whitened in his mind, unsolved: displeased, he let them fade. The shiny links, packed with forcemeat, fed his gaze and he breathed in tranquilly the lukewarm breath of cooked spicy pigs' blood.

A kidney oozed bloodgouts on the willowpatterned dish: the last.

He stood by the nextdoor girl at the counter. Would she buy it too, calling the items from a slip in her hand? Chapped: washingsoda. And a pound and a half of Denny's sausages. His eyes rested on her vigorous hips. Woods his name is. Wonder what he does. Wife is oldish. New blood. No followers allowed. Strong pair of arms. Whacking a carpet on the clothesline. She does whack it, by George. The way her crooked skirt swings at each whack.

The ferreteyed porkbutcher folded the sausages he had snipped off with blotchy fingers, sausagepink. Sound meat there: like a stallfed heifer.

He took a page up from the pile of cut sheets: the model farm at Kinnereth on the lakeshore of Tiberias. Can become ideal winter sanatorium. Moses Montefiore. I thought he was. Farmhouse, wall round it, blurred cattle cropping. He held the page from him: interesting: read it nearer, the title, the blurred cropping cattle, the page rustling. A young white heifer. Those mornings in the cattlemarket, the beasts lowing in their pens, branded sheep, flop and fall of dung, the breeders in hobnailed boots trudging through the litter, slapping a palm on a ripemeated hindquarter, there's a prime one, unpeeled switches in their hands. He held the page aslant patiently, bending his senses and his will, his soft subject gaze at rest. The crooked skirt swinging, whack by whack by whack.

The porkbutcher snapped two sheets from the pile, wrapped up her prime sausages and made a red grimace.

—Now, my miss, he said.

She tendered a coin, smiling boldly, holding her thick wrist out.

—Thank you, my miss. And one shilling threepence change. For you, please?

Which do you think now occupies first place in Bloom's mind: the pork kidney, or the girl from next door?

Mr Bloom pointed quickly. To catch up and walk behind her if she went slowly, behind her moving hams. Pleasant to see first thing in the morning. Hurry up, damn it. Make hay while the sun shines. She stood outside the shop in sunlight and sauntered lazily to the right. He sighed down his nose: they never understand. Sodachapped hands. Crusted toenails too. Brown scapulars in tatters, defending her both ways. The sting of disregard glowed to weak pleasure within his breast. For another: constable off duty cuddling her in Eccles lane. They like them sizeable. Prime sausage. O please, Mr Policeman, I'm lost in the wood.

—Threepence, please.

His hand accepted the moist tender gland and slid it into a sidepocket. Then it fetched up three coins from his trousers' pocket and laid them on the rubber prickles. They lay, were read quickly and quickly slid, disc by disc, into the till.

—Thank you, sir. Another time.

A speck of eager fire from foxeyes thanked him. He withdrew his gaze after an instant. No: better not: another time.

—Good morning, he said, moving away.

— Good morning, sir.

No sign. Gone. What matter?

He walked back along Dorset street, reading gravely. Agendath Netaim: planters' company. To purchase waste sandy tracts from Turkish government and plant with eucalyptus trees. Excellent for shade, fuel and construction. Orangegroves and immense melonfields north of Jaffa. You pay eighty marks and they plant a dunam of land for you with olives, oranges, almonds or citrons. Olives cheaper: oranges need artificial irrigation. Every year you get a sending of the crop. Your name entered for life as owner in the book of the union. Can pay ten down and the balance in yearly instalments. Bleibtreustrasse 34, Berlin, W. 15.

Nothing doing. Still an idea behind it.

He looked at the cattle, blurred in silver heat. Silverpowdered olivetrees. Quiet long days: pruning, ripening. Olives are packed in jars, eh? I have a few left from Andrews. Molly spitting them out. Knows the taste of them now. Oranges in tissue paper packed in crates. Citrons too. Wonder is poor Citron still in Saint Kevin's parade. And Mastiansky with the old cither. Pleasant evenings we had then. Molly in Citron's basketchair. Nice to hold, cool waxen fruit, hold in the hand, lift it to the nostrils and smell the perfume. Like that, heavy, sweet, wild perfume. Always the same, year after year. They fetched high prices too, Moisel told me. Arbutus place: Pleasants street: pleasant old times. Must be without a flaw, he said. Coming all that way: Spain, Gibraltar, Mediterranean, the Levant. Crates lined up on the quayside at Jaffa, chap ticking them off in a book, navvies handling them barefoot in soiled dungarees. There's whatdoyoucallhim out of. How do you? Doesn't see. Chap you know just to salute bit of a bore. His back is like that Norwegian captain's. Wonder if I'll meet him today. Watering cart. To provoke the rain. On earth as it is in heaven.

A cloud began to cover the sun slowly, wholly. Grey. Far.

No, not like that. A barren land, bare waste. Vulcanic lake, the dead sea: no fish, weedless, sunk deep in the earth. No wind could lift those waves, grey metal, poisonous foggy waters. Brimstone they called it raining down: the cities of the plain: Sodom, Gomorrah, Edom. All dead names. A dead sea in a dead land, grey and old. Old now. It bore the oldest, the first race. A bent hag crossed from Cassidy's, clutching a naggin bottle by the neck. The oldest people. Wandered far away over all the earth, captivity to captivity, multiplying, dying, being born everywhere. It lay there now. Now it could bear no more. Dead: an old woman's: the grey sunken cunt of the world.

Desolation.

Grey horror seared his flesh. Folding the page into his pocket he turned into Eccles street, hurrying homeward. Cold oils slid along his veins, chilling his blood: age crusting him with a salt cloak. Well, I am here now. Yes, I am here now. Morning mouth bad images. Got up wrong side of the bed. Must begin again those Sandow's exercises. On the hands down. Blotchy brown brick houses. Number eighty still unlet. Why is that? Valuation is only twentyeight. Towers, Battersby, North, MacArthur: parlour windows plastered with bills. Plasters on a sore eye. To smell the gentle smoke of tea, fume of the pan, sizzling butter. Be near her ample bedwarmed flesh. Yes, yes.

Quick warm sunlight came running from Berkeley road, swiftly, in slim sandals, along the brightening footpath. Runs, she runs to meet me, a girl with gold hair on the wind.

Two letters and a card lay on the hallfloor. He stooped and gathered them. Mrs Marion Bloom. His quickened heart slowed at once. Bold hand. Mrs Marion.

—Poldy!

Entering the bedroom he halfclosed his eyes and walked through warm yellow twilight towards her tousled head.

—Who are the letters for?

He looked at them. Mullingar. Milly.

—A letter for me from Milly, he said carefully, and a card to you. And a letter for you.

He laid her card and letter on the twill bedspread near the curve of her knees.

—Do you want the blind up?

Letting the blind up by gentle tugs halfway his backward eye saw her glance at the letter and tuck it under her pillow.

Why do you think Molly tucks the letter under her pillow?

—That do? he asked, turning.

She was reading the card, propped on her elbow.

—She got the things, she said.

He waited till she had laid the card aside and curled herself back slowly with a snug sigh.

—Hurry up with that tea, she said. I'm parched.

—The kettle is boiling, he said.

But he delayed to clear the chair: her striped petticoat, tossed soiled linen: and lifted all in an armful on to the foot of the bed.

As he went down the kitchen stairs she called:

—Poldy!

—What?

—Scald the teapot.

On the boil sure enough: a plume of steam from the spout. He scalded and rinsed out the teapot and put in four full spoons of tea, tilting the kettle then to let the water flow in. Having set it to draw he took off the kettle, crushed the pan flat on the live coals and watched the lump of butter slide and melt. While he unwrapped the kidney the cat mewed hungrily against him. Give her too much meat she won't mouse. Say they won't eat pork. Kosher. Here. He let the bloodsmeared paper fall to her and dropped the kidney amid the sizzling butter sauce. Pepper. He sprinkled it through his fingers ringwise from the chipped eggcup.

Then he slit open his letter, glancing down the page and over. Thanks: new tam: Mr Coghlan: lough Owel picnic: young student: Blazes Boylan's seaside girls.

The tea was drawn. He filled his own moustachecup, sham crown Derby, smiling. Silly Milly's birthday gift. Only five she was then. No, wait: four. I gave her the amberoid necklace she broke. Putting pieces of folded brown paper in the letterbox for her. He smiled, pouring.

O, Milly Bloom, you are my darling.
You are my lookingglass from night to morning.
I'd rather have you without a farthing
Than Katey Keogh with her ass and garden.

Poor old professor Goodwin. Dreadful old case. Still he was a courteous old chap. Oldfashioned way he used to bow Molly off the platform. And the little mirror in his silk hat. The night Milly brought it into the parlour. O, look what I found in professor Goodwin's hat! All we laughed. Sex breaking out even then. Pert little piece she was.

He prodded a fork into the kidney and slapped it over: then fitted the teapot on the tray. Its hump bumped as he took it up. Everything on it? Bread and butter, four, sugar, spoon, her cream. Yes. He carried it upstairs, his thumb hooked in the teapot handle.

Nudging the door open with his knee he carried the tray in and set it on the chair by the bedhead.

—What a time you were! she said.

She set the brasses jingling as she raised herself briskly, an elbow on the pillow. He looked calmly down on her bulk and between her large soft bubs, sloping within her nightdress like a shegoat's udder. The warmth of her couched body rose on the air, mingling with the fragrance of the tea she poured.

A strip of torn envelope peeped from under the dimpled pillow. In the act of going he stayed to straighten the bedspread.

—Who was the letter from? he asked.

Bold hand. Marion.

—O, Boylan, she said. He's bringing the programme.

—What are you singing?

—*Là ci darem* with J. C. Doyle, she said, and *Love's Old Sweet Song*.

Her full lips, drinking, smiled. Rather stale smell that incense leaves next day. Like foul flowerwater.

—Would you like the window open a little?

She doubled a slice of bread into her mouth, asking:

—What time is the funeral?

—Eleven, I think, he answered. I didn't see the paper.

Following the pointing of her finger he took up a leg of her soiled drawers from the bed. No? Then, a twisted grey garter looped round a stocking: rumpled, shiny sole.

—No: that book.

Other stocking. Her petticoat.

—It must have fell down, she said.

He felt here and there. *Voglio e non vorrei.* Wonder if she pronounces that right: *voglio*. Not in the bed. Must have slid down. He stooped and lifted the valance. The book, fallen, sprawled against the bulge of the orangekeyed chamberpot.

—Show here, she said. I put a mark in it. There's a word I wanted to ask you.

What kind of book do you think Molly has been reading?

She swallowed a draught of tea from her cup held by nothandle and, having wiped her fingertips smartly on the blanket, began to search the text with the hairpin till she reached the word.

—Met him what? he asked.

—Here, she said. What does that mean?

He leaned downward and read near her polished thumbnail.

—Metempsychosis?

—Yes. Who's he when he's at home?

—Metempsychosis, he said, frowning. It's Greek: from the Greek. That means the transmigration of souls.

—O rocks! she said. Tell us in plain words.

He smiled, glancing askance at her mocking eyes. The same young eyes. The first night after the charades. Dolphin's Barn. He turned over the smudged pages. *Ruby: the Pride of the Ring*. Hello. Illustration. Fierce Italian with carriagewhip. Must be Ruby pride of the on the floor naked. Sheet kindly lent. *The monster Maffei desisted and flung his victim from him with an oath*. Cruelty behind it all. Doped animals. Trapeze at Hengler's. Had to look the other way. Mob gaping. Break your neck and we'll break our sides. Families of them. Bone them young so they metamspychosis. That we live after death. Our souls. That a man's soul after he dies, Dignam's soul. …

—Did you finish it? he asked.

—Yes, she said. There's nothing smutty in it. Is she in love with the first fellow all the time?

—Never read it. Do you want another?

— Yes. Get another of Paul de Kock's. Nice name he has.

She poured more tea into her cup, watching it flow sideways.

Must get that Capel street library book renewed or they'll write to Kearney, my guarantor. Reincarnation: that's the word.

— Some people believe, he said, that we go on living in another body after death, that we lived before. They call it reincarnation. That we all lived before on the earth thousands of years ago or some other planet. They say we have forgotten it. Some say they remember their past lives.

The sluggish cream wound curdling spirals through her tea. Better remind her of the word: metempsychosis. An example would be better. An example?

The Bath of the Nymph over the bed. Given away with the Easter number of *Photo Bits*: splendid masterpiece in art colours. Tea before you put milk in. Not unlike her with her hair down: slimmer. Three and six I gave for the frame. She said it would look nice over the bed. Naked nymphs: Greece: and for instance all the people that lived then.

He turned the pages back.

—Metempsychosis, he said, is what the ancient Greeks called it. They used to believe you could be changed into an animal or a tree, for instance. What they called nymphs, for example.

Her spoon ceased to stir up the sugar. She gazed straight before her, inhaling through her arched nostrils.

—There's a smell of burn, she said. Did you leave anything on the fire?

—The kidney! he cried suddenly.

First reaction

3 What is your impression of the Blooms' marriage?

Close reading

4 Look at lines 83–150. Match the line references with the summaries. The first one is done for you.

lines			*summary*
83–90	*e*	***a***	Bloom approaches Larry O'Rourke's place (a combination of pub and shop) and reflects that it is better placed for business than M'Auley's. He exchanges a few words with O'Rourke.
90–106	___	***b***	Bloom wonders how young barmen manage to become owners of their own pubs in such a short time, and speculates about how they make their money.
107–12	___	***c***	Bloom daydreams about a journey in the Orient.
113–35	___	***d***	Bloom passes a school and hears the children reciting their alphabet and Irish geography.
136–46	___	***e***	Bloom crosses to the sunny side of the street, enjoying the warm weather.
146–50	___	***f***	Bloom remembers a witty comment by a politician making fun of a patriotic symbol above the leading article of a newspaper.

5 Now look at lines 151–205 and lines 206–62. Put the following summaries in order. The first ones are done for you.
At the shop (lines 151–205)

- ***a*** Bloom, fantasizing about the servant girl, hopes to follow her. He puts off talking to the butcher about their common background (both come from families of Hungarian Jewish immigrants).
- ***b*** The butcher finishes serving the servant girl, and turns his attention to Bloom.
- ***c*** Bloom watches – appreciatively – his next-door neighbour's servant buying sausages.
- ***d*** Bloom looks in the shop window.

e Bloom picks up a page from a newspaper with an advertisement for a model farm in Palestine, which reminds him of when he used to work in the cattle business.

1 ***d*** 2 ___ 3 ___ 4 ___ 5 ___

On the way back from the shop (lines 206–62)

f The sun comes out, Bloom sees a pretty girl, and he feels better.
g Bloom vaguely recognizes someone. He then makes an ironic mental comment about a watering cart that is passing by.
h The servant girl has gone, so Bloom reads another advertisement for a profit-sharing farm in Palestine while walking along the street.
i Bloom concentrates on resolutions about starting exercises again, noticing the property to let, and looking forward to the comforts of home.
j The sun goes behind a cloud, and Bloom has darker, nightmarish visions of Palestine. Seeing an old woman makes him even more depressed.
k Visions of olive trees on the farm lead him to remember old times, old friends, and have more daydreams about the East.

1 ***h*** 2 ___ 3 ___ 4 ___ 5 ___ 6 ___

6 Look at lines 263–407. In each of the following *two* exercises two statements are *true* and *two* are *false*. Write **True** or **False** next to each one and discuss your choices with a partner before checking with the Key.

a ***1*** Milly writes to thank her father for a new necklace. ______
2 Milly has received some presents from her parents. ______
3 Milly does not seem to be enjoying herself in Mullingar. ______
4 Milly has written to both her parents. ______

b Blazes Boylan is
1 Milly's boyfriend. ______
2 a concert manager. ______
3 Molly's lover. ______
4 someone only Molly knows. ______

Characterization

7 ***a*** Joyce wanted Bloom to be average and ordinary, but complete and 'all-round' at the same time. A friend of Joyce, Frank Budgen, defined Bloom like this:
'Bloom is son, father, husband, lover, friend, worker and citizen.'
Which of these roles do you remember most from the extract? Put them in the appropriate circles and discuss your answer with a partner.

b Would you add anything to Frank Budgen's description of Bloom?

8 Read the following passage from Budgen's book about Joyce.

> 'In the course of many talks with Joyce in Zurich I found that for him human character was best displayed ... in the commonest acts of life. How a man ties his shoelaces or how he eats his egg will give a better clue to his differentiation than how he goes forth to war. Cutting bread displays character better than cutting throats. ... Character, in short, lay not in the doing or not doing of a grand action, but in the peculiar and personal manner of performing a simple one. It lay also in a man's preferences. Does he prefer dogs to cats or does he detest or like both equally? Is he an amateur of beefsteaks, or does he, like Mr Bloom, eat "with relish the inner organs of beasts and fowls"?'
>
> Frank Budgen, *James Joyce and the Making of 'Ulysses'*

a Budgen mentions three 'commonest acts of life' which are not seen in the extract from *Ulysses* you have read. What are they?

b Think of three other 'commonest acts of life' to replace them, so that Budgen's comment describes more closely the extract you have read.

9 Look at the following moments from lines 1–247, and for each make brief notes about what they suggest to you about Bloom's character.

Example: Mr Leopold Bloom ate with relish the inner organs of beasts and fowls. ... which gave to his palate a fine tang of faintly scented urine. (lines 1–5)

Bloom is a man with appetite, and he particularly enjoys meat with a strong flavour. His taste might well be considered 'unrefined' or 'unsophisticated' by some people, and might suggest an interest in things conventionally regarded as 'sordid'.

a Mr Bloom watched curiously, kindly the lithe black form. ... – Milk for the pussens, he said. (lines 21–5)

____

____

b On quietly creaky boots he went up the staircase to the hall, paused by the bedroom door. She might like something tasty. (lines 53–4)

c His hand took his hat from the peg over his initialled heavy overcoat and his lost property office secondhand waterproof. (lines 71–2)

d Somewhere in the east: early morning: set off at dawn. ... Probably not a bit like it really. Kind of stuff you read: ... (lines 90–107)

e Good house, however: just the end of the city traffic. For instance M'Auley's down there: n.g. as position. Of course if they ran a tramline along the North Circular from the cattlemarket to the quays value would go up like a shot. (lines 115–19)

f Stop and say a word: about the funeral perhaps. Sad thing about poor Dignam, Mr O'Rourke. (lines 128–9)

g To catch up and walk behind her if she went slowly, behind her moving hams. Pleasant to see first thing in the morning. (lines 186–8)

h The oldest people. Wandered far away all over the earth, captivity to captivity, multiplying, dying, being born everywhere. It lay there now. Now it could bear no more. Dead: .... (lines 243–6)

10 Choose one of these passages from the extract: lines 248–311 or lines 312–76. Note down some other characteristics of Bloom.

11 Use your ideas from Exercises 9 and 10 and fill in the following chart. Compare your finished chart with a partner's.

THINGS I FIND ATTRACTIVE ABOUT BLOOM	THINGS I FIND UNATTRACTIVE ABOUT BLOOM

12 **Pair work**: For each of the following activities, compare your ideas with a partner.

a Choose some key sentences from the passage about Molly Bloom (lines 276–398), then make notes to interpret them as you did in Exercises 9 and 10.

b Make a chart for Molly as you did for Bloom in Exercise 11.

c Look back to Budgen's definitions of Bloom's roles in Exercise 7. Suggest one or two definitions of Molly's role.

13 Joyce called his novel *Ulysses* because he intended the characters and events to have parallels with Homer's *Odyssey*: Bloom, for example, is a version of Odysseus himself (called 'Ulysses' in Latin). Chapter 4 is related to the 'Calypso' episode in the *Odyssey*: Calypso is a sea nymph who falls in love with Odysseus and keeps him captive as her lover for seven years on the island of Ogygia. Can you think of any possible parallels between the extract from Chapter 4 and the Calypso episode in the *Odyssey*?

14 Draw sketches of Leopold and Molly Bloom, or find pictures of people (from magazines, etc) that you think they might look like. Discuss your impressions with other members of the class.

Language practice – structures

Elliptical sentences

15 a In this chapter from *Ulysses* there are two main **narrators** and two main **points of view** (see Chapter 1, *Anatomy of a Novel*, pages 15–19, if you want to check these terms):

1) A **third-person narrator**: descriptions are from an omniscient point of view.
   Examples: the opening paragraph (lines 1–5); lines 35–40.
   The sentences are grammatically complete. The third person is used to refer to Bloom. The vocabulary is often more sophisticated than in 2 below.
2) Bloom's **interior monologue**: descriptions are from Bloom's point of view.

Example: 'Wonder what I look like to her? Height of a tower? No, she can jump me.' (lines 30–1)
The sentences are often **elliptical**. 'Elliptical' means grammatically incomplete: articles, pronouns, auxiliary verbs or connecting words are omitted. Another feature of interior monologue is the occasional reversal of normal order to put the immediate thought first: for example, 'Thin bread and butter she likes in the morning.' (lines 54–5)

b Mark each of the following sentences 1 or 2 to indicate the two different narrators and points of view. The first two are done for you.

He peeped quickly inside the leather headband. (1) White slip of paper. (2) Quite safe. ( ) On the doorstep he felt in his hip pocket for the latchkey. ( ) Not there. ( ) In the trousers I left off. ( ) Must get it. ( ) Potato I have. ( ) Creaky wardrobe. ( ) No use disturbing her. ( ) She turned over sleepily that time. ( ) He pulled the halldoor to after him very quietly, more, till the footleaf dropped gently over the threshold, a limp lid. ( ) (lines 75–81)

c Choose another paragraph and analyze it in the same way.

16 Convert the following elliptical sentences into grammatically complete sentences and try to make any logical connections explicit. (You may need to look back at the context of some of the sentences.) Make any changes necessary, such as adding words, changing punctuation, combining sentences.

Example: Vindictive too. Cruel. Her nature. Curious mice never squeal. Seem to like it. Wonder what I look like to her. Height of a tower? (lines 28–30)

She's vindictive, too, and cruel. But that's only her nature. It's curious that mice never squeal when she catches them. They seem to like it. I wonder what I look like to her? Perhaps I seem the height of a tower?

a Still perhaps: once in a way (line 55)
b Must get those settled really. Pity. All the way from Gibraltar. Forgotten any little Spanish she knew. Wonder what her father gave for it. Old style. (lines 64–6)
c White slip of paper. Quite safe. (line 76)
d Not there. In the trousers I left off. Must get it. Potato I have. Creaky wardrobe. No use disturbing her. (lines 77–9)
e Make a picnic of it. (line 87)
f Good house, however: just the end of the city traffic. For instance M'Auley's down there: n.g. as position. (lines 115–17)
g No: better not: another time. (line 203)
h No sign. Gone. What matter? (line 206)
i How do you? (line 232)
j No, not like that. (line 237)
k Oldfashioned way he used to bow Molly off the platform. And the little

mirror in his silk hat. The night Milly brought it into the parlour. (lines 313–15)

l The same young eyes. The first night after the charades. Dolphin's Barn. (lines 366–7)

m Cruelty behind it all. Doped animals. Trapeze at Hengler's. Had to look the other way. Mob gaping. Break your neck and we'll break our sides. (lines 371–3)

n Tea before you put milk in. Not unlike her with her hair down: slimmer. (lines 394–6)

17 Joyce once remarked to Budgen 'I try to give the unspoken, unacted thoughts of people in the way they occur'. Compare Joyce's elliptical style of representing Bloom's thoughts with your grammatically complete versions in Exercise 16. Can you think of any reasons why Joyce thought his style might be more successful at representing thoughts?

18 Choose an object or picture and look at it for a while. What thoughts come into your mind?

a Try to write down your flow of thoughts in an interior monologue style (maximum: five lines).

b Exchange what you have written with a partner. The partner changes it into grammatically complete sentences.

c Compare the different versions. Has your partner misinterpreted anything that you were thinking? Are there any other interesting differences?

Language structures – vocabulary

Describing sense impressions

19 For each of the following say which of Bloom's senses – sight, smell, taste, hearing, touch – is involved. (You can choose more than one in each case.)

	SENSES
Example: nutty gizzards (line 2)	***taste***
a gelid light and air were in the kitchen (lines 7–8)	________
b the gloss of her sleek hide, the white button under the butt of her tail, the green flashing eyes (lines 22–3)	________
c her licking lap (line 46)	________
d Drink water scented with fennel, sherbet (line 98)	________
e Night sky, moon, violet, colour of Molly's new garters. (lines 104–5)	________
f the bar squirted out whiffs of ginger, teadust, biscuitmush. (lines 114–15)	________

g strings twanged (line 104) ______
h the lukewarm breath of cooked spicy pigs' blood (lines 155–6) ______
i A kidney oozed bloodgouts on the willowpatterned dish (line 157) ______
j Chapped: washingsoda. (line 159) ______
k The porkbutcher snapped two sheets from the pile (line 180) ______
l Blotchy brown brick houses. (line 254) ______
m the gentle smoke of tea, fume of the pan, sizzling butter. (lines 257–8) ______
n he ... walked through warm yellow twilight toward her tousled head. (lines 267–8) ______
o The warmth of her couched body rose on the air, mingling with the fragrance of the tea she had poured. (lines 328–9) ______

20 Find two or three more expressions from the extract involving each of these senses.

sight

______

______

hearing

______

______

smell

______

______

touch

______

______

21 'The porkbutcher ... made a red grimace.' (lines 180–1) What a vivid way to describe a smile! Make a personal list of five expressions you found most vivid in the extract. Explain to a partner what you like about them.

Extension

22 **Discussion**:

a Which of the following views of the Blooms' marriage do you agree with? Add your own ideas to the list if you like.

- stereotyped rather than realistic
- an average and perfectly normal picture
- tender and affectionate
- perhaps an accurate picture of marriage nearly a hundred years ago, but no longer valid
- a very good compromise between two different people
- sexist: Joyce gives a male vision of marriage

b In what way could the Blooms' marriage be better? In what way could it be worse?

23 Joyce once remarked: 'A writer should never write about the extraordinary. That is for the journalist'.

a Think of some other novels you have read. What happens in them? What are they about? Does Joyce's remark apply to them?
b Give your own definition of what a writer should write about.

24 **Writing**: Choose a favourite time of day – it could be as short as five or ten minutes. Think about the following.

- Where are you?
- What are you doing?
- Are you with anyone?
- What do you see?
- What can you smell?
- What can you hear?
- What can you taste, or imagine yourself tasting?
- What do you touch, or imagine yourself touching?
- What thoughts do you have?

Write a description of this moment. You can use the style of *Ulysses* as a model if you like.

25 **Writing**: A *haiku* is a short poem of three lines (five syllables in the first line, seven in the second, five in the third). It originated in Japan, but Modernist poets often imitated the form. It is an impression of a single moment, often depicting sense impressions.
Example: Gentle smoke of tea,
Kidney in sizzling butter –
Bloom's breakfast calls him.

Write a haiku referring to another scene in the extract from *Ulysses*, or one describing your own sense impressions in the morning.

Beyond the text

26 Read the following extract from Samuel Beckett's novel *Molloy*. While you are reading, try to answer these questions.

- ***a*** Do you think it is worth trying to understand all Molloy's schemes for distributing and circulating his stones?
- ***b*** Why do you think these schemes are described in such detail?
- ***c*** What do the final thoughts (lines 187–99) suggest about Molloy?
- ***d*** When you have finished reading, discuss your ideas with a partner.

Molloy (1951)
Samuel Beckett

Beckett's novel consists of the interior monologue of its main character, Molloy. It opens with Molloy in his mother's room, where he has been for one year, although he has no recollection of how he got there. He is writing a story for a mysterious stranger, who comes once a week to collect what he has written. Eventually he escapes from the room and sets off on a journey in search of his mother, although he has no idea where to look. During the course of his search he finds himself at the seaside ...

See the Glossary section at the back of the book for vocabulary.

I took advantage of being at the seaside to lay in a store of sucking-stones. They were pebbles but I call them stones. Yes, on this occasion I laid in a considerable store. I distributed them equally between my four pockets, and sucked them turn and turn about. This raised a problem which I first solved in the following way. I had say sixteen stones, four in each of my four pockets these being the two pockets of my trousers and the two pockets of my greatcoat. Taking a stone from the right pocket of my greatcoat, and putting it in my mouth, I replaced it in the right pocket of my greatcoat by a stone from the right pocket of my trousers, which I replaced by a stone from the left pocket of my trousers, which I replaced by a stone from the left pocket of my greatcoat, which I replaced by the stone which was in my mouth, as soon as I had finished sucking it. Thus there were still four stones in each of my four pockets, but not quite the same stones. And when the desire to suck took hold of me again, I drew again on the right pocket of my greatcoat, certain of not taking the same stone as the last time. And while I sucked it I rearranged the other stones in the way I have just described. And so on. But this solution did not satisfy me fully. For it did not escape me that, by an extraordinary hazard, the four stones circulating thus might always be the same four. In which case, far from sucking the sixteen stones turn and turn about, I was really only sucking four, always the same, turn and turn about. But I shuffled them well in my pockets, before I began to suck, and again, while I sucked, before transferring them, in the hope of obtaining a more general circulation of the stones from pocket to pocket. But this was only a makeshift that could not long content a man like me. So I began to look for something else. And the first thing I hit upon was that I might do better to transfer the stones four by four, instead of one by one, that is to say, during the sucking, to take the three stones remaining in the right pocket of my greatcoat and replace them by the four in the right pocket of my trousers, and these by the four in the left pocket of my trousers, and these by the four in the left pocket of my greatcoat, and finally these by the three from the right pocket of my greatcoat, plus the one, as soon as I had finished sucking it, which was in my mouth. Yes, it seemed to me at first that by so doing I would arrive at a better result. But on further reflection I had to change my mind and confess that the circulation of the stones four by four came to exactly the same thing as their circulation one by one. For if I was certain of finding each time, in the right pocket of my greatcoat, four stones totally different from their immediate predecessors, the possibility nevertheless remained of my always chancing on the same stone, within each group of four, and consequently of my sucking, not the sixteen turn and turn about as I wished, but in fact four only, always the same, turn and turn about. So I had to seek elsewhere than in the mode of circulation. For no matter how I caused the stones to circulate, I always ran the same risk. It was obvious that by increasing the number of my pockets I was bound to increase my chances of enjoying my stones in the way I planned, that is to say one after the other until their number was exhausted. Had I had eight pockets, for example, instead of the four I did have, then even the most diabolical hazard could not have prevented me from sucking at least eight of my sixteen stones, turn and turn about. The truth is I should have needed sixteen pockets in order to be quite easy in my mind. And for a long time I could see no other conclusion than this, that short of having sixteen pockets, each with its stone, I could never reach the goal I had set myself, short of an extraordinary hazard. And if at a pinch I could double the number of my pockets, were it only by dividing each pocket in two, with the help of a few safety-pins let us say, to quadruple them seemed to be more than I could manage. And I did not feel inclined to take all that trouble for a half-measure. For I was beginning to lose all sense of measure, after all this wrestling and wrangling, and to say, All or nothing. And if I was tempted for an instant to establish a more equitable proportion between my stones and my pocket, by reducing the former to the number of the latter, it was only for an instant. For it would have been an admission of defeat. And sitting on the shore, before the sea, the sixteen stones spread out before my eyes, I gazed at them in anger and perplexity. For just as I had difficulty in sitting on a chair, or in an arm-chair, because of my stiff leg you understand, so I had none in sitting on the ground, because of my stiff leg and my stiffening leg, for it was about this time that my good leg, good in the sense that it was not stiff, began to stiffen. I needed a prop under the ham you understand, and even under the whole length of the leg, the prop of the earth. And while I gazed thus at my stones, revolving interminable martingales all equally defective, and crushing handfuls of sand, so that the sand ran through my fingers and fell back on the strand, yes, while thus I lulled my mind and part of my body, one day suddenly it dawned on the former, dimly, that I might perhaps achieve my purpose without increasing the number of my pockets, or reducing the number of my stones, but simply by sacrificing the principle of trim. The meaning of this illumination, which suddenly began to sing within me, like a verse of Isaiah, or of Jeremiah, I did not penetrate at once, and notably the word trim, which I had never met with, in this sense, long remained obscure. Finally I seemed to grasp that this word trim could not here mean anything else, anything better, than the distribution of the sixteen stones in four groups of four, one group in each pocket, and that it was my refusal to consider any distribution other than this that had vitiated my calculations until then and rendered the problem literally insoluble. And it was on the basis of this interpretation, whether right or wrong, that I finally reached a solution, inelegant assuredly, but sound, sound. Now I am willing to believe, indeed I firmly believe, that other solutions to this problem might have been found, and indeed may still be found, no less sound, but much more elegant, than the one I shall now describe, if I can. And I believe too that had I been a little more insistent, a little more resistant, I could have found them myself. But I was tired, but I was tired, and I contented myself ingloriously with the first solution that was a solution, to this problem. But not to go over the heartbreaking stages through which I passed before I came to it, here it is, in all its hideousness. All (all!) that was necessary was to put for example, to begin with, six stones in the right pocket of my greatcoat, or supply-pocket, five in the right pocket of my trousers, and five in the left pocket of my trousers, that makes the lot, twice five ten plus six sixteen, and none, for none remained, in the left pocket of my greatcoat, which for the time being remained empty, empty of stones that is, for its usual contents remained, as well as occasional objects. For where do you think I hid my vegetable knife, my silver, my horn and the other things that I have not yet named, perhaps shall never name. Good. Now I can begin to suck. Watch me closely. I take a stone from the right pocket of my greatcoat, suck it, stop sucking it, put it in the left pocket of my greatcoat, the one empty (of stones). I take a second stone from the right pocket of my greatcoat, suck it, put it in the left pocket of my greatcoat. And so on until the right pocket of my greatcoat is empty (apart from its usual and casual contents) and the six stones I have just sucked, one after the other, are all in the left pocket of my greatcoat. Pausing then, and concentrating, so as not to make a balls of it, I transfer to the right pocket of my greatcoat, in which there are no stones left, the five stones in the right pocket of my trousers, which I replace by the five stones in the left pocket of my trousers, which I replace by the six stones in the left pocket of my greatcoat At this stage then the left pocket of my greatcoat is again empty of stones, while the right pocket of my greatcoat is again supplied, and in the right way, that is to say with other stones than those I have just sucked. These other stones I then begin to suck, one after the other, and to transfer as I go along to the left pocket of my greatcoat, being absolutely certain, as far as one can be in an affair of this kind, that I am not sucking the same stones as a moment before, but others. And when the right pocket of my greatcoat is again empty (of stones), and the five I have just sucked are all without exception in the left pocket of my greatcoat, then I proceed to the same redistribution as a moment before, or a similar redistribution, that is to say I transfer to the right pocket of my greatcoat, now again available, the five stones in the right pocket of my trousers, which I replace by the six stones in the left pocket of my trousers, which I replace by the five stones in the left pocket of my greatcoat. And there I am ready to begin again. Do I have to go on? No, for it is clear that after the next series, of sucks and transfers, I shall be back where I started, that is to say with the first six stones back in the supply pocket, the next five in the right pocket of my stinking old trousers and finally the last five in left pocket of same, and my sixteen stones will have been sucked once at least in impeccable succession, not one sucked twice, not one left unsucked. It is true that the next time I could scarcely hope to suck my stones in the same order as the first time and that the first, seventh and twelfth for example of the first cycle might very well be the sixth, eleventh and sixteenth respectively of the second, if the worst came to the worst. But that was a drawback I could not avoid. And if in the cycles taken together utter confusion was bound to reign, at least within each cycle taken separately I could be easy in my mind, at least as easy as one can be, in a proceeding of this kind. For in order for each cycle to be identical, as to the succession of stones in my mouth, and God knows I had set my heart on it, the only means were numbered stones or sixteen pockets. And rather than make twelve more pockets or number my stones, I preferred to make the best of the comparative peace of mind I enjoyed within each cycle taken separately. For it was not enough to number the stones, but I would have had to remember, every time I put a stone in my mouth, the number I needed and look for it in my pocket. Which would have put me off stone for ever, in a very short time. For I would never have been sure of not making a mistake unless of course I had kept a kind of register, in which to tick off the stones one by one, as I sucked them. And of this I believed myself incapable. No, the only perfect solution would have been the sixteen pockets, symmetrically disposed, each one with its stone. Then I would have needed neither to number nor to think, but merely, as I sucked a given stone, to move on the fifteen others, each to the next pocket, a delicate business admittedly, but within my power, and to call always on the same pocket when I felt like a suck. This would have freed me from all anxiety, not only within each cycle taken separately, but also for the sum of all cycles, though they went on forever. But however imperfect my own solution was, I was pleased at having found it all alone, yes, quite pleased. And if it was perhaps less sound than I had thought in the first flush of discovery, its inelegance never diminished. And it was above all inelegant in this, to my mind, that the uneven distribution was painful to me, bodily. It is true that a kind of equilibrium was reached, at a given moment, in the early stages of each cycle, namely after the third suck and before the fourth, but it did not last long, and the rest of the time I felt the weight of the stones dragging me now to one side, now to the other. So it was something more than a principle I abandoned, when I abandoned the equal distribution, it was a bodily need. But to suck the stones in the way I have described, not haphazard, but with method, was also I think a bodily need. Here then were two incompatible bodily needs, at loggerheads. Such things happen. But deep down I didn't give a tinker's curse about being off my balance, dragged to the right hand and the left, backwards and forwards. And deep down it was all the same to me whether I sucked a different stone each time or always the same stone, until the end of time. For they all tasted exactly the same. And if I had collected sixteen, it was not in order to ballast myself in such and such a way, or to suck them turn about, but simply to have a little store, so as never to be without. But deep down I didn't give a fiddler's curse about being without, when they were all gone they would be all gone, I wouldn't be any the worse off, or hardly any. And the solution to which I rallied in the end was to throw away all the stones but one, which of course I soon lost, or threw away, or gave away, or swallowed.

27 Choose some phrases which indicate the kind of person Molloy is, and interpret them (as you did for Bloom and Molly in Exercises 9, 10 and 12).

28 What do you think of Molloy? Is he
a completely mad?
b an average but complete man, as Joyce intended Bloom to be?
c an extreme, but very recognizable, representative of humanity?
d your own ideas: ____________________

29 Compare your reactions to the two extracts.

Which did you find	ULYSSES	MOLLOY	I CAN'T DECIDE
more difficult?	________	________	________
more humorous?	________	________	________
more realistic?	________	________	________
more tragic?	________	________	________
your suggestions:			
more ________	________	________	________
more ________	________	________	________
more ________	________	________	________

Authors

James Joyce (1882–1941) was born in Dublin and educated at Jesuit schools before studying modern languages at University College, Dublin. He turned down a chance to enter the Jesuit order, and also refused to play any part in Irish nationalist activities, regarding himself as a rebel against what he saw as the narrow-mindedness of Irish religion, politics and culture. In pursuit of the artistic life he went to Paris in 1902, returned soon afterwards for the death of his mother, but then left again for Europe, taking with him Nora Barnacle, who was to be his partner for the rest of his life (she is the model for Molly Bloom). Joyce earned his living teaching English in Trieste and Zurich and, in 1920, settled in Paris, where he lived till 1940, when the war forced him to move to Switzerland. He died in Zurich a few weeks later.

Despite living abroad for his adult life, Joyce set all his work in Dublin. The fifteen stories in *Dubliners* (1914) describe with mixed affection and criticism the lives of Dublin characters. *A Portrait of the Artist as a Young Man* (1916) is an autobiographical novel following the development of the main character, Stephen Dedalus, from child to young student and his resolution to become a writer and to leave Ireland. *Ulysses* is Joyce's masterpiece, one of the most influential works in 20th century world literature, a book which manages to show life as simultaneously comic and tragic, banal and extraordinary. The first three chapters follow the morning routine of Stephen Dedalus (the same character as in *A Portrait of the Artist as a Young Man*). The central part concerns Bloom and his day's activities: attending a funeral, doing business, walking around Dublin, worrying about his wife's infidelity, and so on. In the last part of the book Bloom and Stephen, whose paths have been crossing all day, but who have not actually met, finally do meet. The parallels with *The Odyssey* (see Exercise 13) suggest a sort of reunion – Stephen needs a father figure and Bloom's son died young – but Joyce leaves it open whether they will meet again. The book close with a long interior monlogue delivered by Molly Bloom where, among many free associations of thoughts, she thinks nostalgically of the early days with Bloom.

Joyce's last novel, *Finnegan's Wake* (1939), pushes experiments with language to such extreme limits that it has become an object of study for Joyce scholars rather than a novel read by the general public.

Samuel Beckett (1906–89) was born and educated in Ireland, although he spent most of his adult life in France. It was while working in Paris as an English teacher at the École Normale Supérieure that he met James Joyce in 1928. His first published work was an essay on Joyce (1929) and their initially academic relationship turned into one of lasting friendship. Beckett wrote both novels and plays in French and English and translated his own works from one language to the other. His best-known work is the play *Waiting for Godot* (1952), in which two men wait by a roadside for someone who never arrives. Although very little seems to happen in the play, it is generally regarded as one of the most important texts of modern times – expressing, among other things, the spiritual loneliness of life in a sceptical, post-religious age. The anguished, helpless condition of individuals in such an age is also the theme of his novels. Two were conceived in English (*Murphy*, 1938, and *Watt*, 1953), while the trilogy *Molloy* (1951), *Malone Dies* (1958) and *The Unnamable* (1960) appeared first in French before being translated by Beckett into English. They are all interior monologues, desolate and bleak, but shot through with black humour. For example, *Malone Dies* opens with the sentence 'I shall be soon quite dead at last in spite of all', and *The Unnamable* ends with '... where I am, I don't know, I'll never know, in the silence you don't know, you must go on, I can't go on, I'll go on'. Beckett's works are abstract, puzzling, symbolic, and filled with subtle philosophical and theological references. They show characters in bleak, extreme situations, yet often manage to be comic, popular, and – as one critic has put it – 'curiously exhilarating'. Beckett avoided publicity, never gave interviews to journalists, and although he accepted the Nobel Prize for Literature in 1969, would not go to Stockholm to receive it. Despite his reputation as a frightening and austere recluse (reinforced by his writings and rather severe appearance in photographs), personal reminiscences show him to have been a man of great warmth and kindness. (A short play by Beckett, *Act Without Words II*, is included in the companion volume in this series, *Modern Plays*.)

8 Future Shock

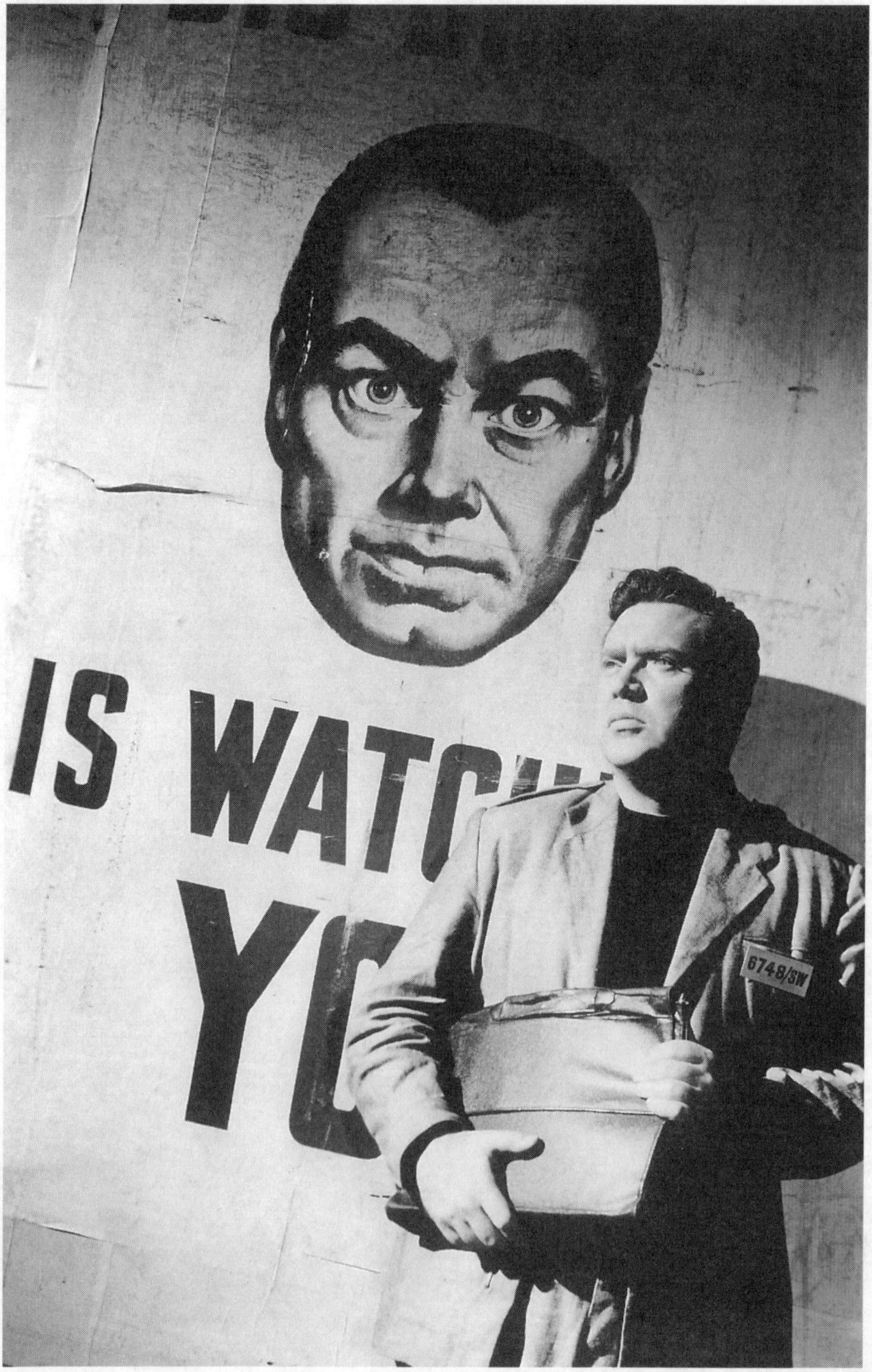

Before you read

1 Look at the film still on the previous page. How would you describe the man's clothes and expression, and the poster behind him? What do you think the purpose of the poster might be?

2 Read the following sentences, using a dictionary if necessary. They are all the openings of novels set in the future. Is there anything about them which seems strange, or which suggests that changes in society have taken place? Make some notes, and compare your ideas with a partner. Check your ideas with the key before going on.

a It was a bright cold day in April, and the clocks were striking thirteen.
Nineteen Eighty-Four, George Orwell

b IT WAS A PLEASURE TO BURN.
Farenheit 451, Ray Bradbury

c We slept in what had once been the gymnasium.
The Handmaid's Tale, Margaret Atwood

d A squat grey building of only thirty-four storeys. Over the main entrance the words, CENTRAL LONDON HATCHERY AND CONDITIONING CENTRE, and, in a shield, the World State's motto, COMMUNITY, IDENTITY, STABILITY.
Brave New World, Aldous Huxley

e The ghost was her father's parting gift, presented by a black-clad secretary in a departure lounge at Narita.
Mona Lisa Overdrive, William Gibson

3 The following passages are taken from the first or second pages of the novels quoted in Exercise 2. Match them with the opening sentences above.

1 'These', he waved his hand, 'are the incubators.' And opening an insulated door he showed them racks upon racks of numbered test tubes. 'The week's supply of ova. Kept', he explained, 'at blood heat; whereas the male gametes,' and here he opened another door, 'they have to be kept at thirty-five instead of thirty-seven. Full blood heat sterilizes.'

2 With his symbolic helmet numbered 451 on his stolid head, and his eyes all orange flame with the thought of what came next, he flicked the igniter and the house jumped up in a gorging fire that burned the evening sky red and yellow and black. He strode in a swarm of fireflies. He wanted above all, like the old joke, to shove a marshmallow on a stick in the furnace, while the flapping pigeon-winged books died on the porch and lawn of the house.

3 On each landing, opposite the lift-shaft, the poster with the enormous face gazed from the wall. It was one of those pictures which are so contrived that the eyes follow you about when you move. BIG BROTHER IS WATCHING YOU, the caption beneath it ran.

4 The ghost woke to Kumiko's touch as they began their descent into Heathrow. The fifty-first generation of Maas-Neotek biochips conjured up an indistinct figure on the seat beside her, a boy out of some faded hunting print, legs crossed casually in tan breeches and riding boots. 'Hullo,' the ghost said. Kumiko blinked, opened her hand. The boy flickered and was gone. She looked down at the smooth little unit in her palm and slowly closed her fingers.

5 We folded our clothes neatly and laid them on the stools at the ends of the beds. The lights were turned down but not out. Aunt Sara and Aunt Elizabeth patrolled; they had electric cattle prods slung on thongs from their leather belts. No guns though, even they could not be trusted with guns. Guns were for the guards, specially picked from the Angels.

1 ____ *2* ____ *3* ____ *4* ____ *5* ____

4 For each extract in Exercise 3 make brief notes about

a the particular situation that is described.
b the general picture of society that is suggested.
c Compare your notes with a partner before checking with the Key.

The Handmaid's Tale (1985)
Margaret Atwood

In this extract the narrator, a young woman who is known as 'Offred', describes a macabre ceremony ...

See the Glossary section at the back of the book for vocabulary.

CHAPTER 42

The bell is tolling, we can hear it from a long way off. It's morning, and today we've had no breakfast. When we reach the main gate we file through it, two by two. There's a heavy contingent of guards, special-detail Angels, with riot gear – the helmets with the bulging dark plexiglass visors that make them look like beetles, the long clubs, the gas-canister guns – in cordon around the outside of the Wall. That's in case of hysteria. The hooks on the Wall are empty.

This is a district Salvaging, for women only. Salvagings are always segregated. It was announced yesterday. They tell you only the day before. It's not enough time, to get used to it.

To the tolling of the bell we walk along the paths once used by students, past buildings that were once lecture halls and dormitories. It's very strange to be in here again. From the outside you can't tell that anything's changed, except that the blinds on most of the

Handmaids at the Salvaging: a scene from Volker Schlöndorff's 1990 film version of *The Handmaid's Tale.*

windows are drawn down. These buildings belong to the Eyes now.

We file onto the wide lawn in front of what used to be the library. The white steps going up are still the same, the main entrance is unaltered. There's a wooden stage erected on the lawn, something like the one they used every spring, for Commencement, in the time before. I think of hats, pastel hats worn by some of the mothers, and of the black gowns the students would put on, and the red ones. But this stage is not the same after all, because of the three wooden posts that stand on it, with the loops of rope.

At the front of the stage there is a microphone; the television camera is discreetly off to the side.

I've only been to one of these before, two years ago. Women's Salvagings are not frequent. There is less need for them. These days we are so well behaved.

I don't want to be telling this story.

We take our places in the standard order: Wives and daughters on the folding wooden chairs placed towards the back, Econowives and Marthas around the edges and on the library steps, and Handmaids at the front, where everyone can keep an eye on us. We don't sit on chairs, but kneel, and this time we have cushions, small red velvet ones with nothing written on them, not even *Faith*.

Luckily the weather is all right: not too hot, cloudy-bright. It would be miserable kneeling here in the rain. Maybe that's why they leave it so late to tell us: so they'll know what the weather will be like. That's as good as reason as any.

I kneel on my red velvet cushion. I try to think about tonight, about making love, in the dark, in the light reflected off the white walls. I remember being held.

There's a long piece of rope which winds like a snake in front of the first row of cushions, along the second, and back through the lines of chairs, bending like a very old, very slow river viewed from the air, down to the back. The rope is thick and brown and smells of tar. The front end of the rope runs up onto the stage. It's like a fuse, or the string of a balloon.

On stage, to the left, are those who are to be salvaged: two Handmaids, one Wife. Wives are unusual, and despite myself I look at this one with interest. I want to know what she has done.

They have been placed here before the gates were opened. All of them sit on folding wooden chairs, like graduating students who are about to be given prizes. Their hands rest in their laps, looking as if they are folded sedately. They sway a little, they've probably been given injections or pills, so they won't make a fuss. It's better if things go smoothly. Are they attached to their chairs? Impossible to say, under all that drapery.

Now the official procession is approaching the stage, mounting the steps at the right: three women, one Aunt in front, two Salvagers in their black hoods and cloaks a pace behind her. Behind them are the other Aunts. The whisperings among us hush. The three arrange themselves, turn towards us, the Aunt flanked by the two black-robed Salvagers.

It's Aunt Lydia. How many years since I've seen her? I'd begun to think she existed only in my head, but here she is, a little older. I have a good view, I can see the deepening furrows to either side of her nose, the engraved frown. Her eyes blink, she smiles nervously, peering to left and right, checking out the audience, and lifts a hand to fidget with her headdress. An odd strangling sound comes over the P.A. system: she is clearing her throat.

I've begun to shiver. Hatred fills my mouth like spit.

What kind of thing do you think Aunt Lydia is going to say?

The sun comes out, and the stage and its occupants light up like a Christmas crèche. I can see the wrinkles under Aunt Lydia's eyes, the pallor of the seated women, the hairs on the rope in front of me on the grass, the blades of grass. There is a dandelion, right in front of me, the colour of egg yolk. I feel hungry. The bell stops tolling.

Aunt Lydia stands up, smooths down her skirt with both hands, and steps forward to the mike. 'Good afternoon, ladies,' she says, and there is an instant and ear-splitting feedback whine from the P.A. system. From among us, incredibly, there is laughter. It's hard not to laugh, it's the tension, and the look of irritation on Aunt Lydia's face as she adjusts the sound. This is supposed to be dignified.

'Good afternoon, ladies,' she says again, her voice now tinny and flattened. It's *ladies* instead of *girls* because of the Wives. 'I'm sure we are all aware of the unfortunate circumstances that bring us all here together on this beautiful morning, when I am certain we would all rather be doing something else, at least I speak for myself, but duty is a hard taskmaster, or may I say on this occasion taskmistress, and it is in the name of duty that we are here today.'

She goes on like this for some minutes, but I don't listen; I've heard this speech, or one like it, often enough before: the same platitudes, the same slogans, the same phrases: the torch of the future, the cradle of the race, the task before us. It's hard to believe there will not be polite clapping after this speech, and tea and cookies served on the lawn.

That was the prologue, I think. Now she'll get down to it.

Aunt Lydia rummages in her pocket, produces a crumpled piece of paper. This she takes an undue length of time to unfold and scan. She's rubbing our noses in it, letting us know exactly who she is, making us watch her as she silently reads, flaunting her prerogative. Obscene, I think. Let's get this over with.

'In the past,' says Aunt Lydia, 'it has been the custom to precede the actual Salvagings with a detailed account of the crimes of which the prisoners stand convicted. However, we have found that such a public account, especially when televised, is invariably followed by a rash, if I may call it that, an outbreak I should say, of exactly similar crimes. So we have decided in the best interests of all to discontinue this practice. The Salvagings will proceed without further ado.'

A collective murmur goes up from us. The crimes of others are a secret language among us. Through them we show ourselves what we might be capable of, after all. This is not a popular announcement. But you would never know it from Aunt Lydia, who smiles and blinks as if washed in applause. Now we are left to our own devices, our own speculations. The first one, the one they're now raising from her chair, black-gloved hands on her upper arms: reading? No, that's only a hand cut off, on the third conviction. Unchastity, or an attempt on the life of her Commander? Or the Commander's Wife, more likely. That's what we're thinking. As for the Wife, there's mostly just one thing they get salvaged for. They can do almost anything to us, but they aren't allowed to kill us, not legally. Not with knitting needles or garden shears, or knives purloined from the kitchen, and especially not when we are pregnant. It could be adultery, of course. It could always be that.

Or attempted escape.

'Ofcharles,' Aunt Lydia announces. No one I know. The woman is brought forward; she walks as if she's really concentrating on it, one foot, the other foot, she's definitely drugged. There's a groggy off-centre smile on her mouth. One side of her face contracts, an uncoordinated wink, aimed at the camera. They'll never show it, of course, this isn't live. The two Salvagers tie her hands, behind her back.

From behind me there's a sound of retching.

That's why we don't get breakfast.

'Janine, most likely,' Ofglen whispers.

I've seen it before, the white bag placed over the head, the woman helped up onto the high stool as if she's being helped up the steps of a bus, steadied there, the noose adjusted delicately around the neck, like a vestment, the stool kicked away. I've heard the long sigh go up, from around me, the sigh like air coming out of an air mattress, I've seen Aunt Lydia place her hand over the mike, to stifle the other sounds coming from behind her, I've leaned forward to touch the rope in front of me, in time with the others, both hands on it, the rope hairy, sticky with tar in the hot sun, then placed my hand on my heart to show my unity with the Salvagers and my consent, and my complicity in the death of this woman. I have seen the kicking feet and the two in black who now seize hold of them and drag downwards with all their weight. I don't want to see it any more. I look at the grass instead. I describe the rope.

Do you think the 'Salvaging' has finished? Might there be anything else to come?

CHAPTER 43

The three bodies hang there, even with the white sacks over their heads looking curiously stretched, like chickens strung up by the necks in a meatshop window; like birds with their wings clipped, like flightless birds, wrecked angels. It's hard to take your eyes off them. Beneath the hems of the dresses the feet dangle, two pairs of red shoes, one pair of blue. If it weren't for the ropes and the sacks it could be a kind of dance, a ballet, caught by flash-camera:

mid-air. They look arranged. They look like showbiz. It must have been Aunt Lydia who put the blue one in the middle.

'Today's Salvaging is now concluded,' Aunt Lydia announces into the mike. 'But …'

We turn to her, listen to her, watch her. She has always known how to space her pauses. A ripple runs over us, a stir. Something else, perhaps, is going to happen.

'But you may stand up, and form a circle.' She smiles down upon us, generous, munificent. She is about to give us something. *Bestow*. 'Orderly, now.'

She is talking to us, to the Handmaids. Some of the Wives are leaving now, some of the daughters. Most of them stay, but they stay behind, out of the way, they watch merely. They are not part of the circle.

Two Guardians have moved forward and are coiling up the thick rope, getting it out of the way. Others move the cushions. We are milling around now, on the grass space in front of the stage, some jockeying for position at the front, next to the centre, many pushing just as hard to work their way to the middle where they will be shielded. It's a mistake to hang back too obviously in any group like this; it stamps you as lukewarm, lacking in zeal. There's an energy building here, a murmur, a tremor of readiness and anger. The bodies tense, the eyes are brighter, as if aiming.

I don't want to be at the front, or at the back either. I'm not sure what's coming, though I sense it won't be anything I want to see up close. But Ofglen has hold of my arm, she tugs me with her, and now we're in the second line, with only a thin hedge of bodies in front of us. I don't want to see, yet I don't pull back either. I've heard rumours, which I only half believed. Despite everything I already know, I say to myself: they wouldn't go that far.

'You know the rules for a Particicution,' Aunt Lydia says. 'You will wait until I blow the whistle. After that, what you do is up to you, until I blow the whistle again. Understood?'

A noise comes from among us, a formless assent.

'Well then,' says Aunt Lydia. She nods. Two Guardians, not the same ones that have taken away the rope, come forward now from behind the stage. Between them they half-carry, half-drag a third man. He too is in a Guardian's uniform, but he has no hat on and the uniform is dirty and torn. His face is cut and bruised, deep reddish-brown bruises; the flesh is swollen and knobby, stubbled with unshaven beard. This doesn't look like a face but like an unknown vegetable, a mangled bulb or tuber, something that's grown wrong. Even from where I'm standing I can smell him: he smells of shit and vomit. His hair is blond and falls over his face, spiky with what? Dried sweat?

I stare at him with revulsion. He looks drunk. He looks like a drunk that's been in a fight. Why have they brought a drunk in here?

'This man,' says Aunt Lydia, 'has been convicted of rape.' Her voice trembles with rage, and a kind of triumph. 'He was once a Guardian. He has disgraced his uniform. He has abused his position of trust. His partner in viciousness has already been shot. The penalty for rape, as you know, is death: Deuteronomy 22:23–29. I might add that this crime involved two of you and took place at gunpoint. It was also brutal. I will not offend your ears with any details, except to say that one woman was pregnant and the baby died.'

A sigh goes up from us; despite myself I feel my hands clench. It is too much, this violation. The baby too, after what we go through. It's true, there is a bloodlust; I want to tear, gouge, rend.

We jostle forward, our heads turn from side to side, our nostrils flare, sniffing death, we look at one another, seeing the hatred. Shooting was too good. The man's head swivels groggily around: has he even heard her?

Aunt Lydia waits a moment; then she gives a little smile and raises her whistle to her lips. We hear it, shrill and silver, an echo from a volleyball game of long ago.

What do you think will happen next? How far do you think Offred will be involved?

The two Guardians let go of the third man's arms and step back. He staggers – is he drugged? – and falls to his knees. His eyes are shrivelled up inside the puffy flesh of his face, as if the light is too bright for him. They've kept him in darkness. He raises one hand to his cheek, as though to feel if he is still there. All of this happens quickly, but it seems to be slowly.

Nobody moves forward. The women are looking at him with horror, as if he's a half-dead rat dragging itself across a kitchen floor. He's squinting around at us, the circle of red women. One corner of his mouth moves up, incredible – a smile?

I try to look inside him, inside the trashed face, see what he must really look like. I think he's about thirty. It isn't Luke.

But it could have been, I know that. It could be Nick. I know that whatever he's done I can't touch him.

He says something. It comes out thick, as if his throat is bruised, his tongue huge in his mouth, but I hear it anyway. He says, 'I didn't ...'

There's a surge forward, like a crowd at a rock concert in the former time, when the doors opened, that urgency coming like a wave through us. The air is bright with adrenalin, we are permitted anything and this is freedom, in my body also, I'm reeling, red spreads everywhere, but before that tide of cloth and bodies hits him Ofglen is shoving through the women in front of us, propelling herself with her elbows, left, right, and running towards him. She pushes him down, sideways, then kicks his head viciously, one, two, three times, sharp painful jabs with the foot, well-aimed. Now there are sounds, gasps, a low noise like growling, yells, and the red bodies tumble forward and I can no longer see, he's obscured by arms, fists, feet. A high scream comes from somewhere, like a horse in terror.

I keep back, try to stay on my feet. Something hits me from behind. I stagger. When I regain my balance and look around, I see the Wives and daughters leaning forward in their chairs, the Aunts on the platform gazing down with interest. They must have a better view from up there.

He has become an *it*.

Ofglen is back beside me. Her face is tight, expressionless.

'I saw what you did,' I say to her. Now I'm beginning to feel again: shock, outrage, nausea. Barbarism. 'Why did you do that? You! I thought you ...'

'Don't look at me,' she says. 'They're watching.'

'I don't care,' I say. My voice is rising, I can't help it.

'Get control of yourself,' she says. She pretends to brush me off, my arm and shoulder, bringing her face close to my ear. 'Don't be stupid. He wasn't a rapist at all, he was a political. He was one of ours. I knocked him out. Put him out of his misery. Don't you know what they're doing to him?'

One of ours, I think. A Guardian. It seems impossible.

Aunt Lydia blows her whistle again, but they don't stop at once. The two Guardians move in, pulling them off, from what's left. Some lie on the grass where they've been hit or kicked by accident. Some have fainted. They straggle away, in twos and threes or by themselves. They seem dazed.

'You will find your partners and re-form your line,' Aunt Lydia says into the mike. Few pay attention to her. A woman comes towards us, walking as if she's feeling her way with her feet, in the dark: Janine. There's a smear of blood across her cheek, and more of it on the white of her headdress. She's smiling, a bright diminutive smile. Her eyes have come loose.

'Hi there,' she says. 'How are you doing?' She's holding something, tightly, in her right hand. It's a clump of blond hair. She gives a small giggle.

'Janine,' I say. But she's let go, totally now, she's in free fall, she's in withdrawal.

'You have a nice day,' she says, and walks on past us, towards the gate.

I look after her. Easy out, is what I think. I don't even feel sorry for her, although I should. I feel angry. I'm not proud of myself for this, or for any of it. But then, that's the point.

My hands smell of warm tar. I want to go back to the house and up to the bathroom and scrub and scrub, with the harsh soap and the pumice, to get every trace of this smell off my skin. The smell makes me feel sick.

But also I'm hungry. This is monstrous, but nevertheless it's true. Death makes me hungry. Maybe it's because I've been emptied; or maybe it's the body's way of seeing to it that I remain alive, continue to repeat its bedrock prayer: *I am, I am*. I am, still.

I want to go to bed, make love, right now.

I think of the word *relish*.

I could eat a horse.

What do you think of Offred's reaction?

CHAPTER 44

Things are back to normal.

How can I call this *normal*? But compared with this morning, it is normal.

For lunch there was a cheese sandwich, on brown bread, a glass of milk, celery sticks, canned pears. A schoolchild's lunch. I ate everything up, not quickly, but revelling in the taste, the flavours lush on my tongue. Now I am going shopping, the same as usual. I even look forward to it. There's a certain consolation to be taken from routine.

I go out the back door, along the path. Nick is washing the car, his hat on sideways. He doesn't look at me. We avoid looking at each other, these days. Surely we'd give something away by it, even out here in the open, with no one to see.

I wait at the corner for Ofglen. She's late. At last I see her coming, a red and white shape of cloth, like a kite, walking at the steady pace we've all learned to keep. I see her and notice nothing at first. Then, as she comes nearer, I think that there must be something wrong with her. She looks wrong. She is altered in some indefinable way; she's not injured, she's not limping. It's as if she has shrunk.

Then when she's nearer still I see what it is. She isn't Ofglen. She's the same height, but thinner, and her face is beige, not pink, She comes up to me, stops.

'Blessed be the fruit,' she says. Straight-faced, straight-laced.

'May the Lord open,' I reply. I try not to show surprise.

'You must be Offred,' she says. I say yes, and we begin our walk.

Now what, I think. My head is churning, this is not good news, what has become of her, how do I find out without showing too much concern? We aren't supposed to form friendships, loyalties, among one another. I try to remember how much time Ofglen has to go at her present posting.

'We've been sent good weather,' I say.

'Which I receive with joy.' The voice placid, flat, unrevealing.

We pass the first checkpoint without saying anything further. She's taciturn, but so am I. Is she waiting for me to start something, reveal myself, or is she a believer, engrossed in inner meditation?

'Has Ofglen been transferred, so soon?' I ask, but I know she hasn't. I saw her only this morning. She would have said.

'I am Ofglen,' the woman says. Word perfect. And of course she is, the new one, and Ofglen, wherever she is, is no longer Ofglen. I never did know her real name. That is how you can get lost, in a sea of names. It wouldn't be easy to find her, now.

We go to Milk and Honey, and to All Flesh, where I buy chicken. and the new Ofglen gets three pounds of hamburger. There are the usual lineups. I see several women I recognize, exchange with them the infinitesimal nods with which we show each other we are known, at least to someone, we still exist. Outside All Flesh I say to the new Ofglen, 'We should go to the Wall.' I don't know what I expect from this; some way of testing the reaction, perhaps. I need to know whether or not she is one of us. If she is, if I can establish that, perhaps she'll be able to tell me what has really happened to Ofglen.

'As you like,' she says. Is that indifference, or caution?

On the Wall hang the three women from this morning, still in their dresses, still in their shoes, still with the white bags over their heads. Their arms have been untied and are stiff and proper at their sides.

The blue one is in the middle, the two red ones on either side, though the colours are no longer as bright; they seem to have faded, grown dingy, like dead butterflies or tropical fish drying on land. The gloss is off them. We stand and look at them in silence.

'Let that be a reminder to us,' says the new Ofglen finally.

I say nothing at first, because I am trying to make out what she means. She could mean that this is a reminder to us of the unjustness and brutality of the regime. In that case I ought to say *yes*. Or she could mean the opposite, that we should remember to do what we are told and not get into trouble, because if we do we will be rightfully punished. If she means that, I should say *praise be*. Her voice was bland, toneless, no clues there

I take a chance. 'Yes,' I say.

To this she does not respond, although I sense a flicker of white at the edge of my vision, as if she's looked quickly at me.

Do you think that the 'new' Ofglen can be trusted?
What do you think has happened to the 'old' Ofglen?

After a moment we turn away and begin the long walk back, matching our steps in the approved way, so that we seem to be in unison.

I think maybe I should wait before attempting anything further. It's too soon to push, to probe. I should give it a week, two weeks, maybe longer, watch her carefully, listen for tones in her voice, unguarded words, the way Ofglen listened to me. Now that Ofglen is gone I am alert again, my sluggishness has fallen away, my body is no longer for pleasure only but senses its jeopardy. I should not be rash, I should not take unnecessary risks. But I need to know. I hold back until we're past the final checkpoint and there are only blocks to go, but then I can no longer control myself.

'I didn't know Ofglen very well,' I say. 'I mean the former one.'

'Oh?' she says. The fact that she's said anything, however guarded, encourages me.

'I've only know her since May,' I say. I can feel my skin growing hot, my heart speeding up. This is tricky. For one thing, it's a lie. And how do I get from there to the next vital word? 'Around the first of May I think it was. What they used to call May Day.'

'Did they?' she says, light, indifferent, menacing. 'That isn't a term I remember. I'm surprised you do. You ought to make an effort …' She pauses. 'To clear your mind of such …' She pauses again. 'Echoes.'

Now I feel cold, seeping over my skin like water. What she is doing is warning me.

She isn't one of us. But she knows.

I walk the last blocks in terror. I've been stupid, again. More than stupid. It hasn't occurred to me before, but now I see: if Ofglen's been caught, Ofglen may talk, about me among others. She will talk. She won't be able to help it.

But I haven't done anything, I tell myself, not really. All I did was know. All I did was not tell.

They know where my child is. What if they bring her, threaten something to her, in front of me? Or do it. I can't bear to think what they might do. Or Luke, what if they have Luke. Or my mother or Moira or almost anyone. Dear God, don't make me choose. I would not be able to stand it, I know that, Moira was right about me. I'll say anything they like, I'll incriminate anyone. It's true, the first scream, whimper even, and I'll turn to jelly, I'll confess to any crime, I'll end up hanging from a hook on the Wall. Keep your head down, I used to tell myself, and see it through. It's no use.

This is the way I talk to myself, on the way home.

At the corner we turn to one another in the usual way.

'Under His Eye,' says the new, treacherous Ofglen.

'Under His Eye,' I say, trying to sound fervent. As if such play-acting could help, now that we've come this far.

Then she does an odd thing. She leans forward, so that the stiff white blinkers on our heads are almost touching, so that I can see her pale beige eyes up close, the delicate web of lines across her cheeks, and whispers, very quickly, her voice faint as dry leaves. 'She hanged herself,' she says. 'After the Salvaging. She saw the van coming for her. It was better.'

Then she's walking away from me down the street.

First reaction

5 ***a*** 'It was better' (line 429). Why was it better for the previous Ofglen to commit suicide?

b Who do you think is in charge of this society? What might make people create such a society?

Close reading

Inferring

6 **Pair/group work:**

a On your own, make a list of ten questions that interest you about the society represented in *The Handmaid's Tale*.

b In pairs or groups, compare your questions. Decide together on the ten questions that most interest you.

7 Look quickly through the questions in Exercises 8 and 9 below. Do they include the ten questions that you decided on in Exercise 6?

8 Using clues from the context, try to answer these questions. Discuss them in pairs or groups. Check your ideas with the Key before going on.

a What are 'Angels' and 'Eyes'?
b What is a 'Salvaging'?
c Where does this Salvaging take place – what did this place used to be?
d What are the women who are 'salvaged' supposed to be guilty of?
e Why is Ofcharles, one of the two accused Handmaids, drugged?
f What is the significance of the rope – what part does it play in the ceremony?
g What is a 'Particicution'? What do you think this word might be derived from?
h What are 'Guardians'? Why is one of them executed?
i 'But I haven't done anything, I tell myself, not really. All I did was know. All I did was not tell.' (lines 408–9) What did Offred know?

9 Now try to make hypotheses about the whole novel. Discuss the following questions in pairs or groups. Check your ideas with the Key before going on.

a What can you infer about the society of *The Handmaid's Tale* from the following?
1 Aunt Lydia's reference to Deuteronomy (line 211)
2 the exchanges between the new Ofglen and the narrator (lines 328–44 and 421–2)
3 the new Ofglen's comments at lines 397–400

b What do you think the following are?
1 Aunts (lines 62–6)
2 Wives and Commanders (lines 120–2)
3 Econowives (line 33)
4 Marthas (line 34)

c *1* What are Handmaids? (lines 34–5)
2 What is their connection with 'Commanders'? (line 120)
3 Why do their names begin 'Of-' ?

d What can you infer about the relationship between Offred and the following characters?

1 Aunt Lydia (lines 67–74)
2 Nick (lines 238; 314–17)
3 Luke (lines 237; 412)
4 Janine (lines 137; 279–90)

Characterization

10 a Look at the following thoughts of Offred. What idea do you get of her character and attitudes?

1 Hatred fills my mouth like spit. (line 74)
2 Obscene, I think. Let's get this over with. (line 104)
3 Wives are unusual, and despite myself I look at this one with interest. I want to know what she has done. (lines 52–3)
4 I try to think about tonight, about making love, in the dark, in the light reflected off the white walls. I remember being held. (lines 42–4)
5 I don't want to see it any more. I look at the grass instead. I describe the rope. (lines 150–1)

b Now choose four or five more remarks from either Chapter 43 or 44 which give an idea of Offred's character and attitudes. Compare your choices with a partner, and discuss your interpretations.

Suspense and surprise

11 a Margaret Atwood creates a considerable amount of **suspense** and **surprise** in this extract (for these terms see Chapter 1, *Anatomy of a Novel*, page 28). Here are some examples from Chapter 42.
suspense: the unexplained references to the hooks (line 7), the three wooden posts (lines 24–5), and the rope (lines 45–50). The reader wonders what exactly these are for, and perhaps suspects a sinister purpose.
surprise: Aunt Lydia's announcement that the crimes will not be described (lines 105–11). Offred is surprised by this, and communicates her surprise to the reader.
Find one or two other moments of suspense from Chapter 42.

b Find some other moments of suspense and surprise in either Chapter 43 or 44. Make a list on your own, and then discuss your lists in small groups. Which moments do you find most effective?

Language practice – structures

Use of present tenses and linking words

12 A **synopsis** is a summary of a novel, play or film. Like Offred's narrative (a transcription of a secret tape-recording she has made), a synopsis is written mainly in the present and present perfect tenses. The following is the first part of a synopsis of *The Handmaid's Tale*. Fill in the gaps with appropriate forms of the verbs given in the box. The first one is done for you

send arrest be set up ~~set~~ impose be call be give declare justify be carry out lead up to be confiscate eliminate

The Handmaid's Tale ***is set*** (a) in the late twentieth century in the United States of America. There __________ (b) a revolution led by white, right-wing, fundamentalist Protestant Christians, who __________ (c) a state which they __________ (d) 'Gilead'. One source of the unrest which __________ (e) this revolution __________ (f) a dramatic fall in the birthrate among the white population. This __________ (g) the result of collateral effects of the AIDS epidemic, and the fear of giving birth to children with deformities caused by the increasing number of leaks from nuclear plants, stockpiles of biological-warfare weapons and toxic-waste disposal sites. Gilead, a repressive, totalitarian state, ruthlessly __________ (h) its authoritarian rule through paramilitary police – the 'Angels' and the 'Guardians' – and secret police – the 'Eyes'. Political opponents and dissidents __________ (i) at public executions, and individuals of little use to the new society __________ (j) as slave-labour to the 'Colonies'. These are areas inside Gilead where pollution from toxic waste or radiation __________ (k) dangerously high. To combat the drastic decline in the birthrate the Government of Gilead, __________ (l) itself by Biblical precedents, __________ (m) that all second marriages and non-marital relationships __________ (n) adulterous, and therefore illegal. Any children of such relationships __________ (o) and given to childless couples of high-ranking officials; the male partners 'disappear', and the female partners __________ (p) and forced to become 'Handmaids'. Responsibility for their training __________ (q) to the 'Aunts', older women who __________ (r) their duties with fanatical devotion to the religious and political philosophy of Gilead.

13 In this second part of the synopsis of *The Handmaid's Tale* linking words have been left out. Use the words given in the box to fill in the gaps. The first one is done for you.

these one evening but despite even though who as a result also where at the moment of such that whose after this however after while whether

After (a) training, the Handmaids are allocated to the households of senior officials – 'Commanders' – __________ (b) their function is to get pregnant by the Commanders and bear children. The narrator of *The Handmaid's Tale*, known to the reader only by her official name 'Offred', is one of __________ (c) Handmaids. __________ (d) doing the shopping, she becomes friendly with 'Ofglen', a member of an underground opposition group known as 'Mayday'. She __________ (e) starts a sexual relationship with Nick, her Commander's chauffeur, __________ (f) the state's rules totally forbid __________ (g) relationships for Handmaids. A greater threat to Offred, __________ (h), comes from her Commander, __________ (i) insists on a relationship which goes beyond the simple aim of procreation prescribed by the regime. __________ (j) he even takes her, against her will, to a clandestine nightclub frequented by politically powerful officials who find the religious precepts __________ (k) Gilead insists on too hard to follow in private life. __________ (l) the attempts at secrecy, the Commander's Wife finds out about __________ (m) relationship, and threatens Offred with revenge. __________ (n), Nick, __________ (o) position probably means he is an 'Eye', __________ (p) who might equally be a double agent working for 'Mayday', arranges for some 'Eyes' to come to the Commander's house and arrest Offred.

__________ (q) the arrest is real, or whether it is part of a 'Mayday' plan to smuggle her to safety in Canada, is not known: __________ (r) her arrest the narrative is interrupted, and her story ends.

14 Write a synopsis of a novel, play or film that you particularly like (about 100–200 words).

Language practice – vocabulary

Politics and language

15 Gilead, the regime described in *The Handmaid's Tale*, has a special set of words for its institutions. Some examples are:

Angels   Salvaging   Eyes   Handmaids   Aunts

a Why do you think the rulers of Gilead have used these words and given them new meanings? What effects did they want to create?
b Find and discuss other examples of similar words (either new ones or existing ones used in new ways) in the extract.

16 **Slogans** are short, memorable phrases used for advertising or political messages. Some well-known examples from political history are:

Votes For Women!
Ban the Bomb!
Power to the People!
Free Nelson Mandela!

Aunt Lydia uses slogans during her speech (lines 95–6) to encourage the Handmaids:

You are the torch of the future!
You are the cradle of the race!

a Why does she use words like 'torch', 'cradle', 'future' and 'race'?

b Invent some more slogans specifically to encourage the Handmaids.

c Invent some other slogans for Gilead, designed to encourage the general public and not just the Handmaids.

17 **Euphemisms** are pleasant-sounding words or phrases used to refer to things that are generally considered unpleasant. In 1974, during the Vietnam war, an official at the the US Embassy in Cambodia was persistently asked for more information about the accidental bombing and destruction of a Cambodian village by American planes. He lost his temper with the reporters, and complained to them: 'You always write it's bombing, bombing, bombing. It's not bombing, it's air support.'

a What was the euphemism used by the official, and why did he prefer it?

b Look at the following expressions, all in current use. Choose some of them, and give a direct, explicit definition of what you think they refer to. Discuss your ideas, then check with the Key.

> *security forces   intelligence   low income groups   downsizing*
> *body count   collateral damage   smart weapons   friendly fire*
> *ethnic cleansing*

c What makes the expressions above sound less unpleasant than the reality they refer to?

d Do you know any other examples of current political euphemisms in your own language or English? If so, what do you think of them?

18 **Pair/group work – inventing political language**: Imagine a fictitious country, *Dystopia*, ruled by a repressive totalitarian regime. There is a secret resistance organization fighting against the regime.

a Members of pairs or groups toss a coin.
heads = imagine that you are a propaganda writer for the regime. Invent names for the various elements and activities of both the regime and the resistance.
tails = imagine that you are a propaganda writer for the resistance. Invent names for the various elements and activities of both the resistance and the regime.

b Compare results with your partner or other members of the group. Decide on the most effective names. Here are some ideas for things you might want to invent names for, but you can add other ideas of your own.

THE REGIME

- the head of the government
- government officials and government ministries
- various ranks among members of society
- various kinds of police and armed forces
- activities (eg making war, spying, arresting, getting confessions, etc)
- slogans

THE RESISTANCE

- the name of the organization
- various parts of the organization
- various roles of members
- ordinary people who support or sympathize with the resistance
- activities (sabotage, propaganda, etc)
- slogans

Extension

Utopias and dystopias

19 *Utopia* is the title of a book about an imaginary ideal commonwealth, written in 1515–16 by the Renaissance humanist Sir Thomas More. The title is a play on words which puts together two possible derivations from Greek: 'outopia', meaning 'no place', and 'eutopia', meaning 'good place'. The first example of this kind of book is Plato's *Republic* (fourth century BC). Recently the word 'dystopia' (meaning in Greek 'bad place') has come to be used to refer to books which describe imaginary – and extremely unpleasant – worlds set in the future, where pessimistic conclusions to present-day social, political or technological tendencies are predicted. Some novels of this kind are quoted in Exercises 1 and 2. Films depicting dystopias (some based on novels) are very common. A few examples are: *Metropolis* (Fritz Lang, 1926), *Alphaville* (Jean-Luc Godard, 1965), *A Clockwork Orange* (Stanley Kubrick, 1971), *Westworld* (Michael Crichton, 1973), *Mad Max* (George Miller, 1979), *Stalker* (Andrei Tarkovsky, 1979), *Blade Runner* (Ridley Scott, 1982), *RoboCop* (Paul Verhoeven, 1987). *The Handmaid's Tale* was filmed in 1990 by Volker Schlöndorff, with a script by Harold Pinter.
Prepare a short talk for the class about a dystopian film or novel that has impressed you (or write a short description). Include

a a synopsis
b your comments on whether it is
- a fantasy
- a warning of what might happen in the future
- a criticism of contemporary society

20 **Writing/discussion**: What are your predictions for the future fifty years from now – what social, political and technological developments might have taken place? Write a short description or tell the class your ideas.

21 Design a cover for a new printing of *The Handmaid's Tale*.

22 **Writing**: Choose one of the following tasks.
- *a* Write a short message for Offred from Ofglen before she died.
- *b* Write the continuation of Aunt Lydia's speech (see lines 93–8).
- *c* Write a report from an Eye on the Salvaging.

Beyond the text

23 As you read the following extract, answer these questions.
- *a* Who is the person accused, and what is he accused of?
- *b* What do you think is the purpose of the 'Two Minutes Hate'?
- *c* Compare your ideas with a partner when you have finished reading.

Nineteen Eighty-Four (1948) George Orwell

Winston Smith, a minor official in the ruling 'Party' of the state of Oceania, is obliged to attend a daily ritual with his colleagues during a break from work.

See the Glossary section at the back of the book for vocabulary.

The next moment a hideous, grinding speech, as of some monstrous machine running without oil, burst from the big telescreen at the end of the room. It was a noise that set one's teeth on edge and bristled the hair at the back of one's neck. The Hate had started.

As usual, the face of Emmanuel Goldstein, the Enemy of the People, had flashed on to the screen. There were hisses here and there among the audience. The little sandy-haired woman gave a squeak of mingled fear and disgust. Goldstein was the renegade and backslider who once, long ago (how long ago, nobody quite remembered), had been one of the leading figures of the Party, almost on a level with Big Brother himself, and then had engaged in counter-revolutionary activities, had been condemned to death, and had mysteriously escaped and disappeared. The programmes of the Two Minutes Hate varied from day to day, but there was none in which Goldstein was not the principal figure. He was the primal traitor, the earliest defiler of the Party's purity. All subsequent crimes against the Party, all treacheries, acts of sabotage, heresies, deviations, sprang directly out of his teaching. Somewhere or other he was still alive and hatching his conspiracies: perhaps somewhere beyond the sea, under the protection of his foreign paymasters, perhaps even – so it was occasionally rumoured – in some hiding-place in Oceania itself.

Winston's diaphragm was constricted. He could never see the face of Goldstein without a painful mixture of emotions. It was a lean Jewish face, with a great fuzzy aureole of white hair and a small goatee beard – a clever face, and yet somehow inherently despicable, with a kind of senile silliness in the long thin nose, near the end of which a pair of spectacles was perched. It resembled the face of a sheep, and the voice, too, had a sheep-like quality. Goldstein was delivering his usual venomous attack upon the doctrines of the Party – an attack so exaggerated and perverse that a child should have been able to see through it, and yet just plausible enough to fill one with an alarmed feeling that other people, less level-headed than oneself, might be taken in by it. He was abusing Big Brother, he was denouncing the dictatorship of the Party, he was demanding the immediate conclusion of peace with Eurasia, he was advocating freedom of speech, freedom of the Press, freedom of assembly, freedom of thought, he was crying hysterically that the revolution had been betrayed – and all this in rapid polysyllabic speech which was a sort of parody of the habitual style of the orators of the Party, and even contained Newspeak words; more Newspeak words, indeed, than any Party member would normally use in real life. And all the while, lest one should be in any doubt as to the reality which Goldstein's specious claptrap covered, behind his head on the telescreen there marched the endless columns of the Eurasian army – row after row of solid-looking men with expressionless Asiatic faces, who swam up to the surface of the screen and vanished, to be replaced by others exactly similar. The dull rhythmic tramp of the soldiers' boots formed the background to Goldstein's bleating voice.

Before the Hate had proceeded for thirty seconds, uncontrollable exclamations of rage were breaking out from half the people in the room. The self-satisfied sheep-like face on the screen, and the terrifying power of the Eurasian army behind it, were too much to be borne: besides, the sight or even the thought of Goldstein produced fear and anger automatically. He was an object of hatred more constant than either Eurasia or Eastasia, since when Oceania was at war with one of these Powers it was generally at peace with the other.

But what was strange was that although Goldstein was hated and despised by everybody, although every day and a thousand times a day, on platforms, on the telescreen, in newspapers, in books, his theories were refuted, smashed, ridiculed, held up to the general gaze for the pitiful rubbish that they were – in spite of all this, his influence never seemed to grow less. Always there were fresh dupes waiting to be seduced by him. A day never passed when spies and saboteurs acting under his directions were not unmasked by the Thought Police. He was the commander of a vast shadowy army, an underground network of conspirators dedicated to the overthrow of the State. The Brotherhood, its name was supposed to be. There were also whispered stories of a terrible book, a compendium of all the heresies, of which Goldstein was the author and which circulated clandestinely here and there. It was a book without a title. People referred to it, if at all, simply as *the book*. But one knew of such things only through vague rumours. Neither the Brotherhood nor *the book* was a subject that any ordinary Party member would mention if there was a way of avoiding it.

In its second minute the Hate rose to a frenzy. People were leaping up and down in their places and shouting at the tops of their voices in an effort to drown the maddening bleating voice that came from the screen. The little sandy-haired woman had turned bright pink, and her mouth was opening and shutting like that of a landed fish. Even O'Brien's heavy face was flushed. He was sitting very straight in his chair, his powerful chest swelling and quivering as though he were standing up to the assault of a wave. The dark-haired girl behind Winston had begun crying out 'Swine! Swine! Swine!' and suddenly she picked up a heavy Newspeak dictionary and flung it at the screen. It struck Goldstein's nose and bounced off; the voice continued inexorably. In a lucid moment Winston found that he was shouting with the others and kicking his heel violently against the rung of his chair. The horrible thing about the Two Minutes Hate was not that one was obliged to act a part, but, on the contrary, that it was impossible to avoid joining in. Within thirty seconds any pretence was always unnecessary. A hideous ecstasy of fear and vindictiveness, a desire to kill, to torture, to smash faces in with a sledge-hammer, seemed to flow through the whole group of people like an electric current, turning one even against one's will into a grimacing, screaming lunatic. And yet the rage that one felt was an abstract, undirected emotion which could be switched from one object to another like the flame of a blowlamp. Thus, at one moment Winston's hatred was not turned against Goldstein at all, but, on the contrary, against Big Brother, the Party, and the Thought Police; and at such moments his heart went out to the lonely, derided heretic on the screen, sole guardian of truth and sanity in a world of lies. And yet the very next instant he was at one with the people about him, and all that was said of Goldstein seemed to him to be true. At those moments his secret loathing of Big Brother changed into adoration, and Big Brother seemed to tower up, an invincible, fearless protector, standing like a rock against the hordes of Asia, and Goldstein, in spite of his isolation, his helplessness, and the doubt that hung about his very existence, seemed like some sinister enchanter, capable by the mere power of his voice of wrecking the structure of civilization. …

… The Hate rose to its climax. The voice of Goldstein had become an actual sheep's bleat, and for an instant the face changed into that of a sheep. Then the sheep-face melted into the figure of a Eurasian soldier who seemed to be advancing, huge and terrible, his sub-machine gun roaring, and seeming to spring out of the surface of the screen, so that some of the people in the front row actually flinched backwards in their seats. But in the same moment, drawing a deep sigh of relief from everybody, the hostile figure melted into the face of Big Brother, black-haired, black-moustachio'd, full of power and mysterious calm, and so vast that it almost filled up the screen. Nobody heard what Big Brother was saying. It was merely a few words of encouragement, the sort of words that are uttered in the din of battle, not distinguishable individually but restoring confidence by the fact of being spoken. Then the face of Big Brother faded away again, and instead the three slogans of the Party stood out in bold capitals:

WAR IS PEACE
FREEDOM IS SLAVERY
IGNORANCE IS STRENGTH

But the face of Big Brother seemed to persist for several seconds on the screen, as though the impact that it had made on everyone's eyeballs was too vivid to wear off immediately. The little sandy-haired woman had flung herself forward over the back of the chair in front of her. With a tremulous murmur that sounded like 'My Saviour!' she extended her arms towards the screen. Then she buried her face in her hands. It was apparent that she was uttering a prayer.

At this moment the entire group of people broke into a deep, slow, rhythmical chant of 'B-B! … B-B! … B-B!' – over and over again, very slowly, with a long pause between the first 'B' and the second – a heavy, murmurous sound, somehow curiously savage, in the background of which one seemed to hear the stamp of naked feet and the throbbing of tom-toms. For perhaps as much as thirty seconds they kept it up. It was a refrain that was often heard in moments of overwhelming emotion. Partly it was a sort of hymn to the wisdom and majesty of Big Brother, but still more it was an act of self-hypnosis, a deliberate drowning of consciousness by means of rhythmic noise. Winston's entrails seemed to grow cold. In the Two Minutes Hate he could not help sharing the general delirium, but this sub-human chanting of 'B-B! … B-B!' always filled him with horror. Of course he chanted it with the rest: it was impossible to do otherwise. To dissemble your feelings, to control your face, to do what everyone else was doing was an instinctive reaction. But there was a space of a couple of seconds during which the expression in his eyes might conceivably have betrayed him.

24 What points of comparison do you notice with *The Handmaid's Tale*? Make notes under these headings.

a the reactions of Winston and Offred

b the reactions of other people

c enemies of the State

d political language

25 **Pair/group work**: Are there any features of today's society – either in your country or abroad – which seem similar to the societies of *The Handmaid's Tale* or *Nineteen Eighty-Four*? Do you think either of these two novels gives a plausible view of the future? Note down your ideas, and compare them with a partner, or in groups, or with the class.

Authors

Margaret Atwood was born in Ottawa, Canada in 1939, and educated at the universities of Toronto and Harvard. She has lectured on English literature and been writer-in-residence at universities in Canada, the USA and Australia. She currently lives with her husband and child in Toronto. Atwood is one of the most eminent of contemporary Canadian writers, and her books have received many awards. Her critical success is matched by popular acclaim: she frequently appears on Canadian TV and radio, and according to one journalist 'people follow her on the streets and in stores'. Her first two volumes of poetry, *Double Persephone* (1961) and *The Circle Game* (1966), both won awards, and since then she has published fourteen volumes of poetry and a study of Canadian literature, *Survival* (1972), in which she distinguishes a specifically Canadian literature, different from its American and British counterparts. She has, however, come to be better known as a novelist: her first novel, *The Edible Woman*, was published in 1969, and has been followed by *Surfacing* (1972), *Lady Oracle* (1976), *Life Before Man* (1979), *Bodily Harm* (1982), *Encounters with the Element Man* (1982), *Unearthing Suite* (1983), *The Handmaid's Tale* (1985, which won both the Governor-General's Award and the Arthur C Clarke Award for Science Fiction), *Cat's Eye* (1989) and *The Robber Bride* (1993).

Both her poetry and prose show evident feminist concerns. The main characters of all the early novels are young women driven to rebellion by the conventions of contemporary North American society, and, when asked to explain why so many of the female characters in her poems are portrayed as suffering, Atwood replied 'My women suffer because most of the women I talk to seem to have suffered'. In *The Handmaid's Tale* the strong feminist theme of earlier books becomes dominant. Atwood has stated that her dystopian state of Gilead is by no means fantasy, but the extrapolation of anti-female tendencies that she has observed in various parts of the world.

Margaret Atwood has also published three collections of short stories: *Dancing Girls* (1977), *Bluebeard's Egg* (1983) and *Murder in the Dark* (1983).

George Orwell (1903–50) was the pen name of Eric Blair. Although born in India, he was sent to the English public schools St Cyprian's and Eton, where he had his first unpleasant experiences of the English class system. He joined the Imperial police in Burma in 1922 and resigned in 1927: the disgust he felt for the oppressive colonialist system can be seen in his first novel *Burmese Days* (1934). In order to gain first-hand experience of the life of the poor, on his return to Europe he lived as a tramp in the slums of Paris and London, an experience described in *Down and Out in Paris and London* (1933).

Orwell fought, and was wounded, in the Spanish Civil War as a volunteer for the Republicans, which he documented in *Homage to Catalonia* (1938). During the Second World War he was war correspondent for the BBC and *The Observer*. He gained an international reputation with *Animal Farm* (1945), a satire on Stalinism, and totalitarianism in general. The animals on a farm, led by the pigs, rebel against the tyranny of the farmer and try to establish a state of perfect social equality. The final result is, however, a new tyranny headed by the pigs.

The title of his last novel, *Nineteen Eighty-Four* (written in 1948: Orwell simply reversed the last figures to invent the date), and the ominous slogan of the ruling party – 'Big Brother Is Watching You' – have passed into the English language as expressions that connote oppressive, totalitarian regimes. In this novel the world is divided into three great powers in a constant state of war: Oceania, Eurasia and Eastasia. In Oceania everything is dominated by 'the Party', which checks every word and action with thousands of telescreens and other instruments of surveillance. Propaganda has replaced truth, and the English language is reduced to a limited number of basic words – 'Newspeak'. The past has been carefully rewritten and where necessary destroyed. The main character, Winston Smith, tries desperately to become an individual, and has an affair with a party member, but after a horrifying experience in 'Room 101', where the 'Thought Police' devise tortures especially adapted to the phobias of each prisoner (in Winston's case, his fear of rats), he too is reduced to an unthinking party member.

Orwell's commitment to free-thinking and non-doctrinaire socialism can also be seen in his *Collected Essays, Journalism and Letters* (published in 1968).

Glossary

2 Mean Streets

Farewell, My Lovely

Exercise 2

1 supercilious: *patronizing, superior*
2 drawlingly: *in a slow, affected way*
4 Check: (US) *That is correct*
6 keep his mouth shut: (colloquial) *not talk to anyone, ie keep a secret*
9 Montemar Vista: *fashionable residential area outside Los Angeles*
13 sidewalk: (US) *pavement*
22 grew icicles: *ie became cold and a little aggressive*
24 a Harvard boy: *Marlowe sarcastically assumes Marriott has studied at Harvard, the oldest University in the USA*
25 itched: *ie wanted to kick Marriott*
25–6 trying to crawl under a duck: *Marlowe means he had so little money in his bank account that you could easily pass it under a duck without disturbing it!*

Main text

3 pelicans: *kind of sea-bird*
3–4 was flying bomber formation: *flying close together, like warplanes*
4 the creaming lip: *the white top part*
8 spur of mountain: *piece of ground projecting from the side of a mountain*
9 sneeze: *violent expulsion of air from the nose and mouth (often done when you have a cold)*
10 box lunches: *cardboard containers for food*
13 galvanized: *covered with metal*
17 awning: *piece of material providing shelter from rain or sun*
20 chided: *reprimanded*
23 grunting: *making a low, rough noise as a result of physical effort*
25 toad: *small amphibian, similar to a frog*
27 offsea: *coming from the sea*
32 yelling: *shouting*
33 salt-tarnished: *lightly covered with salt*
34 imitation coach-lamp: *modern imitation of the old-fashioned lamps on horse-drawn coaches*
37 trimmings: *decorative accessories*
38 coyote: *American wild animal, similar to a wolf*
Winged Victory: *the silver statuette found on Rolls-Royce cars; these cars have a reputation for luxury*
42 clatter: *loud, metallic noise caused by knocking*
45 flannel: *light material, normally used for summer clothes*
satin: *shiny material, similar to silk*
47 cornflower: *small, blue flower*
51 a little on the heavy side: *rather fat*
53 ledges: *layers*
56 lad: (colloquial) *young man*
60 On the dot: *Punctually, Exactly*
61 frowned: *brought his eyebrows together to show he was thinking*
62 phony: (colloquial) *not genuine*
74 crackling: *burning with the noise made by flaming wood or coal*
76 glazed: *shiny*
80 velvet: *thick, soft material, usually considered luxurious*
82 tassels: *groups of short cords tied together at one end, used as decorations on corners of cushions*
83 rough: *violent*
83 damask: *heavy material, usually considered luxurious*
85 absinthe: *strong, green-coloured,*

alcoholic drink with a bitter taste, made in France; usually considered sophisticated
87 squeak: *make a short, high-pitched noise (eg a mouse squeaks); Marlowe implies Marriott's guests don't discuss anything important*
92 Camel: *brand of American cigarette; Marlowe always smokes them*
96 bit: *piece*
98 Klopstein: *not a real sculptor; Marlowe makes up this name*
Warts: *small, hard lumps on the skin*
Fanny: (US slang) *behind, buttocks*
100 He smoothed it out: *He made his face return to normal*
101 somewhat: *rather*
104 slight: *small, unimportant*
108 dimple: *hollow in the cheek or chin*
109 marble: *small glass ball that children play with; Marlowe means that Marriott's dimple is large*
112 blackmail: *demanding money from someone by threatening to reveal a secret they have, or a crime they have committed*
117 aquamarine: *greenish-blue colour*
119 noose: *end of a rope tied in a circle, used for hanging someone*
120 tilted: *moved away from a vertical position*
127 deal: *arrangement*
129 bodyguard: *someone paid to protect a person in case of attack*
130 snicked: *made fall*
139 snubbed out: *put out*
140 twiddled my thumbs: *Marlowe put his hands together and moved his thumbs around each other; it is an action often performed by people who are waiting for something*
144 jerked: *moved suddenly and violently*
146–7 using the edge of his voice: *speaking in a cold and threatening way*
151 risk my neck: *expose myself to danger*
153 got around to: *had time to*
154 dusky: *dark*
157 swift: *quick*
punch: *violent blow delivered with the fist*
158 grinned: *smiled widely*
160 snapped: *spoke quickly*
163 hold-up: *armed robbery*
164 touchy: *sensitive, irritable*
168 jade: *precious green stone, typical of the Orient, often used for making jewellery*
172 workmanship: *artistic skill of the jewellery makers*
175 carats: *units for measuring the weight of jewels*
intricately carved: *decorated in great detail by cutting*
180 the Trocadero: *a night-club*
181 brushed: *touched lightly*
fender: (US) *metal part of the car over the wheel*
185 glimpse: *quick view*
193 ransom: *money paid to a kidnapper or thief to get a person or property back*
199 slid: *moved smoothly*
202 reckless: *not caring about danger or risks*
205 dirt cheap: (slang) *very cheap*
206 thugs: (colloquial) *violent people*
212 hangover: *headache caused by having drunk too much alcohol*
218 plant: *someone, perhaps a policeman, substituting for Marriott*
220 marked: *ie marked with signs that can be recognized by the police*
221 Currency: *Cash, not cheques*
223 black light: *see lines 229–30*
224 cops: (US slang) *police*
226 record: *police files of previous crimes*
227 wrinkled his brow: *made lines appear on his forehead, to show he was thinking*

229 metallic inks: *special inks (coloured liquids) used on banknotes*
glisten: *shine*
234 picked on me: *chose me*
236 boyish: *like a boy*
238 at random: *by chance, without any plan*
241 squashed: *crushed, flattened (Marlowe has been sitting on them)*
245 Uh-huh: (informal) *a written representation of a sound people make to show that they agree, or that they have understood*
253 eight grand: (US slang) *eight thousand dollars*
258 big-hearted: *generous*
259 double-crossing: (slang) *promising to do something, but not keeping one's promise in order to do something to one's advantage; the word is generally used about criminals*
260 heist guys: (US slang) *professional robbers*
264 twitched: *moved rapidly without control*
266 flash: *flashlight, torch*
pulled the stick-up: (US slang) *carried out the robbery*
270 cased: (US slang) *carefully planned*
270–1 They're cased … a gold inlay: *Marlowe means that the robbers have made very careful preparations*
271 dame: (US slang) *woman*
272 stiffly: *uncomfortably and reluctantly*
276 the fewer cups I break: (US slang) *the fewer mistakes I make*
278 play ball: (US slang) *cooperate*
281 shrugged: *moved my shoulders up and down, to show I didn't disagree*
287 conked: (slang) *hit on the head*
291 a spot of: *a little*
292 bucks: (US slang) *dollars*
296 alcove: *small space apart from the main room*
299 Five-Star Martell: *expensive brand of French brandy*
303 zooming: *going very fast*
308 cradled: *put back*
309 hushed: *silent*
drawn: *worried*
311 stiff: *strong*
312 swirled: *made move in circles around the glass*
319 blinked: *reflected*
321 boulevard: (US) *main road*
324 Camino de la Costa: (Spanish) *the coast road*
327–8 made me a fine target: *ie made me easy to see for anyone who wanted to shoot me*
331 manila: *made of strong brown paper*
334–5 four-by-fours: *wooden posts, four inches by four inches wide*
335 dirt road: *road with just earth as a surface*
342 wad: *tighly packed bundle*
344 caved in: *broke*
347 salt-tarnished: *stained with salt*
355 go to bed with the chickens: *ie go to bed very early*
358 brush: *bushes*
360 sage: *aromatic bush, typical of the US*
361 loomed: *came into sight*
365 cut: *switched off*
367 crickets: *brown jumping insects; the male makes a short loud noise by rubbing its wings together*
chirping: *the distinctive noise made by crickets*
371 Sit tight: *Stay sitting, Don't move*
a look see: (colloquial) *a look around*
373 butt: *handle*
375 hacked: cut
377 neck: (US slang) *kiss*
387 night glass: *binoculars for use at night*
396 running board: *board at the sides of cars of this period that you could stand on*
398 tryout: *experiment before the real version*

404 swish: *high soft sound made by something moved quickly through the air*
sap: (US slang) *short thick metal stick covered with rubber or leather, used for hitting people*

The Third Man

4 ushered in: *made him remember*
7 deprecating: *not valuing anybody or anything very much*
7–8 take-it-or-leave-it manner: *ie accept me or not – it's your choice*
11 scoundrel: *villain, bad person*
13 stocky: *short and thick*
14 hunched: *a little raised and bent forwards*
15 rascality: *dishonesty*
18 patted: *touched lightly a few times*
24 known the ropes: (colloquial) *known what to do in every situation*
25–6 the Wheel: *large circular structure, rising vertically from the ground, with carriages (called 'cars' in line 45) on the rim. As it revolves, people in the carriages get taken up and down*
28 poor devils: *an expression of sympathy for people*
30 commiseration: *pity*
32 cross-girders: *large iron bars, part of the structure of the Wheel*
34 Reichsbrücke: *a large bridge in Vienna*
37 smart: (US colloquial) *clever*
42 were on to me: *had discovered things about me*
43 cut me in on the spoils: *share the profits from your criminal activities with me*
45 car: *carriage of the Wheel; Lime and Martins are shown in the car in the photograph on page 53*
47 school-quad: *open area outside a school where children play*
48–9 letting in on it: *sharing the secret with*
51 Marlowe's devils: *the devils in the play 'Doctor Faustus' by the Elizabethan dramatist Christopher Marlowe (1564–1593)*
squibs: *small fireworks that go bang*
52 Peter Pan: *a little boy who never grows up, the main character in a play for children by J M Barrie (1860–1937)*
59 iron-ribbed: *the reference is to the iron girders of the Wheel*
63 dots: *very small round marks (eg full stops at the end of sentences)*
69 stuck to tyres: *continued selling tyres (a previous activity of Lime's)*
72 pop up again: (colloquial) *reappear*
76 shove: *push*
78 carrion: *dead flesh*
84 wrinkled: *with lines (of sunlight) across it*
110 fearful: *terrible*
118 midgets: *extremely short people*
127 mugs: (slang) *idiots*
134 doomed-to-be-victims: *people who will inevitably become victims, either of Harry Lime, or of someone like him*
135 peered: *looked curiously*
138 turn policeman: *work for the police*
140 Bracer: *an old school-friend of Lime and Martins*
144 in a jam: (colloquial) *in trouble*

3 'It Was Never Love'

Women in Love

CHAPTER 9

2 picturesque: *looking very pretty, in a traditional way*
3 Willey Green: *a small village outside the town of Nottingham, in the north of England*

4 colliery train: *train that takes coal away from a mine*
rumbling: *making a continuous low sound*

5 panting: *making a noise like breathing quickly and loudly because of exertion*
hoarsely: *roughly*

6 embankments: *steep sides of earth on either side of the railway line*

9 trotted: *rode (with the horse taking small steps)*

9–10 red Arab mare: *female horse, light brown in colour, from Arabia*

10–11 quivering: *shaking*

13 slender: *delicate*
saluted: *said hello to*

17 well set: *well built*

20 chuffed: *made the noise typical of a steam train*

21 wince away: *move backwards, showing pain*

26 recoiled: *jumped quickly backwards*

29 steel connecting-rod: *piece of metal that joins the part of the steam engine to the wheels and makes them go round*
highroad: *main part of the railway track*
clanking: *making a loud metallic noise*

30 rebounded: *jumped back*

36 black-dilated: *wide open, showing the dark pupils*
spellbound: *as if under a magic spell, hypnotized*

39 clamour: *loud, frightening noise or feeling*

45 buffers: *the projecting pieces of metal that protect the trucks if they hit something*
cymbals: *musical instruments – round metal dishes that you clash together*

47–8 fore-feet: *the front feet of a horse*

48 utterly: *completely*

52 back to the mark: *ie back to the railway crossing*

56 whirlwind: *column of spinning air that creates a violent storm*
faint: *almost unconscious*
poignant: *causing a feeling of sudden sadness*
dizziness: *unpleasant spinning sensation in the head*

63 keen edge: *ie sharp edge of a sword*

65 frenzied: *maddened*
repulsive: *very unpleasant and hateful*

71 treading: *moving slowly and rhythmically*

72–3 grinding and squeaking: *both words describe unpleasant metallic noises*

73 pawed: *hit the air with her feet*

75 encompassed: *covered, controlled*

81 trickles: *small amounts falling down*

83 spurs: *pointed pieces of metal worn on the heels of a rider's boots*
reeled: *went around as though in a circle (ie because of dizziness)*

89 hooded: *covered*

90 diminishing: *getting less as it it went farther away*

92 half-stunned: *half unconscious*

93 unstained: *unmarked, unchanged*

98 trail behind: *follow slowly behind*
receding: *moving away*

101 sprang: *jumped*

102 latch: *the device for closing the gates*

103 asunder: *open*

105 jerked: *moved violently*

106 gull: *sea bird with black and white or grey and white feathers*

109 twisting aside: *moving his body to one side*

111 hoofs: *feet of a horse*

112 drum-like sleepers: *pieces of wood put under the metal of the railway track: here they are drum-like because of the noise made by the horse's hoofs on them*

113 springily: *energetically*
114 hobbled: *walked with a limp*
115 logs: *another word for sleepers (see line 112)*
116 fastened: *closed*
117 jockey: *horse-rider*
his own road: (dialect) *his own way*
121 bully: *rough, threatening boy or man who likes frightening or hurting others*
127 welly: (dialect) *possibly*
131 grand: *important*
136 Harab: *the gatekeeper's pronunciation of Arab*
142 soft black dust: *ie coal-dust*
numbed: *made unfeeling*
145 clenching: *holding tightly*
147 loins and thighs and calves: *loins is the part of the body above the legs and below the waist, including the sexual organs; the thigh is the part of the leg between the knee and where the leg joins the body; the calf is between the knee and the ankle*
148 subordination: *control, exercise of one's will*
151 patterned head-stocks: *some of the machinery of the coal-mine*

CHAPTER 30

159 dropped: *discontinued*
whims: *sudden, small desires to do or have something for no particular reason*
162 cast round: *try to find*
165 stark: *bare, essential*
crouched: *bent her knees and lowered herself toward the ground*
167 mountain-knot: *range of mountains*
168 pivot: *central point on which a situation depends*
172 frost: *white, powdery layer of ice that forms during cold nights*
174 resented: *disliked*
182 darts: *shoots out*
184 mute: *silent*
186 'Are you regretting Ursula?': *ie 'Are you missing Ursula now that she has gone?'*
189 stiffened: *went rigid*
195 flippant: *not serious, joking*
200 *fearful*: *terrible, very bad*
202 unrelenting: *determined, not wanting to give up*
209 strangled: *strange-sounding because of strong emotion*
213 sneer: *facial expression showing strong lack of respect*
219 barren: *sterile, lacking feeling*
222 diabolic: *terrible (ie like a devil)*
228 severing: *cutting*
228–9 Gordian knot: *in ancient Greece the Gordian knot was a knot that was impossible to untie; Alexander the Great finally cut it with a sword; it means a situation impossible to resolve, except by drastic action*
237 counterfoil: *be equal to, challenge, overcome*
238 pleaded: *begged*
240 coaxed: *persuaded gently*
248 Fancy: *Just imagine!*
raillery: *friendly joking*
252–3 swaying … plunging: *both verbs refer to rhythmic, pulsating movements*
254 at the very quick: *deep inside him*
257 waste: *destroy*
261 'You can say you want a dressing room': *Gudrun suggests a way that Gerald can ask for another room without telling the hotel staff the real reason – that they no longer want to share a room*
265 without notice even: *without even informing me first*
270 giddy: *making Gerald's head spin*
271 reeling: *spinning*
275 insentient: *unfeeling*
281 bewildered: *puzzled, confused*
287 clutched: *held tightly*
288 spasmodically: *with quick, sudden movements*
291 forlorn: *unhappy*
298 ghastly: *terrible, awful*

303 soothing: *calming*
spent: *exhausted*
307 fragment: *small piece*
310 doom: *terrible destiny*
311 'thou shalt', 'thou shalt not': (archaic) *in modern English – 'you must', 'you must not'. The Ten Commandments in the Old Testament of the Bible begin with these words; Gudrun means 'a rigid order'*
312 creeping: *moving in a slow, tired, cautious way*
314 see-saw: *situation that moves from one extreme to another (a see-saw is a piece of wood with a central pivot on which children sit at each end and go up and down)*
315 ratified: *confirmed*
nulled: *made nothing*
317 paroxysms: *sudden, powerful expressions of strong feelings*
319–20 leave her in the lurch: *not give her help of any kind*
320 flaw: *imperfection*
326 static: *not moving, still*
331 convulsion: *violent movement*
333 impervious: *incapable of being penetrated*
334 chaos: *disorder*
336 lacking: *missing, not existing*
341 sheer: *complete*
nought: *nothingness*
342 fawn: *flatter, show a lot of attention to*
344 dissipated: *wasted, inexistent*
345 mocking: *joking*
licentiousness: *sexual immorality*
346 rent: *hole made by tearing*
354 forgo: *do without*
355 immune: *not affected by, not suffering*
sheath: *covering, usually the container for a sword*
356 germinated: *started growing*
358 yearning: *strong desire*
363 rebuffs: *refusals of Gerald's approaches*
365 quickening: *coming to life*
370 bud: *the small part of a plant which develops into a flower*
379 keen: *sharp, biting*
380 crimson: *deep red*
381 peaks and ridges: *tops of the mountains*
384 transport: *ecstasy*
387 clamour: *excitement (see line 39)*
394 twilight: *the evening light just before the sun goes down*
grovel: *express exaggerated admiration, at the risk of humiliating oneself*
396 winced: *moved her head backward involuntarily*
violation: *feeling of being damaged or destroyed*
408 debar: *forbid, exclude*
409 straining after: *trying, uselessly, to get*
413 chilled: *cold*
419 do away with: *kill*

A Farewell to Arms

5 orderly: *untrained hospital worker*
10 gravel drive: *path made of small stones*
12 on post: *at my military position*
36 shut: *closed*
43 bridge: *card game*
45 for some stakes: *ie in order to win a prize of some kind*
52 bench: *seat*
57 rotten: *disgusting, unpleasant*
59 Don't be dull: *Don't pretend not to understand*
68–9 I had a very fine little show: *I enjoyed our little game of saying we loved each other*
69–70 gone off: *ie gone off my head; I haven't lost control of my senses*
74 'That's what the priest said.': *Frederic has met an Italian priest earlier in the novel*
90 San Gabriele: *a place outside the town where the fighting is going on*

4 War Games

Catch-22

CHAPTER 4

1 crazy: (US) *mad*
8 snorted: *expelled air violently from the nose to express scorn (see next word)*
scornfully: *with very great lack of respect*
9 gloomy: *sad, unhappy*
10 sneer: *facial expression expressing great lack of respect*
12 draft: *call to compulsory military service*
13 shooting their kissers off: (US slang) *making speeches*
14 the medical game: *the medical profession (Daneeka's choice of words shows his cynicism)*
15 dough: (US slang) *money*
17 sulk: *refuse to speak or smile at people to let them know you are unhappy or angry (children often do this)*
17–18 saturnine: *serious and unfriendly*
18 mournful: *sad*
pouches: *bags of loose skin*
18–19 brooded over: *thought about, worried about*
20 enlisted men: *ordinary soldiers, not officers*
23 stuffed: *blocked (he couldn't breathe very well)*
25–6 reporting on sick call: *saying they were ill and so could not go on duty*
28 gums: *solid pink flesh inside the mouth which teeth are attached to*
28–9 gentian violet solution: *liquid to kill bacteria*
29 laxative: *substance to make you excrete*
36 Major ——— de Coverley: *he has never told anyone his first name, and no-one has dared ask him because of his frightening face! (refer to him as 'Major blank de Coverley')*
pitching: *throwing*
horseshoes: *U-shaped pieces of metal attached to bottoms of horses' feet; the Major plays a game of throwing horseshoes to try to make them fall around a short post fixed in the ground*
37 pit: *enclosed area*
eye patch: *piece of material or plastic to cover the eye*
38 celluloid: *kind of plastic*
41 cornea: *part of the eye; protective covering at the front, inside the white part*
44–5 look him over: *examine him*
49 motor pool: *section in charge of transport (buses, trucks, jeeps, etc)*
52 drastically: *terribly, very*
55 elephantiasis: *disease causing great increase in size of the limbs*
56 dread: *terrible*
63 giving vent to: *expressing*
64 womb: *uterus, organ of woman's body where babies grow during pregnancy*
68 flight log: *official record of flights and passengers kept by a pilot*
69 wheedled: *tried to persuade him to do something by being hypocritically pleasant*
sly: *secretive*
70 conspiratorial: *as though making someone part of a secret plan*
wink: *the closing and opening of one eye to communicate something secret*
75 grease: (literally, *an oily substance to keep machines working easily) Daneeka means a secret exchange of favours*
77 You scratch my back, I'll scratch yours: (idiom) *If you do me a favour, I'll do a favour for you; Yossarian ironically interprets this literally ('to scratch' is to rub a part of your skin that is irritating you)*
84 minute: *very small (pronounced* /maɪˈnjuːt/*)*

86 khaki: *dark yellow-brown cloth, often used for military uniforms*
87 bleached: *with most of the colour removed*
88 laundering: *washing and pressing*
90 unthawed: *unfrozen*
all tucked up into himself: *with the parts of his body closing in on each other*
91 huddled: *moved close together*
96 lament: *complaint*
101 intelligence tent: *tent where intelligence (ie information) about the enemy is gathered and processed (the word 'intelligence' is ironic considering the comments made at lines 111–30)*
eyeglasses: *glasses, spectacles*
102 subversive: *person who tries to harm his own side in a war by giving information to the enemy or (here especially) by destroying his side's morale*
104 *panacea* and *utopia*: *universal cure and ideal society (they are both terms which sound intellectual)*
111–30 *all the questions asked are deliberately without sense, and the short ones are also grammatically deviant*
114 stooped: *with the shoulders bent forward*
mealy-colored: *yellowish coloured*
115 Poppa: (US) *familiar term for father*
merry-go-round: *machine in a fairground that turns round and round and has plastic or wooden animals or vehicles on it that children can ride*
116 trump: *card belonging to the group of cards chosen to have the highest value in a card-game*
117 Ho-ho beriberi: *a nonsense exclamation*
119 Balls: (literally, *testicles*) *slightly offensive term meaning 'Nonsense!'*
122 'Where are the Snowdens of yesteryear?': *Yossarian alludes to a famous line by the French poet Francois Villon (1431–65), 'Où sont les neiges d'antan?', usually translated as 'Where are the snows of yesteryear (ie last year)?'; the line is about the temporary nature of life*
129 *'Où sont les Neigedens d'antan?': Yossarian plays with the fact that 'snow' is 'neige' in French to produce a French version of his question in line 122*
131–2 *'Parlez en anglais, … Je ne parle pas français'*: (French) *'Speak in English, … I don't speak French'*
131 for Christ's sake: *an expression of annoyance and frustration*
134 wring: *extract forcibly*
136 humid: *wet*
coating: *film, covering*
136–7 undernourished: *showing signs of a bad diet*
138 Group Headquarters: *where the commanding officers of this group of pilots and airplanes operate from*
142 a stroke of genius: *a brilliant solution*
152 chaplain: *army priest*
154 banging: *making a lot of noise*
plumbing: *tubes and pipes that carry water in a building*
155 skeet-shooting range: *place for shooting targets made of clay which are thrown into the air*
162 gambling: *playing cards etc for money*
168 homiletic: *with a moral message*
memoranda: *messages sent around to inform everybody in an organization about something (singular form: memorandum)*
172 T. S. Eliot: *well-known poet (1888–1965) who won the Nobel Prize for Literature, author of 'The Waste Land' and 'Four Quartets'*
ex-P.F.C.: *abbreviation for Private First Class, a slightly*

higher rank than Private, which is the lowest rank for a soldier. Wintergreen is 'ex-' because he has been demoted

172–3 mail-sorting cubicle: *place where letters are put in different groups for delivery*

173–4 slammed down: *put down quickly and violently*

175 perplexed: *puzzled, confused*

188 mused: *said rather thoughtfully*

189 funereal: (adjective from 'funeral') *sombre*

191 unctuous: *full of false friendliness*

192 shrewd: *clever*

193 gleamed: *shone*

202 gazed at: *looked for a long time at*

203 level: *total*

204 aide: *assistant*

207 scowl: *angry expression*

208 stocky: *short, but with wide shoulders and chest*

grizzled: *with the hair going grey*

209 tufts: *small bushy collections of hair, ie his eyebrows*

blunt: *square-shaped*

213 bastard: (literally, *an illegitimate person*) *offensive term of abuse*

216 trace: *sign*

224 code: *secret way of communication that the enemy cannot understand*

226 colors of the day: *different daily salutes to the flag*

231 clerk: *office-worker*

232 pretty close to: *quite friendly with*

tipped me off: *advised me*

prose: *writing-style*

233 prolix: *full of unnecessary words*

247 schedule: *timetable*

250 figured out: *calculated*

271 the toll this is taking: *the suffering this is causing*

272 magnanimously: *generously*

275 snigger: *laugh childishly*

292 unhooked: *undone*

brassiere: *piece of women's underwear that supports the breasts; Dunbar says that at high school slight sexual adventures were the most exciting things they could expect from life*

295 Zip!: *a sound representing a very quick motion*

CHAPTER 31

307 missions: *flights*

311 manifest: *list of passengers*

312 struck: *cancelled, removed*

313 roster: *list*

313–14 quivering: *trembling with emotion*

314 trudged: *walked slowly and with effort*

316–17 sepulchral: *suited to a cemetery*

317 roosting: *resting or sleeping (as birds do at night)*

318 orderly room: *room for the hospital assistants*

320 Mudd: *Mudd was supposed to share a tent with Yossarian, but was killed before he even arrived at the base*

323 thornier: *more complicated*

324 stoic: *determined not to show any emotion*

325 bereavement: *sense of loss felt when someone has died*

330 wooden: *showing no emotion*

332 Goddammit: (literally *'God damn it!'*) *a swear word*

expostulated: *complained*

333 exasperation: *frustration*

335 glum: *sad, mournful*

336 sniff: *sharp intake of air through the nose (when you have a cold you sniff a lot)*

337 sulphur pills: *medicine for skin disease*

338 Argyrol: *similar to the solution mentioned in lines 28–9*

downcast: *with eyes looking down, because of sadness*

forlorn: *sad and lonely*

swallow: *small bird with pointed wings and a tail with two points*

342 resentful: *angry about having to accept something*

349 surging: *increasing very quickly*

petrifying: *as though turning into stone*
onrushing: *approaching very quickly*
357 reeling: *turning round and round*
361 War Department: *Government department in charge of the armed forces*
362 yelped: *gave a short shout of fear*
362–3 remonstrate: *protest*
363 edged away: *moved away*
364 repugnance: *dislike and fear*
366 remains: *dead body*
367 Gee: (US colloquial) *an expression of surprise*
371 fuck: (US offensive slang) *offensive person*
374 split: *disturbed*
Staten Island: *area of New York City, where the Daneekas have their home*
375 woeful: *full of sorrow*
lamentation: *cries and tears of sorrow*
380 distraught: *extremely disturbed*
383 a bolt from the blue: (idiom) *something completely unexpected*
386 dumbfounded: *completely puzzled and confused*
387 shaky: *not steady*
390 crinkled: *folded many times*
391 grubby: *rather dirty*
V-mail stationery: (US) *paper used during the war (V stands for Victory)*
391–2 dashed ... off: *wrote quickly*
393 wire: *telegram*
394 touchily: *in an irritated way*
395 sadistic: *causing pain because one likes it*
psychotic: *mad, crazy*
forger: *someone who illegally copies or imitates letters, documents or art*
399 mitigated: *reduced*
400 GI: (US) *General Infantryman; used as a generic term for anyone in the American armed forces in World War 2*
404 Veterans Administration: *Government department in charge of ex-members of the armed forces*
406 demise: (formal) *death*
408 inexorably: *without any possibility of being stopped*
410 provisions: *conditions*
413 burial allowance: *some money to help with the funeral expenses*
418 face value: *the value written in the policy (it could be worth more if invested)*
420 fraternal lodge: *group or society of people created to give help to each other*
421 cemetery plot: *place at a cemetery to bury the remains*
424 flirt: *show sexual interest*
426 piling up: *accumulating, increasing*
432 keep his head above the ground: (idiom) *survive*
dismal: *sad and hopeless*
434 ostracized: *ignored, not allowed to talk to other people or be spoken to*
435 foully: *bitterly, amd with much obscene language*
437 pullulating: *increasing, being born at great speed*
438 PX rations: *food and drink from the canteen*
442 cremated: *burnt as a corpse*
445 baggy-chinned: *with loose folds of skin under the chin*
slovenly: *untidy and dirty*
449 bombardiers: *the airmen in charge of dropping the bombs*
450 ebbing: *decreasing, going away*
under surveillance: *being watched, controlled*
455 ailing: *sick, ill*
rodent: *animal such as a mouse or rat*
456 sacks: *bags, loose skin (see line 18)*
padded: *walked softly and without noise*
457 fruitlessly: *in vain, without getting what he wanted*

ubiquitous: *that goes, or is present, everywhere*
spook: *ghost*
465 plight: *(bad) situation*
470 stunned: *shocked*
471–2 compunction: *guilt*
472 comply: *act according to her husband's request*
478 Lansing, Michigan: *capital city of the state of Michigan in the north-east of the USA; it is not well known; Mrs Daneeka's plan is to escape*
479 forwarding address: *address where any mail arriving at a previous address can be sent*

The Danger Tree

1 Operations truck: *the truck where those in command do the planning and take decisions*
2 grave-faced: *with a serious face*
5–6 as like as two peas: (idiom) *identical*
7 mess: *canteen, where the soldiers eat*
11 awning: *piece of material providing shelter from the sun*
12 stewed tea: *tea that has been left too long, so it has a strong unpleasant taste*
15 a right plague: *the sudden occurrence of a large number of unpleasant things causing harm or damage ('right' is a colloquial way of emphasizing a noun)*
16 flit: *name for a chemical spray to kill flies*
19 bully-beef: *cold beef from a tin*
21 Harriet Pringle: *a friend of Simon's; she has talked to him about the plagues sent by God to persuade the Pharoah to allow Moses and the Israelites to leave Egypt (described in 'Exodus' in the Old Testament)*
23 'a grievous swarm': *the words used in the Authorized Version of the Bible*
25 treacle: *sweet dark thick liquid used in cooking sweet dishes*
27 fly swat: *instrument with a wide flat part attached to a handle which you hit and kill flies with when they have landed on a surface*
33 tarpaulin: *sheet of canvas*
34 bag: (hunting term) *the number of flies killed*
36 veered: *turned*
37 manoeuvring: *moving*
40 manna: *a food which miraculously dropped from heaven and saved Moses and the Israelites from dying of hunger in the desert (another reference to 'Exodus' in the Old Testament)*
46 the heat of battle: *ie when emotions are at their highest*
47 sworn: *promised himself*
51 scrap: (army slang) *battle*
53 Mierir Depression: *place in the North African desert*
54 shelling: *guns firing*
54 holed up: (army slang) *trapped, unable to move*
58 batman: *soldier who is the personal assistant to an officer*
63 brewing: *about to start*
65 Hugman: *Simon's own batman*
67 mine fields: *areas planted with bombs that will explode when you step on them*
75 a tick: (colloquial) *a moment*
78 gun pits: *holes in the ground where the guns are kept*
79 sand devils: *columns of sand that revolve very quickly in the air, caused by the action of the wind*
83 sand fog: *effect of so many particles of sand in the air that it is impossible to see*
86 searing: *sharp and cutting*
89 crimson: *deep red*
104 brew-up: *making tea*
107 mardam: *hard ground of the desert*
108 turrets: *top parts of tanks, resembling small towers, where the guns are*

110 cinder: *the solid form left after something has been burnt*
111 charred: *burnt*
114 batteries: *guns grouped together to give maximum fire power*
124 soaked: *very wet*
131 old chap: (1940s slang) *affectionate term of greeting*
136 mortars: *guns that fire rockets*
137–8 bastards: (literally, *illegitimate people*) *offensive term of abuse*
138 got the lot: *ie killed them all*
140 haemorrhage: *bleeding*
146 wooden pins: (army slang) *artificial legs*
154 furtive: *secret*
156 Rotten luck: (1940s slang) *Bad luck*
161 squaddie: (army slang) *ordinary soldier, not an officer*
167 gritty: *full of sand particles*
173 greenhouse: *building made of glass for growing plants that need warmth and protection*
174 wire: *telegram*
175 rucksack: *bag with straps worn on one's back*
177 NZ: *New Zealand*
185 gulped: *swallowed hard*
187 sobs: *deep breaths made when you are crying*
191 stupefied: *exhausted*
195 fragments: *very small pieces*

5 The White Man's Burden

Heart of Darkness

1 steamer: *ship driven by steam*
blamed: *mild curse expressing disapproval (in modern English: damned)*
5 enigma: *something mysterious and impossible to understand completely*
frowning: (literally, *making lines appear on one's forehead to show worry, annoyance etc*) *here the coast appears to look like this*
6 insipid: *without character or interest*
mute: *silent*
8 grimness: *unattractiveness*
10 fringed with white surf: *the white tops of the waves (the surf) arrive at the edge or limit (the fringe) of the jungle*
11 blurred: *made indistinct*
creeping: *keeping low to sea-level*
mist: *thin fog produced by small drops of water*
13 specks: *small points*
16 pounded: *moved monotonously (with the sound of the engine)*
17 levy toll: *collect taxes*
25 sordid farce: *unpleasant type of comic theatrical play*
26 back-cloth: *piece of cloth at the back of a stage painted to show the scene where the play takes place*
28 languid: *moving slowly*
29 within the toil: *in the effort*
34 paddled: *used paddles (wooden oars) to move a small boat*
43 man-of-war: *warship*
44 shelling the bush: *firing into the jungle*
45 ensign: *flag*
46 muzzles: *barrels of the guns*
47 swell: *upward and downward movement of the sea*
50 Pop: *Sound made by a small explosion*
51 dart: *shoot out*
52 screech: *high, thin sound*
54 lugubrious: *sad, rather mournful*
drollery: *amusement, humour*
dissipated: *dispersed, made to disappear*
55 earnestly: *seriously*
61 still: *without sound or movement*
62 catacomb: *passages and rooms underground where people were buried in the past*
63 ward off: *keep away*
65 slime: *thick, sticky, unpleasant liquid mud*
66 mangroves: *tropical trees typical*

of the jungle and usually found at the side of rivers
writhe: *twist themselves*
69 pilgrimage: *the denotation is a journey made by a believer in a religion to a place where a saint or holy person is buried (you will look at the connotations in Exercise 21)*
70 hints: *suggestions*
71 upwards of thirty days: *a little more than thirty days*
73 farther on: *ie further up the river*
76 bridge: *raised part of a ship where the controls are, and where the captain stands*
77 morose: *unhappy and not very talkative*
77–8 shuffling: *walking without lifting up his feet very much*
78 gait: *way of walking*
wharf: *area where ships load and unload*
82 funny: *strange*
85 athwart: *sideways (ie to look at Marlow better)*
90 opened a reach: *came to a straight part of the river*
92 declivity: *slope, side of the hill*
93 rapids: *dangerous, steep part of a river where the water flows very fast*
94 devastation: *destruction*
95 jetty: *platform extending into a river where boats can tie up*
96 recrudescence: *reappearance*
100 boiler: *piece of machinery, used for heating water for steam engines*
wallowing: *lying on its back like an animal*
103 carcass: *dead body*
104 stack: *pile*
106 stir: *begin to move*
feebly: *weakly*
108 detonation: *explosion*
111 blasting: *causing explosions*
112 clinking: *noise made by pieces of metal hitting each other*
113 toiling: *walking with great difficulty*
116 loins: *part of the body between the tops of the legs and the waist, including the sexual organs*
119 bights: *curves formed by the chain*
120 report: *noise made by an explosion*
122 by no stretch of the imagination: *ie it was impossible to define them as enemies*
125 dilated: *wide open*
128 raw matter: *the denotation is the natural material from which products are manufactured (you will look at the connotations in Exercise 21)*
129 strolled: *walked slowly*
131 hoisted: *raised quickly*
132 alacrity: *speed*
135 rascally: *a rascal is an adult or child who does dishonest things, or things you disapprove of, but whom you don't completely dislike*
139 chain-gang: *group of prisoners tied to each other by chains*
141 fend off: *defend yourself from being hit*
143 blundered into: *got into by mistake*
146 swayed: *moved*
148 flabby: *weak, without real energy*
149 rapacious: *greedy, looking only for profit, even by dishonest means*
151 appalled: *shocked and horrified*
154 divine: *guess*
155 quarry: *hole in the ground made for the excavation of stone or minerals*
158 ravine: *valley with steep sides*
159 tumbled: *thrown carelessly*
160 wanton: *deliberate*
161 smash-up: *act of destruction*
163 Inferno: *Hell*
164 headlong: *with great speed*
166 tearing: *very fast*
167 launched: *ie rotating, moving*
169 effaced: *obscured*

172 shudder: *brief, spasmodic movement*

179 time contracts: *contracts where you are paid a certain amount for a promise to work for a certain length of time (ie alien to contemporary African culture)*

uncongenial: *unusual and unsuitable*

182 moribund: *dying*

186 sunken: *set back deep in the face*

187 orbs: *eyeballs*

192 worsted: *type of woollen cloth*

193 badge: *small piece of cloth (or often metal or plastic) that you wear to show support of an organization or belief, or membership of a group*

194 charm: *object to bring good luck*

propitiatory act: *action to please a person or god who is angry with you*

205 lapped: *drank by putting out his tongue, like an animal*

208 loitering: *passing time*

made haste: *hurried, went quickly*

211 starched: *made stiff because it has been washed in a special chemical*

212 cuffs: *bottom ends of the sleeves, where you button a shirt at your wrists*

alpaca: *thin, high-quality cloth*

clear: *light-coloured*

212–13 varnished: *polished*

217 book-keeping: *keeping the accounts*

225 dummy: *model of a man used for advertising purposes*

226 backbone: *the denotation is the spinal column; here it means strength of character*

227 got-up shirt-fronts: *well-presented shirts*

229 sport such linen: *wear such clothes*

230 blush: *appearance of redness in one's cheeks because of embarrassment*

233 in apple-pie order: (idiom) *in perfect order*

234 in a muddle: *in confusion*

235 niggers: *black people (an offensive word now)*

splay feet: *feet spread wide apart*

236 beads: *small, round coloured pieces of wood or glass with holes in them for putting on string to make necklaces or bracelets*

238 trickle: *small but regular amounts*

ivory: *the precious white material that the tusks of elephants are made of*

241 planks: *long flat pieces of wood used for building*

242 barred: *striped*

245 fiendishly: *savagely*

stabbed: *pushed their stings very deep into the flesh*

247 perching: *sitting*

248 truckle-bed: *low bed on wheels*

250 groans: *noises made by someone in pain*

258 trading post: *place where the Europeans exchange the products mentioned in lines 236–8 in return for ivory*

264 caravan: *a group of people bringing ivory*

babble: *confused noise of many people speaking at the same time*

265 uncouth: *incomprehensible and barbaric*

267 'giving it up': *ie the chief agent had been saying 'I give up', meaning 'I want to abandon this job'*

269 frightful row: *terrible noise*

272 alluding: *indicating, referring to*

280 bulging: *prominent, standing out from the face*

281 somebody in the Administration: *ie an important manager in the company*

282 Council in Europe: *ie the directors of the company*

285 flushed: *with a red face*

290 tramp: *march, journey on foot*

Things Fall Apart

To emphasize the African setting and point of view of his novel, Achebe sometimes uses Ibo words (Ibo is a language of Eastern Nigeria), and sometimes uses Ibo ways of expression and cultural references (there are examples at lines 74–5, 118–19, 144–5, 147 and 155–6).

1 clan: *group of families related to each other by common ancestors*
3 lizard: *kind of reptile with long body, long tail, and four short legs*
6 nine masked spirits: *in Okonkwo's clan nine noble clan-members ritually put on masks and so assume the powers of spirits – this empowers them to act as judges*
10 irreparable: *impossible to make better*
11–12 with a flourish: *in grand style*
14 compound: *property, collection of living and agricultural buildings*
15 barn: *large structure for keeping animals and agricultural produce*
17 ozo: (Ibo word) *the highest rank of society*
19 esteem: *reputation*
22 *chi*: (Ibo word) *personal guardian spirit*
making amends: *compensating*
yams: *vegetables similar to potatoes*
24 sharecroppers: *tenant farmers who receive some of the agricultural produce as wages*
26 resilient: *able to resist*
29 *obi*: (Ibo word) *the room reserved for the head of the family*
31 abomination: *disgrace*
35 curse: *say words or a sentence asking a magical power to make something bad happen to somebody*
43 ailing: *sick, unhealthy*
44 heartache: *sorrow, suffering*
45 buoyant: *happy, high-spirited*
46 snap at: *speak to in short sentences in an angry way (a dog snaps when it tries to bite someone)*
58 half-sister: *ie a daughter of Okonkwo, but by a different mother than Ezinma's mother*
60 wielded: *exerted, had*
69 come forth: *ie present themselves as candidates to marry Okonkwo's daughters*
71 in exile: *sent away by law from the place he lived in*
led many astray: *ie converted many away from the local religion*
72 outcast: *person cut off from the clan because of some offence*
worthy: *noble*
74–5 cut the anklet … cast it away: *ie abandoned his high position in Umuofia society*
77 sacrament of Holy Communion: *bread and wine which symbolize the body and blood of Christ; eating a small piece of bread and drinking a mouthful of wine with this symbolic importance is a Christian religious ceremony*
Feast: *a big meal with a lot to eat and drink*
80 drinking-horn: *the horn of an animal converted into a container for drink*
82–3 District Commissioner: *the chief British administrator of this colonial district*
85 Umuru: *a place not connected culturally or ethnically with Umuofia*
the Great River: *the river Niger*
89 high-handed: *using their power more severely than necessary, without caring about other people's feelings*
90 ash-coloured: *with the colour of the grey powder left when something is burnt*
93 molested: *injured, done harm to*
97 mean: *undignified*

98 They were grieved: *They were made to feel sad and unfairly treated*
mourned: *felt sadness and loss*

100 matchets: *kinds of axes, used for cutting or fighting*

107 bowed: *leaning downward*

113 wiped out: *killed the population of*

123 uphold: *support*

129–30 Aneto … in dispute: *there has been an argument in Umuofia about who owned some land*

136 tongue: *ie language*

147 the wrath of the earth: *the anger of the earth; they believe that murder offends the divinity of the earth*

146 fled: *ran away, escaped (past tense of 'to flee')*

151 flee: *see line 146*

155–6 they have not found … of their suffering: *their suffering is too great to express in words*

6 'Bad Wife!'

The Joy Luck Club

2 banners: *long pieces of cloth with writing on them, hanging from the wall*
fancy room: *ie the room with the best decorations and furniture*

6 standing: *social position*

7 padded dress: *dress with soft, thick cloth inside it to make it bigger and warmer*

8 chop: *cut into small pieces*

12 losing face: *losing the respect and honour of other people*

14 gutting: *taking the insides out of*

21 tricked: *deceived*

25–6 spilled the bowl: *made the contents fall out*

30 sharp corners: *fine, neat points at the corners*

31 embroider: *decorate by sewing*

34 soiled: *got dirty*

37 muddy: *ie with some earth still in it*

39 chamber-pot: *container, usually ceramic, kept under the bed, for urinating in during the night*

41 stuffing: *meat, cut very small, to put inside other items of food*

49 gobble down: *eat quickly and greedily, with obvious enjoyment*

50 bamboo shoots: *typical Chinese food; the young tender plants of a kind of tropical grass*

52 nod: *briefly lower the head to show approval*

54 noodles: *typical Chinese food; long thin strips made from flour and water cooked in boiling liquid, usually served with pieces of meat or vegetables*

63 turned sixteen: *had my sixteenth birthday*
lunar new year: *in the West a year is measured by the time it takes the Earth to travel around the Sun; the Chinese – and Jewish and Hindu – calendars are organized according to the movement of the Moon*

72 *RSVP: abbreviation of 'Répondez s'il vous plaît' (French for 'Please answer'); if it is written on an invitation it means you are asked to write back and say if you accept the invitation or not*

76 dowry: *amount of money or property that a woman's parents give to the man she marries in some societies*

77 water and mud marks: *ie the marks left when Lindo's home was flooded*

78 felicitous: *bringing happiness and good luck*

79 draped: *arranged*

81 palanquin: *ceremonial carriage for one person, without wheels, supported by poles carried on mens' shoulders (see top picture on page 141)*

84 matchmaker: *person paid by*

families to find suitable husbands or wives for their children
87 Shansi: *province of China distant from Lindo's province*
93–4 when she could not wring any more guests out of her hands: *ie when, despite her expressions of despair and frustration, no more guests came*
97–8 dressing table: *small table with a mirror where you brush your hair, put on make-up, etc*
101 Fen River: *the river that runs through the village, and had flooded when Lindo was twelve*
111 scurry: *hurry*
115 yelp: *give short, sharp shouts*
121 scarf: *large piece of material to put around your neck or over your head*
130 poor showing: *low number of guests*
142 carved: *cut into the candle*
145 yanked: *pulled quickly*
147 peacock: *large bird, the male of which has a long tail which it can spread out to show beautiful colours; it is often a symbol of vanity*
148 fanning: *spreading out*
153 ash: *grey powder left when something has been burnt*
159 seal: *unite, join permanently*
168 blankets: *woollen coverings for a bed*
170 Firecrackers: *Fireworks that go bang*
181 courtyard: *open area, surrounded by a wall, outside a house*
191 pebbles: *small stones*
193 the candle flickering: *the flame burning a little unsteadily*
196 Buddha: *the founder of the Asian religion of Buddhism*
197 fluttered: *burned even more unsteadily*
199 burst: *exploded, came out with force*
201 shivered: *trembled*
208 shame-faced: *embarrassed, seeming guilty*
211 do his business: *have sexual intercourse*
227 itch: *uncomfortable feeling that makes you want to rub or scratch yourself*
huffing: *breathing out loudly*
238 gown: *long, loose article of clothing*
267 gossiping: *exchanging information about unimportant things, often about other people's private lives*
scolding: *criticizing*
272 nature: *character, personality*
274 deficient: *not having enough of*
274–5 elements: *in the beliefs of the society described here, the various parts that make up a person*
278 bracelets: *circles of gold or other jewellery worn around the wrist*
288 get rid of: *dispose of, make go away*
292 auspicious: *bringing good luck*
293 Festival of Pure Brightness: *a Chinese festival, described in following sentences in the extract*
295 graves: *places where dead people are buried*
296 hoes: *garden tools to dig up weeds*
297 dumplings: *typical Chinese food; small balls of flour and water cooked in hot liquid; they can be served with meat or vegetables, or with fruit or sugar*
301 wailing: *making long, high sounds of pain or sadness*
305 clutching my mouth: *holding a hand tightly over my mouth*
306 writhing: *twisting*
311 gasps: *short sharp breathings in and out*
321 doomed: *destined to have a bad ending*
324 frowned: *drew her eyebrows together to express disapproval,*

and perhaps to show that she could not understand

333 remorseful: *feeling sorry about what is happening*

336 rotting: *decaying, going bad*

339 mole: *small, dark spot or lump on a person's skin, which stays for a long time, often permanently*

353 pried open: *forced open*

373 struck with: *impressed by*

378 Peking: *capital of China, now referred to as Beijing*

385 twenty-four carats: *units for measuring the purity of gold; twenty-four carats is the purest gold*

The Householder

There are some Hindi words in the extract. There are many languages used in contemporary India, but the official languages of communication which enable people from different parts of the country to communicate with each other are Hindi (a language from northern India) and English.

4 defiant: *proudly refusing to accept authority (in this case, Prem's)*

slam: *noise made when you put something down, or close something, rather violently*

5 pigtail: *the tail formed by hair at the back of the head when long hair is tied together*

8 puris: (Hindi) *typical Indian food; fried cakes made of wheat (a kind of grain)*

sheepishly: *in an uncomfortable, embarrassed way*

11 peer: *look closely*

13–14 Bibiji's: (Hindi) *the familiar title the servant boy uses for Indu (it means 'little mother')*

15 glaring: *looking in an angry way*

17 swami: *Hindu religious teacher; Hinduism is the predominant religion of India, teaching that you must live a good life in order to be reincarnated (born again) into a better life*

19 Sohan Lal: *a colleague of Prem's at the school, who has introduced him to the swami*

21 trivial: *unimportant*

wordly: *everyday, not spiritual*

24 sari: (Hindi) *typical Indian female dress, consisting of many metres of material; one end is wound around the waist to form a skirt, the other end is arranged over the top part of the body and the shoulders or head*

26 bazaar: *word used in Asia for a market*

27 sweetmeat: *cake or sweet very rich in sugar*

frothy: *with lots of small bubbles in it*

28 buttermilk: *sweet drink; it is the liquid left after milk has been converted into butter*

29 syrup: *thick, very sweet liquid made by dissolving sugar in water*

earthenware pots: *containers made out of terracotta (baked mud)*

37–8 'I don't want.': *ie 'I don't want it.' Indu is a Hindi speaker, and speaks English as a second language; she does not speak it perfectly (other examples are at lines 44 and 57)*

42–3 Rasgullas and gulab jamuns and jelabis: (Hindi) *typical Indian sweetmeats (see lines 27–9)*

48 fished for: *looked in the container with her hand to find another delicacy*

52 long for: *desire, want obsessively*

56 shrugged: *raised her shoulders to indicate 'I don't know' or 'It's not important'*

69 vanilla: *sweet substance made from the seeds of a tropical plant*

75 relish: *appetite and enjoyment*

82 the Punjab Mail: *the name of an*

express train (the Punjab is a state in northern India)
86 pickle: *typical Indian food; vegetables or fruit preserved in vinegar or salty water*
87 tonga: (Hindi) *light carriage drawn by one horse*
89 bedding: *mattress, blankets and sheets, for sleeping*
97 annas: (Hindi) *Indian coins of a low value*
99 rebuke: *criticism*
104 bashful: *embarrassed*
hovered: *waited nervously*
107 string-cot: *temporary bed made with ropes or cloth bands*
111 chutneys, guava cheese, sherbet: *typical Indian foods; chutneys are a mixture of fruit, spices, sugar and vinegar, usually eaten with meat or cheese; guava cheese is formed from a pear-like tropical fruit; sherbet is a powder made from fruits (which can be dissolved in water to make a drink)*
119–20 spent too much time at the Club: *Prem's mother criticizes this son-in-law for spending too much time away from his family in the company of male friends at a private club*
122 were lacking in: *did not have enough*
127 recital: *spoken list of information*
128 Ankhpur: *Prem's home town, where his mother has just come from*
130–2 Rajinder, Ganpat, Mr. Williams: *people that Prem knows in Ankhpur*
133 pursed her mouth: *pressed her lips together, expressing disapproval*
136 dwell (on): *go into detail (about)*
136–7 Principal: *the head of the school*
140 grim: *unattractive*
143 U.P.: *Uttar Pradesh, a federal state and administrative region in northern India*
Civil Service: *Government administration*
144 B.A.: *Bachelor of Arts, the title of a degree you get after passing your final exams at a university or institute of higher education*
144–5 the first division: *students with the highest marks in the final exams get a degree in the first division*
145–6 clicked his tongue: *made a noise with his tongue against the roof of his mouth, to express disapproval*
152 gloomy: *sad, unhappy*
164 bare: *without much furniture*
167 flushed: *red because of embarrassment*
170 bun: *long hair collected into a round shape at the back of the head*
173 strangled voice: *unusual, high-sounding voice, because of the emotions he is suffering*
175 heaved: *produced with obvious effort*
187 Mr Khanna: *the name of the Principal referred to in line 184*
191 flung: *threw*
196 mutter: *sound of words said unclearly so as not to be heard*

7 Thinking Aloud

Ulysses

Of all the novelists included in this book, James Joyce plays and experiments most with the English language; he also combines words together in ways that are not normally done in English (eg *liverslices*, *crustcrumbs* (line 3). As usual in this book, the following glossary offers interpretations of the words and expressions as they are used in context, without exploring the range of connotations they have. You will explore Joyce's skill with language in the exercises in this chapter.

In addition to this glossary, Exercises 2, 4, 5

and 6 will help you understand the events and associations of thoughts in this extract.

1 with relish: *with appetite and enjoyment*

2 fowls: *general term for edible birds, such as chickens, ducks, turkeys, etc*

2–4 giblet … gizzards … liverslices … roes: *examples of 'inner organs'*

3 crustcrumbs: *very small pieces of bread, which are used to cover the slices of liver*

5 palate: *taste in the mouth*
tang: *distinctive flavour and smell*

7 righting: *putting in order*
humpy: *not level; the surface is irregular*
Gelid: *Icy, very cold*

9 peckish: (colloquial) *hungry*

13 hob: *surface of a cooker*
squat: *low and fat*

14 spout: *the funnel that the tea is poured from*

16 Mkgnao!: *here, and later, Joyce imitates – with variations – the noises made by a cat*

18 mewed: *made the small noises a cat makes to attract attention*
stalked: *walked slowly and carefully (animals stalk another animal they want to kill and eat)*

21 lithe: *graceful*

22 gloss: *shine*
sleek: *shiny*
butt: *place under which the tail joins the body*

25 pussens: *colloquial and affectionate way of referring to a cat – similar to 'pussy' (Bloom uses 'baby language')*

28 Vindictive: *Cruel, wanting to cause harm*

29 squeal: *make a high-pitched noise*

33 chookchooks: *chickens (more 'baby language')*

35 avid: *greedy*
shameclosing: *the word is an invention of Joyce's; 'shame' means a bad feeling of guilt when you have done something wrong*

35–6 plaintively: *sadly*

38 dresser: *kind of cupboard with drawers and flat surfaces*

42 bristles: *long hairs that grow horizontally and outwards between a cat's mouth and nose*
wirily: *as if they were wires*

43 clip: *cut*

46 lap: *noise made by drinking with the tongue*

47 drouth: (Irish) *drought, lack of rain*

48 mutton: *meat from sheep*

51 porous: *with pores (small holes) that absorb liquid*

53 creaky: *making the noise of an object or machine needing oil*

55 once in a way: *every now and again, occasionally*

60 grunt: *low noise made by people too tired to talk*

61 Mn: *Joyce's representation of a grunt*

63 brass quoits: *flattened rings of brass that form part of the metal net supporting the mattress*

64 jingled: *made a ringing, metallic noise*
settled: *adjusted*

67 a short knock: (colloquial) *a good price*
Hard as nails: (colloquial) *Tough*
Tweedy: *the surname of Molly's father*
at Plevna that was: *at Pleven, in Bulgaria, that used to be called Plevna (Bloom imitates Tweedy's abbreviated way of speaking)*

68 rose from the ranks: *started as an ordinary soldier and then became an officer*

69 make that corner: *do good business, make a profitable investment*

70 farseeing: *clever at predicting future developments*

71 initialled: *with Bloom's initials, LB, written on it*

72 waterproof: *raincoat*
73 Daresay: *ie I daresay, I suppose*
in the swim too: *also involved in making money through other activities*
74 sweated legend: *maker of the hat's sign covered in sweat from being worn*
crown: *the top part*
76 headband: *strip of leather that runs around the inside of the hat at the bottom*
slip: *small piece*
77 latchkey: *key of the door*
81 footleaf: *piece of wood at the bottom of a door that covers the threshold (see next word)*
threshold: *piece of wood or stone on the ground under a door; it is what you step over when you enter a house*
83 cellarflap: *horizontal wooden door in the ground, leading into the cellar (the space under a house)*
84 steeple: *bell-tower*
86 reflects, (refracts is it?): *Bloom looks for but does not find the right word (it should be 'absorbs')*
89 our daily: *abbreviation for 'our daily bread', an expression from the Lord's prayer (a well-known Christian prayer)*
90 turnovers: *variety of bread*
92 steal a day's march on him: (colloquial) *don't let him get a day ahead of me*
93 strand: *seashore*
94 sentry: *soldier on guard*
old ranker: *old soldier, veteran*
95 awned: *with cloth or other material hung above the street to protect people from the sun*
96 Turbaned: *With turbans on, typical oriental head-coverings*
97 Turko the terrible: *name of a Turkish character in popular fiction of the time*
a coiled pipe: *a typical oriental pipe*
98 fennel: *vegetable with a sharp, distinctive flavour*
sherbet: *powdered fruit*
99 Dander: *Wander*
100 Getting on to sundown: *Evening is coming*
101 scroll: *rolled up document*
104 twanged: *made a discordant noise*
105 garters: *circular pieces of elastic, used to keep up stockings*
106 dulcimers: *oriental instruments: boxes with strings stretched over them, which are hit with small hammers*
109 headpiece: *design above the headline*
Freeman: *name of a newspaper*
110 leader: *article where the editor of the newspaper comments on current affairs*
111–12 Ikey touch: (slang) *Clever, amusing comment*
114 flabby gush: *weak-smelling sudden smell*
porter: *kind of beer*
115 squirted out: *came out quickly*
ginger, teadust, biscuitmush: *various items of food and drink*
117 n.g.: *Bloom's abbreviation for 'not good'*
tramline: *route for a tram (form of public transport running on rails)*
119 like a shot: (idiom) *immediately*
120 Cute old codger: (colloquial) *Clever old man*
120–1 canvassing him for an ad: *trying to sell him advertising space*
122 my bold: *Irish expression, equivalent to British 'dear old'*
123 curate: (Irish slang) *barman*
124 takes him off to a tee: *imitates him perfectly ('tee' = 'T')*
screwed up: *closed tightly*
126–7 they'd only be an eight o'clock breakfast for the Japanese: *the Japanese would defeat the Russians easily (a reference to the imminent war between Russia and Japan of 1904–5;*

Larry was right – Japan did win easily)

135 'Tis all that: (Irish expression) *It certainly is*

137 county Leitrim: *a county of Ireland*

rinsing empties: *washing empty bottles and glasses*

141 Put down three and carry five: *Bloom is doing a numerical calculation in his head*

142 bob: *shilling (a coin no longer used, equivalent to a twentieth of a pound)*

dribs and drabs: (colloquial) *small amounts*

142–3 wholesale orders: *the orders from the suppliers*

143 double shuffle with the town travellers: *an illegal arrangement with the suppliers' salesmen to cheat the suppliers*

144 Square it you with the boss: *You make sure the boss agrees*

we'll split the job: *half for you, half for me*

145 tot to: *add up to*

146 stuff: *ie beer*

off: *as a discount*

147 Brats' clamour: *Noise of children*

148 lilt: *a rhythmic way of speaking*

Ahbeesee etc: *represents the pronunciation of A, B, C, etc*

149 Inishturk etc: *places in Ireland*

150 joggerfry: *imitation of children's pronunciation of 'geography'*

Slieve Bloom: *name of a mountain in Ireland*

151 hanks: *loops, circles*

152 polonies: *kinds of sausage*

153 fade: *disappear*

154 links: *parts of a chain*

forcemeat: *finely cut meat used for making sausages*

155 lukewarm: *slighly warm*

157 oozed: *emitted, gave out*

bloodgouts: *drops of blood*

willowpatterned: *with pictures of willow trees on it (a design originating in China and very common in Britain and Ireland)*

159 slip: *piece of paper*

Chapped: *Rough and cracked*

washingsoda: *a substance for washing clothes with*

163 Whacking: *Hitting (to get the dust out)*

163–4 by George: *exclamation of emphasis and approval*

165 ferreteyed: *with eyes like a ferret – a small, fierce animal used for hunting rabbits*

165–6 snipped off: *cut off*

166 blotchy: *with marks of different colours*

Sound: *Solid (implying good)*

167 stallfed heifer: *young cow specially fed to make the meat of good quality*

169 Kinnereth on the Lakeshore of Tiberias: *a place in Palestine in the Middle East*

170 sanatorium: *place where people go to rest and recover their health*

171 blurred cattle cropping: *ie a photograph of cows, out of focus, eating grass*

174 lowing: *noise made by cows*

dung: *animals' excrement*

175 hobnailed: *with nails in the soles to make the boots tough and suitable for the country*

trudging: *walking with difficulty*

litter: *straw etc on the floor*

176 hindquarter: *back part*

prime one: *top quality cow*

176–7 unpeeled switches: *small sticks with the bark (the outer coating) taken off*

177 aslant: *to one side (so that he can look at the girl)*

180 snapped: *took noisily*

181 grimace: *expression made by twisting the mouth (often indicating pain, but here the butcher gives a quick smile)*

183 tendered: *offered*

187 hams: *buttocks and thighs*

188 Make hay while the sun shines: (proverb) *Profit from a situation while it is favourable*

189 sauntered: *walked without hurry*
191 Crusted: *Not cleaned for a long time*
191 scapulars: *long wide band of cloth with an opening for the head worn front and back over the shoulders*
191–2 in tatters: *torn*
193 For another: *And another thing I can think of*
194 cuddling: *caressing, touching*
Eccles lane: *the small road behind where they live, and therefore intimate and dark*
194 sizeable: *big*
197 moist tender gland: *ie the kidney*
199 the rubber prickles: *the rubber mat used for putting money on in the butcher's shop (it has little bits of rubber sticking up from it like thorns)*
200 till: *drawer where the money is kept in a shop*
202 speck: *small point*
208 planters' company: *an agricultural business*
tracts: *pieces of land*
211 Jaffa: *town on the coast of Israel (then called Palestine)*
marks: *German currency*
dunam: *Oriental measure of land*
212 citrons: *term for acidic fruit such as oranges and lemons*
214 sending of the crop: *some of the produce*
219 pruning: *cutting trees to make them grow better*
220 Andrews: *Dublin shop*
222–3 Citron … Mastiansky: *Jewish friends of Bloom's from previous times*
Saint Kevin's parade: *the street in Dublin where Citron used to live*
223 cither: *kind of guitar*
224 waxen: *with a wax-like feel when you touch them*
227 Arbutus place: *where the Blooms used to live*
228 flaw: *imperfection*
229 Levant: *old name for the geographical area including Israel, Palestine and Lebanon*
231 navvies: *workers*
soiled dungarees: *dirty working uniforms*
232 whatdoyoucallhim: (colloquial) *an expression used when you can't remember someone's name*
233 salute: *say hello to*
234 Watering cart: *A vehicle carrying water for public parks and gardens*
235 On earth as it in heaven: *another quotation from the Lord's Prayer (see line 89); it is preceded by the words 'Thy will be done'*
238 weedless: *without any vegetation*
239 Brimstone: *in the Old Testament this was a hot substance like sulphur sent down from the sky to destroy the cities of Sodom,Gomorrah and Edom*
242 hag: *old woman*
243 a naggin bottle: *a small bottle containing quarter of a pint (about 0.14 litre)*
by the neck: *by the top part*
The oldest people: *Bloom refers to the Jews*
246 sunken: *fallen inwards*
cunt: (vulgar slang) *female genitalia*
249 seared: *cut deeply into*
251 cloak: *covering*
252 Morning mouth: *Bad taste in your mouth in the morning*
253 Got up wrong side of the bed: *a common expression meaning 'to wake up in a bad mood'*
253–4 Sandow's exercises: *name of a system of physical exercises*
254 Blotchy: *(see line 166)*
255 still unlet: *ie nobody has rented it yet*
255–6 twentyeight: *ie 28 pounds*
257 plastered: covered, stuck all over
Plasters: *Bandages*
258 fume: *smoke*
ample: *large*

265 Bold hand: *Firm handwriting*
268 tousled: *with the hair in disorder*
270 Mullingar: *place in Ireland where Milly is spending a holiday*
Milly: *the Blooms' daughter*
273 twill: *kind of heavy material*
bedspread: *the top covering on a bed*
276 tugs: *pulls*
277 tuck: *push quickly*
279 propped: *supported*
281 curled herself back: *moved back into a relaxed position*
282 snug: *comfortable*
283 parched: (colloquial) *very thirsty*
285 petticoat: *item of underwear; a light skirt worn under the outside skirt*
285–6 tossed soiled linen: *dirty used underwear thrown onto the chair*
290 Scald: *Warm*
293 tilting: *making it go to one side*
to draw: *to brew (so that the water absorbs the flavour of the tea)*
294 the live coals: *the hot coals*
297 Kosher: *Jewish rules governing preparation of food (eg pork is not allowed)*
300 ringwise: *in a circular motion*
chipped: *slightly broken*
302 new tam: *new cap (one of her birthday presents)*
lough Owel: *lake Owel (in Ireland)*
303 Blazes Boylan: *this person will be mentioned later in line 334 (and in Exercise 6)*
304 moustachecup: *kind of cup*
304–5 sham crown Derby: *cheap imitation of good quality ceramic*
306 amberoid: *imitation of amber, a hard yellow-brown fossil*
310 farthing: *the smallest coin in the old British system of currency: 'without a farthing' means absolutely poor*
311 Katey Keogh: *name of a girl invented by Bloom*
312 Dreadful old case: (colloquial) *Silly old man*
313 courteous: *polite*
bow Molly off: *make a polite gesture of lowering his head to greet or say goodbye to Molly at the railway station*
316 Sex breaking out even then: *She was beginning to be conscious of her own sexuality even at that age*
Pert: *Attractive in a small, firm way*
318 prodded: *quickly pushed*
319 hump bumped: *an expression invented by Joyce, meaning that the tray was unsteady as Bloom carried it (see line 7)*
322 Nudging: *Pushing gently*
325 brasses: *the brass quoits mentioned at line 63*
327 bubs: (colloquial) *breasts*
shegoat's udder: *the breasts of a female goat*
328 couched: *lying down in bed*
330 peeped: *ie a part of it was visible*
dimpled: *not flat, with the impressions made by Molly's head*
336 *Là ci darem*: (Italian) *'There we will hold (each others' hands); opening line from a duet from Mozart's opera 'Don Giovanni'*
337 incense: *substance that is burnt to make a pleasant smell (often used in churches)*
338 flowerwater: *the water that you put cut flowers in*
344 drawers: *underwear covering the area between the waist and the tops of the legs*
345 stocking: *covering for the leg extending as far as the middle of the thigh*
rumpled: *not flat, with many folds and creases*
348 It must have fell down: *it would be grammatically correct to say 'It must have fallen down'*
349 *Voglio e non vorrei*: (Italian) *'I want, and (at the same time) I*

would not like' (another line from the duet mentioned in line 336 – both references ironically refer to Molly's adultery with Boylan)

351 valance: *material hanging from the mattress of the bed as far as the floor*

sprawled: *it was lying there, open*

352 orangekeyed: *with orange-coloured designs in the shape of keys*

chamberpot: *container, usually ceramic, kept under the bed, for urinating in during the night*

355 by nothandle: (Joyce has invented this expression) *ie not by the handle*

357 hairpin: *pin or clip used to keep long hair together*

361 Metempsychosis: *Bloom will explain this word at lines 363–4 and 400–2*

365 rocks: (slang) *expression meaning 'Nonsense! ', 'Speak plainly!''*

366 askance: *sideways*

367 charades: *party game where one person mimes titles of novels etc and the other members of the team must guess the title*

Dolphin's Barn: *name of a place where the Blooms had one of their first meetings*

368 smudged: *with marks of dirty fingers*

Ring: *The circular area in the centre of a circus, where the events take place*

369 carriagewhip: *long whip, a length of leather used for hitting horses*

369–70 pride of the: *ie pride of the ring (see line 368 – Bloom doesn't complete the title in his own mind)*

370 Sheet: *Illustration*

371 *oath: curse, obscene or violent language*

372 Doped: *Drugged*

Trapeze: *A circus act involving swinging from a structure high above the ground*

Hengler's: *name of a circus the Blooms once went to*

373 Mob gaping: *The crowd had their mouths open (both words express disapproval)*

break our sides: *laugh so much that the sides of our bodies will break*

374 them: *ie trapeze artists*

Bone: *Take the bones out of*

metamspychosis: *here Bloom follows a word-game of his own*

378 smutty: *dirty, pornographic*

383 Capel street: *street in Dublin where Bloom's library is*

384 Kearney, my guarantor: *a friend of Bloom's who has promised to pay the library for any books that Bloom loses or does not return*

390 sluggish: *slow-moving*

curdling: *becoming solid*

394 *Photo Bits: a popular illustrated magazine of the time*

395 down: *loose, not tied up*

396 Three and six: *Three shillings and six pence (old currency, about one-sixth of a modern pound)*

397 nymphs: *in Greek and Roman mythology, minor goddesses or spirits in the form of young girls, who live in trees, rivers, the sea, or on mountains etc*

404 arched: *wide-open (to smell better)*

Molloy

1 lay in: *accumulate, collect*

2 sucking-stones: *this is a personal expression of Molloy's (people normally suck sweets or lollipops etc)*

pebbles: *stones that you find at the seaside, made smooth by the action of the sea*

4–5 turn and turn about: *alternately, one after the other*

8 greatcoat: *heavy overcoat*

20 hazard: *chance, piece of (bad) luck*
23–4 shuffled: *moved a group of things around to change their order (eg you shuffle a pack of cards)*
27 makeshift: *temporary arrangement*
28 the first thing I hit upon: *the first idea I had*
43 chancing on: *choosing by chance, accidentally*
46 seek: *look for*
mode: *way, technique*
56 short of: *apart from*
58 at a pinch: *by doing something considered necessary at a certain moment, but not satisfactory*
60 safety-pins: *kinds of pin with a round end into which the sharp end fits, used for holding together pieces of cloth*
62 half-measure: *compromise*
63 wrestling and wrangling: *mental effort involved in considering a lot of solutions*
69 gazed at: *looked at closely, for a long time*
71 stiff: *rigid (Molloy suffers from bad legs)*
74 prop: *support*
ham: *buttock and top of the thigh*
76 martingales: (specialized word) *complex betting systems where what you could win is doubled after each unsuccessful bet*
78 strand: *beach*
79 lulled: *calmed*
dawned on: *started to be realized by*
82 trim: (specialized word) *the exact way a ship is balanced in the water*
84 Isaiah … Jeremiah: *books of the Old Testament of the Bible written by Hebrew prophets*
90 vitiated: weakened
93 assuredly: *of course*
sound: *valid*
102 hideousness: *ugliness*
105–6 the lot: *ie all of them*
110 silver: *collection of silver objects (such as knives, forks, spoons)*
horn: *small curved object to help you when putting on shoes*
119 make a balls of it: (slang) *spoil it by making a stupid mistake*
142 stinking: *with a bad smell*
144 impeccable: *perfect, without any mistake*
149 if the worst came to the worst: *in the worst possible situation, according to the most pessimistic prediction*
drawback: *problem*
152–3 proceeding: *operation*
154–5 I had set my heart on it: *this was what I most desired*
164 tick off: *make a mark like this √ against a thing in a register or on a list to show you have done that thing*
166 symmetrically disposed: *arranged in an organised, mathematical way*
169 delicate: *needing a lot of concentration*
176 in the first flush: (idiom) *in the first, happy moments*
186–7 at loggerheads: *contradicting each other, incompatible with each other*
187–8 I didn't give a tinker's curse about: (Irish expression) *I wasn't at all interested in*
193 ballast: *balance*
195 I didn't give a fiddler's curse about: *I wasn't at all interested in (a variation on the expression in lines 187–8)*
196–7 any the worse off: *at any disadvantage*
197 to which I rallied: *to which I gave my support*

8 Future Shock

The Handmaid's Tale

Some words you might want to know the meaning of, such as Angels, Salvaging,

Eyes, Econowives, Marthas, Handmaids, Aunts, are not given in this glossary. You will be asked to guess their meanings in Exercises 7 and 8 in the *Close reading* section. While you read the extract for the first time try to understand the general meaning of these terms in the context. In this way you will practise 'inferring' – the valuable language skill of guessing the meanings of words that you don't know by using ideas from the context.

1 tolling: *ringing slowly and repeatedly*
4 Angels: *(for the moment, make a guess)*
riot gear: *special uniform and equipment that police use when dealing with crowd trouble*
5 bulging dark plexiglass visors: *the prominent, protective covers in front of the eyes*
6 beetles: *kinds of insect*
clubs: *sticks of wood or metal for hitting people*
in cordon: *in a protective circle*
7 hysteria: *excited madness*
9 Salvaging: *(for the moment, make a guess)*
10 segregated: *either for men only, or for women only*
15 blinds: *covers for windows, made of plastic or cloth*
16 Eyes: *(for the moment, make a guess)*
18 lawn: *level area of grass*
21 Commencement: (US) *the ceremony when university graduates receive their degrees or diplomas*
22 pastel: *light-coloured*
23 black gowns: *the long black piece of clothing worn by graduating students*
25 loops: *the ends of the pieces of rope are tied in circles*
32–4 Wives … Econowives … Marthas … Handmaids: *(for the moment, make a guess)*
36 velvet: *rich, soft material*
49 tar: *thick, black, sticky substance used here for protecting rope from the weather*
50 fuse: *piece of rope or string attached to a bomb that is lit in order to explode the bomb*
51 to be salvaged: *(for the moment, make a guess)*
57 sway: *move unsteadily*
58 make a fuss: *show anxiety*
60 drapery: *loose, flowing clothing*
62 Aunt: *(for the moment, make a guess)*
62–3 Salvagers: *(for the moment, make a guess)*
63 hoods: *pieces of material covering and hiding the head*
cloaks: *long gowns*
64 hush: *become silent, stop*
65 flanked by: *ie the two Salvagers are on each side of her*
69 furrows: *lines*
70 engraved: *ie permanent*
frown: *expression when the eyebrows are drawn together to show worry or annoyance*
blink: *open and close quickly*
71 peering: *looking curiously*
72 fidget with: *nervously adjust*
headdress: *ceremonial head-covering*
73 P.A. system: *public address system; a system of microphone and loudspeakers to amplify the voice so that it is heard by a crowd*
74 shiver: *tremble because of cold, fear or disgust*
spit: *saliva*
76 Christmas crèche: *collection of small figures including the Virgin Mary, Joseph, shepherds and kings, which represents the scene at the birth of Jesus Christ; Christians often arrange and display such scenes at Christmas*
wrinkles: *small lines*
77 pallor: *paleness, white complexion*
78 dandelion: *common yellow wild flower*
81 mike: *microphone*

82 feedback whine: *unpleasant electronic noise made by a P.A. system (see line 73) when it is connected badly*

86 tinny: *metallic-sounding*

87 flattened: *without high or low tones*

91 taskmaster, taskmistress: *somebody who makes you work hard ; she changes it to 'mistress' because she is addressing exclusively women*

94–5 platitudes: *statements made many times before*

95 slogans: *short, memorable phrases used for political messages, and to encourage the Handmaids*

96 cradle: *small bed for babies*

97 cookies: (US) *biscuits*

99 get down to it: *arrive at the main point*

100 rummages: *tries to find something with her hand*
crumpled: *with many irregular folds*

101 scan: *read quickly*

102 rubbing our noses in it: *making us know how important she is*

103 flaunting: *ostentatiously showing*
prerogative: *privilege*

109 rash: *large number of similar events*

111 without further ado: *without any other formalities, immediately*

112 murmur: *low noise of talking*

116–17 left to our own devices: *allowed to do what we wanted*

120 Unchastity: *Having sex*
Commander: *(for the moment, make a guess)*

124 knitting needles: *long thin pieces of metal or plastic used for knitting (eg making pullovers etc)*
garden shears: *cutting tools for grass etc*

124–5 purloined: *stolen*

130 groggy: *unsteady, as if drunk or drugged*

132 wink: *the closing of one eye briefly to communicate something secret*

133 this isn't live: *ie the Salvaging will be recorded, edited, and then shown later on television, with certain scenes cut out*

135 retching: *vomiting*

139 stool: *seat, like a chair without a back*

140 noose: *end of a piece of rope tied in a circle, for hanging people*

141 vestment: *special piece of clothing worn by a priest*

143 stifle: *hide, suppress*

148 complicity: *agreement and involvement*

150 drag: *pull*

153 strung up: *hanging downwards from string or rope*

154 clipped: *with the extremities of the wings cut off, so they cannot fly*

155 wrecked: *destroyed, broken*

156 hems: *the bottom (usually sewn) ends of a dress*
dangle: *hang down*

164 ripple: *small movement of excitement*

167 munificent: *extremely generous*
Bestow: Give an honour or a present; the word has an archaic, biblical favour

168 Orderly: *In good order, with discipline*

173 coiling up: *collecting, winding up*

175 milling around: *forming a crowd*

176 jockeying for position: *trying to get the best position*

178 hang back: *stay towards the back*

179 lukewarm: *not completely committed*
zeal: *enthusiasm*

184 tugs: *pulls*

185 hedge: *line*

189 Particicution: *(for the moment, make a guess)*

192 assent: *agreement*

198 knobby: *with lumps on it*

stubbled: *covered with short, rough hair*
200 mangled: *disfigured*
tuber: *root vegetable, eg potato*
202 shit: (slang) *excrement*
vomit: *food etc coming out of the mouth from the stomach*
203 spiky: *stiff and pointed*
207 rape: *using violence to have sex with a woman against her will*
210 viciousness: *vice, crime*
211 Deuteronomy: *the fifth book of the Old Testament, containing the Laws that God gave to Moses*
212–13 at gunpoint: *using a gun to threaten*
216 clench: *ie her fingers press tightly into her palms*
218 bloodlust: *collective desire for violence*
gouge: *press one's fingers into something to make a hole or to do harm*
rend: *tear into pieces*
220 flare: *open wide*
221 swivels: *turns*
groggily: (*see line 130*)
224 shrill: *high-pitched*
227 staggers: *almost falls over*
228 shrivelled up: *small and unhealthy*
puffy: *swollen*
234 squinting: *looking with difficulty, through almost-closed eyes*
236 trashed: *beaten*
237–8 Luke ... Nick: *these characters' importance in the novel will be examined in Exercise 8 (for the moment, make a guess)*
243 surge: *sudden, massive movement*
246 reeling: *swaying*
248 shoving: *pushing*
251 jabs: *short kicks*
252 yells: *shouts*
258 gazing: *looking intensely*
267 brush me off: *push me away*
269 a political: *opponent of the regime*
276 straggle away: *leave slowly without a sense of purpose*
277 dazed: *not totally conscious*
282 diminutive: *small*
284–90 'Hi there,' etc: *Janine speaks exclusively in common US greetings*
285 clump: *handful*
286 giggle: *childish laugh*
291 Easy out: (US colloquial) *Be dareful, keep calm*
295 scrub: *wash thoroughly (eg with a brush)*
296 pumice: *piece of light, grey volcanic stone used for smoothing or scrubbing*
301 bedrock: *fundamental*
303 *relish: appetite*
304 I could eat a horse: (idiom) *I would like an enormous meal*
309 celery: *vegetable with long thin white stems, often eaten raw*
310 revelling in: *enjoying intensely*
311 lush: *intense*
319 kite: *object, often triangular, made up of a frame covered with paper or plastic, that is flown in the air at the end of a long piece of string*
323 limping: *walking with an injured leg*
324 shrunk: *grown smaller*
326 beige: *pale brown colour*
328–9 'Blessed be the fruit', 'May the Lord open': *open means make ripe; these greetings are in a biblical-sounding style*
328 Straight-faced: *Without expression*
straight-laced: *serious*
331 churning: *going around and around*
335 posting: *position, job*
337 placid: *calm, without emotion*
338 checkpoint: *place where soldiers or police check people's documents*
339 taciturn: *not speaking*
340 engrossed in: *concentrating on*
344 Word perfect: (idiom) *Repeating*

perfectly words that you have learnt

348 Milk and Honey, All Flesh: *names for shops selling dairy products and meat; the names are biblical-sounding (see lines 328–9)*

350 lineups: *queues*

351 infinitesimal: *very small*

nods: *downward movements of the head to show recognition and greeting*

361 proper: *as if making a formal gesture*

364 dingy: *dark and dirty-looking*

365 gloss: *shine*

367 make out: *interpret*

372 *praise be: ie praise be the Lord; another biblical phrase*

373 bland: *without expression*

375 flicker: *quick, sudden movement*

378 approved: *ie official, recommended by the authorities*

378–9 in unison: *synchronized, together*

381 give it a week: *wait for a week*

384 sluggishness: *slow reactions*

385 jeopardy: *state of being in danger*

386 rash: *impulsive*

394 tricky: *difficult*

396 May Day: *the 1st of May, a national holiday in the USA and many other countries*

401 seeping over: *slowly covering*

413 Moira: *a girl Offred used to know*

415 incriminate anyone: *say anyone is guilty or involved*

416 whimper: *small weak sound of pain*

turn to jelly: *tremble all over with fear*

417–18 Keep your head down: *Don't reveal yourself, don't do anything stupid*

418 see it through: *wait till the end*

421 'Under His Eye': *another biblical-sounding phrase*

422 fervent: *very enthusiastic*

425 blinkers: *protruding pieces of material on the sides of their headdresses that prevent them seeing sideways (normally used on horses)*

426 web of lines: *series of fine lines*

Nineteen Eighty-Four

1 grinding: *mechanical noise made when pieces of metal rub against each other*

4 bristled the hair: *made the hair stand on end*

7 hisses: *long sounds like 'sssss', made by people in an audience to show extreme disapproval*

9 squeak: *sudden, high-pitched sound*

mingled: *mixed*

renegade: *someone who has changed their political loyalties*

10 backslider: *someone who has gone back to previous bad habits*

17 defiler: *polluter, spoiler*

18 heresies: *beliefs that are the opposite of official or popular beliefs*

19 sprang directly out of: *derived directly from*

20 hatching: *plotting*

24 diaphragm: *the muscle that separates the chest from the stomach*

26 fuzzy: *hairy*

aureole: *circle*

27 goatee beard: *small pointed beard covering only the chin*

27–8 despicable: *hateful*

31 venomous: *poisonous*

33 plausible: *believable*

35 taken in: *deceived*

38 freedom of assembly: *the right to have public meetings*

45 specious: *seeming believable, but in reality wrong*

claptrap: *nonsense, rubbish*

50 bleating: *noise made by a sheep (see line 30)*

62 refuted: *proved to be wrong*

64 dupes: *stupid people who will believe anybody*

70 compendium: *collection*
72 clandestinely: *secretly*
77 to a frenzy: *to its highest emotional and irrational level*
82 O'Brien: *a leading Party member who is in the audience*
flushed: *red with emotion*
85 Swine!: (literally, *pig*) *an insulting term of abuse*
88 inexorably: *without a possibility of being stopped*
90 rung: *piece of wood, parallel with the ground, connecting the legs of a chair*
95 sledge-hammer: *very heavy hammer, used for knocking down walls etc*
99 blowlamp: *tool with a very hot flame used to remove paint from a surface*
109 hordes: *masses, armies*
111 enchanter: *magician*
119 flinched: *moved involuntarily*
125 din: *intense noise*
144 tom-toms: *drums that you hit with your hands*
149 entrails: *intestines*
153 dissemble: *hide*

Key

1 Anatomy of a Novel

1 open response
2 Durrell suggests many aspects of Alexandria. Your ideas might have included: busy, crowded, ancient, alternately beautiful and sordid, mysterious, etc.
3 ***a*** *4*; ***b*** *1*; ***c*** *3*; ***d*** *5*; ***e*** *2*
4 open response
5 open response
6 In the first extract the narrator gives no indication at all of how the characters speak: the reader must interpret this. There is not even much indication of who is speaking (one example of 'said Fanny'), so the reader must be attentive! In the second extract the narrator uses the full range of techniques to tell us how the characters speak: verbs more explicit than 'say' ('added'); adverbs ('politely, smoothly'); adverbial phrases ('with reflex promptness'); the reaction of characters to things said ('who at this stimulus struggled to his feet'). There is also variety in where the verbs of speaking are placed in the conversation, which indicates pauses. Note that the last line, " 'Not at all,' Dixon said smoothly. 'Mr Welch is just going' " could have been written " 'Not at all. Mr Welch is just going,' Dixon said smoothly.' " but this would change subtly the rhythmn of Dixon's comment. In Chapter 3 you will notice a big difference between the ways that Lawrence and Hemingway present conversation.
7 open response
8 ***a*** You probably noticed the following:
It towered above me and all around me, each blade <u>tattooed</u> (metaphor) with <u>tiger-skins of sunlight</u> (metaphor). It was <u>knife-edged</u> (metaphor), dark, and a wicked green, <u>thick as a forest</u> (simile) and alive with grasshopppers that chirped and chattered and leapt through the air <u>like monkeys</u> (simile).
There are some other things to notice. Mostly one thinks of nouns, or adjectives + nouns, functioning as metaphors, but sometimes adjectives alone can be metaphorical. The adjective 'wicked' is metaphorical here, because it is a word normally associated with people, not with colours: the use here implies the boy had the impression that the grass actually had evil intentions against him. The verb 'chattered' goes with 'monkeys' rather than 'grasshoppers'; the use of this verb is therefore metaphorical, and leads up to the simile with monkeys. The denotation of 'tower' is a high building, so one might think that 'towered' was a metaphor. However, the expression has been used so much that nobody thinks of it as a metaphor any more. Words like this are called *dead metaphors*, and language is full of them (eg 'leg' of a table, 'head' of state).
b The sense of 'terror and bewilderment' of a young child in strange surroundings is presented to the reader by comparing this perfectly ordinary English field with a tropical jungle.
c an adult looking back on childhood experiences; the control of syntax and vocabulary indicates a mature person recreating the experience; a child could never talk or write in this way
d open reponse (note: In all his books, Laurie Lee adopts a 'poetic' style, full of similes and metaphors)
9 ***a*** The 'Rose' and the 'Spring' are conventional symbols. Spring symbolizes the rebirth of nature and life, and – in this context – the rose could also symbolize the rebirth of nature and life, as well as love.
b Among the various symbolic references it has are: Aziz's religion, his feeling of

cultural identity, his spirituality, his artistic sensibility. It is a symbol that helps characterize him, and it also helps define his place in the structure of the novel.

10 ***a*** The Captain sat on horseback, watching. He needed to see his orderly. His helmet threw a dark shadow over his light fierce eyes, but his moustache and mouth and chin were distinct in the sunshine. The orderly must move under the presence of the figure of the horseman. It was not that he was afraid or cowed. It was as if he was disembowelled, made empty, like an empty shell. He felt himself as nothing, a shadow creeping under the sunshine. And, thirsty as he was, he could scarcely drink, feeling the Captain near him. He would not take off his helmet to wipe his wet hair. He wanted to stay in shadow, not to be forced into consciousness. Starting, he saw the light* heel of the officer prick the belly of the horse; the Captain cantered away, and he himself could relapse into vacancy.

*The word 'light' probably denotes agile rather than shining, referring to the Captain's expert control of his horse. However, it might refer to the bright, shining spur on the Captain's heel. In any case, Lawrence probably uses the word deliberately to add to the total effect of the light/dark imagery.

b suggested response: the relationship is one of power and subservience. The Captain has power over the orderly, and he is aware of this and seems to 'need' it. Although the narrator says that the orderly is nor 'afraid or cowed', he is unable to act spontaneously in the presence of the Captain, feels his personality has been taken away, and does not want to be there at all.

11 ***a*** He prefers Jefferson as it used to be.

b The first sentence suggests slight regret, but this become explicit in the long, complex second sentence. The similes, metaphors, imagery and symbolism work together to build up this general picture:

Modern Jefferson = artificial and mechanical: paved streets, trees cut down and replaced with electricity poles, cars instead of people on foot

Jefferson before = authentic and natural: streets made of earth, plenty of trees, more human contact

Here are some particular effects. The listing of the four kinds of shade trees makes an effective visual image and also makes their gradual disappearance seem more like an elegy. The poles that support the electricity wires are described metaphorically as trees, but as unnatural and unpleasant parodies of real trees. The idea of unnaturalness in the word 'ghostly' is reinforced in the word 'apparitionlike'. Notice how the unnaturalness is stressed in the metaphor 'alert and irritable electric horns': people can be 'alert and irritable', not electric horns, yet the cars are described as human beings deliberately to remind us of the lack of human presence (just as the electricity poles replace the trees, yet still remind us of them). Notice that the simile 'with a long diminishing noise of rubber and asphalt like tearing silk' doesn't really describe the noise of a car accelerating: its effect is not so much of imagery of sound as of imagery of touch – the modern materials of rubber and asphalt are contrasted with the softness of silk, with the added idea that the rubber and asphalt destroy the silk.

In the context of this paragraph, the electricity poles and cars become symbols of modernity and the destruction of nature.

12 open response

The following checklist tells you which exercises in this book will enable you to explore in detail the elements of the novel you have looked at in this chapter.

It would be a good idea, when you have finished the chapters of this book, to read quickly through *Anatomy of a Novel* again. You can then use the checklist to remind yourself of more examples of the concepts explained.

Checklist

Elements of a novel	**Chapter**	**Exercises**
synopses	8	12–14
setting	5	7
narrator first person: minor character	5	10–12
narrator first person: main character	6	7–8, 11
	8	10
multiple points of view	3	5–9
	7	15
characters: round and flat	6	9–11
characterization through appearance and possessions	2	10
characterization through everyday actions	2	10c
	7	7 –10
characterization through differences between what is said and what is implied	2	4–9, 20
	3	32
different ways of presenting conversations	3	17–23
characterization through thought	8	10
interior monologue	7	15–18
different ways of presenting thought	6	14–17
complex sentences	4	11–13
denotation and connotation	5	18–22
	8	15 – 18
symbolism	3	24–25
imagery	3	24–25
	7	19–21
suspense and surprise	8	11
narrative structure: flashbacks	4	3, 7
narrative structure: anticipation	5	13
themes	3	13–16
	5	8–9
	6	5–6, 9–10, 12–13

2 Mean Streets

1 open response; background information: the three film stills are from the following films:
(top) *Bullets or Ballots* (1936, directed by William Keighley, with Edward G Robinson, Joan Blondell and Humphrey Bogart)
(bottom left) *Murder, My Sweet* (also known as *Farewell, My Lovely*) (1944, directed by Edward Dmytryk, with Dick Powell as Marlowe)
(bottom right) *Farewell, My Lovely* (1975, directed by Dick Richards, with Robert Mitchum as Marlowe)

2 ***a 1*** You need the money ('my bank account was still trying to crawl under a duck.' – lines 25–6)
2 You find him affected and pretentious. You dislike him so much you would like to kick him! ('The end of my foot itched, …' – lines 24–5)

3 You might want to ask about how much you will be paid, what exactly you will have to do, how long it will take, re-assure yourself of the legality of the business, etc.
b 1 You have heard he is discreet, and you have a rather 'delicate' matter to resolve.
2 You find him rather uncultured (you don't like the way he says 'Check' – line 4) and too blunt, even rude: you don't like his comment 'Not so long as it's legitimate' – line 21. (Perhaps you have something to hide?)
3 You might want to ask how much he charges, whether he has experience of the sort of job you want done, whether he carries a gun, whether he is prepared to work without knowing all the facts, etc.

3 Any hypothesis of yours could be valid, but answer ***b*** turns out to be the case in the novel. The plot of *Farewell, My Lovely* is too complicated to give here: if you enjoyed the extracts, you need to read the complete book!

5 Some questions you might have thought of are: Did you see anybody watching you during the evening, or behaving suspiciously? What is your friend's name? Where does she live? How long have you known her? What kind of relationship do you have with her? What time did the hold-up take place? Where did it take place? What made you stop your car? What kind of car did the robbers have? What did the person / people who got out look like? Could you identify him / them again? What exactly did he / they say? Did he / they threaten you with violence? What was taken? And what was the value? Was there anybody else in the other car? Why didn't you contact the police immediately? Have you had any further contact with the robbers? Have you had any further contact with your friend?

7 ***a*** Accompany Marriott to meet the robbers and give them eight thousand dollars for the return of the necklace.
b One hundred dollars in cash, paid immediately.
c Not perfectly straightforward. There is the risk of violence (lines 259–62; 286–7). Marlowe has reservations (lines 276–9). Is it suspicious that Marriott says 'we' (lines 325–6), or is it just a slip of the tongue? Perhaps Marriott's reticence suggests something suspicious or illegal. And Marlowe is preoccupied at lines 304–5.

8 ***a 2*** or possibly ***1***; ***b 3*** or possibly ***1***; ***c 3***; ***d 2***; ***e 3*** or possibly ***2***; ***f 2*** or ***1***; ***g 1***

9 Suggestions are given, although you might have made equally valid interpretations yourself.
a What a vulgar suggestion! How could you possibly accuse me of such a thing? I'm a respectable person.
b You – and people like you – are just the type. Your 'nice' exterior hides a lot of vices.
c Something doesn't quite convince me in this story.
d You're still hiding something. Are you going to tell me what's really involved?
e I don't care what you think of me.
f Stop being vague. How much are you going to pay me?

10 Remember that Marriott is not described to us from an *omniscient point of view* (see *Anatomy of a Novel*, page 16), but from Marlowe's point of view. Therefore the descriptions also tell us about Marlowe's character and attitudes. But even though the descriptions are not completely *objective* the reader does not distrust Marlowe, and is able to make some judgements. Here are some suggestions:
a This suggests a person who is precise and aware of his appearance (even though it could be 'nature' and not 'art'). Certainly Marlowe finds something to dislike in his appearance.
b 'Appearances are not deceptive' is Marlowe's opinion: he does not think Marriott has a deep personality – the appearance is probably the reality.

c This suggests that Marriott is cultured. Whether his culture is genuine or affected, the reader cannot tell now. Certainly Marlowe seems sceptical: 'metallic-looking bits of sculpture' is a rather pejorative way of describing sculptures.
d This suggests luxury and wealth (because the carpet is thick).
e This suggests that Marriott, and his circle, are pretentious and frivolous, far removed from the realities of life.
f This suggests that he is sensual, aesthetic and not concerned enough with reality.
g This suggests that Marriott is nervous.
h This suggests that Marriott is growing older but not more mature: he still tries to act young, even though he isn't.

11 **A** *like* + noun phrase; *as* + adverb or adjective + *as* + noun phrase
B ***a 10*** (+ *like*); ***b 6*** (+ *like*); ***c 8*** (+ *like*); ***d** 7* (+ *like*); ***e 9*** (+ *as*); ***f 11*** (+ *like*); ***g** 3* (+ *like*); ***h 4*** (+ *as*); ***i 1*** (+ *like*); ***j 2*** (+ *like*); ***k 5*** (+ *as*) (Note that the ironic comparisons are ***e*** + ***9*** (his cunning is so inept it will fool nobody!) and ***g*** + *3* (she is not charming at all!).)

12 **A** *as if* or *as though* + a past tense form of the verb. There is no difference in meaning between *as if* and *as though*. The past tense form ('the unreal past') is used because the comparison is 'unreal', ie a sneeze *will not drop* the houses, opening the door *doesn't dirty* Marriott. In these two examples *as if/though* is preceded by a present participle ('looking') and a past tense verb ('opened'), but the verb after *as if /though* is still in a past tense form. There are other examples at lines 40 and 99.
B open response

13 **A** *the kind of* + noun + relative clause introduced by *where* or *that* (or also by *who, which* or *whose*).
B open response

14 ***c*** open response. Some suggestions are given, but whether you agree with these and what other ideas you have added depends on your concept of 'traditional' heroes and villains.
1 ... he is honest.
2 ... he is not *always* brave (see lines 392–3); he is cynical.
3 ... he is scheming and smooth-talking.
4 ... he is not cruel.

15 ***a*** a good enough man for any world; ***b*** neither tarnished nor afraid; ***c*** a range of awareness that startles you; ***d*** unusual; ***e*** a contempt for pettiness; ***f*** fit for adventure; ***g*** common; ***h*** relatively poor; ***i*** a disgust for sham; ***j*** the best man in his world; ***k*** has a sense of character; ***l*** not himself mean; ***m*** pride; ***n*** is neither a eunuch nor a satyr; ***o*** will take no man's money dishonestly and no man's insolence; ***p*** a man of honour; ***q*** rude wit, a lively sense of the grotesque

16 open response, but some ideas you might have had (the letters refer to the qualities listed in Exercise 15) are:
e lines 251–62; ***f*** lines 276–7, 286–7, 371–2; ***h*** extract in Exercise 2; ***i*** last paragraph in extract in Exercise 2; lines 62–3, 84–7, 98–101; ***j*** lines 115–16; ***k*** lines 251–62; ***o*** lines 147–8, 286–7; ***p*** lines 286–7; ***q*** lines 98–102

18 open response. For your interest, the only description Marlowe gives of his home in *Farewell, My Lovely* is the following:
They locked the lobby door at eleven. I unlocked it and passed into the always musty lobby and along to the stairs and the elevator. I rode up to my floor. Bleak light shone along it. Milk bottles stood at the front of service doors. The red fire door loomed at the back. It had an open screen that let in a lazy trickle of air that never quite swept the cooking smell out. I was home in a sleeping world, a world as harmless as a sleeping cat.

I unlocked the door of my apartment and went in and sniffed the smell of it, just standing there, against the door for a little while before I put the light on. A homely smell, a smell of dust and tobacco smoke, the smell of a world where men live, and keep on living.

20 This question depends very much on personal response. What follows are some ideas you may or may not agree with:
a lines 26–30: his apparent sympathy for the lovers; lines 109–12: his trust in Martins; lines 130–3: his apparent sympathy for humanity; lines 135–41: his apparent nostalgia for old friends and old times and his offer of help to Martins
b lines 60–8: his attitude towards his victims; lines 86–97: he has informed on his girlfriend; lines 106–7: he asks Martins to keep Anna quiet; lines 124–8: his disregard for the people ('the mugs'); lines 131–2: his comments on the dead
c lines 34–5: his friendliness towards Martins – is this genuine or just a conventional formula?; line 39: his praise of Anna – but does he praise her in a cold and patronising way?; line 44: his generosity towards Martins – is this genuine or only something that Lime claims?; lines 99–104: similar to line 39; lines 112–14: he says he would not hurt Martins – but is this a disguised threat?; lines 130–2: he claims he only injures people's bodies, not their souls, and says he believes in 'God and mercy and all that' (the last phrase seems dismissive) – but is this a possible moral attitude, or only cynicism?

21 Both seem to focus on the observation that Lime seems cheerful and young. Perhaps this makes him a more sinister villain?

22–4 open response

3 'It Was Never Love'

1–4 open response (*1* – background information: this represents one of the scenes between Gudrun and Gerald from the second extract from *Women In Love*.)

5 ***a*** ***1*** column 2; ***2*** column 2; ***3*** column 1; ***4*** column 1 *or* column 2; ***5*** column 1; ***6*** column 2; *7* column 2; ***8*** column 2; ***9*** column 1 *or* column 2; ***10*** column 1 *or* column 2
b Gudrun's reactions seem more complex.
c open response

6 ***a*** Mostly neutral, although he could be interpreted as admiring at lines 117–18 and critical at lines 126–8.
b Ursula. Her indignant tone and opinions are the same as before.

7 open response. Gudrun is certainly fascinated by what she has seen, and the description ('thighs', 'loins', 'calves') suggests sexual interest and sensual involvement, but it is difficult to say whether her fascination is for the (sadistic?) domination, the (masochistic?) subordination, or a (sado-masochistic?) combination of both.

8 Sentences like 'It was a repulsive sight' (line 65) and 'like a disgusting dream that has no end' (lines 71–2) certainly condemn, but it is not clear whether they are meant as the narrator's opinions or the opinions of the Brangwen sisters.

13 open response to your crosses on the graph; open response to your choice of three other moments to complete the horizontal axis, but here are three suggested critical moments – lines 368–74: She tortured the open heart … torn open, is destroyed; lines 394–400: 'What does the twilight matter?' … 'you are out of place – '; lines 410–14: 'One day' he said, … 'I am not afraid of your threats!'

14 ***a*** The first two quotations refer to Gerald 'pressing' the horse, the third to Gerald 'pressing' Gudrun.

b 'he pressed upon her' (lines 171–2) recalls Gerald's treatment of the horse (lines 67 and 83) (although 'like a frost' does not continue the similarity). Gudrun's behaviour (lines 201–2 and 241–2) recalls Gerald's treatment of the horse, and the use of the word 'torture' (lines 230 and 232) recalls Ursula's description of Gerald's treatment of the horse (lines 120–2). Gudrun's behaviour: 'her hands clutched his limbs' (lines 287–8) recalls Gerald and the horse (lines 144–6). Gerald's love-making (lines 293–7) recalls his treatment of the horse (eg lines 144–9).
c This suggests that one partner must be in complete control, the other in complete subservience. There is no suggestion of collaboration, sharing, equality or tenderness.

15 open response

16 *a* You might think quotations ***a***, ***c***, and ***m*** might apply – ***a*** particularly for Gerald.
b quotations ***b***, ***f***, ***h*** and ***i***

18 *a* insists; ***b*** doubts; ***c*** admits *or* confesses; ***d*** tells; ***e*** accuses; ***f*** confesses *or* admits; ***g*** begs; ***h*** denies; ***i*** pleads; ***j*** refuses; ***k*** complains; ***l*** asks; ***m*** agree

19 Here are the grammatical patterns that follow the verbs as they are used in Exercise 18: ***1*** tell; ***2*** admit, agree, complain, confess, doubt, insist; ***3*** ask, beg; ***4*** refuse; ***5*** plead; ***6*** accuse; 7 deny
(Note: some of the verbs above can be followed by other grammatical patterns. In contexts other than the sentences in Exercise 18 *deny* can be followed by pattern *2*, *tell* by pattern ***3***, *ask*, *beg*, *agree* by pattern ***4***, and *admit* by pattern 7.)

20 claim (***2***); explain (***2***); order (***3***); promise (***1*** or ***4***); realize (***2***); state (***2***); threaten (***2*** or ***4***); warn (***1*** or ***2***); fear (***2***)

21 *a 1* Gudrun explains that the sunset is the most beautiful thing she has ever seen/that Gerald is insensitive. Gudrun accuses Gerald of being insensitive. Gudrun orders Gerald to leave her alone.
2 Gudrun states that the sunset is more important to her than Gerald/that Gerald has spoilt the pleasure of the sunset for her/that only she can appreciate beautiful things. Gudrun admits that Gerald has spoilt the pleasure of the sunset for her/that the sunset is more important to her than Gerald. Gudrun claims that only she can appreciate beautiful things/that Gerald has spoilt the pleasure of the sunset for her/that the sunset is more important to her than Gerald.
3 Gerald threatens to kill Gudrun/to take his revenge on Gudrun. Gerald promises to take his revenge on Gudrun/to kill Gudrun/Gudrun that he will win. Gerald warns Gudrun that he will win/that he will kill her/that he will take his revenge on her.
4 Gudrun claims that she is not afraid of Gerald/that she is not intimidated/that Gerald does not frighten her. Gudrun denies that she is intimidated/that she is afraid of Gerald/that Gerald frightens her.
5 Gerald realizes that their affair can (will) only end in one way/that he will have the last word/that their affair will finish badly. Gerald promises to have the last word. Gerald fears that their affair will finish badly/that their affair can (will) only end in one way.
b open response

22 Direct speech tends to be more vivid and dramatic: the characters speak with their own voices, instead of being filtered through a narrator. Also, reporting verbs always interpret what is said, whereas with direct speech the reader has to interpret what is going on: this can make the reading experience more stimulating. A particular effect in these extracts from *Women in Love* is that actually saying a formula (such as 'I will love you always') is often made to seem difficult or humiliating.

24 *a* Here are some suggestions for words that might go in the circles ***1–8***: ***1*** light;

2 hard; ***3*** noise; ***4*** heat; ***5*** dark; ***6*** soft; ***7*** quiet; ***8*** cold
b 2 , ***3*** and ***5*** are true; ***1*** , ***4*** and ***6*** are not true.

25 open response

26 ***b***

29 ***a*** At the hotel Gudrun starts a friendship with Loerke, a German sculptor, the complete opposite physically and intellectually of Gerald. Although the attraction between them is intellectual and cultural rather than sexual, it is one more reason for Gerald to feel excluded, and Gudrun uses it as yet another weapon against him. One day Gerald comes across Gudrun and Loerke drinking schnapps in the snow. He loses his temper, knocks Loerke down, and tries to strangle Gudrun. He then walks off into the mountains and, feeling desolate and abandoned, dies of exposure in the night.

30 open response – there are many possibilities. You will find, however, that the definition and example given at ***3c*** (2) , < the dating game >, will be very relevant to the man's attitude in the extract from *A Farewell to Arms.* ('To date' means to go out with a boy or a girl, in a romantic way.)

31 ***a*** He means something like a sport or pastime with rules, the aim of which is pleasure or fun.
b She means something like a pretence or make-believe.
c He seems happy with the game. Note his repetition of 'It was all right', and other comments (lines 37–46).
d She doesn't seem happy with the game (lines 57–62), but seems resigned to it (lines 68–70), and at least recognizes it for what it is (lines (77–8).
e 'Contest' and 'game' both imply competition rather than co-operation, but Lawrence, using the word 'conflict', suggests a far more serious and dangerous struggle for victory, while in *A Farewell to Arms* something less destructive and more playful is suggested.

32 At first Catherine wants to be reassured, and seems to believe what she hears. Then she seems to change her mind – she wants to get at the truth: that the words the man says might be pleasant, but are certainly not sincere. Gudrun, on the other hand, wants to make Gerald say he loves her only to prove that in reality he doesn't.

33 open response; however, it may interest you to know that later in the book they fall deeply and genuinely in love. (This is one of Hemingway's most pessimistic novels, however. Frederic's love for Catherine makes him see the horror and uselessness of war more clearly, and he deserts (runs away from the army). He and Catherine, who is by this time pregnant, escape to Switzerland, but the novel closes with Catherine's death in childbirth and Frederic's despair.)

4 War Games

1 ***b*** open response, but notice that the elephant (probably inspired by *Dumbo*, Walt Disney's1941 cartoon about a flying elephant) is made to resemble a warplane: its trunk is a cannon and bomb doors are located in its stomach. (Background information: the man on the right is Yossarian, the main character in *Catch-22*, and the markings above the elephant are meant to represent bombs – they show the number of bombing missions this crew has flown.)

3 ***a*** 1) d); 2) h); 3) b); 4) j); 5) f); 6) l); 7) a); 8) e); 9) c); 10) k); 11) g); 12) i)
b 2

4 ***a*** 26 characters: Hungry Joe, Yossarian, Doc Daneeka, Gus and Wes, Major——de Coverley, Major Major, McWatt, Clevinger, Captain Blake, the corporal in

eyeglasses, Snowden, Dobbs, Hupple, Colonel Cathcart, Lieutenant Colonel Korn, the chaplain, General Dreedle, Appleby, Colonel Cargill, General Peckem, ex-PFC Wintergreen, Colonel Moodus, Dunbar, Havermeyer, Orr.
(Note: although *Catch-22* is very modern in some respects – eg the narrative technique you looked at in Exercise 3b – the vast number of characters recalls 18th and 19th century novels – eg the novels of Dickens.)

5 open response

7 ***a*** 1) f); 2) b); 3) k); 4) h); 5) c); 6) i); 7) e); 8) g); 9) a); 10) j); 11) d)
b This time the narrative structure is much more chronological. (See Chapter 1, *Anatomy of a Novel*, pages 28–9, for narrative structure.)

8 They are both extremely self-interested. Mrs Daneeka's expressions of grief and relief (lines 373–6 and 389–93) may be genuine, but the exaggerated way Heller describes them, and the fact they do not last very long, perhaps make us suspect them.

9 Here are some examples, but you might have others. Some examples can be included in more than one category.
the enemy = your own side: Doc Daneeka's fear of being transferred (lines 54–8); Captain Black suspecting the corporal and preferring Hitler (lines 101–6); Dreedle's attitude to Peckem (lines 211–14); Group's anger at Dr Stubbs (lines 443–52)
bureaucracy replaces common sense: Gus and Wes' 'exact science' (lines 25–31); Colonel Korn's rule (lines 141–5); the 'T.S. Eliot' episode (lines 172–98 and 213–42); all of the 'Mrs Daneeka' chapter
instinctive dislike and mistrust of other people: General Dreedle's hatred of Colonel Moodus, and his pleasure at calling Peckem (lines 202–14); Peckem's reason for suspecting Dreedle (lines 240–5); Sergeant Towser's reaction to Doc Daneeka (lines 362–6); Gus and Wes' conversation (lines 367–9); Captain Flume, Wes and Gus's rejection of Doc Daneeka (lines 457–60)
self-interest: Doc Daneeka's attitude (lines 8–15 and 22–4); Doc Daneeka (lines 47–50); Doc Daneeka (lines 51–9); Doc Daneeka's answer to Yossarian (lines 79–83); Doc Daneeka (lines 88–97); Sergeant Towser's reason for being upset at Doc Daneeka's 'death' (lines 307–23); the reaction of the husbands (lines 377–9); Mrs Daneeka's reactions to her husband's 'death' (lines 398–404, 424–9, 478–9)
perverse logic: Gus and Wes' 'exact science' (lines 25–31); Captain Black's reason for suspecting the corporal (lines 101–6); the questions (note both the nonsense-grammar and irrelevance) at the educational session (lines 111–20); the rules governing question asking (lines 138–49); perhaps Colonel Cargill's comment (lines 167–71); Peckem's reason for suspecting Dreedle (lines 240–5); the motivation behind the skeet-shooting (lines 243–8); Dunbar's reason for liking skeet-shooting (lines 249–52); the reason for Orr's interruption (lines 276–81); Dunbar's concept of time (lines 282–304); Colonel Cathcart's reason for increasing the missions (lines 305–7); Gus and Wes' conviction that Doc Daneeka is dead (lines 341–61); Group's outrage because Dr Stubbs follows the real regulations (lines 443–52).
mutual incomprehension: Hungry Joe not listening to Yossarian (lines 3–4); incomprehension between Yossarian and Doc Daneeka (is Yossarian making fun of Doc Daneeka?) (lines 75–83); the questions at the educational session, and then Yossarian's questions (lines 111–20 and 122–37); the 'T.S. Eliot' episode (lines 172–98 and 213–42); Dunbar and Clevinger's interchange (lines 253–7 and 263–73); Towser avoiding conversation with Doc Daneeka (lines 313–28); Gus and Wes with Doc Daneeka (lines 339–61); Colonel Cathcart's incomprehensible letter (lines 475–7).

10 open response

11 ***b*** Yossarian knew it was a good one because Yossarian was a collector of good questions and had used them to disrupt the educational sessions [Clevinger had once conducted two nights a week in Captain Black's intelligence tent with the corporal] [in eyeglasses] [who everybody knew was probably a subversive].

Captain Black knew he was a subversive because he wore eyeglasses and used words like *panacea* and *utopia*, and because he disapproved of Adolf Hitler, [who had done such a great job of combating un-American activities in Germany.]

c In general terms, these sentences are packed with apparently irrelevant information, and reflect the chaotic, crowded conditions of a world at war, and the disturbed states of mind of the characters. In Exercise 3b you probably decided that association of ideas and flashbacks instead of chronological order carry the narrative forward: notice how the sentences in ***a*** and ***b*** begin with a link with a previous idea (eg 'the system' referring back to temperature-taking, 'it' and 'a good one' referring back to Doc Daneeka's question 'Why me?' in line 96), yet the link is soon abandoned and the sentences develop in a completely different direction (Major ——— de Coverley's pastime and then his visit to Rome; the educational sessions in Captain Black's tent). The relative clauses are the means by which flashbacks are inserted into the narrative, and the use of the past perfect indicates that the events had happened previously. The relative clauses also allow Heller to leap from character to character, and to include such a great number of characters (see Exercise 4). The considerable number of clauses of purpose and reason ironically contain mostly bizarre purposes and reasons, and serve to emphasize the perverse logic and mutual incomprehension of *Catch-22* (see Exercises 9 and 10).

12 Yossarian went to Doc Daneeka and asked to be grounded because he was crazy and therefore not fit to fly, but Doc Daneeka said he couldn't ground him because of a rule called 'Catch-22'. 'Catch-22' / This rule, which recognized you had to be crazy to keep on flying missions, obliged pilots to *ask* personally to be grounded, and / so as soon as you *asked* to be grounded you proved you weren't crazy, which meant you had to keep on flying combat missions. Yossarian, who had always appreciated intellectual elegance, could not help being impressed by what he called the 'elliptical precision' of this rule, which he compared to good modern art because it was both 'graceful' and 'shocking' at the same time.

15 ***a*** Uniquely funny; comic; knockabout; ironic; bawdy; hilarious; delights; vulgarly, bitterly, savagely funny; with a facility of comic invention; Extremely funny; and above all, funny; Stands comparison with the most memorable works in satire; crazy; written with wit

b macabre; nightmarish; moving, shocking; brutally gruesome; will outrage as many readers as it delights; sad, frightening; a disturbing insight

c mind-spinning; ironic; it will not be forgotten by those who can take it; of deep thought; Stands comparison with the most memorable works in satire; cruelly sane story; a disturbing insight into the larger struggle of today: the survival of mankind

d Remarkable; Wildly original; Devastatingly original novel; Absolutely original

e a dazzling performance; Brilliantly written anti-war novel … a masterpiece; A book of enormous richness and art, … and brilliant writing; deeply impressive

f rave of a novel; illogical, formless, Shavian; wild, exhilarating, raging, giant roller-coaster of a book; wonderful

16 ***b*** Here are some particularly obvious examples: mind-spinning, rave of a novel; wild; giant roller-coaster of a book; Wildly original; Devastatingly original; crazy

19 ***a*** '1: a problematic situation for which the only solution is denied by a circumstance inherent in the problem or by a rule 2 a: an illogical, unreasonable, or senseless situation c: a situation presenting two equally undesirable alternatives'
(from *Merriam Webster's Tenth Collegiate Dictionary*)
'dilemma faced by somebody who is bound to suffer, whichever course of action he takes.'
(from *Oxford Advanced Learner's Dictionary*)

24 ***a*** *The Danger Tree*: the enemy are the Germans. Simon doesn't feel any personal hatred towards them at line 44–7. Peters calls them 'bastards' (lines 137–8) because they deliberately attacked an ambulance.

Catch-22: in the few references to a foreign enemy the attitudes are joky (lines 104–6) and uncomprehending and rather detached (lines 106–8). Principally, the enemy is seen as one's own side. See Key to Exercise 9.

b *The Danger Tree*: constantly with solidarity, kindness, respect and compassion, regardless of rank (officers and men). A brief, perhaps typical, moment of complaining against authority is the man in the cook-house's comment on the CO (lines 15–17), but this seems comic rather than cynical, certainly not the systematic distrust of *Catch-22*.

Catch-22: precisely the opposite of the above. See Key to Exercise 9.

c *The Danger Tree*: Simon is disgusted by his own involvement in killing (lines 45–7) and shocked by the macabre death of the tank crew (lines 110–15), but is initially unmoved (because of shock?) by Hugo's death (lines 131–2 and 156). Then he sees Hugo's death as a premonition of his own (lines 169–71), but full grief comes not with the recognition that Hugo is no longer alive but with recognition of the effect on their parents (lines 172–90). The major (lines 116–27) and Hugman (154–5) show sympathy for Simon rather than explicit grief for Hugo, while Peters is obviously moved (lines 129–48).

Catch-22: the characters respond to death with cynical humour and various forms of crazy, irrational behaviour. At lines 122–37 the men are 'upset', and Yossarian seems to see Snowden's death as an existential problem (death as a phenomenon rather than the death of the individual Snowden seems to be his concern), but his literary joke (line 129) undercuts the seriousness. Doc Daneeka's 'death' is seen as an 'administrative problem' to his colleagues (lines 321–3). Mrs Daneeka's grief (suspiciously exaggerated?) soon gives way to thoughts of money. See Key to Exercise 9.

d *The Danger Tree*: there is some irrational behaviour. Simon's senseless killing of the flies (lines 18–44) derives from boredom and irritation (lines 26–7), and perhaps the stress of war. Emotion and a premonition lead him to go out into the desert alone in a storm (lines 60–88). The prevailing behaviour, however, is rational (notice, for example, Simon's reason for leaving at lines 152–3).

Catch-22: irrational behaviour is everywhere. Yossarian shows a persistent logic which is, however, totally incompatible with the logic of war. See Key to Exercise 9.

25 He finds it completely impossible to communicate the enormity of Hugo's death. *Catch-22* also deals, in a completely different way, with the inability to communicate: contrast Colonel Cathcart's letter (lines 475–7). Both extracts, in their very different ways, imply that events in wartime are senseless and cannot be explained.

5 'The White Man's Burden'

1 open response (the picture of the steamboat is thought to have been taken on a river in Nigeria, West Africa around 1920; the picture of the two white men surrounded by local people with spears is of a hunt for gorillas in a rainforest in Cameroon, West Africa at about the same time)

3 ***a*** He means something like 'The duty that the white races have to bring civilization to the rest of the world'. To do this, many qualities are needed: self-sacrifice (lines 2–4); patience (lines 5, 10); restraint in the use of force (lines 11, 18); humility (line 12); honesty and clarity (lines 13–14); selflessness (lines 15–16); perseverance when your plans fail (lines 21–24).

b They are described in lines 6–8 and 23: fluttered, wild, sullen, Half devil and half child; according to Kipling they embody Sloth and heathen Folly.

7 His first impressions are mostly negative. But note that three moments suggest that he feels some attraction:

a his curiosity about new coasts (lines 4–7): 'Watching a coast as it slips by ... Come and find out.' The 'positive pleasure' in the voice of the surf (lines 30–2). The vitality of the men in the shore boats (lines 34–40): 'A wild vitality ... They were a great comfort to look at'.

Here are some examples that contribute to his negative impression:

b line 7: featureless; line 8: monotonous grimness; line 18: God-forsaken wilderness; line 21: nobody seemed particularly to care; lines 22–3: the coast looked the same, as though we had not moved; lines 25–6: some sordid farce acted in front of a sinister back-cloth; line 28: the uniform sombreness of the coast; lines 29–30: the toil of a mournful and senseless delusion.

8 open response. Here are some ideas that you might have included.

a The work is carried on in a way that is *careless*, *wasteful* and *inefficient* ('I came upon more pieces of decaying machinery, a stack of rusty nails'). Marlow calls the blasting 'objectless' (line 111), ie *pointless*, *useless* and *wasteful*.

b The treatment of the blacks is *cruel* (lines 112–20), and takes away their human dignity ('Black rags ... waggled to and fro like tails'). European values are presented as *inappropriate* and *arbitrary* ('these men could by no stretch of the imagination be called enemies. ... the outraged law, like the bursting shells, had come to them, an insoluble mystery from the sea'). The delegation of authority to natives is presented as *demoralizing* (the guard 'strolled despondently': lines 129–30). The attitude of the guard to white authority is one of fear rather than respect ('This was simple prudence, ...': lines 132–4).

c Complete *indifference* to the suffering of the natives is seen in lines 168–71. The *callous exploitation* of the natives – when they can no longer work they are abandoned – is further described in lines 175–81. *Materialistic* priority given to work instead of human life is criticized in lines 172–4 ('The work was going on. The work! And this was the place where some of the helpers had withdrawn to die.'). The *inappropriacy* of European values – probably again a hypocritical justification, 'legalization' of colonialization – is seen in lines 175–6 ('They were not enemies, they were not criminals...') and 178–9 ('Brought from all the recesses of the coast in all the legality of time contracts').

d Most whites become *demoralized* and seem to let themselves go (lines 225–6). *Confusion* and *chaos*, rather than order and efficiency, dominate (lines 234–5). The trade is clearly *exploitation* – 'rubbishy' material is exchanged for 'precious' ivory (lines 236–8). *Inefficiency* is seen in the way the accountant's office is built (lines 241–4). *Indifference* of the white colonizers towards each other's well-being, and the priority of work over human life, is shown in the accountant's attitude to the sick man (lines 248–50).

9 ***a*** open response
b open response. Particularly in contrast are lines 4–6, 11, 15–16, 19–20 and 22, although all of the poem paints a picture of colonization completely different from Marlow's experience.

10 open response. Here are some suggestions:
b Column 2: I'm used to violence: I believe that it is sometimes necessary. I'm not too scrupulous about what I have to do: I don't make fine moral distinctions.
Column 3: There was no moral ambiguity about this situation: this was unnecessary and purely aggressive violence.
c Column 2: I haven't made many decisions in my life: I take life as it comes.
Column 3: Even to a resigned and accepting person these events were unacceptable and horrific.
d Column 2: I can be moved – for a while – by the sight of suffering.
Column 3: We should be appalled too – and for more than a 'moment'.

11 open response. Marlow's compassion is not in doubt, but readers have had different opinions of his attitude to the Africans. You will be able to consider this again in Exercise 29.

12 open response

13 ***a*** Examples are at lines 220–3; 253–60; 275–82.
b Kurtz is introduced. He is remarkable in that he gets more ivory than all the other agents put together, and the reader wonders how – what kind of man can he be? (We find out later in the novel. When Marlow finally arrives at the Inner Station, he finds that the civilized and educated European, Kurtz, has created his personal kingdom among the Africans, which he rules by barbaric rites – including human sacrifice. Kurtz attempts to justify himself to Marlow, but Marlow persuades him to return with him. On the return journey, however, Kurtz, already ill, dies. In a moment of self-knowledge, he murmurs his last words before dying – 'The horror! The horror!' Marlow is left with two packages to deliver: Kurtz's letters to his fiancée, and his unfinished report for the 'Society for the Suppression of Savage Customs'.)
(*Apocalypse Now*, a film made by the American director Francis Ford Coppola in 1979, is closely based on the plot and themes of *Heart of Darkness.* Set in the Vietnam war, its narrator is an American army captain (played by Martin Sheen) sent on a mission up a river to find a colonel (played by Marlon Brando), who no longer obeys orders from central command and is waging a brutal, unauthorized guerilla war of his own in Cambodia.)

14 ***a*** *In spite of* and *despite* are followed by a noun, while *although* and *even though* are followed by a clause with a subject and a verb. (Note: The expressions *in spite of the fact that* and *despite the fact that* can be followed by a clause with a subject and a verb. *Even though* is more emphatic than *although*. The word *though* is less formal than *although* – it is found more often in spoken than in written English.)
b *Because of* is followed by a noun, while *because* is followed by a clause with a subject and a verb.
c *So* is used before an adjective, while *such* is used before a noun phrase (which may or may not have an adjective in it; ie … had *such an elegant appearance that* Marlow thought … or … had *such an appearance that* Marlow thought …). Both *so* and *such* are often followed by a *that* clause as in the examples here. (Note: *so* can also be followed by an adverb, ie The accountant was dressed *so well* that Marlow thought …)

15 ***a*** A man-of-war was shelling the bush, *even though / although* there wasn't even a shed there.
b *Even though / Although* men on board were dying at the rate of three-a-day, the ship stayed there.
c The Swedish captain suggested the Swede might have hanged himself *because of* the heat.
d The blasting was going on, *even though / although* the cliff was not in the way.
e Marlow felt *such disgust* at the sight of the chain gang *that* he couldn't bear to see them again.
f The treatment, surroundings and food were *so unfamiliar* to the natives *that* they had lost the will to live.
g Marlow mentions the accountant *because* he first heard about Kurtz from him.
h Marlow respected the accountant *because of* his 'backbone'.
i The accountant kept up his appearance *despite / in spite of* the demoralization among the other Europeans.
j The accountant's office was *so badly built that* the light came in.
k The sick agent made *such a (lot of) noise that* the accountant claimed he couldn't concentrate.
l *Even though / Although* the invalid agent from up-country was unconscious, the accountant did not seem concerned.
m The accountant had come to hate the natives *because* they interfered with his concentration.
n The accountant didn't write to Kurtz *because of* his distrust of the messengers.

16 ***b*** because of; ***c*** so; ***d*** that; ***e*** although / even though; ***f*** Although / Even though; ***g*** because; ***h*** such; ***i*** that; ***j*** in spite of; ***k*** because; ***l*** although / even though

17 The following are possible combinations. Other combinations are possible – check with your teacher or a native-speaker if you have written something different.
a *Although / Even though / In spite of the fact that / Despite the fact that* the Church defended the status of South American Indians, no such feelings were extended towards black slaves from Africa.
b Europeans took over nine million black slaves to the Americas *because* they needed them as labourers on their plantations.
c The sugar plantations in the Caribbean became *so prosperous that* piracy of ships returning to Europe became common.
d Until the end of the nineteenth century the interior of Africa, with all its wealth of ivory and gold, remained unexplored *because* disease and climate kept Europeans out.
e Both the use of steam – for railways and ships – and treatment for tropical diseases made *such (great) progress* in the nineteenth century *that* the colonization of the interior of Africa, particularly the Congo, started in the 1880s.
f Europeans had *such (great) confidence* in the superiority of their own religion and customs *that* they thought these should be imposed on their colonies.
g Europeans imposed a wage-earning economy on the peoples they colonized, *even though / although / in spite of the fact that / despite the fact that* the peoples they colonized were used to to a different economy, based on hunting, farming and trading.
h Paradoxically, missionary activity had the effect of encouraging rebellion among natives *because* this showed the difference between the morality of the colonizers and their practice.

19 ***a*** By 'devil' he probably means an immoral or evil force, but a force that is also passionate and energetic. By 'men' he probably means tough, strong and even courageous people.

b By 'devil' he probably means an immoral or even evil person – the opposite of all the positive connotations of the word 'Christian'. By 'child' he probably means someone immature, ingenuous, not yet formed morally and spiritually.

20 *a* The uses in 1 and 3 are still normal today, the use in 2 is not. 'Savage' as a generic term referring to non-European people – implying that they are wild and uncivilized – is unacceptable to most people: today's view is that every race has its own civilization and moral code.

b No. For most people, not belonging to a major religion no longer connotes immorality or 'savagery'.

c open response. Many people would say 'no', because they think it implies that only males can be tough and courageous, and not women. Others might think that 'macho' qualities and attitudes are not admirable under any circumstances, even for men.

21 The suggested responses given here aim to be complete: you are not expected to have mentioned everything included.

a In order to convey the comfort he feels from the surf, he uses the positive connotations of 'brother' – someone familiar, supportive and faithful, someone who shares the same background and attitudes, someone who is loved and who loves in return.

b 'Shape' denotes the outer form, the outline of something. Two ideas might be suggested here: 1) the denotation implies that Marlow can't see the natives very well, and 2) the connotation implies that the natives are so wasted away that they seem more like objects than clearly defined human beings. (Note: Marlow often uses words normally without human connotations, which shows how much the treatment of the natives has taken away their humanity: eg 'things' in line 106, 'shadows' in line 177, 'shapes' again in line 182, 'bundles of acute angles' in line 197, 'phantom' in line 200.)

c 'Raw matter' (or, in contemporary English, 'raw material') denotes a substance such as a metal, mineral or wood used to manufacture something else, which is a 'product'. This use of words therefore suggests that the colonizers do not consider the natives as human beings, but simply use them, with absolutely no humanitarian feelings.

d The denotation of 'pilgrimage' does not apply here – this is not a journey to a holy place, made for religious reasons, by a believer in a faith. Instead, the kind of journey it was and how Marlow felt about it are suggested by the connotations of the word: pilgrimages often involve travel to foreign lands, they are often arduous and long, they test one's endurance, one depends on one's faith to keep going. (In the context of the novel there is perhaps the anticipation that Marlow will eventually have a revelation of some kind.)

e 'Philanthropic' (denotation: inspired by the desire for the welfare of other human beings) only has positive connotations. Yet here Marlow uses the word *ironically*, bitterly suggesting that the motivations of the colonists are exactly the opposite. The word 'criminal' is also used ironically: the denotation and connotations of this word cannot apply to the natives because they are ignorant of the laws they are supposed to have broken, while the colonists use this word to give legality to the slavery that they have imposed on the natives. (Note: Marlow often ironically uses words of positive denotation and connotation to contrast the colonists' moral and legal claims with their actual practice: eg 'enemies' in line 56, 'exalted trust' and 'high and just proceedings' in lines 136–7, 'all the legality of time contracts' in line 179, and 'perfectly correct transactions' in lines 286–7.)

22 open response

26 ***a*** his loss of status and fear of being replaced as a figure of authority (lines 1–9); his son's conversion to Christianity (lines 25–7; 31–6) and the conversion of many villagers (lines 71–8); his disappointment at the loss of his people's fighting spirit (lines 109–20)

b his intention to build up his property, and place his sons in society, and so display his wealth (lines 14–18), leading to the possibility of the highest position for himself (lines 18–20); the fertility of his crops (lines 22–4); his hope in his other sons (lines 27–30); his consolation from his daughters – particularly Ezinma – and hopes for prestigious marriages for them (lines 37–69)

27 You might have included some of the following ideas.

a In the extract from *Things Fall Apart* the law is applied without any knowledge of local customs, 'in ignorance' (lines 83 and 136–8). And not only is it an imposition of an alien code, but it also leads to corruption: bribery of the African staff wins a dispute about land (lines 130–4). The police who arrest people and guard prisoners, the 'Kotma', are not of the same tribe as the victims, and behave arrogantly and with gratuitous violence (lines 83–106). There are similarities with the extract from *Heart of Darkness*: Marlow describes how the Africans cannot understand the white man's law – its arrival is 'an insoluble mystery from the sea' (lines 124–5). He criticizes white law because it is alien, and suggests that it is used for mercenary intentions, in the comment 'all the legality of time contracts' (line 179). A small difference from *Things Fall Apart* is that the native guard seems a rather unwilling collaborator (lines 128–37), unlike the 'Kotma'.

b In the extract from *Things Fall Apart* missionary activity prepares the way for colonization (lines 81–2; 139–41). African converts to Christianity are told that their customs are bad: they adopt not only the religion but the whole social code of the whites, and act against their fellow countrymen (lines 121–7; 136–44; 151–2). Another idea is suggested in the conversion of Ogbuefi Ugonna (lines 73–80): he is portrayed as being ingenuous and not fully aware of the new religion – Okonkwo thinks he is a 'madman' (line 74) – but perhaps there is also criticism of the church for its intention to win converts at any cost, without concern about whether they fully understand their new religion or not. In the extract from *Heart of Darkness* the white man's religion is not mentioned (nor is it in the rest of the novel).

c In the extract from *Heart of Darkness*, Marlow describes free Africans as vital (lines 34–9) and the subjugated Africans as completely passive and resigned (lines 106; 113–20; 125–8; 168–207). The Africans working with the whites are presented as subservient but reluctant (lines 128–37; 230–2). In the extract from *Things Fall Apart* the picture is more detailed. First, Achebe distinguishes between different peoples: the 'Kotma' are a different people to the inhabitants of Umuofa and Mbanta – they willingly accept the role of the white men's policemen, and feel no sympathy for Okonkwo and his people (lines 83–106). Secondly, he says there was an initial benevolent reaction – an acceptance of the whites because they were perceived as 'foolish' (line 141). Thirdly, he distinguishes between the reactions of Okonkwo's people under British rule: those who converted to Christianity accept white rule completely (lines 121–7; 137–44; 151–2), those who did not, react differently, but without the resignation seen in *Heart of Darkness*. For example, Okonkwo wants armed resistance (lines 115–20), although Obierika thinks they are outnumbered (lines 121–7); the prisoners do not behave with the total resignation of Conrad's chain-gang – they make fun of their guards (lines 99–104), and their song becomes a popular 'resistance' song (line 106). Another small difference of detail: Achebe also says that some Africans in prison are unused to the labour and so suffer more (lines 96–9), while Marlow does not take into consideration possible differences of social rank among the Africans.

28 ***a*** It is a patriarchal society – children should obey fathers. Importance is given to males – females are considered 'weak' and less important.
b Social status is important. Being poor or unknown is a social handicap.
c This society tends to be prejudiced against outsiders, although in this case the outsiders behave badly anyway (and perhaps the 'Kotma' behave as they do because of their racial prejudice towards the people of Umuofia).
d Again, rank or class is a feature of this structured society – different classes expect to be treated differently. Organized agriculture is important in the economy.
e Importance is given to property – it leads to quarrels, even murder. But there is a moral / religious code that is respected. (And perhaps this respect for 'the earth' anticipates more contemporary, environmentalist concerns?)

29 open response. Readers who do not agree with Achebe might say that Marlow is not the same person as Conrad (although Achebe sees no difference between the author and the narrator, and we know that Conrad did think Marlow was a decent person – see Exercise 12); that Marlow / Conrad was extremely compassionate, a vast improvement on Kipling; and that terms used by him that are offensive nowadays did not have such offensive connotations at the time of writing. Readers who agree with Achebe might think that expressions such as the following show an attitude of racist superiority: 'black fellows' (line 34), 'they had faces like grotesque masks' (line 36), 'unhappy savages' (line 128), 'with a large, white, rascally grin' (lines 134–5), 'The man seemed young – almost a boy – but you know with them it's hard to tell' (lines 188–9), 'one of these creatures' (line 203), 'his woolly head' (line 206), 'dusty niggers with splay feet' (line 235). Achebe criticized the compassion in the extract you have read in this way: 'The kind of liberalism espoused here by Marlow / Conrad touched all the best minds of the age in England, Europe and America. It took different forms in the minds of different people but almost always managed to sidestep the ultimate question of equality between white people and black people. That extraordinary missionary, Albert Schweitzer … epitomizes the ambivalence. In a comment which has often been quoted Schweitzer says: "The African is indeed my brother but my junior brother." '
(The ending of *Things Fall Apart* carries on Achebe's condemnation of white intervention. When Okonkwo returns to Umuofia, he finds confirmation that Christians have desecrated the local gods. He leads a group of tribesmen to the church where, although they do not harm the missionary, they burn down the building. They are arrested, but then released after paying a fine. During a meeting after their release, 'kotma' messengers arrive to break up the meeting. Enraged, Okonkwo kills the head messenger. Partly through desperation, partly to avoid recrimination on the whole village, he commits suicide by hanging himself. The novel ends with the arrival of the British High Commissioner, who decides to use the incident as a chapter in his book, *The Pacification of the Primitive Tribes of the Lower Niger.* Notice similarities with Kurtz's interest in 'bringing Civilization', and the name of the society Kurtz was writing for – see the Key to Exercise 13.)

6 'Bad Wife!'

1 open response
2 open response. There are many 'messages' in Lindo's story. You will look at this again in Exercise 13.

3 open response, but some ideas you might have had are:
a The social status of a servant (lines 3–6): she is asked to perform the duties of a servant in order to train her as a wife for Tyuan-yu. Examples are: chopping vegetables (line 8); serving at table (lines 25–7); sewing and embroidering (lines 29–31 and 43–4); washing rice (lines 36–7); cleaning chamber pots (lines 38–40); cooking (lines 40–2 and 48–54); washing clothes (lines 43–6); combing her mother-in-law's hair (lines 50–2).
b She is keen to make a good impression (she wears her best dress at line 7); she feels nervous and misses her family, but feels she needs to honour her promise to her parents (lines 9–11); she is worried about doing her duties well and about her mother-in-law's judgement of her, and tries to convince herself she is happy (lines 15–21).
c She becomes resigned to her life at the Huangs, partly because she becomes indifferent to the pain they cause her (lines 47–8), partly because the Huangs seem to have convinced her that she exists solely to give them satisfaction (lines 48–62). Eventually she becomes completely resigned when she realizes that there is nowhere else for her to go anyway (lines 63–7).

4 ***a*** open response, but here are some examples of how Huang Taitai and Tyan-yu treat Lindo:
Huang Taitai doesn't greet Lindo when she arrives (lines 1–3), treating her instead as a servant (lines 3–6). She continues to insist that Lindo learns how to do menial tasks (lines 29–46) – although Huang Taitai herself does not do them (lines 33–5). (Note that she eventually finds her behaviour satisfactory at lines 43–6 and 50–2.)
Tyan-yu doesn't greet Lindo when she arrives (line 3); he does his best to make her unhappy by being arrogant, complaining, making her do unnecessary work and insulting her (lines 22–8). (Note that he eventually finds her cooking satisfactory at lines 52–4.)
b open response

5 ***a*** Lindo's family give their furniture as the traditional 'dowry' (lines 75–7).
b Lindo leaves from a neighbour's house (lines 80–2 and 96).
c Lindo is taken in a red palanquin (lines 81 and 97).
d Lindo wears a beautiful red dress (line 117) and a large embroidered red scarf over her face (line 122).
e It is not specific (the only reference is at line 134).
f The entire village, and friends and family from other cities, are invited (lines 71–2), but most do not come because of fear of the Japanese invasion (lines 86–91). Those who do turn up are the Huang family, the entertainers, a few village people, and some servants and their children (lines 128–33).
g The day chosen is supposed to be a lucky day – the fifteenth day of the eighth moon when the moon is most full – but it rains, which is a sign of bad luck. Added to this, the thunder and lightning are confused with Japanese bombs, so many guests stay at home (lines 86–91).
h The solemnity of the wedding is symbolized by a red candle made to be lit at both ends, with both both Tyan-yu's and Lindo's names written on it. It is supposed to burn all night until nothing is left except ashes; it is a 'marriage bond' symbolizing the eternal union of the bride and bridegroom, even after the death of one of them (lines 141–60).
i a high official (line 137) and the matchmaker (lines 137–41)
j hundreds of dishes (line 75) for a banquet (line 164); entertainers with violins and flutes (line 130)
k jokes; boys hiding under the bed; red eggs hidden between the blankets; the bride and bridegroom have to kiss in public; firecrackers (lines 165–72).

7–8 open response

9 suggested response:

a For the first months of their married life he makes her sleep separately from him, on a sofa (lines 173–6; 209–14). He does not desire her because he is afraid of her, and is immature – Lindo thinks he is afraid of women in general – (lines 239–42). It seems he tries to hide his fear and insecurity behind a show of bravado and arrogance – notice the way he speaks and behaves at line 175.

b At first she is happy that she doesn't have to sleep with him (line 176); for the first months of their married life she is frightened that he will want sex with her (lines 209–11), and feels nausea at the idea. In public she keeps up a show of obedience (lines 215–16), for example, cooking special dishes for him (lines 216–22). She starts to sleep on the bed with him, prepared, if necessary, for a sexual relationship (lines 235–8). Reassured that he has no sexual intentions towards her, she loses her fear of him, and feels protective towards him – she thinks of him as a younger brother rather than a husband (lines 241–5).

c Initially she is pleased by her obedience and deference (line 222), but then she becomes domineering and aggressive: she threatens not to feed or clothe her if she refuses to sleep with Tyan-yu (lines 230–1), and gets angry that Lindo has not become pregnant (lines 249–53). The superstitious measures of keeping Lindo in bed (lines 253–4) and taking away sharp things (lines 258–60), as well as making her take medicine (line 263) also show her domineering nature. The matchmaker's advice to reclaim the jewellery indicates the meannness in Huang Taitai (lines 277–81), rather than generosity towards her daughter-in-law.

d Outward deference – she cooks special dishes for her health (lines 219–22) – but inside she is angry (lines 232–4).

e He lies to her: he tells her that Lindo refuses to sleep with him (lines 230–2). Then he tells her that he has done everything to get Lindo pregnant (lines 251–3). His behaviour seems to be provoked by desire for self-protection and fear of his mother (lines 231–2).

f She seems to have complete faith in her son (lines 230–2; 251–3).

11 open response, but here are some sentences you might have chosen:

Her ability to act a part convincingly, and make people believe her, is seen in the following sentences: 'I was quite convincing, because Huang Taitai drew back and grew small like a scared animal.' (lines 307–8); '… and I patted my cheek as if it already hurt.' (lines 350–1)

Her acting ability, plus her ability to create suspense, and make people want to listen to her, are further seen in the following sentences: 'Oh, it's too terrible to think, too terrible to say.' (line 310); 'Huang Taitai looked impatient as I began to cry softly again.' (line 317); 'Mother,' I called to her in a hoarse whisper. 'Please don't leave me! I am afraid!' (lines 327–8); 'I lay my head down on the pillow as if too tired to go on.' (line 359)

Her ability to invent what people want to hear, and so use their own prejudices against them, is seen in: 'They knew you would not believe me,' I said in a remorseful tone, 'because they know I do not want to leave the comforts of my marriage.' (lines 333–5); 'He said this girl only pretends to come from a bad family. But she is really from imperial blood, and … ' (lines 356–8)

Her insight into human nature, and a sense of humour, is seen in: 'And I knew they were almost caught, two ducks leaning into the pot.' (line 332)

Her powers of observation and invention are seen in: 'I nodded, remembering the painting I had observed on the wall.' (lines 341–2)

12 ***a*** promise; ***b*** promises; ***c*** promise; ***d*** promise; ***e*** forget; ***f*** forget; ***g*** promise; ***h*** forget

13 definitely ***b*** and ***c***; possibly ***d***; there are elements of ***a***, but not to the extent of forgetting one's parents

14 ***a*** **A** attempts to represent the original thought as if it were spoken aloud by the person thinking it, at the time of thinking it. **B** adds a reporting verb (*I wondered*). **C** shifts the tense backwards (*can* → *could*): the interrogative form (*could I*) is maintained. **D** shifts the tense backwards (*can* → *could*) and adds a reporting verb (*I wondered*) followed by an adverb of subordination (*if*); the interrogative form (*could I*) is changed to the affirmative form (*I could*). **E** changes the verb phrase into a noun phrase preceded by a preposition (*if I could be happy with him* → *about my future happiness with him*).

b Most readers and critics tend to think as follows:
When a writer presents thoughts with **A**, **B** or **C** the effect is more immediate, dramatic, precise, vivid, and there is more the effect of a character in dialogue with him/herself. When a writer presents thoughts with **D** or **E** the presence of the writer is more apparent, and the effect is more vague, more a general idea; it is a report, rather than the actual thought. (Note: in grammar books and books on literary style, the five ways **A–E** are usually referred to as follows: **A** = Free Direct Thought (or FDT); **B** = Direct Thought (or DT); **C** = Free Indirect Thought (or FIT); **D** = Indirect Thought (or IT); **E** = Narrative Report of a Thought Act (or NRTA).)

15 ***a*** **D**; ***b*** **E**; ***c*** **B**; ***d*** **C**; ***e*** **D**; ***f*** **C**; ***g*** **D**

16 ***a*** I wondered why it was only my cooking that they appreciated.
b I realized (that) I couldn't run away – the Japanese were everywhere.
c I thought (that) he looked as ridiculous as a young peacock.
d I believed (that) something terrible would happen to me because I'd blown out the candle.
e I was afraid (that) he was going to try and touch me.
f I remembered (that) I had to respect my promise to my parents.
g I knew (that) I didn't have to be afraid of him any more.
h I wondered what it would be like to be that servant girl.
i I thought (that) if I talked about our ancestors, they would believe me.
(Note: the rules for changing tenses in indirect thought are the same as the rules for indirect speech.)

17 open response

18–21 open response

26 Out of context, your interpretations can be open response. However, for your interest, the contexts in the extract are as follows:
a 2 (see lines 171–2); ***b 2*** (see lines 73–4); ***c 1*** (see lines 103–4); ***d 1*** (see lines 85–6); ***e 1*** (see lines 17–18); ***f 1*** (see lines 37–8); ***g 2*** (see lines 113–15); ***h 2*** (see lines 3–4); ***i 1*** (see lines 148–9); ***j 1*** (see lines 132–4)

27 open response, but here are some ideas you might have had:
a Prem towards Indu: embarrassed or awkward (lines 7–8, 31–2, 63–5); apologetic (lines 7–8, 16–17, 35–6); concerned (lines 62–3); generous and indulgent (line 67 – or making up for guilt?; 73–5); guilty (lines 197–8)
b Indu towards Prem: petulant (lines 3–5); sulky (lines 37–8)
c Prem towards his mother: embarrassed or awkward (lines 86, 156); indulgent or patient (lines 116–17 – or afraid of upsetting her?); often there is the crisis of loyalty between wife and mother
d Prem's mother towards Prem: bossy (lines 85–6); a 'martyr' (lines 112–15; 159; 175–6); critical (lines 95–100); complaining (lines 150–1); interfering (lines 193–4); always comparing the past to the present (lines 121–4, 137–8, 143–8); often there is the idea that her son's wife is not good enough for him

e Indu towards Prem's mother: embarrassed (lines 103–4 – perhaps this is simply outward embarrassment?)
f Prem's mother towards Indu: critical (lines 101–2, 154–5, 163–4, 166–7, 169, 171–2); reluctant in praise (lines 106, 154–5)

28–9 open response

31 open response to your personal predictions; however, this is how the novel develops: Prem's mother continues in the same way, but eventually goes home. Prem's worries about his job continue (he never gets his salary rise), but he and Indu become reconciled. The novel ends with their first dinner party, and as their guests compliment Indu, Prem feels satisfaction at having finally become a 'householder' (this is a special term in Indian society describing someone with reasonable wealth and status).

32 open response; notice, however, the differences and similarities in the narrator/point of view. *The Joy Luck Club* has a first-person narrator, while in *The Householder* the narration is in the third person. However, even in *The Householder* the narration is not omniscient: it is limited to Prem's point of view. We are told about his thoughts directly, but we are not told what the other characters are thinking.

7 Thinking Aloud

4 lines 83–90: ***e***; lines 90–106: ***c***; lines 107–12: ***f***; lines 113–35: ***a***; lines 136–46: ***b***; lines 146–50: ***d***

5 (Note: the line references are also given in brackets):
at the shop: 1 ***d*** (151–6); 2 ***c*** (157–64); 3 ***e*** (167–78); 4 ***b*** (180–5); 5 ***a*** (186–203)
on the way back from the shop: 1 ***h*** (206–20); 2 ***k*** (220–31); 3 ***g*** (231–5); 4 ***j*** (236–51); 5 ***i*** (251–9); 6 ***f*** (260–2)

6 ***a 2*** and ***4*** are true, ***1*** and ***3*** are false. The necklace was for an earlier birthday, possibly her fourth (lines 305–7); Bloom's quick look at Milly's letter indicates she has a full social calendar (line 302).
b 2 and ***3*** are true, ***1*** and ***4*** are false. Lines 334–6 refer to Boylan's role as concert manager; lines 264–5, 276–7 and 330 suggest an affair between Molly and Boylan.

7 ***a*** open response, but here are some ideas: Bloom as husband is most evident in this passage. He is presented as a caring father in lines 301–17. On the trip to the shop he behaves like a good citizen, greeting O'Rourke, for example (lines 128–35). Work is never far from his mind (lines 120–1): notice how often he makes financial calculations. He was a friend of Dignam, and he remembers friends affectionately (lines 222–8). Bloom as lover is hinted at in lines 75–6, and as a potential lover in the scene with the girl in the shop (lines 158–64). There is no evidence of Bloom as a son in this extract.
b open response

8 ***a*** tying shoelaces, eating an egg, cutting bread
b open response; there are plenty of examples in the extract: preparing breakfast, making tea, feeding the cat, putting on a hat, greeting an acquaintance, buying something in a butcher's shop, picking up the mail, etc

9 Here are some ideas:
a He is kind, curious, observant and interested in life; he appreciates beauty; he is sentimental about his cat.
b He is considerate, and fond of his wife.
c Either he is careful with money, or does not think clothes are particularly important.

d He has a taste for the exotic and the romantic, and is imaginative and sensual, but he knows how to keep this separate from reality.
e He has business acumen, and is observant.
f He is friendly, polite and sociable, and aware of what to say at certain moments. (Notice that he chooses not to mention Dignam in the following lines: perhaps he thinks the moment is not quite 'right'.)
g Although married, he is sexually attracted to other women.
h He is imaginative, and can be morose and prone to depression.

10 open response, but some characteristics you might have noted could be: He wants to keep fit, but apparently has given up his exercises (lines 253–4). He appreciates home comforts – food and his wife: 'To smell ... Yes, yes' (lines 257–9). He is romantic (lines 260–2). He is observant (lines 276–7). He loves his daughter, and is sentimental about her. He can express himself in a 'vulgar' way: 'Silly Milly's ... *and garden*' (lines 305–11). He notices things, and is suspicious : 'A strip ... the bedspread' (lines 330–1). He is attentive and considerate: 'Would you like the window open a little?' (line 339). He is educated. He seems a patient teacher: 'Metempsychosis ... transmigration of souls' (lines 363–4). He is nostalgic and sentimental, and still admires his wife's looks: 'He smiled ... same young eyes' (lines 366–7). He is not gullible: he is aware of the reality behind appearances. He doesn't like the sight of unpleasant or dangerous actions. He thinks many people can be uncompassionate and selfish: 'Cruelty ... break our sides' (lines 371–4). He speculates about 'big' ideas. He is human, compassionate: 'Our souls ... Dignam's soul' (lines 375–6).

12 open response, but some ideas are:
a eager to read Boylan's letter, sly (lines 276–7); demanding (lines 283, 290 and 324); untidy (lines 285–6 and 343–5); appetitive (line 340); not very educated (not because of not knowing 'metempsychosis' – few people would – but note for example her grammar: 'must have fell' instead of 'must have fallen' in line 348); not particularly clean (line 356); plain-speaking (lines 362 and 365); unsophisticated taste in reading (lines 368–71 and 378–81). Notice also how often she seems to ignore Bloom (lines 275–9 and 339–41). Bloom finds her sensual and attractive (lines 325–9, 366–7 and 395–6).
c wife, mistress, mother, worker (as a singer)

13 As Odysseus is captive to Calypso, Bloom is captivated by love of Molly. (Note: most critics and readers agree that the parallels with the *Odyssey* make *Ulysses* a richer and more entertaining novel, but that one can enjoy the novel without being aware of this parallelism. For readers who are aware of it, there is the added bonus of picking up Joyce's ironic jokes. Here, for example, the discussion of metempsychosis and the picture of the nymph over the bed (lines 393–8: nymph = Calypso / Molly) ironically relate modern, everyday life to the epic events of the *Odyssey*. Joyce is also very free in his parallels: the novel describes just one day in Dublin, instead of ten years' wandering around the Mediterranean by Odysseus, and although here Molly relates to Calypso, for most of the book she relates to Odysseus' wife Penelope (but an ironically unfaithful version of the patient, faithful Penelope).

15 ***b*** He peeped quickly inside the leather headband. (1) White slip of paper. (2) Quite safe. (2) On the doorstep he felt in his hip pocket for the latchkey. (1) Not there. (2) In the trousers I left off. (2) Must get it. (2) Potato I have. (2) Creaky wardrobe. (2) No use disturbing her. (2) She turned over sleepily that time. (2) He pulled the halldoor to after him very quietly, more, till the footleaf dropped gently over the threshold, a limp lid. (1)

16 Here are some grammatically complete versions of the examples of interior monologue, but you might have written equally valid versions. (Note: ( ) = optional words. / = alternative expressions.)
a Still, perhaps, once in a way (= every now and again) she might like something special for breakfast.
b I really must get those (quoits) settled. It's a pity: the / that bed came all the way from Gibraltar. She's / Molly's forgotten any little Spanish she knew. I wonder what her father gave for it / that bed? It's an old style bed.
c There's / I've got the white slip of paper. It's quite safe.
d The key / It is not there. It is / must be in the trousers (that / which) I left off. I must get it. I have my / the potato. (But) the wardrobe (door) is creaky. There's no use disturbing her (just for a key).
e A light suit / That would make the funeral look too much like a picnic / would make it look as if I was going to a picnic (, not a funeral).
f It's a good house, however, because it's just at the end of the city traffic. For instance M'Auley's down there is not good as far as position goes / is concerned.
g No, I'd better not say anything (about our both being Jews). I'll say something another time / Another time will do.
h There's no sign of her. She's gone. (Well,) what does that matter?
i How do you do?
j No, it / Palestine is not like that.
k He used to bow Molly off the platform in an old-fashioned way. And he used to keep / have a little mirror in his silk hat. I remember the night Milly brought it into the parlour.
l She's got the same young eyes. I remember the first night after the charades in Dolphin's Barn.
m There's cruelty behind it all. The animals are doped. I remember the trapeze at Hengler's. I had to look the other way. The mob was gaping. 'Break your neck and we'll break our sides' they seemed to be thinking.
n She likes you to pour the tea before you put the milk in. The nymph in the picture is not unlike her with her hair down, but / only slimmer.

17 Some reasons why Joyce's style might be more successful at representing thoughts: it gives an impression of the rapid flow of thoughts (eg lines 64–70, 90–112, 218–35). It focuses on the central images and thoughts and gives importance to them (eg lines 14, 46–9, 206). Because it is less explicit it is less restrictive, and can therefore suggest the rich, ambiguous nature of thoughts (eg lines 85–7, 265, 375–6). The fragmented grammar reflects the fragmentary nature of some thoughts (eg the discontinued thoughts of lines 230–1). 'Complete' grammar is more a feature of writing rather than speech (just listen to people speaking); Joyce's style is closer to the way people speak (although whether we think in 'words' or not is completely open to discussion).
(Compare your impressions of Joyce's way of representing thought with the ways used by Amy Tan for the representation of Lindo's thoughts in Chapter 6, Exercises 14–17.)

19 ***a*** touch (and perhaps also sight); ***b*** sight (and perhaps 'gloss' and 'sleek' also suggest touch); ***c*** hearing; ***d*** taste and smell; ***e*** sight; ***f*** smell; ***g*** hearing; ***h*** smell (and taste in 'spicy'); ***i*** sight; ***j*** sight (the 'chapped' hands also suggest touch); ***k*** hearing and sight; ***l*** sight; ***m*** smell, hearing and sight: ***n*** touch (in the 'warm' twilight) and sight (the twilight is visualized as 'yellow', and her head is 'tousled'); ***o*** smell and touch (in 'the warmth of her body')

20 Some examples you might have found are:
sight: The coals were reddening (line 10); She blinked … milkwhite teeth. … green stones. (lines 35–7); he watched the bristles shining wirily in the weak light (line 42); staring at the hanks of sausages, polonies, black and white. … The figures whitened in his mind, unsolved: displeased, he let them fade. The shiny links, packed with forcemeat, fed his gaze (lines 151–4); His eyes rested on her vigorous hips (lines 160–1); Whacking a carpet on the clothesline. (line 163); with blotchy fingers, sausagepink (line 166); blurred cattle cropping (line 171); and made a red grimace (line 181); behind her moving hams. Pleasant to see first thing in the morning (lines 187–8); A speck of eager fire from foxeyes thanked him. (line 202); those waves, grey metal, poisonous foggy waters (line 239); Grey horror … with a salt cloak (lines 249–51) (the horror is visualised as 'grey'); a girl with gold hair on the wind (line 262); He looked calmly down on her bulk and between her large soft bubs, sloping within her nightdress like a shegoat's udder (lines 326–7); A strip of torn envelope peeped from under the dimpled pillow. (line 330); the orangekeyed chamberpot (line 352); her polished thumbnail (line 360); glancing askance at her mocking eyes (line 366).
hearing: Mkgnao! (line 16); The cat mewed in answer (line 18); Mrkgnao! the cat cried (line 26); Mrkrgnao! the cat said loudly (line 34); Gurrhr! she cried (line 41); A sleepy soft grunt answered (line 60); He heard then a warm heavy sigh … the bedstead jingled (lines 62–4); Creaky wardrobe (lines 78–9); Cries of sellers in the street (lines 97–8); She calls her children home in their dark language (lines 103–4); Brats' clamour (line 147); Whacking a carpet on the clothesline. (line 163); the page rustling (lines 172–3); the beasts lowing in their pens (line 174); flop and fall of dung (line 174); slapping a palm on a ripemeated hindquarter (lines 175–6); sizzling butter (line 258); Its hump bumped as he took it up (line 319); She set the brasses jingling as she raised herself briskly (line 325)
smell: faintly scented urine (line 5); From the cellar grating floated up the flabby gush of porter (lines 113–14); lift it to the nostrils and smell the perfume. Like that, heavy, sweet, wild perfume. (lines 225–6); Rather stale smell that incense leaves next day. Like foul flowerwater (lines 337–8); inhaling through her arched nostrils. There's a smell of burn, she said (lines 404–5)
touch: Scratch my head (line 20); Why are their tongues so rough? (lines 50–1); Be a warm day … black clothes feel it more … happy warmth (lines 85–8); His hand accepted the moist tender gland (line 197); Nice to hold, cool waxen fruit, hold in the hand (lines 224–5); Grey horror … with a salt cloak (lines 249–51); Be near her ample bedwarmed flesh (lines 258–9)

26 ***a*** open response
b It shows his obsessional nature.
c It shows that, deep down, he doesn't really care about his schemes. Perhaps they are a way of killing time, or of occupying his mind. (Your response to this will be relevant for Exercise 29.)

28 open response; Beckett does not make any judgements, nor do we see Molloy in any different stage of development elsewhere in the novel. It ends with him back in his room, writing again, his search for his mother unfulfilled.

8 Future Shock

1 Background information: this a film still from the 1955 version of of George Orwell's *Nineteen Eighty-Four* (another version was filmed in 1984!). Note the man's badge, which shows a number followed by the initials of his name (in reverse order), Winston Smith: this kind of badge is typical of military or prison uniforms. The man looks very worried, perhaps frightened. The poster behind him represents the political leader 'Big Brother'. The caption reads 'Big Brother is watching you'.

2 ***a*** The twenty-four hour clock is, of course, very common nowadays, but clocks in public places which strike the hour (generally found on churches and historical buildings) still use the twelve hour clock rather than the twenty-four hour clock. 'The clocks were striking thirteen' therefore seems strange.
b This could of course be spoken by a criminal or a psychopath (and could therefore refer to anyone 'outside' society). But if it refers to a feeling shared by a community or group of people, the pleasure in burning and destroying certainly seems strange.
c This simply suggests that the gymnasium is no longer used for physical exercise, and that the building (perhaps a school or sports centre) has been converted. But there may also be a suggestion of over-population, or of emergency measures, as in war or a natural disaster.
d Thirty-four storey buildings are nowadays considered high, certainly not 'squat' (= low)! 'HATCHERY AND CONDITIONING CENTRE' seems strange. A 'World State' is still a long way in the future.
e Giving a ghost as a present is certainly strange!

3 ***1 d**; **2 b**; **3 a**; **4 e**; **5 c***

4 ***1 a*** The creation of 'test-tube babies' is described: babies are created in the laboratory, rather than naturally.
b This suggests a technologically advanced, but perhaps less 'human' society.
2 a A house and books are being burnt, with pleasure, by someone in a position of authority or a member of an institutionalized group – the special helmet leads us to infer this. (Note on the title: Farenheit 451 is the temperature at which paper catches fire and burns.)
b This suggests a brutal society.
3 a A poster of a leader is displayed inside a building. The caption seems menacing.
b It suggests a repressive, police state.
4 a The ghost seems to be a hologram controlled by a small unit in the girl's hand.
b This suggests a technologically advanced society.
5 a The 'we' described seem to be imprisoned, and there is the threat of violence towards them. The immmediate guards seem to be female ('Aunts'), while the guards with more authority (picked from the 'Angels') might be men.
b It suggests a repressive, police state.

5 ***a*** By killing herself she avoids being caught, tortured, and executed at a Salvaging. During torture, she might well have given away the names of fellow conspirators.
b Exercises 8, 9, 12 and 13 will clarify these questions.

8 ***a*** 'Angels' are riot police; 'Eyes' are secret police.
b A 'Salvaging' is a public execution which Handmaids are forced to attend. It is also filmed for television (see lines 26–7; 132–3).
c This Salvaging takes place in what used to be a University (see lines 12–13; 18–24; 55–6).
d The two Handmaids might have been condemned for 'Unchastity' or attempting to kill their Commanders or their wives (see lines 120–1); the Wife for attempting to kill a Handmaid or for adultery (see line 126). Both might have been condemned for attempted escape (line 127).
e Ofcharles is probably drugged so that she does not violently resist and so spoil the spectacle.
f The Handmaids have to touch the rope to show their agreement with and

participation in the execution (see lines 144–8). They are therefore publicly seen to show solidarity with the State and its repressive laws rather than with the condemned women with whom they secretly sympathize (see lines 105–14).

g A 'Particicution' is an execution conducted by the spectators, not by executioners. It probably derives from 'participate' + 'execution', with perhaps also a derivation from 'part' or 'particle' since the victim is torn to pieces.

h 'Guardians' are male state officials whose duty is to 'guard' the Handmaids. This Guardian is publicly accused of the rape of two Handmaids (see lines 207–15), but his real crime is that he was a political dissident, a member of an anti-government conspiracy (see lines 269-72).

i Offred knew about the conspiracy of which Ofglen, the executed Guardian and others were members. She claims, however, she was not an active member.

9 You are not expected to be able to arrive at all the conclusions given here: the aim of this exercise is to stimulate you to do some 'educated guessing'.

a 1 This reference suggests a society governed by religious law. (Deuteronomy is a book of the Old Testament of the Bible which codifies Mosaic law.)

2 The religious flavour of the language again suggests how important and pervasive religion is in this society.

3 This suggests that people are not supposed to make references to how things used to be.

b 1 Aunts are older women in a position of power: they are in charge of training Handmaids.

2 Wives are the wives of Commanders, who are senior state officials.

3 Econowives are the wives of minor state officials (the derivation is probably from 'economy'+ 'wife').

4 Marthas (another Biblical reference: Martha was the sister of Lazarus, and gave Jesus hospitality) are the housekeepers in Commanders' households.

c 1 Handmaids are young women who are still able to have children.

2 Handmaids are allocated to senior state officials (Commanders) for the purposes of procreation. Sexual pleasure is not supposed to be involved in this relationship.

3 Handmaids are not called by their real names: they are given names composed of 'Of' (in the sense of 'belonging to') plus the first names of their Commanders.

d 1 Aunt Lydia (see lines 67–72) was in charge of the institution where Offred was trained to become a Handmaid. (She was the head Aunt in the institution described in Exercise 3 (*5*).)

2 There is clearly some kind of clandestine relationship between Offred and Nick, the chauffeur at the household where Offred lives (see lines 314–17). They have, in fact, become lovers. (It is Nick that Offred refers to in lines 42–4 and 302.)

3 Luke (see line 412) was the man Offred used to live with. He is the father of the child she refers to in line 410.

4 Offred and Janine were trained together to be Handmaids, so they have known each other some time (see lines 137; 279–90).

10 ***a*** Her disgust at the Salvaging is explicit (remarks ***1*** and ***2***), but despite this she does show interest in the proceedings (remark ***3***), although this is probably interest in the fact that a higher-ranking member of the society has done something 'criminal', rather than morbid curiosity. She tries to ignore the ceremony rather than openly rebel: she thinks of more pleasant things (remark ***4***), or simply looks elsewhere (remark ***5***).

b Some ideas you might have considered are: Offred's caution and instinct for self-preservation (line 182); her momentary hatred of the accused man (lines 216–18: does this mean she is susceptible to the state's propaganda, a victim of mass hysteria, or searching for a target for her indignation?); her indignation against Ofglen for having participated (lines 262–6), although this might also show her ingenuousness; her mixed feeling about needing to distance herself, yet not being proud of herself for this instinct (lines 291–3); her concentration on other things to block out the horror (lines 298–304, 308–13); her need to find out what happened to Ofglen (lines 380–89: is this just curiosity or courageous loyalty to Ofglen?); her instinct for self-preservation when she mentally distances herself from the Resistance (line 408–9); her acknowledgment that she is not heroic (lines 413–18).

11 ***a*** Other moments of suspense are: Offred's comment 'I don't want to be telling this story' (line 31). The reader wonders why, and imagines that something horrible is going to happen. The reader wonders what the Wife has done (lines 52–3). The reader does not know what a 'Salvaging' is yet, and might wonder why the women should make a fuss. What does 'things' mean exactly (line 59)? The reader wonders what Aunt Lydia is going to say (lines 101–3).

b Some examples of moments that create suspense and surprise, in the order in which they occur in the extract: Chapter 43 – *suspense*: what is Aunt Lydia going to announce (lines 161–5)? *suspense*: we don't know what is going to happen, but it will be unpleasant (lines 182–4). *suspense*: what has the accused man done? (lines 204–6). *suspense*: why is the man behaving in this way (lines 227; 234–5)? *surprise*: Ofglen takes part in the Particicution (lines 248–51; 262–4). *surprise*: the Guardian was a member of the underground (lines 268–71). Chapter 44 – *suspense*: will Ofglen come? Then, when she is arriving, why has she changed? (lines 318–24). *surprise*: there is a 'new' Ofglen (lines 325–7). *suspense*: what has happened to the 'old' Ofglen (lines 331–5)? This suspense continues for the whole chapter, until line 429. *suspense*: how will the 'new' Ofglen respond (line 375)? *suspense*: the conversation between Offred and the 'new' Ofglen might at any moment end with the 'new' Ofglen denouncing Offred (lines 386–403). *suspense*: what will happen to Offred (lines 410–18)?

12 a) is set; b) has been; c) have set up; d) call *or* have called; e) has led up to *or* led up to; f) is *or* was; g) is *or* was; h) imposes; i) are eliminated; j) are sent; k) is; l) justifying; m) has declared; n) are; o) are confiscated; p) are arrested; q) is given *or* has been given; r) carry out

13 a) After; b) where; c) these; d) While; e) also; f) even though; g) such; h) however; i) who; j) One evening; k) that; l) Despite; m) this; n) As a result; o) whose; p) but; q) Whether; r) at the moment of

15 ***a*** Angels, Salvaging, Handmaids and Aunts all sound less frightening or sinister, and perhaps more respectable, than the reality they refer to: they all have positive *connotations* which hide ugly *denotations* (for a description of these terms see Chapter 1, *Anatomy of a Novel*, page 24). Eyes stresses that Secret Police are everywhere and can see everything.

b Other examples are: the Wall; Salvagers; Particicution; Econowives; Marthas; Commanders; Wives; Guardians.

16 ***a*** All these words flatter the importance of the Handmaids: 'future' and 'race' stress the dependence of the state on the Handmaids; 'torch' is a traditionally 'heroic' *symbol* for a source of illumination, discovery, leadership, etc; 'cradle' is a *metaphor*, and suggests that the Handmaids occupy a central, maternal role. (For the terms *symbol* and *metaphor*, see Chapter 1, *Anatomy of a Novel*, page 25.)

17 ***a*** 'air support'. This term does not contain the idea of violence: it also emphasizes collaboration among members of one side rather than aggression against the other side.

b security forces = the police, or the army, navy or air force; intelligence = spying, or the information gathered from spying; low income groups = the poor, people who earn little money; downsizing = dismissing employees from a company; body count = the number of dead soldiers in a battle; collateral damage = civilian victims of a bombing raid; smart weapons = weapons guided by radar / computer that are supposed to hit exclusively the intended target; friendly fire = fire from one side in a battle which accidentally kills its own soldiers; ethnic cleansing = genocide, mass killing of a racial or cultural group

c You will probably have discussed each expression in some detail, but in general terms they are are all very *abstract* or *positive-sounding* terms (ie with positive *connotations*) for the unpleasant realities of death, violence, poverty, etc.

23 ***a*** Emmanuel Goldstein is accused of various crimes: of having left the Party and instigating counter-revolutionary activities (lines 9–20); of collaborating with Oceania's current enemy, Eurasia (lines 21–2; 43–50); of founding the underground organization called the 'Brotherhood' and writing a subversive book (lines 67–76). Note his demands at lines 36–40 – that these democratic ideas should be considered subversive shows the repressive nature of Oceania.

b The obvious purpose is to express collective hate against the enemies of the state, but, as in *The Handmaid's Tale*, other purposes are to encourage solidarity among party members and to allow an expression of strong emotions which might otherwise be turned against the state.

24 Here are some ideas you might have considered:

a Both Winston and Offred suppress any public show of disgust for these ceremonies, doubtless for reasons of self-preservation. But the extent of their participation, and how they try not to become involved in the mass hysteria, are different. Winston's mixed reactions are seen at lines 24–35, 88–92, 97–112 and 149–56. He feels intellectual attraction towards Goldstein and fears that other people will be taken in by the propaganda, yet he can still find Goldstein's face 'despicable, with a kind of senile silliness'. He finds participation in the Hate irresistible, but is able to switch his hatred towards Party members instead of towards Goldstein. He feels horror at the chanting of 'B–B!', and it is during this that he is vulnerable – people might notice he is not sincere. Offred feels sympathy and solidarity for the accused women, even curiosity, about what they have done. She participates only to avoid suspicion (eg lines 144–8), but momentarily is convinced of the guilt of the accused man and shares in the general blood-lust (lines 216–22). One way she tries to block out the ceremony is to think of being elsewhere, eg making love or eating (lines 42–4; 298–304).

b In *Nineteen Eighty-Four* other people seem to participate fully in the ceremony (lines 7–9, 51–3, 77–87, 93–7, 134–49), although the reader cannot tell whether they are sincere, pretending, or momentarily involved in the way that Winston is. In *The Handmaid's Tale* the reactions of other people are more various: nervousness (lines 83–4); dissent and solidarity with the accused women (lines 112–15); curiosity about the supposed crime of the women (lines 116–27); revulsion of an individual (line 135); enthusiasm of some and disgust of others at the Particicution (lines 174–81); belief in the regime's version of events, and therefore shock at the man's supposed crime (line 216); collective revulsion at the accused man (lines 232–3); mass hysteria (lines 243–54). The reactions of the higher ranks – Wives, Daughters and Aunts – are more detached: some leave, some stay to watch but not participate (lines 169–72, 256–9), perhaps out of morbid or sadistic curiosity. Two individuals are mentioned: Ofglen ostensibly participates, but only to save her fellow conspirator from suffering (lines 248–51), while Janine is deranged by the experience (lines 279–90).

c In both extracts the reader suspects that the enemies are on 'the right side' against the regime, and that the regime deliberately lies about their 'crimes'. The regimes vilify them and encourage general participation in hatred against them.
d Examples of the political language in *Nineteen Eighty-Four* are: Enemy of the People, Two Minutes Hate, Big Brother, the Party, Newspeak, Thought Police, Brotherhood, and the slogans at lines 129–31. Use of capital letters and the comforting connotations of the family (Aunts and Big Brother, although the underground is also called the Brotherhood) can be seen in both extracts. The ubiquity of the Secret Police is also stressed – Eyes and Thought Police. The slogans of Oceania are less obvious and perhaps more intellectually and morally perverse than those of Gilead: they seem to encourage the public to accept that the reversal of conventional ideas and civil liberties is something positive.

List of Film Versions

Below is a list of the novels in this book which have had films based on them. The names of the film company, the director and the main actors are given in order to help you if you want to buy or hire a video version.

Chapter	Novel	Film version(s)
2	*Farewell, My Lovely*	a) *Murder My Sweet* (also released under the title *Farewell, My Lovely*) (RKO, 1944) director: Edward Dmytryk; actors: Dick Powell, Claire Trevor b) *Farewell, My Lovely* (Avco Embassy, 1975) director: Dick Richards; actors: Robert Mitchum, Charlotte Rampling
	The Third Man	*The Third Man* (British Lion, 1949) director: Carol Reed; actors: Orson Welles, Joseph Cotten, Trevor Howard
3	*Women in Love*	*Women in Love* (United Artists, 1969) director: Ken Russell; actors: Glenda Jackson, Jennie Linden, Alan Bates, Oliver Reed
	A Farewell to Arms	a) *A Farewell to Arms* (Paramount, 1932) director: Frank Borzage; actors: Gary Cooper, Helen Hayes b) *A Farewell to Arms* (TCF, 1957) director: Charles Vidor; actors: Rock Hudson, Jennifer Jones c) *Force of Arms* (Warner Brothers, 1951) director: Michael Curtiz; actors: William Holden, Nancy Olson (loosely based on Hemingway's novel, rather than a faithful film version of it)
4	*Catch-22*	*Catch-22* (Paramount, 1970) director: Mike Nichols; actors: Alan Arkin, Martin Balsam, Richard Benjamin, Art Garfunkel, Jack Gifford, Bob Newhart, Anthony Perkins, Jon Voight, Martin Sheen, Orson Welles
5	*Heart of Darkness*	*Apocalypse Now* (Omni Zoetrope, 1979) director: Francis Coppola; actors: Martin Sheen, Marlon Brando, Robert Duvall (inspired by, rather than based on, Conrad's novel; the setting is completely different, but the structure and themes are similar; for more details see the Key to Exercise 13b, Chapter 5)
6	*The Joy Luck Club*	*The Joy Luck Club* (Buena Vista, 1993) director: Wayne Wang; actors: Kieu Chinh, Tsai Chin, France Nuyen, Lisa Lu, Ming-Na Wen
	The Householder	*The Householder* (Contemporary Films, 1963) director: James Ivory; actors: Shashi Kapoor, Leela Naidu, Durga Khote
7	*Ulysses*	*Ulysses* (Walter Reade, 1967) director: Joseph Strick; actors: Milo O'Shea, Maurice Roeves, Barbara Jefford
8	*The Handmaid's Tale*	*The Handmaid's Tale* (Virgin/Cinecom/Bioskop Film, 1990) director: Volker Schlöndorff; actors: Natasha Richardson, Robert Duvall, Faye Dunaway
	Nineteen Eighty-Four	a) *Nineteen Eighty-Four* (Holiday, 1955) director: Michael Anderson; actors: Edmond O'Brien, Michael Redgrave, Jan Sterling b) *Nineteen Eighty-Four* (Umbrella/Rosenblum/Virgin, 1984) director: Roger Deakins; actors: John Hurt, Richard Burton, Suzanna Hamilton